A History of Rock Music: The Rock & Roll Era

Preliminary Edition

D0223170

Glenn Gass

Indiana University
School of Music

McGraw-Hill, Inc.
College Custom Series

New York St. Louis San Francisco Auckland Bogotá
Caracas Lisbon London Madrid Mexico Milan Montreal
New Delhi Paris San Juan Singapore Sydney Tokyo Toronto

A HISTORY OF ROCK MUSIC: THE ROCK & ROLL ERA

15 16 17 18 19 HAM HAM 15 14 13 12 11

ISBN 0-07-022988-0
ISBN-13: 978-0-07-022988-4

Cover Photos of Elvis Presley and Jerry Lee Lewis courtesy of UPI/Bettmann.

Editor: Jan Scipio

Cover Design: Jenny L. Friedman

Printer/Binder: HAMCO Corporation

A History of Rock Music: The Rock & Roll Era

Glenn Gass

- Outline of Contents -

A History of Rock Music: The Rock & Roll Era

Glenn Gass

- Brief Contents -

"Got my mojo working": Muddy Waters and President Jimmy Carter

[1] ROCK ROOTS

Since colonial days and the tragedy of slavery, white and black Americans have viewed each other with a mixture of fear and fascination—so close and yet so far apart. The slaves arriving from Africa brought along a world view and set of customs radically different from those of the European settlers, a difference clearly heard and felt in the hypnotic rhythms of the music that accompanied the slaves' daily life. Plantation owners were so worried about the messages that might be encoded in those "jungle rhythms" that drumming was often forbidden and a close and nervous watch was maintained on the slaves' mournful work songs, eerie chants, frenzied dancing and other mysterious means of communication that seemed so threatening and yet, at the same time, so strangely alluring.[1]

Alluring enough, in fact, that by the 19th century white entertainers were blackening their faces with burnt cork and performing caricatures of the slaves' songs and dances in "minstrel" shows. Meanwhile, the slaves were adapting to their new surroundings and incorporating white styles and customs, though not without a certain measure of bemused mockery. The "cakewalk," for example, started as a comically exaggerated promenade that ridiculed the slave owners' stilted manner and pompous gentility. Fascinated by the strange dance, and oblivious to the irony, white dancers mimicked the parody of their own movements and the cakewalk became a minstrel show staple and a full-blown dance craze in the ragtime era. Variations on the cakewalk scenario were replayed with the Fox-trot, Charleston, Black Bottom, Jitterbug, Twist and all the other dance steps fueled by an infatuation with the African-derived rhythms of ragtime, jazz, boogie-woogie, swing, rhythm & blues, rock & roll, soul, funk, disco, rap...

By the time Elvis led a band of crazed rebels into the pop charts, everything and nothing had changed—so close and yet still so far. The rising popularity of black rhythm & blues, now dubbed "rock & roll," among white teenagers had created a new generation of drum-fearing white folks, now called "parents," who listened with alarm to the strange, hypnotic rhythms and coded messages ("a-wop bop a lu bop"?!) that were driving their children into fits of uncontrolled frenzy and irresponsible behavior. To thwart this menace, or at least cash in on it, Pat Boone and his clean-cut compatriots donned musical blackface and performed pasteurized caricatures, now called "covers," of black music on modern-day minstrel shows. Further south, a more daring and freewheeling bunch of "rockabillies" inherited their ancestors' forbidden fascination with black music and culture and added their own feverish determination to find that spark in themselves.

Musical boundaries—and a good many racial and cultural boundaries—crumbled around rock & roll. The music was a varied and fascinating hybrid of styles, shaped by Elvis and the rockabillies' mixture of country and blues, Chuck Berry's mix of blues and a comic "hillbilly" style, Little Richard's manic marriage of gospel shrieks and rhythm & blues, Fats Domino's musical New Orleans gumbo, Buddy Holly's blend of pop and rock, the Everly Brothers' polite country rock and the various shadings of gospel, R&B and pop blended into "soul" by Ray Charles, Sam Cooke, Jackie Wilson and James Brown. Although its days as a liberating threat to the moral fabric of our society were relatively short-lived, rock & roll's blend of black and white redefined the meaning of and audience for "popular music." (And just when it seemed that the danger had passed, a bunch of *British* kids churned it all up again, with yet another unexpected twist.) The vitality of American music, like America itself, has always reflected the rough edges and incredible variety of its cultural melting pot, and nowhere have these central tensions and undercurrents more fully confronted and transformed each other than in that startling music called "rock & roll."

"Rock Around the Clock"

Asked to identify the "first rock & roll song," most people tend to think of Bill Haley's 1955 hit, "Rock Around the Clock." They are at least partly right: "Rock Around the Clock" *was* the first rock & roll song to go to #1 on the *Billboard* pop charts, making rock & roll a fact that the music industry could no longer ignore or try to whitewash away. "Rock Around the Clock" was a call to arms and to the dance floor: to "rock! rock! rock! till the broad daylight!" It was the first celebration of rock & roll itself, and though it may sound merely quaint today, it punctured a hole in the smug conformity of the 1950's and seemed like a thrilling act of open defiance from the Paul Revere of the Rock Revolution.

"Rock Around the Clock" was released in 1954 but became a hit the following year when it was blasted over the opening and closing credits of *The Blackboard Jungle*, a movie about teenage delinquency and the clash of generations in an urban classroom. A key scene of that movie shows a group of troublemakers smashing a teacher's collection of classic jazz 78's, mocking his beloved Bix Beiderbecke and demanding some Sinatra and Joni James(!) Before rock & roll, there was no "teenage" music and, for that matter, no clear cultural definition of a "teenager." Although the scene captures the kids' contempt for authority and tradition, the musical "battle" rings a little hollow. Like James Dean in *Rebel Without a Cause*, the teenagers in *The Blackboard Jungle* are in full rebellion, though with no particular focus beyond their own inner turmoil and their rage at their stifling environment. Had the movie been made just a year or two later, "Sinatra" would have been replaced by "Elvis" and the *cause* would have been clear: the raucous rhythms of rock & roll. As it was, "Rock Around the Clock" was added as an afterthought, but the song made the rebellion explicit and millions of kids took their cue and chimed in with their own impromptu versions of their new anthem in hallways and on street corners around the country—particularly in the cities, where this new "urban folk music" struck its initial chord.

"Rock Around the Clock" was indeed a landmark, but it was certainly not—by any just measure—the "first rock song": it was the first important *white* rock song, a crucial distinction given the racial climate of America in the 1950's. Although no single song could fully claim the honor, there are plenty of legitimate "first rock song" contenders: the Crow's "Gee," the Midnighter's "Work with Me Annie," the Penguin's "Earth Angel" and the Chord's "Sh-Boom" (all from 1954); the Orioles' "Crying in the Chapel" and Big Mama Thornton's "Hound Dog" (from 1953); the Dominoes' "Have Mercy Baby" and Lloyd Price's "Lawdy Miss Clawdy" (from 1952); Jackie Brenston & the Ike Turner Band's "Rocket 88" and the Dominoes' "Sixty Minute Man" (from 1951); Cecil Gant's "We're Gonna Rock," and any number of other rhythm & blues records that pre-date "Rock Around the Clock," including Goree Carter's "Rock Awhile" (1949), Roy Brown's "Good Rockin' Tonight" (1947), Wild Bill Moore's "We're Gonna Rock, We're Gonna Roll" (1947), and the many blues and boogie numbers with strong dance beats and references to "rocking" and "rolling" in their titles and lyrics. One could even trace it all the way back to songs like Trixie Smith's "My Man Rocks Me (With One Steady Roll)," from 1922, since "rock" had long been a euphemism for sex, partying and raucous music making.

Rock's roots run deep into the folk and popular music's of 20th century American (and much deeper still if one traces its sources back to African and European headwaters). Country & western, boogie-woogie, gospel, jazz, swing and pop all played a significant role in rock's development, along with the later stimuli reflected in Bob Dylan's folk-rock and beat poetry, the Beatles' excursions into classical music and Indian ragas, the psychedelic embrace of avant-garde jazz and all the other far-flung inspirations that rock came to claim as its own. In the beginning, though, "rock & roll" was just another name for rhythm & blues, and the journey back to its origins is a direct shot back to the South and to the blues.

THE BLUES

The blues was the musical wellspring for rock & roll and the primary source of rock's urgency and emotional resonance. The direct, unadorned expression at the core of the blues—the emphasis on *feeling* above musical niceties and polished technique—informs the best rock music, while the flattened notes of the blues scale, the bent "blue notes" (the "notes between the notes" sung naturally by the human voice and mimicked by bent guitar strings and sliding saxophones, and approximated in black and white piano keys banged together) and other expressive devices of the blues lent musical grit and emotional depth to nearly all of the popular styles of the 20th century.

The blues was also the main source of rock's specific musical vocabulary. Most of the classic rock guitar lead, riff and rhythm patterns, for example, are directly descended from the rural acoustic blues of the Depression era and the electric urban blues of the post-war years, which also imparted the powerfully masculine imagery of the guitar itself. The rough-hewn, natural voices and emotional, note-bending singing styles of the blues were a further, liberating inspiration to young singers who had no time or talent for polite pop crooning. In contrast to the happy escape offered by popular entertainment, the blues seemed *real*, confronting the hardest times head-on and challenging its adherents to summon up the same tough stance in themselves.

The blunt sexuality of blues lyrics was certainly quite a contrast to the restraints of other styles: a country or popular or, Lord knows, gospel performer would never have dreamed of singing a blues staple like "you can squeeze my lemon till the juice runs down my leg..." The aggressive sexuality and macho posturing of the blues was mimicked with increasing boldness by rock performers who coveted the blues' expressive range and welcomed the controversy and devilish image the blues had always engendered. (The Rolling Stones, for example, built on their love for the blues to write songs and project an image very different from the pop-based cheeriness of the Beatles.)

The Outsider stance of the blues singers—an inescapable byproduct their skin color—was also refashioned to fit rock's rebellion, where the "struggle" was redefined in the context of young vs. old rather than black vs. white. The blues informed rock's sense of itself as a subculture outside of and even oppressed by the Establishment, a view that gained at least some credence during the Vietnam and Civil Rights era. And if a true blues "authenticity" was beyond the musical and experiential reach of young white singers like Elvis Presley or Mick Jagger, at least the spirit, intensity and rebellious individuality of the blues was theirs to claim and reshape in their own image.

The 12-Bar Blues

The musical form most associated with the blues—the 12-bar blues—was also borrowed frequently by other popular styles and was the musical framework for nearly all pre-Beatles rock & roll.[2] The 12-bar blues reflects the music's roots in the interaction between a leader and a group—a work crew or church congregation—that characterized both the slaves' "field holler" work songs and the repetitive "ring shouts" and "call-and-response" format of African-American religious music. This interaction is imbedded in the alternation between singing and instrumental "answers" and in the *aab* text format of a classic 12-bar blues, which consists of one line, sung twice, followed by a kicker, as in Robert Johnson's "Crossroads Blues":

> Standin' at the crossroad, I tried to flag a ride
> Standin' at the crossroad, I tried to flag a ride
> Nobody seemed to know me, everybody passed me by.

The lyrics are set to a fixed sequence of accompanying chords that repeats, with new lyrics, every twelve measures:

- the first line (*a*) is sung to the home or "tonic" chord (the "**I**" chord; in the key of E, an E chord), followed by an instrumental answer or "response";

- the first line (*a*) is then repeated against a new, "subdominant" chord (the "**IV**" chord; in the key of E, an **A** chord—four steps up the scale from E), followed by a return to the home (I) chord and another instrumental response;

- the new line of lyrics (*b*) is sung to a new, climaxing "dominant" chord (the "**V**" chord; in the key of E, a **B** chord), which is resolved by a final return to the home chord and a preparation for the next 12-bar phrase.

Although the vast majority of blues songs utilize the 12-bar blues form, 8-bar, 16-bar and other adaptations are also fairly common, and many songs dispense with chord changes altogether and are instead shaped by a repeating riff (as in Howlin' Wolf's "Smokestack Lightnin'" and Muddy Waters' "Mannish Boy") or hypnotic rhythm (as in John Lee Hooker's "Boogie Chillen" and almost any Bo Diddley song). In any case, the exact musical labels and theory are less important than the *feel* of the 12-bar blues (and it is certainly more complicated on paper than it is in the music). The overall motion and sense of inevitability created by each new chord and line of lyrics allows for unlimited repetitions without tedium, and highlights the individual expression each artist brings to this shared musical framework. In a similar way, blues lyrics, themes and phrases ("baby, where'd you stay last night," "that's all right, mama," "you're gonna need my help someday," and so on) formed a shared *lingua franca* that highlighted individual voices and visions against a shared language and context. As deceptively simple and evocative as a sonnet or Japanese haiku, the blues is supremely adaptable—unchanging and highly stylized, yet always fresh and capable of great expression.

Blues Roots

The roots of the blues stretches back to Africa and through the work songs, and dance accompaniments of African-Americans who, like their ancestors, viewed music as a part of everyday life and expression. Born in the cotton fields and the agony of slavery, the blues provided a common language for poor southern blacks. The music of the black church had a strong influence as well, both in the frenzied, hypnotic "ring shouts" and in the slow, stately spirituals that required an added measure of emotion that took the form of slurs, shouts, moans and bent, sorrowful blue notes: "the key note of blues and jazz, and the most haunting sound of the new world."[3]

Religious songs and the blues both drew on real experience and provided a vision of escape—to a better life in heaven (or, perhaps, Chicago)—and a means of voicing pain with dignity and beauty. The slow, gloomy, solitary blues and the communal sorrow and celebration of black church music may have occupied opposite ends of the social and moral scale, but they were really two sides of the same emotional coin and a constant influence on each other, as the rural blues sound of gospel singer-guitarists like Blind Willie Johnson attests. (Not that one would admit to a fondness for blues in church, where it was viewed as Devil's music, or around the more "respectable" members of the black community who tended to view it as the product of backwards rural people.)

The term "blues" dates back to "Blue Devils," a 16th century expression for depression or melancholia. By 1900 it was associated with a musical style as well, though no blues recordings were made until 1920 and the exact genesis of the blues remains something of a romantic mystery. Itinerant "songsters" and other 19th century blues predecessors played a variety of folk, popular, dancing, minstrel and religious songs on banjo, guitar, fiddle, mandolin and other mobile instruments (an eclectic folk tradition that was passed along in this century by Huddie Ledbetter, better known as Leadbelly). Blues singers built on that tradition but developed strikingly individual styles and plaintive voices that lent a visceral chill to their accounts of love and hope lost. Their mournful "sung speech" melodies—sung within a narrow vocal range and punctuated by bending blue notes, growls, falsettos wails and aggressively rhythmic phrasing—were certainly very different from conventional European singing, pointing again to their earliest origins in the work songs that served as a means of expression and solace.

Ragtime & Jazz

The novel mixture of European harmonies with African-derived rhythmic syncopations sparked a craze for ragtime music at the turn of the century, making it the first widely-popularized blend of black and white in the post-minstrel era, and the first of many styles of black-based music—including blues, jazz, boogie-woogie, swing, rhythm & blues, rock & roll, soul, funk, disco, rap—to capture the general public's ear and imagination. Ragtime's piano roll precision and one-dimensional cheeriness limited its expressive range, but the increasing influence of the blues on pianists and ragtime bands inspired a more flexible and exciting music, dubbed "jazz," which gained popularity in the 1910's and then fueled the Roaring Twenties.

Meanwhile, in 1914, the year ragtime king Scott Joplin published his last piano rag, **W. C. Handy** published the classic "St. Louis Blues" and helped trigger a similar blues mania. A successful dance band leader, Handy heard the blues in the Mississippi Delta in 1903, then borrowed ideas from his rural counterparts and began writing and publishing his own original blues, beginning with 1912's "Memphis Blues." Handy's publishing success brought the blues to a wide audience and inspired a flood of popular songs from Tin Pan Alley that included "blues" in the title and lyrics, however ludicrously, to cash in on the craze.

"Classic Blues"

Recordings of vocal blues began in 1920, three years after the first jazz recordings were made by the Original Dixieland Jass (*sic*) Band, a typically earnest group of white musicians who found themselves "pioneering" a well-established black musical form. The surprise success of Mamie Smith's "Crazy Blues," however, alerted the still-young recording industry to the existence of a large black audience, or "race market," eager for blues recordings. Mindful of the popular styles of the day, the first blues recordings were a mixture of vaudevillian novelties and jazz arrangements, and nearly all were recorded by female singers. It would be many years before anyone thought to record the rough rural blues of the Mississippi Delta. In the meantime, the "classic blues" of the twenties brought the blues to a wide audience and even gave it an aura of glamour and speakeasy class.

The early blues queens, including Gertrude "Ma" Rainey, Alberta Hunter, Victoria Spivey, Sippie Wallace, Edith Wilson, Clara Smith, Trixie Smith and Memphis Minnie, hailed from the South and worked their way around the country on the tent show and black theater circuits. The spreading jazz boom brought them into the white clubs and cabarets of the North, backed by the hottest pianists and jazz bands of the time. Their material ranged from popular Tin Pan Alley "blues" to expressive laments, with plenty of sexual references peppering their unapologetic toughness. Just as the blues gave voice to men's sufferings in life and love, the female blues singers communicated these harsh realities along with the extra measure of hardship they faced as women, and used the blues to express feelings that were otherwise not condoned in "polite" society.

> You never get nothing by being an angel child,
> You'd better change your way an' get real wild.
> I wanta' tell you something, I wouldn't tell no lie,
> Wild women are the only kind that ever get by.
> Wild women don't worry, Wild women don't have the blues.
>   - Ida Cox, "Wild Women Don't Have the Blues" (1924)

Bessie Smith

Bessie Smith gave classic blues a deeply personal voice and raised blues singing to the level of an art. Smith was born in 1894 in Chattanooga, Tennessee. She "apprenticed" with Ma Rainey in a traveling troupe and was a veteran performer by the time she made her first record in 1923, "Down Hearted Blues" ("I never loved but three men in my life: my father, my brother, and the man that wrecked my life"). The "Empress of the Blues" ruled through the 1920's and became the measure by which all other blues singers were judged.

Smith was raised in dire poverty and was well-acquainted with physical and emotional suffering throughout her life. The inner torment that drove her to bad relationships and bad habits also infused her best blues with an intensely felt emotion. Her 1925 version of W.C. Handy's "St. Louis Blues" is one of her best-known recordings, featuring sublimely sorrowful singing and an inspired call-and-response between Bessie's growling, brassy voice and Louis Armstrong's trumpet.

Smith's career fell into a steep decline during the Depression years. She died in a car crash in 1937 near Clarksdale, Mississippi, and was buried in an unmarked grave in Philadelphia. Smith is still considered one of the finest singers of any style ever recorded, and her fusion of technique and emotion has only rarely been matched. The tradition of strong female presences which she exemplified continued through a line of great jazz, gospel, rhythm & blues and soul singers, such as Billie Holiday, Ella Fitzgerald, Dinah Washington, Mahalia Jackson, Marion Williams, Ruth Brown, Etta James and Aretha Franklin. A similarly bold white female artist did not emerge until a young singer from Texas modeled herself (in too many ways) on Bessie Smith: Janis Joplin even paid for the tombstone that finally marked Bessie's grave in 1970.

RURAL BLUES

In contrast to the relative urbanity of classic blues, the lonely and timeless sound of rural blues came straight from the farm fields and cotton plantations of the rural South. The field holler singing and acoustic guitar backing—often played slide-style with a knife or bottleneck, supplemented by an occasional harmonica—of rural blues were a stark contrast to the jazz stylings of the classic blues it pre-dated and influenced. W.C. Handy, for one, had his musical life altered by his first rendezvous with the rural blues of the Mississippi Delta, which happened one desolate night in 1903 in the Tutwiler, Mississippi, train station. While Handy dozed off waiting for a train that was nine hours late, a tattered black man with "the sadness of the ages"[4] etched on his face began singing and playing a guitar, sliding a knife across the strings to get a slurred, mournful sound that mirrored his voice. Robert Palmer describes the fateful encounter: "Handy woke up to this music, and the first words he heard the man sing were 'Goin' where the Southern cross the Dog.' The line was repeated three times, answered in each case by the slide guitar. Politely, Handy asked what it meant, and the guitarist rolled his eyes mirthfully. In Moorehead, farther south near the Sunflower River in the heart of the Delta, the tracks of the Yazoo & Mississippi Valley Railroad, known to the locals as the Yellow Dog, crossed the tracks of the Southern at right angles. The man was on his way to Moorehead, and he was singing about it."[5]

Handy stumbled onto a fully-formed style that night in Mississippi, although two more decades would pass before the rough lyrics and "primitive" music of the rural blues were finally recorded.[6] The first downhome blues recordings were made in 1925 by Blind Lemon Jefferson, a Texan whose songs included "Match Box Blues" (later turned into a rockabilly standard by Carl Perkins), "That Black Snake Moan" and "See That My Grave's Kept Clean." The success of Jefferson's recordings and those of another blind singer, Blind Blake, from Georgia, inspired further digging on the part of the record companies that uncovered a treasure trove of rural blues styles. Jefferson's single string leads and jazzy rhythmic feel helped establish the distinct Texas blues style, while Blake's recordings (including the much-covered "Diddie Wah Diddie") were in a more melodic, ragtime-ish dance style that was popular in the Southeast. The records of Blind Willie McTell ("Statesboro Blues"), Skip James ("I'm So Glad"), Leroy Carr ("How Long—How Long Blues"), Kokomo Arnold ("Milk Cow Blues"), the Mississippi Sheiks ("Sitting On Top of the World"), Big Joe Williams ("Baby, Please Don't Go"), Big Bill Broonzy, Peetie Wheatstraw, Lonnie Johnson, Scrapper Blackwell and many other great bluesmen illustrate the rich diversity of rural blues styles throughout the South in the twenties and thirties.

Mississippi Delta Blues

The cotton fields and plantation towns of the Mississippi Delta were home to the deepest blues of all. The Delta blues, and the urban styles it spawned upriver, made an especially easy transition to rock & roll with the addition of a band and a bit of amplification, as evidenced by the many rock covers of Delta blues songs, especially those of the legendary Robert Johnson. (The lead riffs and driving boogie-bass figures of Johnson's "Dust My Broom," for example, formed a virtual blueprint for Chicago blues and hard rock guitar.)

An expanse of flat, fertile land stretching from Memphis to Vicksburg, the Mississippi Delta remains a mythic landscape of towns (Clarksdale, Rosedale, Friars Point, Yazoo City, Helena), roads (the infamous Highway 61), rivers and railroad lines immortalized in songs more than a half century old. The decaying plantations, abandoned sharecropper shacks and desolate crossroads retain a haunting power to this day, and it still seems that it would be entirely possible make a deal with the Devil himself on any dark night. The Delta bluesmen, like the one in the Tutwiler train station, sang so eloquently of their everyday life that the landscape seems strangely familiar to any blues fan, yet it is still hard to believe that this small, bleak area was once the scene of one of America's truly great and spontaneous explosions of talent. Roebuck "Pop" Staples, founder of the Staple Singers, recalls the old days in the Delta: "On Saturday afternoons everybody would go into town and those fellows like Charley Patton, Robert Johnson, and Howlin' Wolf would be playin' on the streets, standin' by the railroad tracks, people pitchin' 'em nickels and dimes."[7]

The Delta blues had an aggressive intensity unmatched in other blues styles: the best players could very nearly turn their acoustic guitars into an entire band, with driving rhythms and bass figures, strong chords and cutting bottleneck-slide leads all simultaneously propelling the equally intense half-shouted vocals. The lyrics, too, took on an unmatched expressive intensity, ranging from simple destinations ("Goin' where the Southern cross the Dog") that took an eerie, ominous feel, to utter tragedies and meetings with the Devil depicted as chillingly mundane, everyday events. Most were about love—in other words, about sex, despair and/or revenge—and were expressed bluntly and peppered with indecipherable slang and haunting voodoo imagery. The spontaneous poetry of the Delta was often violent (the harsh sexism of the blues is one of its unhappier legacies to rock & roll), never prettified and never very popular beyond its southern base, but its influence has been far-reaching and its ability to astound is undiminished by the decades.

The blues of the Mississippi Delta reached a peak in the 1936-37 recordings of Robert Johnson, though he was more a brilliant synthesizer of existing styles than an originator. Charley Patton ("Founder of the Delta Blues") was nearly 50 and had been playing for decades by the time he began recording in 1929. Although the unrecorded origins of the music are lost to history, Patton, Son House and Willie Brown are three famous influences on Johnson, and their astonishing music, like that of Tommy Johnson, Willie Newbern, Bukka White and other Johnson predecessors, provides a glimpse into the rich musical world of the Delta in the first decades of the century.

Robert Johnson: King of the Delta Blues

The "King of the Delta Blues," Robert Johnson, has also been referred to as the "Father of Rock & Roll," in a nod to the crucial influence of the Delta blues. Johnson soaked up the influence of his Delta peers and predecessors and along with the influence of bluesmen from other areas who reached him via recordings (particularly Kokomo Arnold, Peetie Wheatstraw and Skip James). His fusion of technique and emotion matched Bessie Smith's, though on a darker and more disturbing level. The raw power and possessed intensity of Johnson's music lends some romantic credence to the legend that he "sold his soul to the Devil" in exchange for his talent. (By all accounts, Johnson was a mediocre and uninspired player before he disappeared for a period of time; he returned with a jaw-dropping talent and a colorful story for those who wanted an explanation for the miraculous change.) Johnson may have believed it himself, or at least seemed to see it as an apt metaphor for the inner demons that drove his furious playing and singing and his equally hell-bent life. A sense of foreboding and dread colors even his lightest efforts, and the blues seems a palpable, terrifying *presence* in his most riveting songs, such as "Preaching Blues":

> I's up this morning, blues walking like a man,
> I's up this morning, blues walking like a man,
> Worried blues, give me your right hand.

The blues is a low-down shakin' chill
The blues is a low-down shakin' chill
You ain't never had 'em—I hope you never will.

Johnson's guitar playing inspires and mystifies today's great players just as it astounded his peers, and provokes the same displays of unabashed awe and envy. His simultaneous mix of rhythm and lead playing was a dazzling perfection of Delta styles, while the sheer focused intensity of his playing lifted it into another realm altogether. Johnson's wonderfully evocative lyrics, too, transcended the disjointed songs and shared common phrases of the blues and entered the realm of poetry, as in "Love In Vain":

I followed her to the station with a suitcase in my hand,
I followed her to the station with a suitcase in my hand,
It's hard to tell, it's hard to tell, when all your love's in vain,
All my love's in vain.

When the train rolled up to the station, I looked her in the eye,
When the train rolled up to the station and I looked her in the eye,
I was so lonesome, I felt so lonesome, and I could not help but cry,
All my love's in vain.

When the train left the station with two lights on behind,
When the train left the station with two lights on behind,
The blue light was my blues, and the red light was my mind,
All my love's in vain.

Robert Johnson's rambling life and early death in 1938—poisoned by a jealous husband at the age of 27—added to his legend when his recordings were reissued in the 1960's and a new generation fell under his spell.[8] Cream's version of "Crossroads," the Rolling Stones' "Love in Vain" and "Stop Breaking Down," and the many other Johnson covers join his original recordings as testimony to his influence and legacy. Eric Clapton summed up his admiration this way: "Robert Johnson to me is the most important blues musician who ever lived... I have never found anything more deeply soulful. His music remains the most powerful cry that I think you can find in the human voice." Or as Rolling Stone Keith Richards put it: "Everybody should know about Robert Johnson. You want to know how good the blues can get? Well, this is it."[9]

URBAN BLUES

In the years after World War I, southern blacks began a mass exodus northward in search of better jobs and a better life. The move from the cotton fields to the factories continued through the Depression and World War II years, and was reflected in a shift from acoustic rural blues played in tiny "juke joints" to amplified urban blues, played on electric guitars with a band backing and a strong beat to fill the noisy city clubs and dance floors.

The electric guitar was introduced on jazz and blues records in the late 1930's. Charlie Christian and Eddie Durham pioneered the horn-like single-string jazz style that elevated the guitar from its traditional supporting role in the rhythm section of jazz bands. **Aaron "T-Bone" Walker** spent his early years leading Blind Lemon Jefferson around Texas towns, then played in several jazz bands before recording under his own name in 1942. Walker, who had his signature hit with 1943's "Stormy Monday," was the first to really exploit the new possibilities offered by electricity—the variety and control of tone colors, volume, sustain, special effects etc.—and was largely responsible for developing the classy, jazz-tinged "uptown" urban blues that was most accessible to later blues and rock players.

Memphis

Memphis was a natural hub for blues musicians, just upriver and up Highway 61 from the Delta and home to **Beale Street**, an area thronged with blues clubs that offered steady employment to the many Delta bluesmen who settled in Memphis or spent time there en route to Chicago. Although now something of a glossed-over blues "theme park," Beale Street was once a thriving musical center at the confluence of rural and urban blues styles, and was witness to the exciting changes as the blues moved from the rural past into the urban present.

Memphis also had the advantage of a hometown recording studio that provided further opportunities for blues players. The tiny studio run by independent producer **Sam Phillips** in a converted radiator repair shop was the only place a black man could make a record in Memphis, and Phillips was personally responsible for preserving much of the city's rich musical heritage. After leasing his recordings to outside labels, Phillips launched his own Sun label in 1953 and, in another stunning bit of musical foresight, discovered Elvis Presley and put Memphis and Sun Records at the center of the rock & roll map.

B. B. King

B. B. King built on T-Bone Walker's jazz-laced style to develop his own emotional blend of crying, gospel-inflected vocals, virtuosic single-string guitar solos and polished big band arrangements. Born Riley King in 1925, he moved from Indianola, Mississippi, to Memphis, Tennessee, in 1949 and landed a disc jockey spot on WDIA, the first station in the nation to go to an all-black format. King took the name "Beale Street Blues Boy," which was then shortened to "B. B.," and embarked on the most successful of all blues careers in 1951 with "Three O'Clock Blues," a #1 R&B hit that was recorded in independent producer Sam Phillips' newly-opened Memphis studio and leased to the Los Angeles-based Modern Records.

King and his trusty guitar, "Lucille," have been the blues' ambassador to the mainstream without sacrificing his heritage or losing touch with his emotional roots, whether playing in a rowdy blueshall or a black tie nightclub. The amiable, constantly touring King was the most popular blues performer on the "hippie" circuit during the blues revival of the late sixties and early seventies, and even enjoyed a string of pop hits in the period, including 1969's "The Thrill Is Gone," a classic pleading blues in a lush modern soul setting. King's influence on later blues and rock guitarists, like Otis Rush, Buddy Guy, and Eric Clapton, was so pervasive that it is really inseparable from the influence of the blues itself.

Howlin' Wolf

Another Delta native, the peerless Howlin' Wolf (b. Chester Burnett, 1910; d. 1976), also began a daily radio broadcast in Memphis in 1949, though in every other way he represented the opposite end of the blues spectrum from the forward looking sophistication of B. B. King. Howlin' Wolf grew up on the Dockery Farms plantation near Cleveland, Mississippi, which was also home to Charley Patton and as good a candidate as any for the actual birthplace of the Delta blues. Wolf played with and learned from Patton, Son House, Robert Johnson and the other Delta giants, but was still splitting his time between farming and playing the blues when he decided to move to Memphis and begin a serious music career at the age of 39. Howlin' Wolf remained firmly rooted in pure Delta blues—no jazzy licks or uptown gloss for the Wolf—and used electricity to amplify and further strengthen the raw intensity of the Delta blues. The recordings he made at Sam Phillips' studio from 1950 through 1952, including "Moaning at Midnight" and "How Many More Years," rank as some of the most electrifying records ever made, driven by Willie Johnson's brutal, distorted guitar playing and Wolf's soul-piercing, microphone-shredding vocals and unearthly trademark howls. Sam Phillips recalls the intensity of a Howlin' Wolf session: "...the greatest show you could see to this day would be Chester Burnett doing one of those sessions in my studio. God, what it would be worth on film to see the fervor in that man's face when he sang. His eyes would light up, you'd see the veins come out on his neck, and, buddy, there was *nothing* on his mind but that song. He sang with his damn soul."[10]

Together, the contrasting styles of B. B. King and Howlin' Wolf present the musical extremes of urban blues styles and hint at the rich vitality of Memphis and Beale Street in the early fifties. A decade later, the Stax studio made Memphis the soul music capital of America, though the blues still made its presence felt in the form of **Albert King**, who recorded with the Stax house band, Booker T. and the MG's. King's soul-spiked blues was the most direct influence on Eric Clapton's late-sixties work with Cream, who covered his "Born Under a Bad Sign," and, via Clapton, on the guitar styles of an entire generation of blues-rockers.

John Lee Hooker

Most notable among the other cities that developed their own blues scenes were Houston, home to Albert Collins ("The Freeze"), Lightnin' Hopkins ("Short Haired Woman") and the Duke record label, where Bobby "Blue" Bland ("Farther Up the Road") and Junior Parker ("Next Time You See Me") recorded; St. Louis, home to Ike Turner, Little Milton Campbell and pre-Stax Albert King; and Detroit, where Clarksdale, Mississippi native **John Lee Hooker** recorded "Boogie Chillen" in 1948, a classic one-chord rhythmic riff that has been endlessly copied and elaborated upon (most admirably by Canned Heat and ZZ Top). Hooker's hypnotic rhythmic drones, half-spoken storylines and casual spontaneity formed one of the blues' most distinct individual styles. Other oft-covered originals include "Crawling King Snake Blues," recorded by the Doors, and "Boom Boom," a 1962 R&B hit that was covered by the Yardbirds (featuring Eric Clapton) at their first recording session. Hooker lived long enough to reap the accolades—in the form of covers, recorded tributes and a slew of jams and duets—of his rock descendants, and he remains the official Living Legend of the blues.

Sweet Home Chicago

Oh baby, don't you want to go
Oh baby, don't you want to go
Back to the land of California, to my sweet home Chicago

So sang Robert Johnson in 1936, and wherever it was, Chicago was definitely *out there* somewhere far enough from the dying farms and dreary life of the Delta to seem like a beacon of hope. By World War II, Chicago was home to a huge community of transplanted Delta residents, including many blues artists who were lured by the factory jobs and, later, by the hope of recording for **Chess Records**, the great urban blues label founded by Leonard and Phil Chess in the late forties.

Chicago's promise of jobs and opportunity had lured southern blacks and fueled the dreams of musicians ever since an influx from New Orleans turned Chicago into the jazz center of the early twenties. By the 1940's, Chicago was home to Big Bill Broonzy, Tampa Red, John Lee "Sonny Boy" Williamson, Peetie Wheatstraw, Kokomo Arnold and many other southern bluesmen who were recording with small band backings and playing in a variety of popular styles ranging from straight blues to jazz, jump and novelty numbers meant to appeal to the changing tastes of an urban audience. In spite of the changes, however, black Chicago remained a very southern community: the sprawling South Side and social centers like the Maxwell Street market were filled with displaced, homesick southerners who still loved their blues hard and straight, Delta-style. Chicago inherited the Delta's blues heritage as a link to the past but used it to help shape the future, in the Chess Records releases by Muddy Waters, Howlin' Wolf and the other greats who made Chicago synonymous with the bar band style of urban blues that fed—and still feeds—directly into rock & roll.

Muddy Waters

Muddy Waters (b. McKinley Morganfield, 1915; d. 1983) was first recorded in 1941 at his home on the Stovall Plantation near Clarksdale, Mississippi, by Library of Congress archivist Alan Lomax. His style was directly descended from Robert Johnson and classic Delta bottleneck blues, and it remained strongly rooted in the Delta even after his move to Chicago in 1943 and his switch to electric guitars. Muddy Waters' first hit, "I Can't Be Satisfied," an electrified update of one of his early Lomax recordings, was released in 1948 on the Aristocrat label, which was renamed Chess Records in 1949. Chess launched its long run as the premiere blues label with a series of Muddy Waters hits in the early fifties—"Louisiana Blues," "Honey Bee," "She Moves Me," "Still a Fool"—that featured a full band backing and a fully-realized urban blues sound.

The toughened sound provided by electricity and amplifiers was further strengthened on Muddy's records by Leonard Chess' experiments with echo and reverb, intentionally over-driven microphones and the amplified harmonica that is as strong and menacing a presence as Muddy's singing and slide guitar. Waters and harmonica player Little Walter Jacobs were joined by guitarist Jimmy Rogers, pianist Otis Spann, bassist Willie Dixon and drummer Elgin Evans, all Delta refugees, in Chicago's first great blues band—probably the greatest blues band ever assembled. The dark, brooding, fiercely electric sound of Muddy Waters' music defined urban blues and astonished his fellow blues players and Chicago audiences. The music seemed startlingly new yet familiar, as if the ghost of Robert Johnson had reappeared in the guise of a thoroughly modern blues band. A decade later, Waters' records had an equally electrifying impact on a small but devoted band of blues devotees in England, who viewed coming even *close* to the sound of a Muddy Waters record as the ultimate accomplishment. (Muddy Waters liked the Rolling Stones' version of "I Just Want to Make Love to You" and declared them "my boys," to the great delight and relief of the group who had taken their name from one of his songs.)

Willie Dixon and Howlin' Wolf at Chess

Muddy Waters was the blues world's equivalent of a rock star, and his larger-than-life, "hoodoo stud" image was cemented by the sexual bravado and stop-time swagger of his biggest hits: "Hoochie Coochie Man," "I Just Want to Make Love to You" and "I'm Ready." All three songs were written for Waters in 1954 by Chess Records' resident bass player, A&R man, songwriter, arranger, producer and talent scout, **Willie Dixon**. Dixon (b. Vicksburg, Mississippi, 1915;

d. 1992) was the author of the greatest modern blues, including a long string of hits for Muddy Waters, "My Babe" for Little Walter, "I Can't Quit You Baby" for Otis Rush, and most of the Chess hits for Howlin Wolf.[11]

Howlin' Wolf moved to Chicago in 1953 and made music at the Chess studio that was even more ferocious than his Memphis recordings. The shivering dread of 1954's "Evil" and the hypnotic riff and eerie howls of his 1956 signature song, "Smokestack Lightnin'," staked his turf as Muddy Waters' only serious rival. Wolf hit full stride in the early sixties with his own "Killing Floor" and a slew of Willie Dixon numbers, including "Wang Dang Doodle," "Back Door Man," "Little Red Rooster" and "Spoonful," all covered to the point of being rock standards. (The piercing snarl of Howlin' Wolf's voice was copied as well, most obviously by Wolfman Jack, most creatively by Captain Beefheart.)

Jimmy Reed and Elmore James

Howlin' Wolf and Muddy Waters were the Twin Towers at Chess, though nearly all of the Chicago blues greats recorded for the label during its heyday. Two notable exceptions were Delta veterans Jimmy Reed, who recorded for Chicago's Vee Jay Records, and Elmore James, who recorded for a number of labels (including Chess). Reed was one the best-known bluesmen among white audiences, thanks largely to the frequent covers of his songs. (Elvis Presley, for one, covered Reed's "Big Boss Man," "Ain't That Lovin' You Baby" and "Baby, What You Want Me to Do.") Elmore James' slash & burn slide guitar harkened back to the deepest blues of the Delta—back to the days when he traveled with Robert Johnson. James played the hardest rocking, most straightforward and accessible style of bar band blues, and had a huge influence—probably the biggest of all the blues players—on rock guitarists, who have habitually copied his style and covered "It Hurts Me Too," "Shake Your Money Maker" and his electrifying version of Robert Johnson's "Dust My Broom."

Hound Dog Taylor, Son Seals, Otis Rush, Buddy Guy, Junior Wells and many other great singers and players have kept Chicago blues alive through changing times and tastes. Today's wide and largely white audience for the blues obscures the fact that, for all the brilliance of the music and musicians, the blues appealed to a relatively small audience of older black listeners during its explosive peak in the 1950's. Undiluted blues was completely foreign to most white listeners, young or old, through the fifties, and was considered old-fashioned by younger black listeners who preferred the dance beat and happier feel of *rhythm* & blues. Times got even tougher for the blues artists when rhythm & blues crossed over and turned into rock & roll, taking away more of their audience and venues. Ironically, Chess Records was home to two of the early shaping forces of rock & roll: Chuck Berry and Bo Diddley. This significant contribution has earned Chess praise for helping to "invent" rock & roll, though it had already done that long before Berry and Diddley arrived.

The Blues Had a Baby and They Named it 'Rock & Roll'

While initially viewed as a threat and a thankless imitation, rock music was eventually responsible for bringing the blues to a wider audience than it had ever enjoyed or dreamed of. Many of the surviving originals, like Son House, Sonny Boy Williamson and John Lee Hooker, were rediscovered during the late fifties and early sixties as the booming popularity of folk music sent young aficionados digging further into their musical roots. The mid-sixties British Invasion heightened interest in the men who had inspired so many rock guitar heroes and recorded the original versions of so many current hits. The Rolling Stones, for example, began as a blues covers band and sang the praises of their heroes to anyone who would listen—they performed Howlin' Wolf's "Little Red Rooster" on the *Ed Sullivan Show* and insisted that Howlin' Wolf himself be included as a guest when they appeared on the television show *Shindig*. Blues guitarists like B. B. King, Elmore James, Albert King and Albert Collins achieved even greater popularity in the late sixties when they were embraced by the psychedelic scene that, thanks to Hendrix and Clapton, had developed a new appreciation for the blues and for virtuoso guitar playing.

Elvis Presley began his career singing a blues song in Sam Phillip's Memphis studio, and the thin line separating the blues and rock has been blurred ever since. The blues formed the foundation for the guitar rock of the Rolling Stones, the Yardbirds, Cream, John Mayall's Bluesbreakers, Jimi Hendrix, the Paul Butterfield Blues Band, Canned Heat, Led Zeppelin, ZZ Top, Johnny Winter, Stevie Ray Vaughan, and so on down an endless list, and it remains a source of rejuvenating energy and inspiration. Always adaptable yet timeless and unchanging, the blues is rock's soul and conscience. While other rock "influences" can be pointed out and traced with some definition, the influence of the blues is so deeply imbedded that it is much more than a mere "influence." As Muddy Waters once sang, "the blues had a baby and they named it 'rock & roll'."

COUNTRY & WESTERN

The blues and its rhythm & blues offspring were the most direct influences on rock & roll, but other musical genres contributed as well and brought added dimensions that kept it from being merely an imitation of R&B. At its best, country music resonated with all the depth and emotional honesty of the blues. It was the native sound of the rural white South and the home style of Elvis Presley, Jerry Lee Lewis, Carl Perkins, Buddy Holly and all of the other "rockabillies" who brought a distinctly country accent rock & roll.

It makes sense that the South was the region where white musicians were first able to incorporate an essentially black style to create their own brand of rock & roll. The blues, country music, gospel and other "folk" music's of the South always existed side-by-side, and though racial hatred was a fact of life, coexisting was a fact as well—much more than in the supposedly "equal" but very separate racial worlds of the North. And while the audiences may have been segregated, the music never was: southern musicians had borrowed from and influenced each other since the music of the slaves first caught the plantation owners' nervous and fascinated ears, and country musicians and blues musicians had borrowed from each other before either music had a name.

"The Sources of Country Music," a mural by Thomas Hart Benton at the Country Music Hall of Fame and Museum, depicts country music's varied roots, showing Appalachian dulcimers and fiddles, a banjo played by rural black man, a guitar playing cowboy, a church choir, a riverboat and train passing by, a cowboy saddle, a moonshine jug... Country music's heritage runs deep into America's past, back to the early settlers and to British folk songs and other European folk styles that were brought to America and gradually transformed by the harsh new land and by new musical ideas and cultural settings.

Bill Monroe (b. 1911), the founder of bluegrass music, recalls the varied sources and influences on even his style: "It's got an old-time fiddle and string band feeling, but I put the hard rhythm drive in there with my mandolin. There's a feeling of the Methodists and Baptists singers in the music, too, and Scotch bagpipe playing and southern blues, too—I always loved the blues, and I wanted to put the feeling of the blues in my music."[12] The timeless sound of bluegrass was literally invented by Monroe in the early 1940's, and despite its varied sources and the breakneck virtuosity that balanced its "high, lonesome sound," bluegrass remained the most self-consciously traditional of country styles, sticking with acoustic instruments and traditional themes while other country styles adapted and moved ahead.

Even Bill Monroe made a mark on rock & roll, however: his 1946 classic, "Blue Moon of Kentucky," took an unlikely leap into rock history as the flipside of Monroe fan Elvis Presley's first single. ("He came and apologized for the way he changed it around, and I told him he was gonna sell a lot of records with that and I was for him a hundred percent."[13]) The other side of the single was "That's All Right," a rural blues by Arthur Crudup that also dated from 1946, and it was the bold surprise of a "country boy playing the blues" that helped ignite rock & roll. And while Elvis' fusion of blues and country seemed—and was—startlingly new in 1954, it was also the culmination of many decades of white borrowings from the blues.

The Carter Family

Country music in the early 1900's consisted largely of Appalachian string bands who had already incorporated the African-derived banjo and the influence of black styles of fiddle and guitar playing. With the rising popularity of radio and recordings in the 1920's, country music began reaching a wider audience and vocalists began to dominate the sound. The widely famous country artists were the Carter Family and Jimmie Rodgers, who both launched their recording careers in 1927 in Bristol, Tennessee.

The Carter Family consisted of A. P. Carter on fiddle and his wife Sara and sister-in-law Maybelle on vocals, autoharp and guitar. Between 1927 and 1941 the Carter Family recorded over 300 songs, preserving a rich heritage of traditional country and folk material—sacred and secular—along with A. P. Carter's original songs. (Carter wrote several classics but also copyrighted many traditional songs under his own name, reflecting the same liberal interpretation of "authorship" found among blues singers.) The Carter Family built their group style around the alternating strumming and thumb-picking of Maybelle's guitar playing, which mixed melodic bass lines with strummed chords and established an entire school of country guitar picking.

The Carter Family embodied the musical values and social conservatism of the South, rooted firmly in tradition and God-fearing Christianity. Although they occasionally recorded songs in blues forms (usually denoted by a "blues" in the title, as in "Worried Man Blues"), their enduring popularity was based largely on the upright sentiment and the reassuring evocation of the past reflected in songs like "Will the Circle Be Unbroken," "Wabash Cannonball" and "Wildwood Flower." Maybelle and her daughters continued performing as the Carter Family into the 1970's, reaching new audiences through daughter June's marriage to Johnny Cash, who booked them on his tours and television shows. (Granddaughter Carlene Carter now keeps the seventy-year family dynasty alive.)

Jimmie Rodgers

Jimmie Rodgers (1897-1933) was a friend and fellow traveler of the Carter Family and a similarly encyclopedic collector of traditional songs and styles. Rodgers grew up in Mississippi, however, not in the Virginia hills that were home to the Carter Family, and he grew up familiar with both black and white styles and was at home with the blues to a degree unprecedented among recorded white artists. Rodgers was also tuned to the latest Tin Pan Alley hits, risqué novelty songs and sentimental ballads, and was not at all shy about mixing up his styles and audience, but he laid his greatest claim to the future with his convincing appropriation of black styles—by popularizing the black borrowings that had informed white folk music for years, and by formulating the country-plus-blues equation that eventually equaled rock & roll. (The blues players were equally attuned to their white counterparts: several of Rodgers' songs joined the blues vernacular, and his influence even extended to artists as far afield from country as Howlin' Wolf, who claimed that he "wanted to yodel like Jimmie Rodgers" but couldn't, so he howled instead.)

Rodgers wrote a good portion of his own material and often mixed blues licks and bent notes into his country style or fit his country style into an earthy 12-bar blues peppered with stock blues phrases and his trademark "blue yodels," as in his "**Blue Yodel #1**," recorded in 1927:

> T for Texas, T for Tennessee,
> T for Texas, T for Tennessee,
> T for Thelma—that gal that made a wreck out of me.
>
> If you don't want me mama, you sure don't have to stall,
> If you don't want me mama, you sure don't have to stall,
> 'cause I can get more women than a passenger train can haul.
>
> I'm gonna buy me a pistol, just as long as I'm tall,
> I'm gonna buy me a pistol, just as long as I'm tall,
> I'm gonna shoot poor Thelma, just to see her jump and fall.

And so on... Each verse is capped—almost dementedly so, considering poor Thelma—with the carefree yodel he made his trademark, while the even strumming rhythm and alternating low string bass notes of his guitar are clear blueprints for the basic feel of country music. The 12-bar form and earthy lyrics, however, were lifted straight out of the blues. (All of the song's verses were taken from the blues vernacular; the second, for example, can be found in Bessie Smith's 1924 recording of "Ticket Agent, Ease Your Window Down.") This prescient blending of blues and country styles earned Rodgers a spot alongside Robert Johnson in the first round of inductions to the Rock & Roll Hall of Fame's "Early Influences" category.

Jimmie Rodgers projected the image of a vagabond loner, riding the rails from town to town, tavern to tavern and woman to woman, hell-bent on living every moment his advancing tuberculosis allowed him. His romanticized, hard-living lifestyle and larger-than-life image was an important part of his appeal, as it would be for later country and rock stars, and represented the *other* side of country music and southern culture—the Saturday night side that fueled the Sunday morning guilt and repentance. Often called the "Father of Country Music," Rodgers was the first true country *star*, and he exerted a tremendous influence on those who followed: Roy Acuff, Bill Monroe, Ernest Tubb, Hank Snow, Gene Autry and many other country giants began their careers singing his songs and copying his style (even his yodels, which were a key emotional element of many cowboy songs). While the Carter Family helped preserve the roots and rich heritage of country music, Rodgers' eclectic borrowings and personal imprint pushed country toward a bigger world and broader expressive palette.

Western Swing

The traditional string bands, autoharps and dulcimers of Appalachia gave way to newer styles as country music's popularity grew and spread throughout the South and Southwest. Nashville, Tennessee, emerged as country music's capital city, but other areas added their own flavor to country music, including Jimmie Rodgers' adopted home state of Texas, where "country" was expanded into "country & western." Country music's rustic, "common folk" appeal, coupled with the image of the drifting loner popularized by Rodgers, blended easily into the romantic cowboy and western themes popularized in songs and movies. Free from the "hillbilly" stigma of other country styles, "Singing Cowboys" like Gene Autry, Tex Ritter, Roy Rogers and the Sons of the Pioneers brought a smooth and sentimental version of country music to a wide audience during the Depression and World War II years, when the image of tough American cowboys held a particularly strong and patriotic appeal. The cowboy songs were stocked with the requisite references to "little dogies," "Old Paint," jingling spurs, ropin' and ridin' and wide-open spaces and were generally sung with smooth voices sweetened by strings, choirs and Hollywood orchestras. (Cowgirls were popular as well: Patsy Montana yodeled her way to the first country music hit for a female singer in 1935 with "I Want to Be a Cowboy's Sweetheart.")

"Western" meant more than Singing Cowboys, however. Texas, Oklahoma and the surrounding areas were dotted with bars and dance halls in the 1930's, thanks to an oil boom that softened the blow of the Depression. Like the juke joints of the deep South that were home to the blues, the "honky-tonks on the outskirts of town" spawned a subculture fueled by hard working, hard drinking and hard dancing, and by a musical style tough and rhythmic enough to keep it all going. Although the term "western swing" was not widely used until the mid-forties, a big-beat dance style swept the Southwest and gained national popularity in the late thirties and through the War years. With a mandate to make people dance and forget their troubles, western swing musicians looked beyond country music to a more obvious source of earthiness and rhythmic vitality—to the blues, jazz and to the big band music that put the "swing" in "western swing."

Bandleader **Bob Wills** (1905-75), the "King of Western Swing," began his recording career in 1929 with a version of Bessie Smith's "Gulf Coast Blues.". He continued to incorporate black styles, adding the influence of Dixieland jazz and band leaders like Kansas City's Count Basie to his country two-step sound and sentimental popular selections. With star vocalist Tommy Duncan up front, Wills' gradually expanded his group, the Texas Playboys, to include piano, accordion, and sax and horn sections modeled after big band swing. The Texas Playboys further shocked the crowd at the *Grand Ole Opry* in 1945 by being the first to use drums on the show—blasphemy to country purists, but a key ingredient in Wills' rhythmic dance style.

The guitar remained the premier instrument in western swing, however. (The prominence of the guitar is another feature that links country music and the blues and distinguished them both from pop, jazz and rhythm & blues, where the guitar remained primarily a supporting rhythm instrument.) Country music developed its own distinct guitar sound, partly due by a fad for the exotic wave-like sound of the Hawaiian guitar, created by fretting the neck of the guitar with a steel bar. A similar "steel guitar" style became one of country music's defining traits, with the added influence of the bottleneck slide styles developed by the blues players. (The playing styles were quite different, however: blues players usually held the guitar normally, while country steel players usually held the guitar in their laps or, later, stood to play the free-standing electrified versions.)

The steel guitar, manufactured by the National and Dobro companies beginning in the late 1920's, was used in all country styles. It's not surprising, however, that western swing groups were the first to exploit *amplification* as a way of further expanding their big band sound. The electric steel guitar was first manufactured in 1931 and was commonly used in western swing bands by late thirties. Here, too, the influence of jazz was pronounced: early solos, by pioneers like Texas Playboy Leon McAuliffe and Bob Dunn of Milton Brown and His Musical Brownies, often mimicked jazz sax solos in timbre and style. The bent and blue notes of the blues was also a natural influence on the steel players, who, in turn, influenced Charlie Christian, T-Bone Walker and other early electric jazz and blues guitarists in a continuing cross-pollination between the styles. The mid-forties saw the introduction of further advancements: the pedal steel guitar, which offered a rich new range of timbres, and solid body electric guitars, the most popular of which were made by Californian Leo Fender (who also introduced an electric bass guitar in 1951).

The Grand Ole Opry

Western swing remained popular mainly in the Southwest and in California after World War II, though it did directly influence rock & roll via Bill Haley and His Comets—a western swing combo from the Pennsylvania that was originally called Bill Haley and His Saddlemen, until their bandleader fell under the spell of Louis Jordan and rhythm & blues. The "purer" country music of the South and Southeast reclaimed its predominance in the 1940's and reached a wide audience via recordings and radio broadcasts. Nashville cemented its place at the center of the country world with the live shows and radio broadcasts from the *Grand Ole Opry*, the "Mother Church of Country Music." Live radio broadcasts were crucial to the growth of country music, just as they helped spread jazz, blues and swing music. Chicago's WLS beamed a "Barn Dance" program throughout the Midwest beginning in 1924. A year later, Nashville station WSM launched its own "Barn Dance," which was renamed the *Grand Ole Opry* in 1927. The show was dominated by old-time string bands in the early days, and benefited from Nashville's proximity to country's Appalachian headwaters. Its first notable personality was Uncle Dave Macon, a banjo playing comic who relied on down-home humor and a vast storehouse of country, folk, minstrel and vaudeville songs.

Roy Acuff and Ernest Tubb

The first true singing star of the *Grand Ole Opry* was Roy Acuff (1903-92), who came to the Opry in 1938, straight from his home in the Appalachian foothills of Eastern Tennessee. Acuff was an institution in Nashville for over half a century, as both an entertainer and as the co-founder, with Fred Rose in 1942, of the Acuff-Rose publishing house, the first publisher devoted exclusively to country music.[14] Acuff's best-known songs, including "The Great Speckled Bird" and "The Precious Jewel," were sung with a guileless sincerity and respect for tradition that packed a powerful emotional punch, especially during the War years: "When Roy Acuff raised his voice in his mournful, mountain style, he seemed to suggest all the verities for which Americans were fighting: home, mother, and God."[15] The war itself brought young Americans of all backgrounds and from all regions together, and was a major factor in the nationwide spread of country music's popularity. In fact, Roy Acuff won a popularity poll among servicemen sponsored by the Armed Forces Network, which beamed country music alongside the music of Frank Sinatra and the swing bands. In one famous incident on Okinawa, the Japanese charged the American lines hurling the worst insults they could think of: "To hell with Roosevelt! To hell with Babe Ruth! To hell with Roy Acuff!"

Texan Ernest Tubb came to the *Grand Ole Opry* in 1943 after scoring his first hit in 1941 with "Walking the Floor Over You." Tubb began his singing career as a Jimmie Rodgers clone, until the removal of his tonsils in 1939 also removed his ability to yodel and forced him to develop his own style. The "honky-tonk" style he perfected became the model for Hank Williams and other honky-tonk exponents who would dominate country music for over a decade. Tubb's choked acoustic guitar style, played as much for the backbeat rhythm as for the chords, set the feel for the dance beat of honky-tonk, which was created without the benefit of a drummer (much as Elvis Presley's rhythmic acoustic guitar playing grounded his drum-less early rockabilly recordings). Tubb's style also popularized the use of the electric lead guitar in the Southeast, while his flat, folksy singing epitomized the casual warmth and honesty that appealed to country fans and invited the scorn of more "sophisticated" ears. Ernest Tubb was second in popularity only to Roy Acuff through the forties, though the dancing beat and the cheatin', drinkin' and heartache imagery of his songs seemed far removed from Acuff's Smoky Mountain piety.

Hank Williams

Those two prevalent strands of country music—Acuff's homage to tradition and Tubb's rootless honky-tonk—were fused by Hank Williams, one of America's great artists and still a looming presence in country music, over four decades after his death. A folk poet and musical synthesizer in the league of Robert Johnson, Williams marked the culmination of a passing era and thoroughly redefined country music for modern times, pushing well beyond any "hillbilly" and cowboy clichés. Born in 1923 in rural Alabama, Williams was solidly rooted in rural Southern tradition, but his rambling life, his addictions to alcohol and pain killers (begun as treatment for a chronically aching back) and his turbulent, consuming marriage to Audrey Sheppard kept his eyes open to a darker and rootless world. Although his catalog of good-humored uptempo songs includes favorites like "Hey Good Lookin'" and "Jambalaya," he was at his best in the personal songs pulled from his own heartaches—the melancholy weepers that continue to resonate with anyone who has survived the ravages of love.

Williams wrote and sang with absolute sincerity and artful insight: he *lived* the songs he sang, or seemed to, and was able to capture universal emotions in a few plainspoken words. In doing so, he expanded country music's expressive range immensely, just as Robert Johnson breathed unexpected new life into traditional blues and just as Bob Dylan would expand rock's poetic possibilities. "Your Cheatin' Heart," "Cold, Cold Heart," "I Can't Help It If I'm Still in Love With You," "Take These Chains from My Heart" and so many other Hank Williams classics earned country music the title of "the white man's blues." Like the greatest folk artists of any style, Williams gave voice to the hopes, fears, dreams and *realities* of the lives of his listeners. And like a great poet of any art form, he was able to perfectly capture a mood and freeze an image, collapsing a broad emotional expanse into a few well-chosen words, as in "I'm So Lonesome I Could Cry," where his internal sorrow colors a desolate external tableau:

> Hear that lonesome whippoorwill, he sounds to blue to fly,
> The midnight train is whining low, I'm so lonesome I could cry.
>
> I've never seen a night so long, when time goes crawling by,
> The moon just went behind the clouds to hide his face and cry.
>
> Did you ever see a robin weep when leaves begin to die?
> That means he's lost the will to live, I'm so lonesome I could cry.
>
> The silence of a falling star lights up a purple sky,
> And as I wonder where you are, I'm so lonesome I could cry.[16]

Hank Williams' first country hit was 1947's "Move It On Over" (which uncannily anticipated the beat and melody of "Rock Around the Clock"). He became a regular on the *Louisiana Hayride* radio show, broadcast throughout the South from Shreveport, Louisiana, in 1948, then moved up to the *Grand Ole Opry* the following year with the huge success of "Lovesick Blues."   An unending stream of country classics, supported by constant touring and a well-publicized soap opera life, made Williams a country superstar and brought country music to a much wider audience, through his own recordings and through cover versions of his songs recorded by popular mainstream artists (including Tony Bennett, who recorded "Cold, Cold Heart" in 1951, and Rosemary Clooney, who recorded "Half as Much" the following year).

Williams was fired from the *Opry* in 1952 for drunkenness and unreliability.   Still a hero, he returned to the *Louisiana Hayride*, but his anguish increased with his divorce and a rapid remarriage that was "performed" before audiences in New Orleans' Municipal Auditorium, in ironic recognition of how public his private life had become. The sheer pain of living that can fuel great art inevitably takes its toll, and it seems that tormented souls like Hank Williams (or Robert Johnson or Bessie Smith, or Charlie Parker, Billie Holiday, Janis Joplin, Jimi Hendrix, Mozart...) are somehow predestined for an early demise. Williams' "I'll Never Get Out of This World Alive" was on the country charts when his heart gave out in the back of a Cadillac late one night on a lost highway in West Virginia, on his way to a New Years Day 1953 show in Canton, Ohio. Williams was a very old and world-weary 29 when he died.

Hank Williams' death—like Buddy Holly's, six short years later—symbolized the end of an era. Williams left musical offspring all over the South who mimicked his style then took his influence on a detour that went further into the blues than ever before (though Williams, too, had continued the tradition of borrowing blues forms in songs like "Honky Tonk Blues"). Elvis Presley even followed in Williams' footsteps as a regular on the *Louisiana Hayride*, where he was a huge success, and in a disastrous appearance at the *Grand Ole Opry*, where he was booed by country fans who weren't quite ready for the unholy marriage to the blues called "rock & roll."

Country Music in the Rock Era

A restless younger generation *was* ready, however, and they defected in droves to rockabilly and rock & roll, depriving mainstream country music of many great talents and much of its audience and commercial network. The challenge of rock & roll and the overpowering legacy of Hank Williams made a change of direction necessary for country music's survival. In the late-fifties a new "Nashville Sound" emerged, crafted mainly by producers Chet Atkins and Owen Bradley, who dispensed with the traditional trappings of fiddles, steel guitars and country twangs in favor of a more pop-oriented sound sweetened by strings, choirs and polished productions. Eddy Arnold, Faron Young, Tennessee Ernie Ford, Marty Robbins, Jim Reeves, Conway Twitty, Patsy Cline and several other country singers managed to cross over into the pop mainstream while retaining a country base, though a notable few, such as George Jones, Lefty Frizzell and Ray Price, stayed true to the honky-tonks and the legacy of Hank Williams (though even George Jones felt obliged to give rockabilly a try).

The purist honky-tonk sound of Buck Owens and Merle Haggard made Bakersfield, California, a prominent alternative to Nashville in the 1960's, an era that saw further country inroads into the mainstream, including the pop success of Roger Miller ("King of the Road," "Dang Me") and Johnny Cash and Glen Campbell, who both had broad enough appeal to land their own television shows at the end of the decade. Television also helped keep traditional, hardcore country alive in the 1960's: *The Wilburn Brothers Show*, *The Porter Wagoner Show*, *Hee Haw* and other popular shows mixed great music with cornball humor that resurrected the unfortunate "hillbilly" images from the past and reflected country music's ambivalent attitude toward change. Tammy Wynette's 1968 hit, "Stand By Your Man," captured country's prevailing conservative winds, although her success did nudge the country establishment further along in its grudging acceptance of female artists.

Country music clung to an increasingly romanticized image rooted in a rapidly dying rural culture—in sharp contrast to the blues, which expressed no such nostalgia about the harsh realities of the past. The country audience was at the opposite end of the spectrum from the rock counterculture in the 1960's, when issues like the Vietnam War and the civil rights struggle polarized the country. It was something of a shock, then, when Bob Dylan released an album in 1969 called *Nashville Skyline*, which featured straightforward country stylings and duets with Johnny Cash. Dylan, the Byrds, Buffalo Springfield, Poco, Gram Parsons and the Flying Burrito Brothers were at the forefront of rock's incorporation of country styles, which paved the way for the highly successful California "country rock" of Linda Ronstadt, the Eagles and other seventies superstars. Back in the South, the Allman Brothers, Lynyrd Skynyrd, Charlie Daniels, the Marshall Tucker Band and others fashioned an updated blend of guitar-based country, blues and boogie, while a group of self-styled country "outlaws"—Waylon Jennings, Willie Nelson, Kris Kristofferson, Hank Williams, Jr., and Jerry Jeff Walker—responded with a rock-derived sound and lifestyle and singer-songwriter sensibilities that were an open rebellion against the conservative Nashville hierarchy.

The *Grand Ole Opry* moved from its traditional home in downtown Nashville's Ryman Auditorium to a new "Opryland" theme park outside of town in 1974. The change was an apt metaphor for the direction country music was taking. Kenny Rogers and Dolly Parton led country's crossover assault on the pop mainstream in the 1970's, with a smooth "countrypolitan" sound and an image bland enough for the seventies mainstream, where pop and watered-down country mingled easily enough for middle-of-the-road entertainers like John Denver, Anne Murray and Olivia Newton-John to be passed off as "country." In reaction, the 1980's saw a revival of traditional country styles that overlapped with the similarly inspired "roots rock" movement. Ricky Scaggs, George Strait, Clint Black, Randy Travis and other "New Traditionalists" fashioned modern images with retro-country styles, while veterans like George Jones and Johnny Cash found their styles back in fashion and their audience bigger than ever.

The lines between rock, pop and country have been thoroughly blurred, with Garth Brooks outselling Michael Jackson and country earmarks such as fiddles and steel guitars woven into rock songs as naturally as blues licks. (The country-roots sound was popularized by John Mellencamp in the mid-1980's and was widely adopted as a badge of musical honesty in the age of synthesizers and sampling.) Rock fans, especially older ones unable to relate to rap or heavy metal, have embraced country's reassuring emphasis on adult emotions and straightforward singing and songwriting, while country fans matter-of-factly claim rock & roll as their own and don't miss a beat when a country band breaks into "Johnny B. Goode" or "Honky Tonk Women."

Country music and the blues have both moved well beyond their traditional audience: country threatens to be more popular than pop, while upscale white babyboomers seem to be the core audience for blues these days. Nonetheless, both country music and the blues still derive much of their appeal from a sense of tradition and continuity and respect for their proud heritage. The indigenous styles of two "outsider" cultures, blacks and poor southern whites, the blues and country once spoke to and for a specific audience, reflecting the reality of their lives and hopes, dreams and values. As "folk" music in the broadest sense, the honest, direct expression of both styles was a stark contrast to the changing whims and mass-marketed blandness that characterized most popular entertainment.

Rock & roll rendered meaningless any remaining distinctions between "folk" and "popular" music (just as, a decade later, *Sgt. Pepper* and other lofty achievements blurred the line between "popular" and "fine" art). Rock fought its battles on the pop charts and its success there was its great victory and the requisite foundation for its power as a cultural force. It gained its emotional urgency and sense of communal empowerment, however, from having America's two great folk styles as its spiritual parents, and the blues and country music remain a source of renewal and inspiration to which rock periodically returns to stake its own claim to authenticity.

---

[1]The fervored, rhythmic "ring shouts" and other African-derived means of expressing religious fervor were equally unsettling. The plantation owners felt less threatened by the devout spirituals the slaves began singing as they adopted more melodic, European-derived styles, though they *would* have worried had they been aware of the "secret messages" that inspired an extra

measure of emotion here as well. "Swing Low Sweet Chariot" ("... comin' for to carry me home"), for example, was a coded reference to Harriet Tubman and underground railroad, and "home" could be read as both deliverance to heaven and deliverance to freedom in the North.

[2]A short, merely representative list of songs employing the 12-bar blues includes "Rock Around the Clock," "Hound Dog," "Blue Suede Shoes," "Johnny B. Goode," "Long Tall Sally" (and virtually every other Chuck Berry and Little Richard song), "Whole Lot of Shakin' Going On," "What'd I Say," "The Twist" and "Wipe Out." The only other commonly used chord patterns in early rock & roll were the I-vi-IV-V pop-ballad progression, used on "Earth Angel," "Breaking Up Is Hard to Do" and most other doo-wop ballads and early sixties pop songs, and the I-IV-V-IV "garage rock" progression, used in "La Bamba," "Louie Louie," "Twist and Shout," etc.

[3]Tony Heilbut, liner notes for "The Gospel Sound," Columbia Records.

[4]W. C. Handy, "Father of the Blues" (New York: Macmillan, 1944), p. 184.

[5]Robert Palmer, "Deep Blues" (New York: Viking, 1981) p. 45.

[6]ALthough known as "The Father of the Blues," Handy certainly did not "invent" the blues any more than Elvis Presley invented rock & roll. He was, however, the first to publish, commercialize and popularize the blues, and for this he is honored with a statue in Handy Park on Beale Street, the legendary blues district of Memphis. At the other end of Beale Street there is, appropriately enough, a statue of Elvis, the man who commercialized and popularized the blues beyond Handy's wildest dreams.

[7]Robert Palmer, "Deep Blues" (New York: Viking, 1981) p. 61.

[8]Johnson's voodoo spell seemed to reach through the ages for his spiritual godson, Jimi Hendrix, and the equally hard-living Janis Joplin and Jim Morrison, who all died at the age of 27, and for Elvis Presley—another great American synthesizer of styles—who died on August 16, the same day as Johnson.

[9]Clapton and Richards quotes from liner notes for the 1990 Columbia Records release, *Robert Johnson: The Complete Recordings*.

[10]Palmer, p. 233-234.

[11]Dixon's "You Need Love" was the subject of an extended and ultimately successful lawsuit with Led Zeppelin, who lifted much of the song for their own "Whole Lotta Love."

[12]Bill Monroe, in conversation with the author, September, 1992.

[13]ibid.

[14]The success of Acuff-Rose prompted other publishing houses and record companies to follow suit and open offices and recording studios in Nashville, solidifying the city's stature in the late forties.

[15]Bill Malone, "Country Music U.S.A." (Austin: University of Texas Press, 1985), p. 192.

Photo courtesy of THE BETTMAN ARCHIVE

Hank Williams

Photo courtesy of THE BETTMAN ARCHIVE

Louis Jordan

Photo courtesy of UPI/BETTMAN

Bill Haley and the Comets

[2] RHYTHM & BLUES

Rhythm & blues was an offspring of the blues, built on the musical language, 12-bar formal structure and emotional directness of the blues, though it was a rather rambunctious child. While the blues remained a relatively constant and self-contained musical form, rhythm & blues pulled from a variety of sources—blues, boogie-woogie, jazz, swing, gospel, pop—and changed with the times and trends.[1] The term "Rhythm & Blues" replaced the offensive "Race Records" label in *Billboard* magazine in 1949, the same year that "Country & Western" was substituted for "Hillbilly." (The two styles and audiences were originally lumped together in a "Western & Race" category, reflecting the view of black and southern white audiences as fringe elements outside of the mainstream represented by the "Popular" charts.) Like "race records," rhythm & blues was really just a catchall term that covered everything from Ink Spots ballads to Joe Turner shouts and meant little more than "black music aimed at a black audience," and even that definition was rendered inadequate when white teenagers discovered R&B and claimed it as "rock & roll."

As the name implies, rhythm & blues was propelled by stronger and faster rhythms made for the dance floor. The rollicking beat and bass lines of rhythm & blues came largely from piano boogie-woogie and big band swing music, which also spawned R&B's jazz-based instrumentation and band arrangements, while the vocal styles and emotional expression of R&B mixed blues urgency with pop's polish and gospel stylings. The livelier dance rhythms were complemented by upbeat and often sexual and humorous lyrics that appealed to a younger audience of urban blacks who were starting to view traditional blues as an uncomfortable reminder of times best forgotten. Rhythm & blues rolled right over the self-torment of the blues, just as rockabilly jettisoned the guilt that always accompanied the good times in country music. The rise of rhythm & blues in the years after World War II reflected the high spirits and the new feeling of optimism with which black Americans looked to the future and to a rightful place in a nation that had just won a war in the name of freedom and justice. The actual changes proved to be painfully slow in coming, but the music itself ended up playing a major role in bringing them about.

Boogie-woogie

A landmark pair of concerts, called "Spirituals to Swing," were presented in Carnegie Hall in 1938 and 1939. The concerts showcased all styles of black music and were an important watershed point for black music in America. The wide-ranging lineup included Big Bill Broonzy (a substitute for Robert Johnson, who died before he could be reached with an invitation to perform), gospel singer Sister Rosetta Tharpe, the blues-based swing of the Kansas City Six (featuring Count Basie and Lester Young), blues shouter Joe Turner, boogie pianists Pete Johnson, Albert Ammons, Meade Lux Lewis, and many others. The pianists caused the biggest sensation: their rollicking rhythms ignited a craze for boogie-woogie music that, like the ragtime and blues fads before it, was spread from cafe society to the masses via records and sheet music, and was soon adapted by popular white entertainers (the Andrews Sisters' "Boogie Woogie Bugle Boy" was one of the more obvious examples).

The origins of boogie-woogie are obscure as those of the blues, though the music seems to have originated in the saloons surrounding the lumber and turpentine camps in Texas and Louisiana in the early part of the century. Boogie-woogie found its urban base in Chicago, where the music was first recorded and where it was in constant demand for bars and "rent parties," which raised money for both the pianist and the landlord. Boogie-woogie was essentially a piano version of the 12-bar blues, derived from blues guitar styles, church piano styles and the ragtime and barrelhouse jazz styles of the New Orleans pianists. While shaped by the influence of the blues, boogie-woogie placed its emphasis on the dance beat and *rhythm*, rather than on the lyrics and personal expression, and on a good-times party mood that was a sharp contrast to the inward melancholy of the blues. (The term "boogie" came to be used by guitarists as well, to describe a particularly rhythmic style, and was eventually used to refer to dancing and partying in general.) The boogie-woogie players mixed the musical outlines of the 12-bar blues with pounding dance rhythms, driving left-hand bass patterns and fancy right-hand flourishes that were as idiomatic on the piano as bent strings and slide styles were on the guitar. And while it took a talent like Robert Johnson's to evoke an entire band with a single guitar, any enthusiastic piano player could smack keys, pound pedals and hammer out a constant "eight-to-the-bar" boogie bass to keep the dancers moving and the spirits high.

The term "boogie-woogie" was first used on record in 1928 by Clarence "Pine Top" Smith, who recorded "Pine Top's Boogie Woogie" in the form of a party song and dance lesson. Other early boogie innovators included Cow Cow Davenport, Albert Ammons, Meade Lux Lewis and **Jimmy Yancey**, the "Father of Boogie-woogie" who crystallized boogie style in the 1920's but did not make any recordings of his own until 1939. In a welcome acknowledgment of the formative influence of boogie-woogie, Jimmy Yancey joined Jimmie Rodgers and Robert Johnson as the first three inductees into the Rock & Roll Hall of Fame's "Early Influences" category. That influence is heard most clearly, of course, in the manic boogie of rock & roll piano, as exemplified by Little Richard and Jerry Lee Lewis, but it is also heard in rock's boogie-derived rhythms and bass lines and in the chugging rhythm and riffing lead styles that formed the essentials of rock & roll guitar as defined by Chuck Berry. (Berry adapted much of his guitar style from a piano playing bandleader, and called his own playing "boogie-woogie" until "rock & roll" became an operative term.)

Big Band Swing

En route to rock & roll, boogie-woogie helped turn jazz into swing music and put the *rhythm* in rhythm & blues. In the early 1930's, the New Orleans style of "Dixieland" jazz gave way to bigger bands and a more dance-oriented style pioneered by Fletcher Henderson in New York and Benny Moten and Count Basie in Kansas City (along with the great and unclassifiable Duke Ellington). Big band "swing" music was a pop phenomenon by the late 1930's, helped along by the lessening effects of the Depression and by a mania for dancing that swept the country in the years before and during World War II. The popularity of swing music was also aided by the repeal of Prohibition in 1933, which brought liquor—and jazz—out of the speakeasies and into the ballrooms and dance halls.

Swing music was one more example in a long line of black styles adopted by white audiences and white artists. Not surprisingly, the most commercially successful big bands were led by white bandleaders who had learned the lessens of the originators well, including Paul Whitehead, who was dubbed the "King of Jazz" in the twenties, and swing era stars Glenn Miller, Jimmy and Tommy Dorsey, and Benny Goodman, the nominal "King of Swing." (To his credit, Goodman was acutely aware of the racial bias that pronounced him the "King," and helped fight it by bringing black players into his bands and leading the fight to integrate jazz. He was helped and encouraged in this by producer and talent scout John Hammond, who organized the "Spirituals to Swing" concerts and played a major role in promoting the careers of Goodman, Count Basie, Billie Holiday and many others, including later discoveries like Bob Dylan, Bruce Springsteen, Aretha Franklin and Stevie Ray Vaughan.)

The big bands were made up of many players divided into brass, reed and rhythm sections. A typical line-up consisted of five brass players (trumpets and trombones), four reed players (saxophones and clarinets) and a four-man rhythm section made up of piano, guitar, bass and drums. (As rock's detractors were fond of pointing out, the basic rock band lineup was merely the *rhythm* section of a swing band.) Big bands were often broken down into smaller units as well, such as those led by Count Basie and Benny Goodman, that retained the rhythmic drive of the large groups and formed the foundation for the rhythm & blues bands of the late forties. Not all "swing" bands could really swing, however, and many concentrated instead on commercial novelties, polite dance numbers ("society music") and sweet sentimental favorites in the mode made famous by Paul Whiteman, Guy Lombardo and Lawrence Welk. But the most popular bands knew how to move a dance crowd, and the terms "big band" and "swing" became virtually interchangeable.

Swing music's lively dance rhythm was built over evenly stressed, four-to-the-bar beats that produced a more fluid rhythmic feel than the two-beat, "oom-pah" march of ragtime and Dixieland, a change of feel highlighted by the switch from tubas and banjos to string basses and guitars. The beats were often emphasized by a "walking" bass line that moved up and down the scale, or accelerated to double-time (eight-to-the-bar) by a boogie-woogie bass. Swing music featured plenty of hot soloists but was largely driven by tight, harmonized melodies played by entire instrumental sections, punctuated by short melodic fragments—"riffs"—that were tossed back and forth between sections in a propulsive call-and-response. (Glenn Miller's "In the Mood" is a good, famous example of riffing sections laid over a 12-bar blues, and a driving bass and dance beat.)

For an exciting few years, the stars of the swing bands were the *bands* themselves—the tight, intricately woven playing of the entire ensemble—and the instrumental soloists, including bandleaders like trombonist Glenn Miller on trombone and clarinetist Benny Goodman, and spotlighted band members: saxophonists Lester Young and Coleman Hawkins, trumpeter Roy Eldridge, drummers Gene Krupa and Buddy Rich, and guitarists Eddie Durham and Charlie Christian were among the many great players who gave swing music a personal stamp and, in the latter cases, helped bring the electric guitar to prominence as a featured solo instrument.

Big band swing was, at first, primarily a non-vocal instrumental form crafted by the bandleaders and arrangers (to the great consternation of the Tin Pan Alley songwriters and publishing houses). Even when singers were included, they were merely considered "featured vocalists" and did not necessarily stand out in the public's mind any more than, say, a trumpet soloist. (Indeed, much of the art of big band singing lay in making the voice an "instrument" and mastering all the subtle nuances of tone and phrasing displayed by the great instrumental soloists.) The focus inevitably changed with the arrival of great voices able to blend the popular song tradition with the jazz depth and rhythmic drive of swing. The featured vocalists eventually became the real stars, as great singers like Billie Holiday, Ella Fitzgerald, Ethel Waters and Sarah Vaughan rose to fame with various shadings of jazz, blues and popular styles.

Frank Sinatra

Once again it took a white artist to move a mass audience: Frank Sinatra set off an outpouring of hysterical adulation unmatched until Elvis came along. Sinatra (b. 1915) rose to prominence during the World War II years as the featured soloist with the Harry James and Tommy Dorsey big bands. His success did the most to shift the focus from the band leaders and instrumentalists to the star singers, while the sheer unprecedented *level* of his success defined new goals for all popular entertainers. Rock & roll may have learned its most important musical lessons elsewhere, but its measure of success came from the riches of the pop charts and the adoration of the pop audience—and Sinatra represented the ultimate measure of that success (just as Elvis defined the goals for the Beatles, and they in turn defined the goals, or fantasies, for everyone since). Along with Bing Crosby's cool, aloof croon, Sinatra's expressive singing served as a model and measuring stick for popular singers, including a good many envious rockers who shaped their style around their best efforts at imitating Sinatra's impeccable sense of melody and timing. Sinatra himself matured into an incomparable artist and avid rock hater. At least he earned the right to scoff: his lush 1950's collaborations with arranger Nelson Riddle stood outside and above the fray, unmoved either by rock & roll or by the generic banalities that had consumed mainstream popular music.

Nat "King" Cole

One of the first black artists to achieve widespread popularity with white listeners was Nat "King" Cole. Nat Cole was born in Montgomery, Alabama, in 1919, but he defined his sound and established his career in California, where the Nat Cole Trio pioneered a soft "club blues" style built around Cole's smooth, jazz-laced piano playing and a light bass & brushed drums accompaniment that served as a model for other scaled-down "lounge" groups. Cole's style included uptempo numbers like "Straighten Up and Fly Right" and "Route 66" that were the very definition of "hepcat" cool, but he moved in an increasingly middle-of-the-road direction in the late forties and early fifties with string-drenched hits like "Mona Lisa," "Too Young," "Unforgettable" and the ever-popular "Christmas Song" ("Chestnuts roasting on an open fire").[2]

Cole's clear-voiced, crooning interpretations of sentimental standards made him quite a rarity for his time—a black artist more popular with white audiences than with black, though the mature romance and sophisticated stylings of his music were beyond the experience and interest of the teenage market. His wide appeal and gracious manner did not place him beyond the hatred of racist bigots, however, even in his home state: Cole was dragged from the stage and savagely beaten during a 1956 concert in Birmingham, Alabama.

Nat "King" Cole remained enormously popular with the adult market until his death from lung cancer in 1965. His 1950's recordings with arranger Nelson Riddle stand with those of Capitol Records labelmate Frank Sinatra as high-water marks of sublimely produced popular music.

Popular Music

"Sublime" is not a word commonly associated with the popular music of the early 1950's, however, or the popular music of any era for that matter. Popular music was meant to entertain and to provide a brief escape from reality and a few memorable melodies to whistle or sing in the shower. Like all forms of "popular" entertainment, it was produced for mass consumption and meant to appeal to as wide an audience as possible. Before the swing era, hit songs came largely from the world of the musical theater, which developed out of the minstrel shows, music halls and vaudeville variety shows of the 19th and early 20th century, and grew into the glamour of Broadway musicals and Hollywood extravaganzas. The music was popularized by traveling troupes and sheet music sales, then took a quantum marketing leap with the arrival of radio broadcasts, jukeboxes, 78 r.p.m. recordings and other 20th century technologies that revolutionized pop culture, continuing into the 1950's with the advent of the 45 r.p.m. "single" and 33 1/3 r.p.m. "album" formats and the arrival of television, which grew up alongside rock & roll.

Popular hits of the first half of the 20th century were supplied by the songwriters of "Tin Pan Alley," who celebrated the boom years and Roaring Twenties and provided a dreamy escape from the harsh realities of the Depression and two World Wars.[3] Cole Porter, Hoagy Carmichael, Irving Berlin, George Gershwin, Rodgers & Hart, Jerome Kern and many other great writers left an indelible imprint on the popular imagination during the "Jazz Age," crafting memorable melodies and sly, literate turns of romantic phrases that were, indeed, sublime. For all the notable exceptions, however, the popular music industry was also cluttered—as it always is—with long-forgotten hacks cashing in on the latest fads and spewing out sentimental weepers and cute novelty numbers aimed at the bland tastes of the American mainstream.

The impetus of jazz and boogie-woogie in the thirties moved popular music away from the light entertainment offered by the publishing houses and toward a more exciting and dance-oriented style that made the swing era a true golden period. As the big bands died out, however, and the star singers again grabbed the spotlight, the professional songwriters found their services again in demand to provide material for a flood of new singers. (Unlike blues and country singers, popular singers rarely wrote their own material in the pre-rock eras.) Without the drive of jazz supporting it, and with post-war America too busy rebuilding lives and starting a baby-boom to waste time dancing, popular music turned back to lightweight sentimental songs and cute novelty music sung by smoothly polished voices and backed by sweetly generic instrumental arrangements. It would take the impetus of another black style–rhythm & blues–to put some fire back into the pop charts. In the meantime, the music industry's assembly line of songwriters, publishers, A&R men, arrangers, studio musicians, song-pluggers and record promoters worked overtime turning out pleasant entertainment that seemed to fit the comforting predictability of life in the most prosperous country in the world.

Not everyone shared in the prosperity, needless to say, but the 1950's *were* a good time to be a white, middle-class American. The post-war years brought an unprecedented prosperity and confidence to America and to a new generation of young people who couldn't remember the Great Depression (or, soon enough, even World War II). The popular music of the early 1950's mirrored life in mainstream America: bland, predictable and reassuring, which didn't seem at all bad after a devastating Depression and horrifying war, at least not to the adults who lived through those hard years and now actually *enjoyed* listening to Perry Como, Patti Page, Doris Day, Teresa Brewer, Rosemary Clooney, Kay Starr, Dean Martin, Connie Francis, Fontane Sisters, McGuire Sisters, Lawrence Welk...

An unending stream of polite, popular white entertainers filled the fifties with music that sounded (and still sounds) either charming or nauseating, depending largely on your age. A subculture called "teenagers" was forming in the midst of the Eisenhower America, united by a vague feeling of boredom and by an undercurrent of restless energy that had no outlet—certainly not in the popular music their parents enjoyed, which seemed as bland and wholesome as the family homilies of *The Adventures of Ozzie and Harriet* and the single beds in *I Love Lucy*. After all, the #1 song of 1953 was Patti Page's treacly "Doggie in the Window"(!)

Only **Johnny Ray** and, to a lesser extent, Frankie Laine ("That's My Desire") seemed to sing with anything approaching the level of feeling the black singers took for granted. In fact, Johnny Ray was at first mistaken for black, even by black record buyers, who sent his 1951 hit "Cry" to the #1 spot on the R&B charts. The overt emotion of Ray's singing and live theatrics caused quite a sensation, as this *New York Times* review attests: "Ray sings like a man in an agony of suffering. Drenched in tears... His hair falls over his face. He clutches at the microphone and behaves as if he were about to tear it apart. His arms shoot out in wild gesticulations and his outstretched fingers are clenched and unclenched."[4]

Ray's overwrought histrionics sounds a bit laughable now, but it was enough to make him positively thrilling in the early fifties. (When Elvis hit, Ray was the only white precedent that came to most minds.) Most of the popular music of the era was made up of virtually interchangeable singers and arrangements, as demonstrated every week on *Your Hit Parade*. This popular fifties show gave audiences the chance to see all of the week's best-selling songs sung by a nondescript group of singers backed by a nondescript studio band, with the occasional appearance of an actual star to sing his or her nondescript hit in person. The appearance of rock & roll caused big problems, however, as the show's cast of white-bread singers and band members were forced to make some sense of "Rock Around the Clock"—which hit #1 on the pop charts and thus had be dealt with—and all the subsequent rock & roll hits that refused to be kept in their place.

Your Hit Parade finally went off the air in 1959, after several years of embarrassing attempts to deal with the popularity of a music that flew in the face of the guiding principal of the show and of popular music in general: that the *Song* sells, not the *Singer*. While the individual styles of the popular singers varied from the cool croon of Perry Como to the hyper-emotion of Johnny Ray, popular music clung to the basic idea that fed the publishing companies through the years of sheet music and piano rolls and parlor songs: the idea that what really counted was the song, not the specific "rendition" of the song, however pleasing it might be. Rock & roll turned this equation on its head and placed the Singer above the Song and declared that the "genuine article" was not a lifeless piece of sheet music to be "interpreted" but was, instead, the individually-etched *performance* and persona that brought the song to life and was thereafter inseparable from the song itself. The sound and feel of rock & roll were certainly as important as the notes and words. Imagine "Tutti Frutti" reduced to sheet music! (Refer to Pat Boone's cover for the results...) Clearly that sound and feel came from somewhere beyond the horizons of "Que Sera Sera." That "somewhere" was rhythm & blues.

RHYTHM & BLUES

The big bands died out during the World War II years for a number of reasons, including the War itself, which depleted the bands and made touring and recording virtually impossible due to the rationing of tires, gas, shellac and other materials. In addition, wartime taxes forced many clubs to close and made large bands impractical and smaller units a necessity. A musicians' union recording ban in 1942 and 1943—a doomed effort to combat the "threat" of the juke box and pre-recorded radio broadcasts—contributed to swing's decline as well. The end was further hastened by restless musicians who were tired of the strict arrangements and forced anonymity of the big bands, and anxious to explore newer and more personal terrain. The **bebop** style of jazz pioneered by Charlie Parker and Dizzy Gillespie took jazz out of the ballrooms and put it into intimate clubs where serious aficionados went to *listen*, rather than dance, to bebop's complex rhythms and melodies. The music itself had little influence on rock & roll, which occupied the other end of the difficulty spectrum, but the subculture that surrounded bebop—the "beats" and the jazz-paced poetry, the hipster slang and dress, and the Bohemian lifestyle chronicled by Jack Kerouac, Allen Ginsburg and other writers—served as a fertile source of imagery for the rock subcultures to come (and provided yet another installment of white fascination with black music and style).

Dancehall Rhythm & Blues

Plenty of people still wanted to dance, however, and as the popular singers and bebop players each, in their way, moved further from the dance beat, a third offshoot of the swing era brought that beat to a new prominence. As the big bands broke into smaller units, jazz and the blues went their separate ways into bebop units and dancehall R&B—or "**jump blues**"—bands that played straightforward music with a big dance beat and broad appeal (along with enough contrasting mellow ballads mixed in to give couples a chance to slow-dance—the bands often traveled with designated "ballad singers" and "shouters"). The jump bands began as smaller, stripped-down versions of swing bands, consisting of a rhythm section and a couple of horns—a sax and trumpet, or two saxes—that played hard-driving riffs and solos over blues progressions, and a boogie-derived (or shuffle) bass and beat. The overall rhythm was punched up by accented backbeats (one TWO three FOUR, instead of ONE two

THREE four) that demanded motion on the dancefloor. The featured soloists were usually sax players who abandoned the finely-tuned finesse of jazz for a raucous wail that matched the energy of the music. In similar fashion, the great R&B shouters, like Joe Turner and Ruth Brown, lacked the subtleties of the jazz singers but packed a wallop that could rise above a full-tilt band.

The Count Basie and Lionel Hampton bands were important bridges between swing and R&B: the lean, aggressive energy of Basie's 1937 "One O'Clock Jump," from 1937, and Hampton's 1942 recording of "Flying Home" were exciting signposts of things to come. Roy Milton's "R. M. Blues" and Joe Liggins' "The Honeydripper," both released in 1945, were a further shift away from the sophistication of jazz to a backbeat and boogie-dominated sound and party mood. The million selling success of both records also signaled the presence of a revitalized "race" market after the Depression and War years, and hinted at a significant number of white record buyers as well. Other jump-era landmarks included Amos Milburn's "Bad Bad Whiskey" and Jimmy Liggins' "The Shuffleshuck," both from 1950, and Roy Brown's 1947 hit "Good Rockin' Tonight" (also recorded by Wynonie Harris the same year, and by Elvis Presley in 1954). "The Hucklebuck," a 1949 hit that popularized a dance of the same name, also made inroads into the white market in its original version by Paul Williams, in competing R&B versions by Roy Milton and Lionel Hampton, and in later versions recorded by white stars Frank Sinatra and Tommy Dorsey, anticipating the "crossover" pop hits by R&B artists and the white "cover" versions that were the first volleys of the 1950's rock & roll revolution.

Louis Jordan

Louis Jordan was the most popular jump blues bandleader of the late forties, and one of the few black entertainers of the time to consistently reach both white and black audiences. Born in Brinkley, Arkansas, in 1908, Jordan moved to New York and played alto sax in several big bands before starting his own smaller, streamlined group in 1938, which he dubbed the "Tympani Five" (though the number of players usually ranged from six to eight). Jordan combined swing riffs and arrangements, boogie bass lines, shuffling dance beats, catchy tunes, clear singing and humorous storytelling lyrics, and created a crowd-pleasing act that defined jump blues and expanded its audience. "With my little band, I did everything they did with the big band. *I made the blues jump.* After I got into the public, they said I should straddle the fence. I didn't know what they meant at first. But they meant that I shouldn't play just for Negroes, but for the world. Then I decided that when you come to hear Louis Jordan, you'd hear things to make you forget what you'd had to do the day before and just have a good time, a great time."[5]

Jordan specialized in upbeat novelty-style numbers in the comic vein of singer and bandleader Cab Calloway, who had demonstrated the prejudice-softening appeal of humor in the 1930's. A great showman, Jordan never went for comic effect at the expense of his music, but used humor to punctuate the great riffs and dance beats of hits like "Caldonia" (1945), "Choo Choo Ch'Boogie" (1946) and "Saturday Night Fish Fry" (1950), and he never lost sight of his core audience in his attempt to amuse everyone. His entertaining style remained rooted in the blues of his southern youth, and his songs were filled with "jive" talk and funny, lovingly-etched depictions of black life that amused both rural and urban black audiences along with his large following of white converts. Jordan's style was a decisive influence on Bill Haley and was the catalyst for Haley's transformation from western swing to rock & roll. Jordan was also a major influence on rock archetype Chuck Berry, who has often credited Jordan as an inspiration for his witty, rapid-fire lyrics and clear diction. (Berry also cites Jordan's guitar player, Carl Hogan, as an influence on the trademark chiming guitar riffs that open most Chuck Berry classics.)

The "Majors" and "Indies"

Louis Jordan's success was due in part to the fact that he recorded for Decca Records, a well-established major label with clout and connections that helped open doors to the white market. The Mills Brothers and the Ink Spots were also on the Decca roster, while Capitol Records was home to Nat "King" Cole, the only other black artist able to consistently crack the white market in the 1940's. Aside from these significant exceptions, the large record labels—the "**majors**"—lost interest in the black market after a slump in sales during the Depression. The void was filled by many small independent labels—"**indies**"— devoted to black music and aimed at a black audience.[6]

The indies posed little threat to the music establishment, or so it seemed until the indies and R&B began crossing over to the pop charts and pop audience on a large scale in the 1950's, siphoning sales and profits away from the large record labels. The indies formed something of a grassroots network that was the stomping ground for most rock & roll. The most famous small labels—Chicago's Chess Records, Memphis' Sun Records, Cincinnati's King Records—are now enshrined in rock legend, while others, most notably Atlantic Records, grew to be "majors" themselves. Other important indies of the era included the Savoy, Jubilee and Deluxe labels in New York; Modern, Aladdin, Imperial and Specialty in Los Angeles; Peacock and Duke in Houston; Vee Jay in Chicago; and, a bit later, the greatest indie success story of all, Detroit's Motown Records.

While the major labels snoozed and let the indies sneak away with the future of popular music, the large publishing houses of Tin Pan Alley and their performance rights organization, ASCAP (American Society of Composers, Authors and Publishers), suffered a similar blow in the 1940's with the formation of BMI (Broadcast Music Incorporated). BMI was formed as an alternative licensing organization by radio broadcasters tired of ASCAP's stuffy monopoly and the high fees they were charged for playing any songs licensed by ASCAP, which nearly all popular hits were. In response, BMI licensed R&B, country and, eventually, rock & roll songs that ASCAP considered beneath its dignity, much to its later regret. The indies and BMI gave rhythm & blues a crucial outlet and a voice within the music industry that grew louder and louder until the Big Guys were finally forced to listen.

The West Coast & Johnny Otis

The presence of several independent record labels made Los Angeles a particularly important center for the development of rhythm & blues. Bandleader and talent scout Johnny Otis recalls the scene and the style: "Now, R&B started here in L.A. Roy Milton was here, Joe Liggins was here, T-Bone Walker was here, Charles Brown was here, I was here, and others, too. By '48 or '49 it was set—we had an art form, though we didn't know it then... It was a hybrid form that began to emerge. It surely wasn't big band; it wasn't swing; it wasn't country blues. It was what was to become known as rhythm & blues, a hybrid form that became an art form in itself. It was the foundation of rock & roll... Rock & roll was a direct outgrowth of R&B. It took over all the things that made R&B different from big band swing: the afterbeat on a steady four; the influence of boogie; the triplets on piano; eight-to-the-bar on the top-hat cymbal; and the shuffle pattern of dotted eighth and sixteenth notes."[7]

The intimate "club blues" style popularized by the Nat "King" Cole Trio in the forties was carried on by other performers on the West Coast, including Charles Brown ("Drifting Blues," 1945; "Trouble Blues," 1949), Cecil Gant ("I Wonder," 1945), Percy Mayfield ("Please Send Me Someone to Love," 1950), and a young Ray Charles, who began as a Nat Cole imitator before finding his own style. (Billy Eckstine and, later, Johnny Mathis echoed the mainstream crooning side of Cole's appeal.) Soft club blues combos shared popularity with dancehall R&B bands on the West Coast, including Johnny Otis' own Caravan of Stars, a touring company that was both the last of the great big band touring groups—a single band that backed a number of singers—and the forerunner of the rock & roll package shows that crisscrossed the country with a full roster of stars.

A Greek-American from the Los Angeles area, Johnny Otis grew up in the black community and felt so at home there that he simply called himself "black" and has done so ever since (with no argument on either side). He was one of the great bandleaders and talent scouts of the 1950's: Otis discovered Etta James, Little Esther Phillips, Big Mama Thornton, Jackie Wilson, the Midnighters, Little Willie John, Mel Walker, the Treniers, the Robins (later renamed the Coasters) and long list of other R&B stars, many of whom were featured singers on the Caravan of Stars. Otis was also a talented songwriter and producer. His biggest hit under his own name was 1958's "Willie and the Hand Jive," but he was also responsible for many hits for members of his troupe, including Etta James' "The Wallflower (Roll With Me Henry)" and Willie Mae "Big Mama" Thornton's original version of "Hound Dog," which he produced and co-authored with Jerry Leiber and Mike Stoller, a pair of young white songwriters who had a feel for the blues and a great future as the premiere songwriting team of the 1950's.

"Hound Dog" vs. "Doggie in the Window"

Big Mama Thornton's "Hound Dog" was a #1 R&B hit in 1953, while another "dog" song, Patti Page's "(How Much is That) Doggie in the Window," was the year's top pop seller. "Hound Dog" and "Doggie in the Window" pretty well defined the extremes of the early fifties, from tough blues to sugary pop, from black to white and young to old, BMI to ASCAP, small indie label, Peacock, to major giant Mercury...

While "Hound Dog" was recorded in Los Angeles, Thornton was a refugee from the Deep South and her deep, uncut blues growl was a perfect vehicle for the snarling lyrics, while the gutbucket guitar, bass and drums backing sounds straight out of the Delta—more blues than rhythm—and equally appropriate. By contrast, Page's French canary singing and "heavenly" strings & woodwinds arrangement sounds straight out of Nowhere—the land of polite entertainment with no personality. Actually, "Doggie in the Window" is sung well and quite cute and is even somewhat interesting as an early example of double-tracking, which allowed Page to sing each part of the song's sweet two-part harmonies (an effect she also used effectively on her biggest hit, 1951's "Tennessee Waltz"). Still, anyone who would prefer "Doggie in the Window" over "Hound Dog" is either *very* young or *very* old... One embodied a noble past while looking to the future of popular music, while the other embodied all the reasons why a new style of popular was so desperately needed, at least for anyone between the ages of ten and twenty.

Of course, no one in 1953 could have predicted that a song like "Hound Dog" would ever appeal to *teenagers*, especially white teenagers, but then no one could have imagined Elvis Presley in their wildest 1953 dreams either, or imagined how different "Hound Dog" could sound. Elvis turned it into one of the defining songs of rock & roll in 1956, and in the process reaffirmed rock's allegiance to the blues even while he was moving the music further away from it. The "Hound Dog" saga is often invoked as an example of a white artist stealing and profiting from black music, which it certainly is. It's worth remembering in this particular case, though, that the song was written by a pair of young white kids and a Greek-American who was only "black" because he said he was—and that Elvis' version was actually inspired by a *lounge* act he saw doing the song as a novelty number in Las Vegas(!) With all that in mind, the "Dog" songs saga does indeed cover and confuse a lot of bases...

"Rocket 88"

The gritty southern sound of Thornton's "Hound Dog" was heard in full-band glory two years earlier in "Rocket 88," another #1 R&B hit that touched a lot of interesting bases. The song was recorded by singer **Jackie Brenston** backed by

Ike Turner & the Kings of Rhythm, a young traveling troupe out of Clarksdale, Mississippi, in the heart of the Mississippi Delta, and was recorded in Sam Phillips' studio in Memphis then leased to Chicago's Chess Records because Sam had yet to start his own Sun label. Thus the "Rocket 88" saga brings together the Mississippi Delta (home of rural blues), Memphis (home of Beale Street), Chess (home of the greatest urban blues), Sam Phillips' Union Avenue studio (future home of Elvis, Jerry Lee Lewis, Carl Perkins, Johnny Cash...) and Ike Turner (pivotal bandleader and future partner, for better or worse, of Tina Turner) and, of course, Jackie Brenston, a sax player for The Kings of Rhythm who really didn't have much of a future but did secure his place in rock history when he stepped up to sing lead on one of the consensus candidates for any list of "first rock songs."

Most interesting of all is the song itself, an over-amped, manic Delta version of jump blues that keeps an equal emphasis on "rhythm" and "blues" and really does sound like rock & roll, complete with a big booming beat and raucous saxophone and hyper-boogie Jerry Lee-style piano from Ike Turner. The boastful car lyrics and swaggering vocals would have suited Jerry Lee as well, and the aggressive overall sound of the backing wouldn't have seemed at all out of place behind Little Richard (who did credit "Rocket 88" with being the inspiration for "Good Golly Miss Molly"). Driving it all is a hard-boogie riff from a distorted "fuzzed" guitar—the result of a guitar amp's tumble off the top of the band's car—that is the crowning touch of the song's claim to rock status. As Sam Phillips recalled to Robert Palmer, "When it fell that burst the speaker cone. We had no way of getting it fixed... it would have taken a couple of days, so we started playing around with the damn thing. I stuffed a little paper in there where the speaker cone was ruptured, and it sounded good. It sounded like a saxophone. And we decided to go ahead and record."[8] The "fuzz box" would not be invented for over a decade and wasn't popularized until Rolling Stone Keith Richards used one for the "Satisfaction" riff in place of the horn line he originally had in mind, much as Phillips opted for the distortion that "sounded like a saxophone." Phillips made a decision to go with the *feel* of the band and music at the expense of production niceties—a lesson he would apply to his explosive Howlin' Wolf recordings and, of course, to the experiments with Elvis and so many others in that same little room.

"Rocket 88" offered a prophetic look into the future, and was even covered, like "Hound Dog," by a white rocker often credited with "inventing" rock & roll. Bill Haley recorded "Rocket 88" in 1951 in a very early and extraordinary example of a white artist attuned to the sounds of rhythm & blues. The record went virtually unheard, however, and Haley would have to wait several more years for that same equation to click in his cover of Joe Turner's "Shake, Rattle & Roll." Ike Turner made many recordings in the 1950's that showcased his explosive piano and guitar playing, though none sold well and he was better known, like Johnny Otis, as a wide-ranging and brilliant talent scout, A&R man and bandleader. He settled in St. Louis in 1956 with a revamped

Kings of Rhythm, married Annie Mae Bullock and embarked on a new career phase as "Ike & Tine Turner" with 1960's "A Fool in Love."

Atlantic Records

The crude sound of "Rocket 88" did not have universal appeal by any means, even within the rhythm & blues market. The R&B that came from the South was rougher and rawer than the dancehall blues of urban centers on the coasts, where the jazz influence was stronger and the audiences were more "refined" in their tastes. The classiest R&B came from Atlantic Records, a small indie label founded in 1947 by Ahmet Ertegun, the son of a Turkish ambassador to the United States, and his friend and fellow rhythm & blues fan, Herb Abramson. Long before it became a mega-label, home to the likes of Led Zeppelin, the Rolling Stones and Crosby, Stills, Nash & Young, and even before it dominated the soul music of the 1960's with Aretha Franklin, the Queen Herself, heading the way, Atlantic was the best of the R&B indies, with a roster that included Ray Charles, the Drifters, the Coasters, LaVern Baker and many R&B giants, and a reputation for well-crafted productions, well-engineered recordings and a welcome and genuine concern for their music and musicians.

Ertegun and Abramson were joined by Tom Dowd and Jerry Wexler, and by Ahmet's brother Nesuhi Ertegun, who developed the label's extensive jazz roster. The earliest Atlantic releases were mainly jazz-oriented jump blues, though the label's first bit hit came with the downhome "Drinkin' Wine Spo-Dee-O-Dee" by "Sticks" McGhee. A couple of trips to New Orleans at the end of the 1940's led to sessions with the legendary Professor Longhair and convinced the Atlantic brain trust that they had to incorporate some of the city's Latin-tinged boogie and gutsy sound. (Southern styles were an equally big inspiration in Atlantic's move to soul music a decade later.) Staff arranger Jesse Stone could not quite re-create the earthy New Orleans sound with Atlantic's more sophisticated and jazz-oriented group of New York sessionmen, but in the process of trying he created the polished grit of the "Atlantic Sound," which supported all of the label's singers with great, boogie-based sax-led band arrangements that were an integral part of the song rather than afterthoughts or mere accompaniments to the vocals.

The biggest stars of Atlantic's early years were Ruth Brown and Joe Turner, along with two vocal groups—the Clovers and the first incarnation of the durable Drifters—who were a link between the adult pop of the Ink Spots and the streetcorner sounds of doo-wop.

Ruth Brown

Ruth Brown was the flagship artist of Atlantic's early years—important enough to the label's success that some took to calling Atlantic the "house that Ruth built." The twenty-year-old "Miss Rhythm" was signed by Atlantic in 1948 and began her string of 24 R&B hits with "So Long" in 1949, after injuries from a car wreck delayed her debut by nearly a year. One of the great singers of her era, Brown mixed blues shouts, sultry pouts and a wide range of dramatic inflections, including the signature "squeaks" that sounded both cute and sexy.

Brown's **"Mama, He Treats Your Daughter Mean"** was a big R&B hit for Atlantic in 1953 and was among the early rumblings of records penetrating the white teen consciousness with its earthy beat and sound. Again, the year's "Dog" songs provide a good context for comparison. "Mama, He Treats Your Daughter Mean" was raw and earthy indeed compared to "Doggie in the Window." Ruth Brown had everything Patti Page seemed to lack: a gutsy voice, a tough sound and beat behind her and a song that actually deserved some emotional involvement. On the other hand, compared to the deep blues growl of "Hound Dog," Brown's jazzy backing, nuanced vocalisms and sassy knowing-wink delivery seemed positively urbane and sophisticated.

With Ruth Brown, Atlantic Records staked out a middle ground between pop and rhythm & blues, blending the polish of jazz and pop with the rough emotion of R&B. Her subsequent Atlantic hits included "Teardrops from My Eyes," "5-10-15 Hours" and "Wild, Wild Young Men" and other great songs that were, unfortunately, still too R&B-oriented for the general pop market and too "adult" for the emerging white teenage audience. The jazz band flavor of Brown's Atlantic recordings served her voice well but limited her appeal in the crossover era. Brown was never able to parlay her R&B success into a "rock & roll" career (unlike LaVern Baker, who came to Atlantic in 1953 and was positioned for the crossover market from the start). She finally did have a pair of minor pop hits later in the decade with "Lucky Lips" and "This Little Girl's Gone Rockin'," pop singalongs that were far removed from the sassy confidence her groundbreaking R&B hits.

Ruth Brown led a list of great female R&B singers who were unable to follow lesser voices into the riches of the pop world, including Big Mama Thornton (who recorded the original versions of both "Hound Dog" and Janis Joplin's hit "Ball & Chain"), Big Maybelle (who recorded "Whole Lotta Shakin' Goin' On"), Faye Adams ("Shake a Hand") and the eclectic Dinah Washington, who was the most successful black female singer of the 1950's but was likewise unable appeal to the rock & roll audience.

Joe Turner

Big Joe Turner was similarly unable to reach the rock & roll market, even though he recorded a one of rock's early defining classics: "Shake, Rattle & Roll." Turner was born in 1911 in Kansas City, home of Benny Moten, Count Basie and the other great Kansas City bandleaders who put fire into jazz and made it swing. Turner and boogie-woogie pianist Pete Johnson were featured in the 1938 "Spirituals to Swing" concerts in Carnegie Hall, where their "Roll 'Em Pete" served as a rollicking invocation of the wide-open spirit of their hometown. Turner's combination of blues shouting with an upbeat boogie-woogie beat and spirit formed the basic equation of all R&B shouters, but Turner was not a star himself until signed to Atlantic in 1951 and produced "Chains of Love," "Honey Hush," "TV Mama" (featuring blues slide master Elmore James), "Shake, Rattle & Roll" and its musical twin, "Flip, Flop & Fly," and other blues-shout anthems.

"Shake, Rattle & Roll" was recorded in 1954 and was soon discovered by white teenagers who loved the song's big beat and singalong refrain and made a cult star out of the surprised 43-year-old Turner—for a few brief moments, that is, until Bill Haley & His Comets scored their first big hit with the song and completed its transformation to "rock & roll." Joe Turner continued recording and performing and never lost his big, booming voice. He died of a heart attack in 1985 after a half-century career that put him at the birth of both rhythm & blues and rock & roll.

VOCAL GROUPS

Vocal group singing was the most popular style of rhythm & blues in the early 1950's and was the first music to be called "rock & roll." Always a feature of popular styles—white and black, sacred and secular—vocal groups achieved their greatest popularity when they helped usher in the rock & roll era and then, as doo-wop, supplied it with some of its most memorable moments.

The Ink Spots

The broad pop appeal of Nat "King" Cole was pre-dated by and indebted to the success of the Ink Spots, who sang similarly soothing versions of familiar pop standards and tasteful new material with no discernible blues inflections. The broad popularity of an earlier black group, the Mills Brothers, in the 1930's inspired the Ink Spots and they, in turn, inspired countless other groups and established pop and ballad-oriented group singing as the best avenue for reaching white listeners.

The Ink Spots came together in 1934 in New York City and first recorded for Victor Records in 1935. They switched to another major label, Decca, the following year and had their first hit in 1939 with "If I Didn't Care," a romantic ballad that introduced the high, silky-smooth tenor of lead singer **Bill Kenny** and the group's beautifully blended overall sound. The record also introduced a favorite Ink Spots device—a "talking bass" soliloquy in the middle of the song by bass singer Orville "Hoppy" Jones that elaborated on the mood and feeling of intimacy. (Talking bass interludes became something of a cliché; Elvis Presley's "Are You Lonesome Tonight" is one of the more famous examples.) "If I Didn't Care" formed the blueprint for the Ink Spots ballads to come—"My Prayer," "Maybe," "We Three," "When the Swallows Come Back to Capistrano"—and established the basic vocal group style for the secular groups that followed.

The Ink Spots proved that with a smooth, non-threatening sound and some well-chosen songs, success in the white world was *possible*. Their sentimental lyrics and pop and light-jazz sound owed much more to Tin Pan Alley than to dancehall R&B, and it was certainly *far* removed from the harsh realism of the blues. Although the timbre and emotion of Bill Kenny's voice pointed gently to the group's true color, the Ink Spots' appeal was largely based on their ability to sound "white." Nonetheless, their success in the popular mainstream was a source of great pride in an age when black artists too often seemed simply invisible to white America, and was an inspiration for countless young singers who began forming their own groups and emulating their heroes. Soul singer Jerry Butler: "The Ink Spots were the ultimate. They were the first of our race to achieve that kind of fame. To someone singing doo-wop on the corners or any place, the dream was to be and sound like the Ink Spots. Because of the name—the imagery of the black spots on white paper—the tonality of the tenor voice, the spoken words of the bass and the beauty of the harmony and guitar on their records, the Ink Spots were cherished by the black community with the same sort of pride that we had in Joe Louis being the heavyweight champion of the world. The Ink Spots were the heavyweight champions of quartet singing."[9]

The Ravens and The Orioles

The Ravens and the Orioles were important transitional groups of the late forties and early fifties—and the inspiration for a flood of other "bird groups": the Larks, Penguins, Pelicans, Sparrows, Crows, Wrens, Cardinals, Swallows, Robins, Falcons, Blue Jays, Meadowlarks, Flamingos...

In contrast to the crooning tenor of the Ink Spots' Bill Kenny, the Ravens featured the lead vocals of **Jimmy Ricks**, a deep-voiced singer who defined the booming "Mr. Bassman" style. Most of their recordings, like their 1947 hit version of "Old Man River," fell into the "café au lait" style of popular songs with just the faintest hint of color. More influential was the bluesier, dance-oriented material like 1950's "**Gotta Find My Baby**," which features Rick's basso profundo over a 12-bar blues, a strong dancebeat and propelled by a jazzy club blues accompaniment and wordless background vocals that mimic a riffing sax section. The Ravens' success was largely confined to the R&B market, but their uptempo R&B styles had a big influence on younger groups who wanted more excitement than the Ink Spots seemed to offer.

The Orioles focued mainly on ballads and took the smooth sound of the Ink Spots as their reference point, then peeled away some of the pop finesse for a more emotionally-direct feeling. Originally from Baltimore, the Orioles moved to New York and established themselves as show-stopping regulars at Harlem's Apollo Theater with lead singer lead singer **Sonny Til** up front. The group's first hit came in 1948 with "**It's Too Soon to Know**," an unadorned ballad with a plaintive lead and simple accompaniment that moved from the colorless pop croon of the Ink Spots to a more "untutored" and emotional R&B sound.

In contrast to the Ink Spots, the Orioles sounded unmistakably black, a fact that kept them from reaching a white audience—until, that is, the surprise success of their version of **"Crying in the Chapel"** in 1953. The stately and pious ballad song was actually a re-recording of a religious white *country* song—a typically confused history—and was a highly unlikely candidate for being a landmark in rock history. Had it confined itself to the R&B charts, where it was a #1 hit, it would merely have been another in a long line of great Orioles ballads. But "Crying in the Chapel" also hit #11 on the *pop* charts, the highest chart showing of any black act up to that point, confirming the trend toward an increased acceptance of black styles.

"Crying in the Chapel" was the first **crossover** song of real magnitude: the first R&B record to "cross over" to and climb that far up the pop charts. In other words, the first record by a black act, aimed at a black audience, to sell to white record buyers in sufficient numbers to place it a notch away from the Top Ten on the national charts. *Young* white record buyers, to be more exact: Sonny Til's emotional singing was an exciting revelation to young white listeners in 1953 (which was, once again, the year of "Doggie in the Window"). In fact, a large underground of hip white teenagers had already noticed that there was life beyond the Hit Parade. They had been listening to rhythm & blues for a long time before "Crying in the Chapel" broke, searching it out on jukeboxes and in record stores, and even finding it on the radio sometimes—beamed in from some distant station when the atmosphere was just right and then shared with a select group of like-minded friends in secret societies of white kids who had discovered the exciting, forbidden, sexy music called rhythm & blues.

Alan Freed and the Birth of "Rock & Roll"

Some white teens were luckier than others: some lived in cities with large enough black populations to justify rhythm & blues programming. The luckiest of all lived in Cleveland, where they didn't even have to eavesdrop on someone else's party to hear it, because disc jockey Alan Feed played rhythm & blues especially for *them* every night on his "Moondog Rock & Roll Party." Freed didn't call it "rhythm & blues," however: he called it "rock & roll." With the sensibilities of his young white audience (and their parents) in mind, Freed coined the "new" term in order to avoid the racial overtones attached to "rhythm & blues." Although Freed is rightly credited with giving "rock & roll" its specific musical association, the expression itself had been around for many years in the black community as a slang for sex in particular and for "partying" in general, and "rockin'" and "rollin'" had become commonly used phrases in R&B songs. With considerable irony, then, Freed lifted the risqué term from the music, then applied it *to* the music in order to avoid controversy(!) In any case, the most important point remains clear: "rock & roll" was, at first, just another name for rhythm & blues, plain and simple.

Freed was certainly not the first disc jockey to play R&B, but he was the most important and the most active and vocal in his support of the music and musicians. Freed was playing classical music(!) on Cleveland's WJW, a 50,000 watt clear-channel powerhouse, when he was first alerted to the existence of a network of white teen R&B fans by Leo Mintz, a record store owner who witnessed the phenomenon every day. Freed convinced the station to let him try an R&B show for his white audience, and officially launched his "Moondog Rock & Roll Party" in June of 1951.

Alan Freed was the original Wildman DJ, playing "drums" on his microphone and singing and shouting along with the records he played and launching into a high-energy jive-talking spiel between songs to keep the energy from slipping. Freed loved rhythm & blues, especially the vocal groups, and he hosted the first of his landmark live shows in 1952 in the Cleveland Arena with a bill that included the Orioles, Moonglows, Dominoes and other popular groups. The "Moondog Coronation Ball" attracted over 20,000 fans and a good deal of national attention, as did similar shows the following year which attracted equally large numbers and elicited gasps from newspaper readers around the country with pictures of Freed's racially mixed audiences dancing and cheeering their black heroes together.

Freed moved on to a bigger audience and bigger fame in 1954 when he signed on at WINS in New York City and began building a huge radio following and promoting his famous rock & roll package shows at Brooklyn's Paramount Theater. Freed quickly became the biggest star-maker of the music industry and would remain in power until the payola" scandal brought him down at the end of the decade for participating in (and refusing to lie about) the standard practice of accepting money for playing certain records. Freed was a flawed hero, to be sure, but he was a hero nonetheless. He truly loved rock & roll: no amount of money could make him play a record he didn't like, and nothing could keep him from crusading for the ones he loved. Most of all, he never forgot where the music came from and always championed the black originators over any white imposters. Alan Freed was the leading advocate for black music at a crucial time, and he probably opened more doors for black artists than any other single figure in rock's history. He waged many battles for the music he loved—and he won. As he was fond of saying, "Anyone who says rock & roll is a passing fad or a flash in the pan has rocks in his head, dad!"

1951: The Clovers and Five Keys

Freed's rock & roll debut pointed to—was made possible by—the growing number of white teenagers who were bored with the popular music of the time and eager for more exciting sounds and styles. Vocal groups remained the most accessible of R&B forms, due to the immediacy of the voices and sentiment, and were the music of choice for the teens and disc jockeys. 1951 saw a wave of new groups following the lead of the Ravens and Orioles, including the Larks ("My Reverie"), the Cardinals ("Shouldn't I Know") and the Swallows ("Will You Be Mine"). More significant was the arrival of **The Clovers**, who launched their career with a pair of hits written by Ahmet Ertegun, "Don't You Know I Love You So" and "Fool, Fool, Fool," that presented a new, rhythmically-oriented style of vocal backing woven into the jazz-based Atlantic production sound. **The Five Keys'** recording of "The Glory of Love" was similarly progressive on the ballad side, taking the Orioles model in a still-more plaintive and emotional direction. The record's close-miked intimacy and even vocal blend—with the background singers more evenly matched with the lead—influenced the sound of the vocal group ballads that followed (such as the Harp-Tones' 1953 hit "A Sunday Kind of Love"). The most striking new sound of the new decade, however, came from Billy Ward & The Dominoes, who shocked the music world and then, with everyone's attention diverted, reinvented the sound of vocal group R&B.

Billy Ward & His Dominoes

The Orioles' breakthrough into the pop charts was surprising and threatening only because the group was black and recorded for a small indie label, thereby collecting profits that "rightfully" belonged to the major labels. Another record, released two years earlier on the King/Federal label out of Cincinnati, caused more consternation: Billy Ward & The Dominoes' "**Sixty Minute Man**" was downright *shocking*, all the more so because it made it up to #23 on the pop charts—the first significant showing of the new era and clearly all due to sales to teenagers. "Sixty Minute Man" was a textbook example of all the reasons parents did *not* want their children listening to rhythm & blues, or "that music." The sheer sound of Bill Brown's deep "Mr. Bassman" vocal (an echo of the Raven's Jimmy Ricks) seemed brash and vulgar, and was balanced at the top end by a leering guitar obbligato and a moaning high voice that both seemed altogether too suggestive. But the lyrics and intentions of the song went well beyond being merely "suggestive":

> Look-ee hear girls I'm telling you now
> They call me Lovin' Dan
> I rock 'em, roll 'em all night long
> I'm a sixty minute man!
>
> If you don't believe I'm all I say
> Come up and take my hand
> When I let you go you'll cry,
> "Oh yes, he's a sixty minute man!"

Clearly the references to "rock" and "roll" in "Sixty Minute Man" hearkened back to the earlier meaning of the term... (Alan Freed began using the term a month later, and was probably inspired most directly by this song.) Civic groups and PTA's around the country had a field day with "Sixty Minute Man," holding it up as an example of the type of "smut" that would surely lead to a nation of juvenile delinquents. The Dominoes were the 2 Live Crew of 1951, caught in a swirl of controversy and free publicity that only drew more attention to their song, while "respectable" citizens expressed moral outrage that only thinly disguised the scarier *racial* fear that lay just beneath it. The Dominoes' producer, Ralph Bass, recalls the furor: "I was being lambasted for dirty lyrics on 'Sixty Minute Man'... The problem was that white kids were listening to those things for the first time. It was all right so long as blacks were listening, but as soon as the whites started listening, it was no good. Then it became a big political thing."[10]

    "Sixty Minute Man" had an open and unapologetic sexuality presented by "uncultured" voices over a "dangerously strong" beat that would inevitably drive impressionable young people to move parts of their bodies that they shouldn't even be aware of... In short, "Sixty Minute Man" was a threat to everything America held dear, or seemed that way for a few weeks, anyway. Ultimately it was viewed as a fluke and a novelty and the real threat of the crossovers was delayed for a few more years. But the seeds and fears were sown, and the reaction took shape in expressions like these, published in various papers throughout the Land of the Free:

STOP!
Help Save the Youth of America
DON'T BUY NEGRO RECORDS!

If you don't want to serve Negroes in *your* place of business,
then do not have negro records on your juke box
or listen to negro records on the radio.

The screaming idiotic words, and savage music of these records
are undermining the morals of our white youth in America.

Call the advertisers of radio stations
that play this type of music and complain to them!
Don't Let Your Children Buy Or Listen To These Negro Records!

    America in 1951 was a deeply divided country, on the verge of hysteria about "communists" and digging more deeply into the national wellspring of racial mistrust and hatred. Rosa Parks wouldn't demand her seat on the bus in Montgomery, Alabama, for four more years, and it would be three more before the Supreme Court even went on record against segregated schools, and three more after that before the National Guard was required to simply put that decision into effect in Little Rock, Arkansas. Against this backdrop, it is easy to see how threatening the image of nice white children listening to "that negro music" could be to adults, and how exciting listening to "that negro music" could be to the adventurous kids looking for something beyond the stifling conformity their parents seemed to offer. Rock & roll did not free its followers from prejudice: the rock community has always been full of fans who are devoted to black music yet still unable to see a connection between the music they love and the people they hate. Still, rock & roll *did* bring the races together on the dancefloor and in a shared passion that went a long way toward easing the fear and mistrust on both sides. The Supreme Court itself could not have mandated such a sweeping change, but crusaders like Alan Freed made it happen.

Gospel Influences

Who would have thought that this same band—The Dominoes—would make bigger history in the long run with their incorporation of *gospel* styles? They did, largely because leader Billy Ward had the foresight to hire an 18-year-old gospel singer named **Clyde McPhatter**, one of the first real "stars" of rock & roll. McPhatter sang the high moans on "Sixty Minute Man" but came to the fore on subsequent releases, as on "**Have Mercy Baby**," a song commonly referred to as the birth of the "rhythm & gospel" mixture of gospel singing over rhythm & blues that put a new fire into vocal group styles and eventually led to soul music.

"Have Mercy Baby" is set to a straightforward 12-bar blues and is backed by a strong beat and a grinding, saxophone-led R&B band. The song is also sexy like its predecessor, though not overtly so this time—the sensuality is more in McPhatter's voice and pleading delivery, and *that* came straight from the church. McPhatter's singing seems loose and freely emotional and is set against a constant echo from the background singers that drives the song forward. That "**call-and-response**" was clearly a gospel device, used in group singing and in the interplay between a lead voice and a church choir, or between a preacher and the congregation. McPhatter's improvisatory singing style also illusrates his gospel background: he plays with the melody throughout the song, bending it to fit his heightening emotion until he finally breaks down into overwhelmed sobs at the end of the song. (McPhatter's shrieking sobs became his trademark: the sorrow of a man overwhelmed with the Spirit and the Grief. Usually reserved for the church, that overt emotion was taken to a melodramatic extreme for "The Bells," which is set as a girlfriend's "funeral," complete with an intoning preacher, a church organ, somber backing vocals and a shattered, weeping McPhatter.)

The specifics of McPhatter's style—the phrasing and "melismas," or single syllables stretched expressively over a number of notes—and the sheer level of his emotional involvement were also clearly gospel-derived to listeners within the black audience, as were the pleading lyrics themselves:

> Have mercy mercy baby, I know I done you wrong
> Have mercy mercy baby, I know I done you wrong
> Now my heart is full with sorrow, so take me back where I belong

I've been a good-for-nothin', I've lied and cheated too
I've been a good-for-nothin', I've lied and cheated too
But I reaped it all, my darlin', and I don't know what to do.

The song is a clear *aab* 12-bar blues but it reads like—and is—a plea for forgiveness: aimed at the Woman rather than the Lord, but sung with the same urgency. As writer Barry Hanson put it, "The title summarizes the whole rhythm & gospel idea: "Baby" is interchangeable with "Lord." In fact, the entire lyric could be transformed back into a gospel prayer with very little effort."[11] This same "blues + gospel" formula, with the "Lord" and the "Woman" as essentially interchangeable parts, was elaborated in the work of Ray Charles, James Brown and the others who completed R&B's transformation into soul.

"Have Mercy Baby" was #1 R&B hit in 1952, and its success alarmed many in the black community with its bold leap over the line between secular and sacred—the Devil and the Lord—that had always kept the blues and gospel apart, regardless of how closely related their musical languages were. Gospel music itself had once been the subject of much debate and disapproval as its growing popularity displaced the older spirituals, such as "Amazing Grace," that had been the vehicle for black religious expression. The term "gospel" was popularized in the twenties and thirties by songwriters who wrote new religious songs with popular influences and an emotional appeal that stretched beyond the church. **Thomas A. Dorsey** was the W. C. Handy of gospel: the author of "Precious Lord," "Peace in the Valley" and many other gospel standards and the founder of the first publishing house devoted to black gospel music. And like the early blues, many of the greatest gospel singers were strong-voiced women— Clara Ward, Mahalia Jackson, Marion Williams, Bessie Griffin, Sister Rosetta Tharpe—who sang their praises to the Lord with same passion that fueled Bessie Smith and the other "classic blues" singers, and the same passion that would mark the style of their most famous disciple, Aretha Franklin.

Vocal groups had been a prominent feature of black gospel music for many years as well, and were coming to the fore on the gospel circuit, as they were in the rhythm & blues world, in the late 1940's and early 1950's. Groups like the Five Blind Boys, Dixie Hummingbirds, Swan Silvertones and the Soul Stirrers were enormously popular and their effect on R&B groups was inevitable. While the influence of gospel was heard in earlier R&B singers (in Roy Brown's "crying" delivery of "Good Rockin' Tonight," for example, or in the eclectic style of Dinah Washington, who sang jazz, blues and pop with a style rooted in her early years as a gospel singer), the influence was felt most fully and significantly in the vocal groups. Of particular importance were the **Soul Stirrers** and their lead singer, R. H. Harris, who popularized the falsetto singing so common in soul music, and pioneered a freely emotional lead style set against repetitive, rhythmic "vamps" from the backing singers: exactly the type of embellished lead against a stable backing response that drives "Have Mercy Baby." (Harris would never have sung to the 12-bar blues that the Dominoes' harmonies outline so clearly, however. He could not even abide by the "worldly ways" of his fellow Soul Stirrers and left the group in 1951. He was replaced by a young Sam Cooke.)

The golden age of gospel music—1945-1960—paralleled the era of rhythm & blues and shared its network of independent records labels and mirrored its "chitlin circuit" in a network of concert halls and tabernacles devoted to gospel music. By the end of the 1950's the assimilation of gospel—both the sorrowful laments and the shouts of celebration—into R&B was so complete that a new term, "soul," became necessary and the lines between the two were nearly dissolved. The inspiration of gospel music was felt most widely in the 1960's, when soul music and the civil rights struggle both came of age and the music and the black church served as rallying points for social change.

Clyde McPhatter & the Drifters

Billy Ward's vision of fusing gospel styles with R&B brought a wide new range of expression to vocal group singing and to all rhythm & blues. Meanwhile, however, Clyde McPhatter was starting to feel that it made little sense to be the lead singer and star of a group still billed as "Billy Ward & The Dominoes": those who didn't know better simply assumed that the great singer out front was Ward himself. He ran afoul of taskmaster Ward and was fired from—and gladly left—the group in 1953. (Billy Ward hired the unknown Jackie Wilson to take the McPhatter's place.) Ahmet Ertegun wasted no time in bringing McPhatter to Atlantic Records and assembling a group for him to front. The group was called "The Drifters," the longest-running act in the rock & roll era, though "their" career was marked by so many personnel changes that they eventually overpopulated the "oldies" circuit with a bewildering number of groups legitimately billing themselves The "Drifters." (The Drifters famous for later hits like "Up on the Roof" and "Under the Boardwalk" were a completely different set of singers; the earliest line-up of the group is usually referred to as "Clyde McPhatter & the Drifters.")

"**Money Honey**" was the first in a run of 43 hits for various Drifters line-ups. The "blow harmonies," or "bagpipe harmonies," that back Clyde McPhatter are the distinctive feature of the arrangement, though guitar great Mickey Baker, saxophonist Sam "The Man" Taylor and the rest of the great house band gave the record a typical Atlantic sheen. The loose feel of the group and, especially, of McPhatter's free-ranging lead vocals point again to the crucial influence of gospel styles, which were the catalyst for moving beyond a sound world bounded by the Ink Spots' mainstream ballads and the older jump-based uptempo group styles. (A comparison of the Drifters sleek modern sound and the Clover's more weighted R&B style illustrates the difference between the two feels.)

Written by arranger Jesse Stone, "Money Honey" is a clever song about the eternal quest for cash, given an appealingly deadpan delivery by McPhatter and highlighted by a singalong refrain that appealed to both pop and R&B fans. The Drifters' other big hit with Clyde McPhatter appealed as well, though for the wrong reasons in many minds. **"Honey Love"** was banned by many radio stations and banished from the juke boxes in many areas., though it still made it to #1 on the R&B charts and reached a good many thrilled white ears as well with its invocation of the non-stop, 'round the clock pleasures of "honey love."

Clyde McPhatter was drafted in 1954, in an unfortunate stroke of bad luck and bad timing. He returned to Atlantic in 1956 and continued as a solo act. He had several solo hits—his biggest was 1958's "A Lover's Question"—but was never able to fully regain the inspired and effortless sound of his Dominoes and Drifters recordings. His influence was felt most clearly in Smokey Robinson's high, graceful voice, but it really was immeasurable. The "first soul singer" died of a heart attack in 1972, at the age of forty-one.

The "5" Royales

The Cincinnati-based **King Records** and its subsidiary Federal label rivaled Atlantic Records for great rhythm & blues, and had a broad roster of artists that represented all styles of R&B and even white country & western music. The label's first successful vocal group was The "5" Royales, led by songwriter and guitarist Lowman Pauling, had a first R&B hit in 1952 with "Baby, Don't Do It" while they were still with Apollo Records (they came to King in 1954). Always a star attraction on the R&B circuit, The "5" Royales never cracked the pop market, but they did write and record the original versions of several songs that were hits for an eclectic array of later artists, including "Dedicated to the One I Love," which was covered by the Shirelles and the Mamas & Papas, "Tell the Truth," which was covered by Ray Charles and Eric Clapton, and **"Think,"** a prophetic look to the future of soul that was covered by King labelmate James Brown. ("Think" was a hit twice for Brown, in fact, in two different versions separated by the immense expanse of the 1960's. The "5" Royales' 1957 original and James Brown's 1960 and 1973 covers serve as a good and handy illustration of the progression from R&B to soul to funk.)

Hank Ballard & the Midnighters

Hank Ballard & the Midnighters—another in a long line of Johnny Otis discoveries—also recorded for King Records and dropped their original name, the Royals, to avoid confusion with The "5" Royales. Like many other young singers not suited well to ballads, Ballard was thrilled by the Dominoes and Drifters and inspired to create his own mix of raunchy lyrics sung with a gospel wail over a 12-bar blues and an R&B band backing punctuated by rhythmic "bagpipe harmonies." The result was 1954's **"Work With Me Annie,"** the song that earned the Midnighters a spot right next to the Dominoes in the horrified hearts of parents. Lines like "Annie please don't cheat, give me all my meat" and the refrain of "Work with me Annie, let's get it while the gettin' is good!" were not likely to please Mom and Dad, but they certainly delighted teenagers, who passed the song around like a dirty joke so obvious that it was funnier without the punch line. And just in case there *was* any doubt about the real meaning of the song, the Midnighters followed with "Annie Had a Baby (Can't Work No More)," which contained a memorable explanation and moral to remember: "That's what happens when the gettin' gets good!"

The "Annie" saga reached the point of diminishing returns with "Annie's Aunt Fannie" and "Henry's Got Flat Feet (Can't Dance No More)," but not before inspiring an "answer" song from 16-year-old Etta James, co-authored and produced by (who else?) Johnny Otis. "Roll With Me Henry" featured the future author of "Louie Louie," Richard Berry, playing the role of "Hank" in a teasing, call-and-response invitation to more "work" that was renamed "The Wallflower" for popular consumption (and further sanitized as "Dance With Me Henry" by white singer Georgia Gibbs).

Hank Ballard & the Midnighters continued with "Sexy Ways," "It's Love Baby (24 Hours a Day)" and other songs of wonderfully questionable taste and indisputably great dance beats, most featuring electric guitar leads that were a striking contrast to the sax-dominated sound of other group backings. Ballard had his biggest influence in a more roundabout way, however, when a note-for-note copy of a two-year-old Midnighters record started a national craze in 1960: Ballard wrote and recorded "The Twist" in 1958, then released it as merely the B-side of a ballad called "Teardrops on Your Letter." While Chubby Checker was forever associated with the song, the dance craze it triggered pulled Ballard's original up to #28 in the pop charts (mostly the result of kids who accidentally bought the "wrong" version) and inspired a few Twist-tempo follow-ups, including the 1960 pop hits "Finger Poppin' Time" and "Let's Go, Let's Go, Let's Go," which were good, catchy dance numbers but a long way from the great bump-and-grind of his "Annie" days.

CROSSOVERS AND COVERS

"One of the most meaningful developments in years on the music-record scene has been the mass acceptance of rhythm & blues—its emergence from narrow confines and its impact on the broad field of pop music... Notwithstanding the opposition of entrenched facets of the music business, this exciting form of musical expression, together with its notable body of artists, could not be relegated to a relatively unimportant niche.

"In the last analysis, it was, of course, the kid with the 89 cents in his pocket who cast the deciding vote. He considered the repertoire, listened to the imaginative arrangements of the artists and repertoire men, critically weighed the merits of the artists—and found them all good." (*Billboard* magazine, 1955)

"Work With Me Annie" caused a flurry of controversy reminiscent of the "Sixty Minute Man" scandal, though this time it was not possible to write off the record's success as a mere "fluke." 1954 was the Year of the Crossover, when it became apparent that the rhythm & blues "fad" had more force than any previous white infatuation with a black style. The success of "Crying in the Chapel" the previous year had opened the floodgates for a torrent of new songs from an unending spring of new groups inspired by the Orioles' success (as their generation of groups had been inspired by the Ink Spots). The popularity of songs like "Work With Me Annie" also showed that the groups no longer had to restrict themselves to ballads to reach beyond their R&B following. The young rock & roll fans liked their music with a beat and didn't mind a few suggestive lyrics either, or anything else that could make their parents mad. Still, as the makeup of both the audience and the groups grew younger, the music itself grew "younger" as well. The harsh edges, overt sexuality and adult attitudes of rhythm & blues began to soften and move in a more melodic and innocent pop direction with the new teenage audience in mind. (The pronounced gospel influence remained, however, and was even heightened by the move to more "idyllic" and beseeching love lyrics that were not far removed, in spirit, from religious songs and sentiment.)

"Gee"

The Crows 1954 hit "Gee" was one of the first signposts of the new direction. The record was actually released in 1953, but was not a hit until 1954, after a prominent disc jockey rescued the song from oblivion by playing it over and over on his show (not because he *liked* the song, mind you: his girlfriend had just left him and *she* liked the song, and he wanted her back).

"Gee" is yet another in the long list of "first rock songs," due to both its crossover success on the pop charts (it made it to #14) and to its young, happy sound and enthusiastic voices—an unadorned lead singer backed by a chanting singalong of rhythmic nonsense syllables that anyone could imitate in the locker room or on the streetcorner. The lyrics, too, were easy to relate to and could be sung without embarrassment, or at least without the type of embarrassment that a rendition of "Sixty Minute Man" or "Work With Me Annie" might engender. While those songs were great for a shared laugh and thrill, and certainly great for a shared dance, black groups became more successful in crossing over to the pop charts when their themes became younger and more universal. In other words, when idyllic LOVE returned as the focus once again. Not that the parents (or the Ink Spots) would ever like a song like "Gee." However wholesome its values, it was still "trash" at best, but then the admiration and respect of the adult world was not the goal. Music that "the kids" could love and relate to was the goal, and a more innocent and idyllic view of love fit more easily into the experience of the young crossover market.

The music also reflected the changing times and tastes in a gradual move away from the jazz flavor and jump blues echoes of older R&B groups toward a simpler and more immediate style of instrumental backing. The arrangements thinned out to make way for the voices, and the instruments became almost unnecessary as the sax riffs, rhythmic bass lines and other instrumental features were taken over by the background singers, or "by the fellows who didn't get to sing lead and got tired of singing nothing but "aaaaah," as Barry Hansen put it.[12] Instead of "aaah" or "ooh," background singers turned to ever-more elaborate patterns of vocal sounds and rhythms that could create a strong beat and a full sound without conflicting with the lead singer's words or melody. Why bother with a saxophone when you have two or three background singers who are perfectly capable of singing "ooh-wah" or "dum-dee-dum"? Or **"doo-wop,"** for that matter, the term that was later applied to the vocal group sound of the rock & roll era to distinguish it from the earlier and more adult-oriented styles of the R&B vocal groups.

"Sh-Boom"

"Gee" was just the beginning of a string of crossover hits for black groups in 1954. The Chords' "Sh-Boom" followed "Gee" up the charts in the Spring of 1954 and made it even higher, peaking at #5 on the pop charts—an astonishing showing for a black act. "Sh-Boom" is a good-natured uptempo song, much like "Gee" in spirit, driven by a spirited, scatting lead voice that yields to a deep "Mr. Bassman" interlude in the middle of the song, and by the chanted nonsense syllables that gave the song its name.

Actually, the version of "Sh-Boom" that *most* people heard was bland and corny and sounded like a barbershop quartet... <u>That</u> version was a **#1** pop hit for the Crew Cuts, a white group that recorded for Mercury Records, one of the industry giants that was starting to become alarmed by the quickening crossover pace. Working on the age-old pop assumption that the *Song* sold, not the Singer, Mercury decided to have the Crew Cuts record a pop version of an R&B hit. The idea was simple: jump on a newly-released song, record it and crush the original version with all the industry might that a major label had at its command—the vast distribution network, the publicity budget, the ties to important radio and television shows, the inside connections and favors owed...

First, of course, they had to find a song. Needless to say, "Work With Me Annie" would not do. The whole point was to make an R&B song palatable to all varieties of pop ears—to keep enough of the beat and feel of the original to satisfy the teenagers while cleaning up the sound, the singing and (if necessary) the lyrics enough to have it appeal to Mom and Dad as well. "Sh-Boom" fit the bill, and in short order the arrangers and producers at Mercury were able to remove everything that had made the Chords' version exciting and replace it with a bland, generic sound that *still* stood out enough to make it a hit but not enough to offend anyone (unlike the sore thumb the original seemed compared to "Doggie in the Window" or "The Yellow Rose of Texas"). On sheet music, the originals and covers would look the same: same melody, same tempo, same chords... The practice of covering highlighted all the intangibles—the feel, the emotion, the sheer *sound*—that made rock & roll so special, so hard to contrive and hard to explain to anyone who just didn't get it.

Rock & Roll Under Covers

The success of the Crew Cuts' "**cover**" version of "Sh-Boom" set the pattern for the industry's response to the crossover trend: if you can't beat 'em, steal 'em. After all, if the gullible teenagers were going to listen to junk, they at least ought to listen to well-produced, politely sung versions of that junk that would earn profits for the respectable major labels rather than for some small "indie" that catered to that *other* audience and was responsible for the junk in the first place... Once it became clear that the R&B "fad" was not going to vanish anytime soon, the "entrenched facets of the music business" jumped on the covers bandwagon as a way to stop the hemorrhaging of their profits and audience.

In a way, the covers trend was simply an updated version of the music industry's response to the earlier ragtime, jazz, blues and boogie-woogie "fads," though on a much larger scale and with a faster response time and a more predatory attitude. "Covers" were nothing new, in any case: there had always been many different recordings of popular songs on the market (there were countless versions of "White Christmas," for example, though Bing Crosby's is best-remembered). And there were many earlier examples of covers reaching across stylistic boundaries, such as Woody Herman's anemic big band version of Louis Jordan's "Caldonia," or Tony Bennett's crooning take on Hank Williams' "Cold, Cold Heart."

The R&B covers of the 1950's were more malicious in nature, however, as they were competing for the same market and specifically trying to hijack the sales of current hits—trying to beat the originals to the pop market. To that end the major labels employed A&R men who monitored every release from every small indie label for any songs that might have pop appeal. The majors knew that the indies could not compete with their connections and clout, and that most radio listeners would never even *hear* the original versions of their covers, or even realize they *were* covers.

"Roll, er, Dance With Me Henry"

The originals were always better than the covers, and were always outsold by them.[13] The pop charts of 1954 and 1955 were littered with stalled crossovers and undeserving hit covers. The McGuire Sisters, for example, rendered the Spaniels' "Goodnight, Sweetheart, Goodnight" and the Moonglows' "**Sincerely**" safe for young America, while the Fontane Sisters did the same to "**Hearts of Stone**," an R&B hit for the Charms (which was itself a "cover" of another black group, the Jewels). The uptempo "Hearts of Stone" and the elegant ballad "Sincerely" were both successful crossovers—the Charms went to #15 on the pop charts, the Moonglows to # 20—and interesting examples of the vocal group style at the midpoint between R&B and doo-wop. Such distinctions were obliterated, however, in the comically whitewashed cover versions, which both went to #1(!)

The Penguins' "**Earth Angel**" was the slow-dance flipside of "Gee" and the song that completed the transition from rhythm & blues earthiness to doo-wop innocence. The record remains one of rock's most beloved oldies, while the cover by the irritating Crew Cuts was forgotten long ago, though that is of little consolation to the Penguins, who never had another hit and had to watch the Crew Cuts sail past them up the pop charts with the one hit they could claim. (In a field littered with "one-hit wonders," most groups never recovered from having their one shot taken from them.) The Crew Cuts only climbed to #3 with "Earth Angel," however, since the McGuire Sisters' cover of "Sincerely" and Georgia Gibbs' cover of "Tweedlee Dee" were socked into the top two spots (an illustration of how prevalent the covers mania had become). Georgia Gibbs was even able to turn Etta James' risqué "Roll With Me Henry" into an innocuous and laughably asexual toe-tapper called "Dance With Me Henry."

And then there was **Pat Boone**, the King of the Covers, who launched his wholesome career in 1955 with "Two Hearts," an R&B hit for the ever-reliable Charms, then hit #1 on the pop charts with "Ain't That A Shame," a dreary cover of the great Fats Domino's first crossover hit. He followed with the El Dorados' "At My Front Door," then completed his one-two punch with a cover of Little Richard's first hit, "Tutti Frutti." (Little Richard later recalled that he wanted to "find and kill" Pat Boone when he heard Boone's polite cover of his gloriously unrestrained song.) In his defense, Pat Boone brought at least a watered-down version of rock & roll to a wide audience—at least the entire nation *heard* "Tutti Frutti," and many were then a little more open to the real thing when it finally came their way. Anyway, it's hard to judge Pat Boone too harshly. After all, who would ever think that a <u>white</u> singer really *could* sing rock & roll?

BILL HALEY & HIS COMETS

Bill Haley didn't "invent rock & roll" any more than Columbus "discovered America," but he *was* the first white artist to play it well and "**Rock Around the Clock**" *was* the first rock & roll hit of any color to go to #1 on the pop charts. This was no cover: it was a song written for Haley and *about* rock & roll, and was clearly aimed right at the crossover market with a big dance beat and no references to any world bigger than or beyond the sock hop. The success of "Rock Around the Clock" confirmed the existence of an audience of teenagers (adults certainly didn't buy it) far bigger than even the biggest crossover successes had hinted at—teenagers who found their voice and an expression of their world in rock & roll.

Best of all, it paved the way for the cataclysmic arrival of Elvis Presley on RCA in 1956, which ended the era of the crossovers and covers by rendering each concept obsolete. Elvis sealed rock's triumph and also ushered in a new level of acceptance of the black originators like Little Richard, whose "Long Tall Sally" was the first rock & roll single to hit the charts after Elvis' arrival. Little Richard's original outsold Pat Boone's cover: the reign of the cover songs had ended. Once rock & roll *defined* the market, it was ludicrous to call Little Richard a "crossover," and foolhardy to attempt a "cover" when the kids wanted real rock & roll.

It is the fate of Bill Haley, who liked to call himself the "Father of Rock & Roll," to be always remembered as a mere prelude to Elvis, the *real* white rocker. Of course, there shouldn't have been a need for a "white rocker" to begin with. Chuck Berry, Little Richard, Fats Domino, Bo Diddley and the other great *black* rockers who debuted in 1955 were certainly exciting enough. But the realities of both American society and the music industry dictated otherwise, and assured that the black acts would remain "crossovers" and rock & roll would remain a "fad" and that it would all continue to be swept away by polite covers until the danger had passed. Only a white star of enormous magnitude could give rock & roll access to the mainstream. No one expected or imagined an Elvis, of course, and there might not have *been* an "Elvis" if Bill Haley hadn't proven that such a thing was possible: that a white singer could really capture the sound and feel of rhythm & blues—that a white artists could really play rock & roll. In the light of the harsh realities of the times, "Rock Around the Clock" was a crucial watershed point, and the subsequent arrival of Elvis Presley a nearly miraculous instance of perfect timing.

Shake, Rattle & Roll

Bill Haley & His Saddleman were a small-time western swing combo from Chester, Pennsylvania, when their leader fell under the spell of Louis Jordan and began to reshape their music to accommodate the influence of Jordan's jump blues. Their 1951 recording of "Rocket 88" and subsequent covers of R&B songs were far ahead of their time, in concept if not in music. Renamed Bill Haley & His Comets, they recorded the first white rock & roll hit, "Crazy Man Crazy," in 1953, then joined with Decca Records and producer Milt Gabler and had a Top Ten hit with a cover of "Shake, Rattle & Roll" the following year.

A comparison of Bill Haley & the Comets' version of "Shake, Rattle & Roll" with Joe Turner's original reveals all of the damnable offenses that covers usually perpetrated on their hapless prey. For a start, the lyrics were "cleaned up" and de-sexed (no references to the "sun shinin' through dresses" or the "Devil in nylon hose" in Haley's cover—even the reference to the "bed" at the beginning of Turner's original was deleted); the arrangement was similarly cleaned and polished into a bright and cheery pop sound with clearly-sung melodies that are miles away from Turner's bluesy adult shout; the beat was cleaned and brightened as well, moved from booming lows to a brittle high-end of snare and cymbals, while the song itself was reshaped to allow the singalong title refrain—the "hook"—to appear earlier and more often in order to penetrate the attention span of Haley's teenage audience... And *that* was the difference between Haley and all previous cover artists: Haley loved rhythm & blues and his version was aimed directly at the the rock & roll market, not at appeasing Mom and Dad, and his goal was to retain and hopefully increase the excitement of the original rather than gloss it over. Haley kept the beat big, strong and danceable and kept the energy level high in a way the Crew Cuts could never even have attempted.

See You Later, Alligator!

Bill Haley & the Comets recorded "Rock Around the Clock" before "Shake, Rattle & Roll," but they had to wait until 1955 for *Blackboard Jungle* to turn the forgotten B-side into the battlecry of a new generation. "Rock Around the Clock" made Haley the biggest star in popular music, but he never had another hit that even approached its impact. "See You Later, Alligator," a #6 hit in 1956, was his last big hit. The record is a fun fifties period piece, but it also a good example of the type of post-jump blues arrangements and strained "dig it, daddy-o" hepster image he used to try to stay "in" with a style and a generation that he really wasn't a part of. Haley was old—nearly 30!—and married with children by the time "Rock Around the Clock" became a hit, and he looked it, with a dumb spit curl on his forehead and the Comets' tacky matching outfits and a showbiz smile that seemed exciting until kids got a glimpse of Elvis' sneer.

Declining sales and fortunes at home led Bill Haley & His Comets to embark on a famous tour of England in 1957. His visit was the first from a real American rock & roll star, and the fans were in a frenzied state of anticipation by the time Haley arrived. The frenzy escalated into full-scale riots at Haley's concerts, fueled by a surge of pent-up energy that was too much for the lightweight music and star too absorb. The British fans discovered what American teens already knew: Bill Haley, the Father of Rock & Roll, was a dork.

Bill Haley was definitely in the right place at the right time, but he was ultimately the wrong guy. He was what he seemed to be: a good entertainer who *performed* rock & roll. Elvis *lived* rock & roll, and was the genuine article while Haley was, in the end, an "authentic cover."

Haley simply didn't seem very exciting for very long, but the news that a white artist could play real rock & roll *was* exciting. Opening the pop market to black artists had created "rock & roll" and was one of its great triumphs; ironically, Haley's great triumph was opening up the rock & roll market for *white* artists. He confirmed that rhythm & blues *was* rock & roll, and then proved that rock & roll was "popular music" as well.

Bill Haley died bitter, paranoid and half-crazed in 1981 after many depressing years on the oldies circuit playing "Rock Around the Clock" until he hated the song. The song was his Moment, however, and was the turning point for rock & roll and the dividing line between the past and present. Rock's roots led to and ended—and its future began—with "Rock Around the Clock." Haley had other hits, but none of them mattered. He may not have been the Father of Rock & Roll, but he was definitely the greatest of all "One-hit Wonders."

[1]In this sense, one could distinguish between the blues as a "folk" music and R&B as a "popular" music, though those types of distinctions remain vague at best.

[2]Cole's 1951 recording of "Unforgettable" was revived four decades later in an overdubbed "duet" with daughter Natalie Cole.

[3]The term "Tin Pan Alley" referred loosely to the theater and publishing districts in New York, but was more a catchall term for the publishing and musical entertainment business in general.

[4]David Ewen, "All the Years of American Popular Music" (Englewood Cliffs: Prentice-Hall, 1977), p. 535

[5]Arnold Shaw, "Honkers and Shouters" (New York: Macmillan, 1978), p. 74.

[6]The indies were generally owned by white men, though a few were owned and operated by blacks, most notably Don Robey's Houston-based Peacock label , Vivian and James Bracken's Vee Jay Records, a Chicago rival of Chess Records, and of course Berry Gordy's Motown.

[7]Shaw, "Honkers and Shouters."

[8]Robert Palmer, "Deep Blues" (New York: Viking, 1981) p. 222.

[9]*Rolling Stone* magazine, February 1989, #545

[10]Shaw, p. 243.

[11]Barry Hansen, "Rhythm & Gospel," in "The Rolling Stone Illustrated History of Rock & Roll," ed. Anthony DeCurtis, rev. ed. (1976; rpt. New York: Random House, 1992), p. 18.

[12]Barry Hansen, "Doo-Wop," in "The Rolling Stone Illustrated History of Rock & Roll," ed. Jim Miller, rev. ed. (1976; rpt. New York: Random House, 1980), p. 83.

[13] The original groups were usually left with little or nothing to show for their efforts, even if they had written the song to begin with. While cover versions had to give credit and pay royalties to the "songwriter," more often than not the groups sold the song's copyright—gladly—to the record label owners in exchange for the chance to make a record, and then received no songwriting royalties from either their own recording or the hit cover version. (The label owners didn't necessarily fare much better, since they often had to sell most of their stake in the song to a publisher in order to get it recorded by an established star.)

Photo courtesy of UPI/BETTMAN

Young Elvis

[3] ELVIS PRESLEY

Sunrise

If one *really* had to pick a single place and date as the Birth of Rock &
Roll, it might as well be a Memphis, Tennessee, on July 5, 1954. That hot
summer night found Elvis Presley, Scotty Moore and Bill Black recording at
Sam Phillips' Sun Records studio, struggling through a country ballad and
trying to figure out why nothing seemed to be coming together. Tense and
frustrated, the band took a break from recording and launched into a frenzied,
clowning rave up of an old blues song to let off steam. Elvis threw off his
inhibitions and tore into Arthur "Big Boy" Crudup's **"That's All Right"** like a
schoolboy smashing a window. Following his lead, Bill slapped and jumped
all over his standup bass while Scotty fired off lowdown blues guitar licks that
would have gotten him fired from the country band he and Bill played in. Sam
burst through the control room door, asked what they were doing and told the
slightly embarrassed trio to "do whatever it was again" so they could put it on
tape.

To his great credit, Sam Phillips recognized the future when he heard
it. For years he had recorded some of the great Memphis bluesmen, and for
years he had repeated what is now rock's most famous line: "If only I could find
a white man who had the Negro sound and the Negro feel, I could make a
million dollars." Suddenly there He was, that "white man with a Negro feel,"
and suddenly it seemed so obvious and natural. The fusion of white and black—
country and blues—that had seemed impossibly remote just a few minutes
earlier was now standing right in front of him having the time of his life. It is
wonderfully appropriate that this crucial version of rock & roll was born in the
spirit of fun and letting loose. In one spontaneous, unconscious moment Elvis
reached into his soul and musical heritage and turned the old into the
stunningly new. While the East Coast version of rock & roll developed
gradually and with some discernible logic out of rhythm & blues, the
sprawling, diverse musical traditions of the South exploded into rock & roll in
one fiery blast.

Not that it was a Shot Heard 'round the World. It would be 18 months
before mainstream America surrendered to Elvis, but it was all there that day
in July—all the urgency, excitement and liberating freedom of rock & roll. Had
that strange boy with the pink pants and sideburns simply gone back to driving
a truck, "That's All Right" would still be a remarkable, revelatory record.
Instead, he became the King of Rock & Roll, and the record was nothing less
than revolutionary.

Elvis and Us

Young Elvis Presley remains rock's most indelible image, eternally
young, hip and inspiring despite the tragic mess he made of his later life. The

appearance of Elvis was *the* Moment for the rock era, perfectly timed, now timeless. Rock & roll would have happened—was already happening—without him, but it would have been very different and would never have reached the spectacular heights and had the sweeping impact that it did. Elvis was far greater than the sum of his singles: he was rock's first larger-than-life Hero, and with him began the shared dreams and myths and personal identification that have shaped rock culture ever since. The message of Elvis was, it's the Singer, not the Song. To dress like Elvis or affect his sneering self-confidence or hang his poster in your bedroom meant more than "I like his music." In Elvis, millions of young people found more than a new entertainer: they found themselves, or at least an idealized image of themselves that stood in stark, liberating contrast to the repressed atmosphere of 1950's America. Bob Dylan recalled that hearing Elvis for the first time "was like busting out of jail."[1] Or as fellow fan Springsteen put it, "It was like he came along and whispered a dream in everybody's ear and then we dreamed it."[2]

Elvis gave rock's first generation a standard-bearer in the battle against the mainstream—against Perry Como, Doris Day and Mom & Dad's other favorites, and against Pat Boone, the Crew Cuts and the rest of the clean-cut covers crowd passing itself off as "rock & roll." Had America lived up to its own ideals, of course, it would not have taken a white performer to lead the charge, but the stark realities of the 1950's assured that no black artist could have the wide appeal, music industry support and access to the media that Elvis enjoyed. That blunt fact is cause for both condemnation and celebration—condemnation of the *need* for an "Elvis," and celebration that one appeared.

The sheer force of Elvis' popularity and talent broke through previously impenetrable barriers and forced rock & roll down the mainstream's throat. He gave rock a center of gravity and source of momentum and single-handedly created the context that made it possible to talk about rock as something more than a "passing fad for rhythm & blues." While he was at his peak, rock exploded with and around him; when he "retired" to the army and the movies, it started to whither: without an overriding force like Elvis to keep things moving in the early sixties, rock was at the mercy of *American Bandstand* and the "teen idol" pretenders to the throne. The audience scattered, waiting, as it turned out, for the Beatles to shape rock's second generation as Elvis had the first.

Elvis never really reclaimed his throne after leaving for the army, but he never relinquished it either. Through all the passing years and changing times, a central fact remains unchanged: there's only one King of Rock & Roll, and that's Elvis.

Elvis and the South

Elvis Aron Presley was born on January 8, 1935 in Tupelo, Mississippi. (Elvis later added an extra "a" to his middle name. his twin brother, Jessie Garon, died at birth.) Elvis grew up an only child, surrounded by as much love and pampering as the family's resources would allow, which wasn't much— Vernon and Gladys Presley were desperately poor. In 1948, tired of barely scraping by in Tupelo, the family moved to Memphis and settled into the dreary Lauderdale Courts public housing project. They did not find much of the better life they'd sought in the city, however, and by the time he finished high school Elvis had already begun a series of dead-end jobs and was settling into a life that seemed to offer little beyond more hard times with some fun along the way.

Elvis was, by all accounts, a painfully shy and introverted youth who revered his mother and treated his elders with humble deference. He was also a high school rebel who wore long sideburns, slicked-back hair and outrageous, hepcat clothes from the black stores on Beale Street that made him stand out like the sore thumb he already felt he was. Years before he made his first record, Elvis was already creating the image that would both project him to and protect him from the world. First as a poor rural kid in the big city and later as a hillbilly southerner trying to make it in mainstream America, Elvis' basic stance—which became rock & roll's basic stance—was that of the Outsider, a little awkward and out of place, desperately wanting acceptance but determined to win that acceptance on his own terms.

Looking back, it seems almost inevitable that so many of rock's Founding Fathers came from the South, with its rich legacy of contrasting cultures and musical styles. Country music was everywhere, of course, and all roads and all the dreams of young white musicians led to Nashville and the *Grand Ole Opry*. The South was also home to the blues, however, and to a fringe element of crazed rednecks who were fascinated by the blues and bold enough to try creating their own version. Although it is certainly true that the South of the fifties was severely segregated and rife with racial hatred, on a practical day-to-day level, southerners—especially *poor* southerners—of both races intermingled much more closely and with a much deeper awareness of each other than their counterparts in the North. That awareness extended to the music, and a good many white southerners of Elvis' generation felt that the emotional depth and earthy sensuality of the blues and R&B spoke more directly to their youthful energy and frustrations than the traditional values and emotional restraints of country music. The fact that, given the racial climate, it was "forbidden fruit" made it all the more exciting. Adopting black musical styles and other aspects of black culture, such as wild "cat clothes" and jive slang ("Go cat go!"), helped to give expression to their own feelings of alienation and their own desire to be different. Although rockabilly is often called—and was—a fusion of blues and country, the "country" part of the equation was simply a reflection of the rockabillies' heritage and natural musical accents. What made it different and exciting was their attempt to mimic the blues and sound "black": the defining musical traits, image and outsider stance of rockabilly drew heavily from black music and culture.[3]

Gospel music, black and white, was also a big part of the South's musical spectrum and an important influence on Elvis and rockabilly. Gospel styles ranged from quietly devotional to joyous and celebratory, but fast or slow, quiet or loud, the crucial ingredient was a heartfelt emotion—singing as if your very life and immortal soul depended on it. Singing in church was Elvis' first musical memory, and gospel music remained a part of his repertoire throughout his career. For poor southerners like Elvis, church was a place to let your feelings out, to escape your troubles for an hour or two and sing of a promised land where all your sufferings will be rewarded—to sing with exactly the sense of release and liberation that Elvis brought to his Sun recordings.

The native blues, gospel and country music of the South spoke with a direct honesty and real-life authenticity that was lacking in the pop music or even the more sophisticated rhythm & blues from the North. There was a strong regional identity in the music that found its way into rock & roll as well ("rockabillies" were "rockin' hillbillies," after all). Inasmuch as early rock & roll was an emotionally direct and authentic "folk" music, it owes much to its southern roots. The raw, rough-edged music of Elvis, Jerry Lee, Carl Perkins, Little Richard, Buddy Holly and other giants of rock's first wave simply could not have come from the North.

With all this in mind, we find young Elvis walking into Sam Phillips' studio in the summer of 1953 to make a record as a present for his mother. On that day, Elvis chose to record two Ink Spots ballads in the style of his idol— that epitome of the pop establishment, Dean Martin(!) For all his southern roots, it's important to note that unlike, say, Carl Perkins or Jerry Lee Lewis, Elvis also loved mainstream popular music and dreamed of crooning like Dean Martin and becoming a movie star, and that his Sun recordings include versions of pop chestnuts like "Blue Moon," "I Love You Because" and "I'll Never Let You Go" side-by-side with the blues and country songs. In essence, Elvis had a pop voice and a pop musical sensibility that drew on his love of country, blues and gospel to form an entirely new conception of "pop." And for all his celebrated shyness and self-deprecating manner, he had grand pop dreams and ambitions that heightened his impatience with lesser classifications ("C&W," "R&B") and fueled his—and rock's—triumphant assault on the pop charts and popular culture. By the time he first set foot in a studio, Elvis was a uniquely balanced bundle of contradictions, and a musical time bomb waiting to explode.

The Sun Years: 1954-55

Sun Records was a relatively small-time operation that had a huge impact on rock & roll. It's owner and operator, **Sam Phillips** (born 1923), is a legendary figure in his own right. With a roster of artists that included Elvis Presley, Jerry Lee Lewis, Carl Perkins, Johnny Cash, Charlie Rich and Roy Orbison, along with many of the great southern blues artists, Phillips' importance to the development of rock & roll cannot be overstated. Simply discovering those artists would have been enough to secure his place in history, but all of them went on to make some of the very best—if not *the* best—music of their careers with Phillips at the controls.

Phillips genuinely loved the music he recorded and believed in his artists, and they, in turn, believed in and respected him. He had a great knack for helping his artists discover their own unique style and hidden talents, and he fostered an air of casual camaraderie that helped make inspired "accidents" like "That's All Right" possible. As Carl Perkins later recalled, "You just forgot about making a record and tried to show him. I'd walk out on a limb, I'd try things I knew I couldn't do, and then have to work my way out of it. I'd say 'Mr. Phillips, that's terrible.' He'd say 'That's original.' I'd say, 'But it's just a big original mistake.' And he said, 'That's what Sun records *is*!'"[4]

Memphis was a hotbed of blues talent at the beginning of the 1950's, with a vibrant club scene on Beale Street, where Elvis soaked up the sights and sounds he would soon mimic, and a well-established presence of black radio station stations that kept blues, R&B and gospel sounds just a flick of the dial away from the *Grand Ole Opry* broadcasts. Sam Phillips opened the Memphis Recording Service in 1950 to provide an outlet for the city's great blues and R&B talent, and made some of the first recordings by B. B. King, Howlin' Wolf, Bobby "Blue" Bland, Elmore James, Ike Turner, James Cotton, Junior Parker, Walter Horton and Rufus Thomas. After first leasing his recordings to outside labels (the classic "Rocket 88," for example, was issued by Chess Records), he began his own **Sun Records** label in 1952. Although he was painfully aware of the prejudice that limited its commercial potential, Phillips loved black music and realized that it had an intensity and vitality that was sorely lacking in the stagnant pop music of the time. Now if only he could find a white artist who could capture that same drive and spirit...

Meanwhile, to help finance his blues recordings, Phillips continued the Memphis Recording Service's other functions: mobile recordings and an in-studio, do-it-yourself operation that let anyone off the street come in, pay $4 and walk out with his own record. In the summer of 1953, Elvis walked in to do just that, after many long minutes of pacing the sidewalk in front of the studio to work up his nerves. After witnessing the spectacle, Sam's bemused office manager, Marion Keisker, took Elvis' payment and asked him who he sounded like and what type of song he wanted to record. The shy teenager politely—and prophetically—replied, "I don't sound like nobody," then recorded "My Happiness" and "That's When Your Heartaches Begin" to his own guitar accompaniment.

Sam Phillips sensed something different about the nervous but sincere young singer—something promising enough to prompt him to make his own copy of the recordings for future reference. It certainly wasn't the magnetic charisma that Elvis would soon be known for, as Phillips later recalled: "Elvis Presley probably innately was the most introverted person that [ever] came into that studio. He didn't go to this little club and pick and grin. All he did was sit with his guitar on the side of the bed at home. I don't think he even played on the front porch."[5] Elvis was a fully-realized product of his own imagination: he never "jammed" with friends or sang with a band before coming to Sun, and he invented a look for himself that invited years of ridicule before becoming the Look of a generation. Like so many other lonely and alienated young people, Elvis created a fantasy world for himself and an idealized image of what he wanted to be. Unlike all others, he made that dream real, forcing the music to bend to his vision and creating a wholly original style in the process.

The Sun Recordings

Elvis was in the back of Sam's mind for nearly a year before he was finally called for a real audition. Phillips hooked him up with guitarist **Scotty More** and bassist **Bill Black**—the other heroes of the Sun Sessions—and began the search for the right song and the right style for the young truck driver. The search ended—and the future began—abruptly on July 5 when the little band launched into "That's All Right."

The group reconvened the next evening, July 6, and recorded again, now experimenting with and defining a style that hadn't existed—even in their wildest dreams—just 24 short hours earlier. After "That's All Right," Sam, Elvis, Scotty and Bill knew they were breaking new ground with every step, and the excitement and enthusiasm of Elvis' Sun recordings reflects that sense of discovery. Existing rehearsal tapes and outtakes show they were constantly experimenting with the tempo, style and feel of the songs, and mixing up old styles to create new possibilities. At the end of a slow, bluesy rehearsal of **"Blue Moon of Kentucky,"** for example, Sam can be heard saying, "fine, man... hell, that's different, that's a pop song now!" A bluegrass classic by Bill Monroe, "Blue Moon of Kentucky" was chosen for the flipside of "That's All Right," though the fast, aggressive released version was completely different from the early rehearsals, reflecting the anything goes atmosphere at Sun, and establishing the pattern of blues-country pairings that was used for the remainder of Elvis' Sun singles.

Elvis never really wrote a song of his own, but at his best he reworked and revitalized the songs he sang so thoroughly that he might as well have written them. He ignored the lamenting overtones of Crudup's original "That's All Right," and turned Junior Parker's dirge-like "Mystery Train" into a celebration. (Parker mourns the fact that the train "took my baby, and it's gonna do it again," while Elvis' train "took my baby, but it NEVER WILL AGAIN.") In similar fashion, Roy Brown's classy jump-blues "Good Rockin'

Tonight" became a battle cry for a new era, while Arthur Gunter's timid "Baby Let's Play House" was transformed into a musical and sexual cataclysm.

Elvis' **"Milkcow Blues Boogie"** is a combination of an old Kokomo Arnold blues standard and "Brain Cloudy Blues," a western swing number by Bob Wills and His Texas Playboys. Although loosely a blues "cover," his inspired vision of the song is as far from the blues as his "Blue Moon of Kentucky" was from bluegrass, though he begins "Milkcow Blues Boogie" with a playful false start of slow, straight blues. Elvis cuts the intriguing opening short with a challenge to the band: "Hold it fellas! That don't <u>move</u> me. Let's get real, real GONE for a change." He then plunges into the song for real, with a hopped-up tempo and an daredevil vocal performance that erases the false start from memory and mocks the notion that he, Elvis Presley, could ever be confined to old-time blues any more than he could confine himself to the staid bluegrass of Bill Monroe. "I don't sound like nobody," indeed. Elvis' Sun Sessions were a triumph of instinctive, self-creating talent, and are pure rock & roll—the purest rock & roll, standing at the crossroads of the pre-rock past and the decades of music they helped spawn. Elvis reinvented himself in one blinding flash, and fused his influences so seamlessly that total effect of the Sun recordings is that of a slate wiped clean, where anything and everything was possible.

Rockabilly Style Traits

The unbridled energy and raw sound of Elvis' Sun recordings formed the blueprint for the distinctly southern brand of rock & roll called **rockabilly**. "Keep it simple" was Sam Phillips' first rule: no horns, strings, superfluous instruments or even background singers to get in the way of the emotion and spontaneity. Everything was stripped to the barest essentials, yet the records sound amazingly full, thanks largely to Phillips' tape-delay "slapback" echo, in which the recorded voice or instrument was immediately fed back on itself through a tape delay circuit. The split-second lag, coupled with the natural ambiance of the Sun studio, created the "echo" and a focused, magnified sound (unlike the distant, "empty concert hall" sound of normal "reverb") that became Phillips' trademark, much copied but never quite duplicated anywhere else.[6]

The full sound of the Sun recordings is even more impressive in light of the fact that there was no drummer in the band for the majority of his stay at Sun, in keeping with the drum-less tradition of country music. The percussive "drum" sound so prominent in these recordings is actually a "slapping bass," another rockabilly trademark. Paul Burlison, of the Johnny Burnette Trio, explains the technique: "You loosen that top string, the big E, about half way. You don't even tune it. It's got to be real loose to where you can pop it with the palm of your hand against the neck. You pop it first and hear that slapping sound, and then pull your fingers across your D and G strings. Slap, then pull."[7]

In addition to "slapping," Bill Black alternated between a simple country-style bass and bluesy walking bass figures. Scotty Moore played a similar mix of country and blues, working gritty bent strings and blues licks into his Chet Atkins picking style, often mixing styles within the same lead break (as in "That's All Right," where the country figure that opens the solo dovetails into the "blue notes" and then out again, or in the bright country solo that jumps out of the middle of the bluesy "Milkcow Blues Boogie"). Moore's brilliant stylistic synthesis and lean, piercing sound added a crucial ingredient to Elvis' Sun style and, along with Carl Perkins' twangy picking, established the basic attack of all rockabilly guitarists.

The rhythmic foundation of the Sun recordings came from Elvis' acoustic guitar, which he—like Hank Williams—played hard and percussively, as much for the rhythm as for the notes or chords. Although he later used the guitar mainly as a prop, Elvis was a fine, energetic guitarist, and one of the many delights of the Sun Sessions is listening to Elvis pound away, skipping beats and surging ahead on his guitar with the same nervous energy and intensity that fueled his singing, which, of course, was the focus of it all. Against such a sparse backing, Elvis had plenty of room to develop the nuances and impressive range of his voice, which could shift from loud to soft, high to low, shouting to crooning at a moment's notice.

"Baby Let's Play House" is a textbook of Elvis' vocal styles: the low, sensual vibratos and inexplicable little hiccups ("Oh Baby, baby, bab-EE"), the chopped, breathless syllables, the sweep up to a high, pure tenor and the dramatic plummet back down to a sexy, quavering growl. His versatility and his willingness to let go and have fun with his voice gave his songs a wonderfully elastic and playful quality (note the self-mocking laugh in the final chorus of "Baby Let's Play House"). Elvis' voice was central to his appeal, though his looks—those eyes, that sneer—certainly contributed as well! Joined together in one astonishing package, and given the right music as a medium, his sensual voice and equally sensual image made for a viscerally powerful combination.

The Hillbilly Cat

Elvis, Scotty and Bill were as surprised as anyone by "That's All Right," and had no idea what kind of reaction to expect when people first heard this country boy singing the blues. The night the record was first aired on Memphis radio, Scotty confidently predicted they'd be "run out of town," while Elvis was so nervous he tuned in the station on his family radio, told his parents to listen and then took off to hide in a movie theater. He needn't have worried. The request lines lit up immediately, and WHBQ disc jockey Dewey Phillips (no relation to Sam) played the record over and over, all night long.

Dewey Phillips, who was white, was at first hesitant to spin the record since he only played black R&B on his show. His mixed audience included a lot of young whites, like Elvis, who tuned in to hear the latest R&B and Phillips' crazed, rapid-fire hepcat delivery. To ward off any confusion, Phillips had Elvis rounded up from the movie theater for an on-air interview, where the first order of business was to clarify his color (he simply got Elvis to say where he'd gone to high school—a clear sign in those segregated days). Still, no one knew quite what to make of the song or the singer. He was dubbed the "hillbilly cat" which, as Greil Marcus put it, meant the "white Negro." Or as Elvis later recalled, "...when the record came out a lot of people liked it, and you could hear folks around town saying, 'Is he, is he?' and I'm going, 'Am I, am I?'"[8]

Elvis quickly became a local star, then began working his way through the South in an endless string of one-nighters in high school gyms, National Guard armories and city parks. As the fan reaction got wilder and wilder, so did Elvis, who discovered that the more he shook his legs and moved his hips, the louder the girls screamed. Elvis recalled: "My very first appearance, I was on a show in Memphis [July 30, 1954]... I was scared stiff. I came out and I was doing a fast-type tune and everybody was hollering and I didn't know what they were hollering at... I came offstage and my manager told me they was hollering because I was wiggling. And so I went back out for an encore and I did a little more. And the more I did, the wilder they went."[9] After a disastrous appearance on the *Grand Ole Opry*, where he was advised to go back to driving a truck (the good folks of Nashville told him they didn't want "any of that nigger music around here"), Elvis became a regular on the weekly *Louisiana Hayride* radio show in Shreveport, Louisiana, which beamed him into households throughout the South.

Elvis' popularity grew steadily during his year and a half at Sun, though it was still limited to the South and the country market (*Billboard* named him the nation's "most promising young country singer" in 1955). Meanwhile rock & roll was exploding around the country: Chuck Berry, Little Richard, Fats Domino, the Platters and Bo Diddley all hit the pop charts in 1955, as did Bill Haley's "Rock Around the Clock," which proved that a white artist could capture that same beat and feel. The time was right for Elvis to make a move. **Col. Tom Parker**, his new manager, negotiated the sale of Elvis' contract to RCA for a whopping $40,000—a lot of money in 1955 for a relatively unknown and unproven talent.[10]

For Elvis, the move to RCA meant a move to the Bigtime: the "struggle," such as it was, was over. In a few short months "Heartbreak Hotel" would hit the top of the national charts and Elvis would be the biggest thing to ever hit the entertainment scene. To mainstream America it seemed that Elvis became a star overnight, but some of his greatest music was already behind him by the time most of the nation first heard his name. At RCA, his massive fame and ambition, the demands of popular taste and the weight of his all-consuming image would distance Elvis further and further from his own talent, and would add an element of self-consciousness and calculation to his songs and performances that was gloriously lacking in the free-for-all of his Sun days. The "Sun Sessions" provide a last glimpse of undiluted young Elvis at his breathtaking best.

The Glory Years: 1956-58

One night in 1957, Elvis took the stage at a large outdoor concert and asked the audience to rise with him and "sing our national anthem." As hats came off and hands went over hearts, he knelt solemnly, eyed the crowd, took a deep breath and tore into "Hound Dog!" Perfect! And he was right—as far as teenage America was concerned, it WAS our national anthem.

Elvis made his first television appearance on the Dorsey Brothers' *Stage Show* on January 28, 1956 His performance—his hips and "suggestive movements"—caused a storm of controversy and prompted a rash of angry calls from parents shocked at the display of unchecked emotion. If this sort of thing caught on, could rampant juvenile delinquency be far behind?

Elvis' appearance also sent shock waves through Young America. This wasn't some anonymous R&B vocal group or a middle-aged Bill Haley presenting rock & roll as "entertainment for the kids." This guy was one of *us*, young and bristling with energy, and he seemed to *live* rock & roll, not just perform it. To the horrified parents and delighted teenagers alike, Elvis seemed like James Dean incarnate—a rebel, though With a Cause this time: the raucous new rhythms of rock & roll.

50,000,000 Elvis Fans Can't Be Wrong

Elvis took over where Frank Sinatra left off, then kept going up into uncharted realms of success. The Gold Record award for sales, for example, was essentially invented for Elvis (the mind-numbing hallway of gold records at Graceland, Elvis' Memphis home, is the high point of a tour there, or at least the most pertinent reminder of why Elvis continues to matter so much). The army of Elvis fans multiplied as rock & roll spread and grew to a point where RCA could release an album entitled *50,000,000 Elvis Fans Can't Be Wrong* without risking any accusations of exaggerated hype.

For the fans and for the flood of new singers who followed in his wake, Elvis completely defined what it meant to be a rocker, or at least a white rocker. When Gene Vincent, Eddie Cochran and Ricky Nelson, for example, came out looking and sounding like Elvis clones, it was no more a matter of "ripping off" Elvis than to say the Rolling Stones or the Byrds were simply "copying the Beatles" by growing their hair. Elvis simply defined the fifties rock image. His southern brand of rock & roll became the dominant style and that impossible little curl in his lip, a harmless natural trait present even in his baby pictures, became the defiant sneer of an entire generation. His aura of bored but polite disdain for the adult world, and his ability to laugh at it and at himself with equal ease, gave rock & roll a model of both driving ambition and free-spirited fun. Most of all, his brooding sensuality defined the male ideal for both the swooning girls and their envious boyfriends, who tried their hardest to create that look of moody magnificence in themselves.

The visual image was a key ingredient in Elvis' popularity, and has been a central aspect of rock's appeal ever since. To feel Elvis' full impact you had to *see* him sway and shake and work himself into a seemingly uncontrollable frenzy. That image of wild, passionate abandon was then etched in the listener's mind, inseparable from the music itself. Elvis' explosion in the national consciousness was the first fully-televised ascent to stardom, and his arrival forever linked rock and television, the two beacons of popular culture. The visual flash and excitement of rock & roll was perfectly suited for the camera, and no one was more perfectly suited than Elvis, who attracted cameras like a magnet and repaid the interest with an ever-fascinating and evolving image of perfection.

Elvis dominated the fifties as the Beatles would the sixties, giving rock & roll a broad appeal and opening up the turf for others to follow or create their own niche in. Elvis' success showed white singers that they, too, could rock out—that they didn't have to become Pat Boone to have a hit. And contradictory as it may seem, his success gave a big boost to the black artists as well. Elvis certainly covered black artists, but he sang the songs because he loved the music and never tried to steal a hit or compete with a song that was currently on the charts (a number of his covers were even big hits on the R&B charts). His covers naturally created interest in the original artists, giving them a wider audience as well: having Elvis wail "Tutti Frutti" on national TV was almost as much a victory for Little Richard as for Elvis. Soul singer and Sun veteran Rufus Thomas says that despite the resentment his success generated, "Elvis created an acceptance for black music that had never been there before—he opened a lot of doors."[11]

Still, the racism lurking beneath the surface of Elvis' coronation as the "King" of rock & roll remains a sad indictment of America's social attitudes. It should have been an easy matter for black artists to break through on their own, but it wasn't, and it is very obviously true that the black artists received less—and Elvis and his peers more—credit than they were due. Although black music was the main impetus for rock & roll, a white singer became the "King of Rock & Roll," just as Paul Whiteman and Benny Goodman became the "Kings" of Jazz and Swing. In spite of this blatant injustice, rock & roll did bring black performers into the mainstream to a far greater extent than ever before, and it's role in breaking down the racial barriers in our society is one of its happier legacies. At the very least it brought white and black kids together on the same dance floor, something years of court rulings and good intentions had failed to do.

Rebel in the Mainstream

1956 and 1957 were the glory years for Elvis Presley. After signing with RCA, his career spiraled upward with dizzying speed: by April of 1956, "Heartbreak Hotel" was at the top of all three charts (Pop, C&W and R&B), beginning a string of #1 hits that continued through Elvis' induction into the army in 1958. By then, though, things were already changing and the rough edges of his image and music—and of rock & roll in general—had begun to soften. In an effort to broaden his appeal and fulfill his most cherished dream, Elvis began work on his first movie, *Love Me Tender*, in August of 1956. The movie and its saccharine title song did broaden his appeal, but at the expense of his rebel image and commitment to rock & roll. Elvis made four movies in the fifties: *Love Me Tender, Loving You, King Creole* and *Jailhouse Rock*. They weren't bad—the latter two were surprisingly good—but they distracted him from his recording and performing career and were, in retrospect, warning signs of the dismal decade to come.

There were other signs as well. Elvis made his last televised appearance of the fifties at the end of 1957 on the *Ed Sullivan Show*. Disturbed by the complaints (those hips again) that followed his previous appearances, Sullivan decided to blunt the criticism by only filming Elvis from the waist up. (The last song Elvis sang that night was the Thomas Dorsey gospel classic "Peace in the Valley"—from the waist up!) To cap it off, Sullivan appeared at the end of the show to tell the country that Elvis was a "real decent, fine boy," giving him, in effect, the Good Housekeeping Seal of Approval. A short time later he was in the army. The battle was lost.

Elvis' transformation from rebel hoodlum to decent all-American boy was remarkably swift. You can follow the changes in his TV clips, as his southern accent fades and the jeans and oversized hepcat suits give way to gold jackets and plugs for his latest movie. But along the way he made some great music and won a great victory for rock & roll. At least he was *on* national TV, shaking his hips (when they showed them), singing rock & roll and bringing an exuberant sexuality right into America's living rooms. And he was now on RCA, bringing huge profits to the label and sending the other majors scurrying to sign their own authentic rockers. After years of countering with covers and hoping that it would simply go away, Elvis' success at RCA forced the music industry to concede defeat and surrender to rock & roll.

Elvis at RCA

Elvis racked up an impressive string of #1 hits in two short years: "Heartbreak Hotel," "I Want You, I Need You, I Love You," "Don't Be Cruel," "Hound Dog," "Love Me Tender," "Too Much," "All Shook Up," "Teddy Bear," "Jailhouse Rock," "Don't," and "Hard Headed Woman." During that period Elvis held down the #1 position for a staggering 58 weeks. The statistics for his entire career are equally impressive: 41 gold albums, 18 #1 singles, 38 top ten and 107 top forty hits. Only the Beatles even came close to Elvis' domination of the charts.

Looking at the above list of songs, or any collection of Elvis songs, its hard not to be struck by the diversity and inconsistency of the material. "Hound Dog" and "Jailhouse Rock" are as tough and exciting as rock & roll gets, while "Love Me Tender" and "I Want You, I Need You, I Love You" are mawkish ballads that would have made Johnny Ray or Pat Boone proud; "Too Much" and "Hard Headed Woman" have a bluesy sexuality while "Teddy Bear" seems barely out of puberty; and the eerie sound and adult sensibilities of "Heartbreak Hotel" are a sharp contrast to the sock-hop pop of "Don't Be Cruel" and "All Shook Up."

The true merits of Elvis Presley's music have always been the subject of some dispute. Elvis couldn't write songs or play the guitar like Chuck Berry, Carl Perkins and Buddy Holly, couldn't sustain the rock & roll fire of Little Richard and Jerry Lee Lewis, lacked the consistency of Fats Domino... But no one else could have appealed to such varied tastes and united a nation fans the way Elvis did. If you hated "Love Me Tender," then you probably loved "Hound Dog"; if not, then you *had* to love "Don't Be Cruel." From schmaltzy ballads through mainstream pop to hard-edged rock & roll, Elvis covered all the bases—and when he was at his best, he was indeed the King of rock & roll. At his worst, he was nearly unlistenable, and he was always capable of turning out mediocre, half-hearted material at RCA, where the pressures of sustaining his success and image inevitably had an effect on his music, especially with the added demands of the movies and the requisite soundtrack songs. Eventually he covered too many bases, and diluted his talent in his attempt to appeal to everyone, though it is also that grand, sweeping attempt to be all things to all people that makes Elvis Presley such a spectacular and uniquely American success story. In any case, that the same man could record "Hound Dog" and "Old Shep," with equal conviction, is just one of the many apparent contradictions that make Elvis so fascinating and so exasperating.

"Heartbreak Hotel"

Elvis got off to a great start at RCA with "**Heartbreak Hotel**," which started its steady climb up the charts in January 1956. The Elvis of "Heartbreak Hotel" sounds as if he's suffocating in some twisted after-hours club in the Twilight Zone, backed by a half-demented jazz bass and piano and a distorted guitar that rails against the desolation of the song's lyrics and mood. "Heartbreak Hotel" is unlike anything he recorded at Sun: big, spacious and massively reverberated where the Sun sound was lean and focused, set with an instrumental arrangement punctuated by stops, starts and dynamic subtleties that seem a world away from the full-speed-ahead feel of rockabilly, and sung with a brash, worldwise voice that already seems far removed from the innocence of his wide-eyed Memphis celebrations.

Scotty Moore and Bill Black made the dramatic change with Elvis and remained the core of his band at RCA, along with drummer **D. J. Fontana**, who had toured with Elvis since they met at the *Louisiana Hayride*. At RCA, the band was usually augmented to include a piano, an extra guitar and a gospel-style backing vocal group, the **Jordanaires**, who had a knack for adding ludicrously polite harmonies to even the hardest rock songs.[12] Still uncertain about Elvis' style and appeal, RCA first chose their Nashville studios as the logical place to tap his Memphis rockabilly. (Elvis continued to record in Nashville throughout his career, alternating with sessions in New York and Hollywood.) Nashville wasn't Memphis, however, and Elvis was no longer a "rockabilly," and the results were markedly different.

The Rockers

The songs Elvis chose to record ranged from hard-edged *rock* to catchy *pop* and sentimental *ballads*, and his overall output can be loosely divided into those three styles. He cut through the dense guitar and drums clatter of his hardest rockers with a raucous voice that he, and everyone else, borrowed from Little Richard. This hard rocking side of Elvis included most of his cover songs, such as "Hound Dog," "Blue Suede Shoes," "Lawdy Miss Clawdy," "Shake, Rattle and Roll" and his many Little Richard covers, and some of his most riveting original performances, including "Jailhouse Rock" and "A Big Hunk O' Love."

Elvis' version of "**Hound Dog**" serves as a good illustration of the difference between "rockabilly" and "rock & roll." Rockabilly was, of course, inseparable from—was a version of—rock & roll, and its influence is clearly felt in the instrumentation and the sheer energy and tough sound of "Hound Dog." On the other hand, the rough, aggressive vocals, the huge drum sound, added hand claps, distorted guitar, pop-styled vocal backing and big, slick production make the record very different from the lean minimalism of his Sun style, while the blues and country mixture that fueled rockabilly is only faintly audible, if at all. Rock & roll was developing a tradition of its own and, like Elvis, was already a giant step removed from its roots.

"Hound Dog" was originally recorded by Big Mama Thornton in 1952, though Elvis' version was actually based on a comic rendition by a Las Vegas lounge band—much of the humor derived from the male rendition of the song's female point of view, though this element of humor was vaporized in the ferocity of Elvis' attack. The song was written by the team of **Jerry Leiber and Mike Stoller** (with uncredited help from Johnny Otis), who then began supplying Elvis with hits written specifically for him, including "Jailhouse Rock," "Loving You," "Love Me," "Don't," "Treat Me Nice" and "(You're So Square) Baby I Don't Care." Elvis left the ancient blues and country behind at RCA, first turning to covers of more recent R&B and rock & roll songs, then to new material written for him as his popularity and appeal to songwriters grew.[13]

Leiber and Stoller wrote "**Jailhouse Rock**" for the 1957 movie of the same name. Like the rest of his movie songs, it was written to order—the script called for a production number in a jail—in the manner that was largely responsible for the decline of Elvis' material in later years. In the hands of Leiber and Stoller, however, the song became an aural jail break that transcended the plot and inspired a full-throttle performance from Elvis, backed by a syncopated drum beat meant to sound like convicts busting rocks on a chain gang. Elvis also choreographed the song's production number for the movie, and danced one of his best routines to its beat, happily mocking the outlaw role that much of America had hoisted upon him.

"**A Big Hunk O' Love**" was recorded in June 1956 during a leave of absence from the army shortly after Elvis' induction. (RCA was anxious, to say the least, about their star's departure, and wanted to make sure they had a supply of Elvis to release during his absence. "A Big Hunk O' Love" wasn't released until 1959.) The session featured new backing musicians, including guitarist Hank Garland, bassist Bob Moore, pianist Floyd Cramer and drummer Buddy Harman, who would continue with him upon his return from the service. (Scotty and Bill felt increasingly ignored and superfluous at RCA, and broke with Elvis shortly before his induction. Scotty returned to front his sixties bands, but Bill left for good and started his own Bill Black Combo. He died of a brain tumor in 1965.) Highlighted by stop-start guitar riffs and high, rapidfire piano runs, the full sound and streamlined energy of the arrangement prompted a great performance from Elvis, who made the most of the song's sexual undercurrent and bluesy feel. "A Big Hunk O' Love" is ample proof that Elvis had lost none of his taste and talent for pure rock & roll, and ample reason to lament the arrival of his draft notice.

The Pop Songs

"Hound Dog" was just one half of an amazing 1956 single: the flipside was "**Don't Be Cruel**," a pairing that resulted in the highest selling single record of the 1950's. The double-sided hit also offers a good comparison of Elvis' uptempo styles. While the straight rock of "Hound Dog" emphasizes a big beat and raucous sound over a 12-bar blues, the pop-oriented "Don't Be Cruel" has a lighter beat and gentler accompaniment that focuses attention on the clever melody and lyrics. Memorable melodies, catchy "hooks" and romantic lyrics have always been the hallmarks of pop, and the difference between the sexually aggressive "Hound Dog" and the playfully innocent "Don't Be Cruel" is roughly the difference between rock and pop, though not in any sense that Mom and Dad might have recognized. "Don't Be Cruel" is clearly more different from Perry Como or any other earlier pop style than it is from "Hound Dog." The immediacy of the Elvis' performance and the song's eminently danceable beat, teen-oriented lyrics and unadorned sound—no strings, horn section or heavenly choir—placed it squarely in the world of "Hound Dog" and Little Richard. "Don't Be Cruel" represented a new conception of "pop," redefined within the context of the rock audience and rock & roll aesthetics.

The pop-rock feel of "Don't Be Cruel" was echoed happily a year later in "All Shook Up." Both songs are propelled by a gently rolling boogie-bass line and an airy sound and infectious beat (which was actually created by Elvis tapping the back of his guitar while D. J. Fontana "played" a guitar case with his hands). The screaming guitars and drums of "Hound Dog" are nowhere to be found, and their absence left plenty of room for Elvis to glide, swoop, quaver, hiccup, stretch and clip his syllables and use all the signature effects from his Sun days to full advantage. The relatively sparse accompaniment also leaves more room for the ever-present Jordanaires, who actually make sense on a record like "Don't Be Cruel."

"Don't Be Cruel" and "All Shook Up" were both written by **Otis Blackwell**, who also supplied Elvis with "Paralyzed" and "Return to Sender." Other standouts in Elvis' pop vein included "Treat Me Nice," "Teddy Bear," "I Got Stung" and "(You're So Square) Baby I Don't Care." For many fans, and most Elvis imitators, this is the most distinctive Elvis style.

The Ballads

Elvis' ballads fit more easily within the "old" definition of "pop," though Elvis' vocal style and the sparse backing arrangements of the "rock-a-ballads" were still far removed from the syrupy strings-and-harp settings and vibrato-laden singing of earlier popular ballads. The songs range from the very touching and beautifully sung, such as "Love Me Tender," "I Was the One" and "Loving You," to cloying and schmaltzy melodramas like "I Want You, I Need You, I Love You," "Love Me," "That's When Your Heartaches Begin."

"**Love Me Tender**," the title song from Elvis' first movie, is backed by a gently strummed acoustic guitar and sentimental, humming-by-the-campfire background voices that fit the Western setting of the movie. Elvis sings the song in a sincere and fairly unadorned style, close-miked for an extra feeling of intimacy. Sung to the tune of "Aura Lee," an old folk ballad of the 1860's, "Love Me Tender" did much to broaden Elvis' appeal to both younger pre-teen fans and older listeners (much as the Beatles' "Yesterday" expanded their audience).

Elvis had always loved sentimental ballads and he sang them with the same conviction he brought to rock & roll. Still, it is in the ballads and some of the more lightweight up-tempo material that Elvis began to display questionable judgment, to put it kindly, and a loss of musical focus. Given good material, like "A Big Hunk O' Love," Elvis could always rise to the occasion and make a great record. But as the good material began to dry up, or be buried under the flood of demotapes from every hack writer around, so did Elvis' interest, and his recording sessions began to take on the feeling of perfunctory routine—a far cry from the thoroughly absorbed conviction of the Sun and early RCA days. The problem was certainly compounded by his manager, Col. Parker, who heard only the sound of cash registers in Elvis' music. He knew that the mainstream was where the money was, and he firmly pushed his impressionable and success-hungry young client in that direction.

But rock & roll defined itself *against* the mainstream, even while it was succeeding within it. That tension between acceptance and defiance gave (and continues to give) rock & roll much of its power to challenge and threaten, as well as its tendency, too often, to descend to mere product. That tension was always present at the heart of Elvis' image and music. His desire to appeal to everyone (he even released an album called *Something for Everybody*) was always at odds with his urge to throw off all constraints and get "real, real gone." Elvis had the mind of a polite entertainer and the soul of a true rocker, and these "two Elvises"—the polite southern boy who desperately craved respectability and the rebel who sneered at it—battled each other throughout his career.

In the end it was a draw: the distinctions were simply smoothed over and rendered meaningless in the last years of his life. In a sense, Elvis' career encapsulated the course of rock music itself through the decades. Rock has now been so absorbed into the mainstream that it has simply *become* the mainstream. If it can rebel at all, it can only rebel against itself, which is all Elvis could do in his last decades.

The Army: 1958-60

"Elvis the Pelvis" became Private Presley, U.S. Army, in March of 1958. For the following two years he was out of circulation, serving first at Ft. Hood, Texas, and then in Friedberg, West Germany. From today's perspective, it seems almost unbelievable that Elvis would go into the army at the peak of his powers and popularity. He *was* drafted, of course, but it was a peacetime draft and it would have been fairly easy for Elvis to either avoid it altogether or to arrange to serve in the Special Services, singing for the troops, promoting the army and otherwise going on as if nothing had happened. Instead, Elvis chose to serve his time like any other inductee, cutting his salary from over $100,000 to $78 a month and completely abandoning his recording and performing career.

Or perhaps more to the point, Col. Parker recognized the public relations value of G.I. Elvis. There would certainly have been howls of indignant outrage from rock-hating parents if it seemed that Elvis had received any sort of "preferential treatment." In addition, the army provided an escape from the intense pressures of superstardom. By exiting at the peak of his popularity, Elvis could sidestep the possible embarrassment of watching that popularity decline. Since no one had ever been in his position before, it was impossible to know how long his luck could last or what kind of future an "aging" rock star could expect. In any case, and contrary to the glowing press releases, Elvis was fairly miserable during his army stay. He worried about his career and missed home terribly; most of all, he missed his beloved mother, who died shortly after Elvis was inducted, casting a gloom over his stay in Germany and the rest of his life.

For better or worse, serving in the army had a sanitizing effect on Elvis' image that all the money and publicity in the world couldn't have bought. Photographs of Elvis getting his hair shorn, riding tanks and peeling potatoes were flashed across the country, and suddenly this once threatening symbol of juvenile delinquency became a shining example of patriotism and decency, willing to give up his riches and fame for the honor of serving his country. Even the kids who were mourning the loss of their idol watched it all with admiration (the army was still a popular destination in 1958) and listened in astonishment as their parents began chiding them with "Why can't you be more like Elvis?!"

Hollywood: 1960-68

By the time Elvis emerged from the army, and at least partly because of his absence, rock & roll had gone into a tailspin. The rough edges and raw nerve that had made it so exciting were being smoothed over and softened in an attempt by the music industry to make rock & roll safe and controllable. Rock had dissolved back into harmless pop and the airwaves were dominated by cleancut, watered-down, sexless Elvises who seemed to have forgotten—if they ever knew—that rock & roll came from the blues.

Unfortunately, Elvis seemed to have forgotten as well, though he once knew it better than anyone. More to the point, he no longer saw himself as a "rock & roll star" and was now intent on pursuing a career as a movie star and "all-around entertainer." A strong desire for mainstream acceptance and respectability had always been the flipside of his rebelliousness—that tension is part of what made him so exciting—and in moving away from rock & roll he was simply adapting to the changes that had happened in his absence and to his own view of himself as a "maturing" artist. In any case, it's too bad. Elvis still had the talent, power and popularity to rally the rock troops for a second time, and he could have single-handedly kicked rock & roll back into gear by exchanging his army uniform for a leather jacket and rocking back onto the charts.

Instead he opted out and became, irony of ironies, essentially a watered-down Elvis imitator himself, turning out harmless ballads and an unending stream of forgettable movies. His looks and his voice were still beautiful, but the sex, threat and energy were nearly gone. Jerry Lee Lewis, himself a casualty of the teen idol trend, held Elvis largely responsible for leaving rock's direction in the hands of Dick Clark and the teen idol machines: "We kept cutting rock & roll records, though nobody would play them. Elvis started singing like Bing Crosby. Don't get me wrong, I love Elvis and he's a great talent, but I think he let us down."[14] After his release from the army, Elvis performed at a couple of charity benefits and made a TV appearance on a Frank Sinatra special, eyes firmly fixed on the middle of the road. He then abandoned live appearances altogether and spent the next eight years buried in Hollywood while the music world changed dramatically.

Even the movie years need not have been so dismal. Elvis could actually act quite well, given a good director and a believable script (as *Flaming Star* and handful—a small handful—of other movies proved). Similarly, he could still, given good material, make a great record. Unfortunately he rarely had the chance to live up to his talents in either endeavor. Songwriters Doc Pomus and Mort Shuman provided "Little Sister," "(Marie's the Name) His Latest Flame," "Surrender," "She's Not You" and other sixties standouts, but most of his post-army hits were ballads like "Are You Lonesome Tonight," "Can't Help Falling in Love" and the operatic "It's Now or Never": huge hits, beautifully sung, but a long way from rock & roll. Things got progressively worse as he descended further into Hollywood and soundtrack albums filled with trivial songs that were embarrassing enough in the movie. Only the gospel songs from this period were of consistent quality and sung with real conviction. In any case, it's more than a little painful to hear the King of Rock & Roll reduced to singing "Do the Clam" or "Old MacDonald," and one can only wonder at the monumental lapse of pride that could lead Elvis to record a piece of drivel like "Rock-a-hula Baby" at the same session that produced a classic like "Little Sister." Col. Parker and the movie studios aside, Elvis could still have taken control of his musical direction, but he simply didn't seem to have one, and worse, he didn't really seem to care.

The 1968 Comeback

After sleepwalking through Hollywood for eight years, Elvis' following had dwindled to a still large but rapidly shrinking and aging group of die-hard fans. Meanwhile, Elvis Presley was little more than a joke, and a bad one at that, to the new generation of rock fans. In the era of the Beatles, Rolling Stones and Bob Dylan, his movies and music seemed to epitomize exactly the type of showbiz sellout that the sixties rockers scorned. With the exception of 1965's "Crying in the Chapel," Elvis hadn't scored a Top Ten hit since 1963—since the arrival of the Beatles and a new rock era.

Painfully aware of his diminishing stature, Elvis decided it was time to get in front of an audience again and prove, to himself as much as anyone else, that he was still the King. An hour of prime time was booked on NBC for a Christmas special to be aired on December 3, 1968. Col. Parker envisioned a wholesome hour of Christmas songs and family entertainment, which would have been perfectly in keeping with Elvis' image at that point. For once in his life Elvis put his foot down, overruled the Colonel and came out rocking, determined not to go down without a fight.

He fought hard—and he won, maybe because for the first time in over a decade he *had* to fight. Elvis was, by his own admission, terrified of facing a live crowd after such a long absence from the stage. For the first time since he walked into Sun Studios or onto *Stage Show*, he was an Outsider again, with a lot to lose and a victory he would have to *win*, not merely act out. To the delight of his old fans and the astonishment of all those who had given up on him, he did it: for one last time, Elvis was really ELVIS again.

The Christmas special had its share of corny production numbers, but the centerpiece of the show featured a leather-clad Elvis, slimmed to perfection, singing his heart out in an informal jam session with a small circle of old friends, including Scotty Moore and D. J. Fontana. It was the very essence of rockabilly again: everything on the line, with no big bands or background singers, no theatrics and no movie script or anything else to hide behind. Elvis reached into himself in a way he hadn't since those distant Sun days, and blasted through his old hits with exactly the passion and urgency that had been missing in all the years that had come in-between. In his excellent book, "Mystery Train," Greil Marcus summed up the unexpected power of Elvis' performance this way: "It was the finest music of his life. If ever there was music that bleeds, this was it. Nothing came easy that night, and he gave everything he had—more than anyone knew was there."[15] Including, no doubt, Elvis.

The *Memphis Record*

Fueled by the success of the show and his own renewed confidence, Elvis decided to ease out of the movies and concentrate again on live performances. He also went through a long overdue recording renaissance. In January and February, 1969, Elvis recorded two albums worth of material, now known as *The Memphis Record*, at Chips Moman's American Studios in Memphis—his first recordings in Memphis since leaving Sun. (Though he recorded and made movies elsewhere, his Graceland mansion in Memphis remained his home until his death, and is now his burial site.)

Recording on home turf once again, Elvis seemed to rediscover his musical heritage. Backed by veteran Memphis session players with roots similar to his own, Elvis again infused his pop style with the expressive immediacy of the blues, country and gospel music. It was not really a "return" to his old style but an updating of it, from a new, mature vantage point. The blues and country songs were now full and modern sounding with big, contemporary arrangements, while the gospel elements—now called "soul"— were more prominent than ever. Above all, the songs reflected adult sensibilities and adult realities; Elvis was finally taking care to choose songs that struck a personal chord with him—songs that inspired and deserved the passion of his voice. Having reclaimed and redeemed his past with the TV special, it seemed that Elvis was finally free to grow up and move on to the next stage of his career and life.

The *Memphis Record* material sealed Elvis' comeback and his claim to artistic vitality, and yielded a number of hits, including the socially-conscious "In the Ghetto" and "**Suspicious Minds**," his first #1 hit since 1962's "Good Luck Charm." "Suspicious Minds" serves as a good example of Elvis' mature style: the emotionally direct lyrics are supported by a country-rock guitar and rhythm section, gospel-styled backup singers, and a big pop string and brass arrangement, and are sung with grand drama and utter conviction. Elvis' changing personal life surely contributed to the soulful depth of his new music. He married Priscilla Ann Beaulieu in 1967, longing for the security and sense of family he had missed since his mother's death. Instead, the troubled marriage ended in divorce in 1973 (a daughter, Lisa Marie, was born in 1968), and the emotional turmoil is felt in the emotion of his best recordings from that era. "Suspicious Minds," "Any Day Now," "Kentucky Rain," "Only the Strong Survive," "Long Black Limousine" and other standouts from the 1969 sessions are sung with a deeply resonant adult voice that would have been far beyond the emotional and physical grasp of the 19-year-old at Sun.

The triumphant return to form revealed in the Memphis recordings became the basis for Elvis' return to the stage. Unfortunately, they didn't always translate well to his elaborate live shows, where the size and spectacle of the show often overshadowed the music. The emotional power of the new material was quickly lost in the giant halls while his old rock & roll hits suffocated under the glossy new big band arrangements. Elvis had won another great victory at the end of the sixties. In depressingly familiar fashion, he then began throwing it away. Instead of the army, this time he went to Las Vegas.

The Final, Sad Decline

The grand ballrooms of Las Vegas were the setting for Elvis' return to full-time performing. Elvis played 57 shows at the Las Vegas International Hotel in July and August of 1969, and made Las Vegas his performing home base through the early seventies. The decision says much about what had become of Elvis' image and audience. He was at the height of his rock & roll powers when he made his first appearance in Las Vegas in 1956, and he flopped. It was a disastrous case of bad booking: rock & roll flew in the face of the glitter and schlock that Las Vegas exemplified, and the high-rolling crowds were as foreign and threatening to Elvis as he was to them. Now, in 1969, he was perfectly at home with the glitzy neon settings, jeweled Liberace jumpsuits and all the other gaudy trappings of American success that so quickly replaced the leather jacket and raw intensity of the '68 special. The two sides of Elvis—the artist and the entertainer—were still battling, and the wrong one was winning again.

Elvis' return to the stage was initially a great triumph, supported by good new material, a good backup band (led by guitarist James Burton) and a renewed sense of musical direction. To his credit, Elvis re-established himself as a contemporary star, not a nostalgia act, singing new material alongside his old hits and performing concerts, not revival shows. Of all the surviving fifties giants, only Elvis and Jerry Lee Lewis retained any real semblance of artistic vitality and growth, sporadic as it may have been.

It was certainly sporadic in Elvis' case, and depressingly short-lived. Soon enough it all became too easy and boring again. He toured constantly through the seventies, branching out from Las Vegas to giant arenas around the country, but the tours became yet another movie set and Elvis the man and artist became almost a bit player in the ongoing drama of his larger-than-life myth. He was eventually trapped by his consuming fame and by a mindlessly adoring public that was thrilled by a big belt buckle and a few half-hearted karate kicks, and would probably have cheered if he'd simply gotten onstage and gargled. As the atmosphere at his concerts, and in his personal life, became more surreal and circus-like, his commitment to his music faded into the background again. The great country-rocker **"Burning Love,"** which hit #2 in 1972, was the last major hit of his life.

Elvis' last days were the sad final chapter of the most wildly successful—and the most tragic and lonely—American success story of them all. It is easy to judge the final period of Elvis' life too quickly and harshly. Watching video clips of a grotesquely obese and lethargic Elvis slurring his way through his last performances, it's hard to imagine how anyone, let alone anyone with his talent, could let himself slip so far. But it's even harder for anyone else to imagine the kind of claustrophobic life he lived and the pressure he felt in trying to live up to the idealized image of "Elvis" while the real-life man aged and crumbled. The abuse of prescription drugs that hastened his death began as a desperate attempt to lose weight and keep the image alive, and ended as an even more desperate attempt to block out the pain of having failed. Only the Beatles could possibly understand the type of maddening pressure Elvis lived with, and they, at least, had each other. Elvis didn't have a John or Paul to challenge his creativity or preserve his sanity. Apparently he didn't even have a friend compassionate or courageous enough to tell him he was killing himself or keep him from doing it. Elvis Presley died in Memphis on August 16, 1977.

Elvis Is Everywhere

The reaction worldwide was one of stunned disbelief: a mixture of empty numbness for all the years it had been since he'd really seemed to matter, and genuine shock and sorrow for the suddenly distant times when he had mattered most of all. The King of Rock & Roll—dead?! As several generations aged overnight, the King's passing became a metaphor for rock's lost innocence and Elvis became, once again, forever young. Bob Dylan: "I broke down... One of the few times. I went over my whole life. I went over my whole childhood. I didn't talk to anyone for a week after Elvis died. If it wasn't for Elvis and Hank Williams, I couldn't be doing what I do today."[16] That feeling of personal loss was shared by millions of fans and by millions of others who hadn't thought of Elvis for years but now felt as if they'd lost a part of themselves. The loss was echoed on a communal level as well, as the rock world said good-bye to one of the few forces that really had united it (as it would say a collective good-bye just three years later after the murder of John Lennon). As Lester Bangs so memorably put it, "I can guarantee you one thing: we will never again agree on anything as we agreed on Elvis. So I won't bother saying good-bye to his corpse. I will say good-bye to you."[17]

Even in death, the two Elvises—the artist and the icon—battle it out, as reissuings of his great music alternate with "Elvis sightings" and endless tabloid articles. (When his image finally graced a United States postal stamp, even the government felt compelled to address the issue and ask the public to vote for *which Elvis*—young rocker or adult entertainer—would be depicted. In a rare display of good judgment, the young Elvis won out.) He finally did succeed in becoming all things to all people: everyone has their own unique image of Elvis, it seems, and the endless fascination with both the man and his myth shows no sign of abating. Ultimately, though, it is all a footnote to what really matters: that perfect image of young Elvis in the 1950's—the timeless music he made and the revolution he helped create. It is *that* Elvis who will matter as long as rock & roll matters, and it is that Elvis who will forever be the King.

---

[1]Dylan quote from August, 1987 *US* magazine.

[2]Greil Marcus, "Dead Elvis, " (1991; New York: Doubleday), pg. 129.

[3]The 1960's rock "counterculture" employed an equally spirited appropriation of black culture to articulate its stance as Outsiders oppressed by the Establishment. Much of the language and imagery ("brother," soul handshakes, power salutes, etc.) were borrowed from the black community and civil rights movement (with a dose of American Indian imagery—love beads, hippie "tribes"—thrown in for good measure).

[4]Peter Guralnick, liner notes for *Elvis: The Sun Sessions*, (RCA Compact Disc, 1987).

[5]Guralnick, *Sun Sessions* liner notes.

[6]It is also interesting to consider the "artificial" sound created by the slapback echo as the first of a long history of experiments and developments in recording technology that have enhanced rock & roll and, from the very beginning, made

the Record more than merely a live performance captured on tape. (Elvis' live performances could not, of course, take advantage of the studio enhancements, though his formidable visual appeal more than made up for the thinner sound!)

[7]Paul Burlison qoute from 1983 *Musician* magazine.

[8]Greil Marcus, "Mystery Train," rev. ed. (1976; New York: Dutton, 1982), p. 181.

[9]Guralnick, *Sun Sessions* liner notes.

[10]Though he never made his fortune off his "white man with the negro feel," Sam did quite well as one of the initial investors in the Memphis-based Holiday Inn chain.

[11]In conversation with the author. The blues and R&B artists on the Sun roster had a particularly immediate reason for resenting Elvis, since his success led Sam Phillips into rockabilly and away from the black music that had started it all.

[12] The extra guitar at some of the first sessions was played by Scotty's hero, Chet Atkins; Nashville veteran Floyd Cramer played piano on "Heartbreak Hotel," and regularly recorded with Elvis through the sixties.

[13]Although Elvis never actually wrote a song himself, his name mysteriously appeared as co-author on a number of songs. This partly reflected the fact that Elvis would often re-work the songs to fit his style and feel. Mainly, though, it reflects a type of "payola" that was rampant in the fifties; quite simply, co-authorship credit would bring more royalties to Elvis. The writers rarely complained, since half of the songwriting royalties from an Elvis hit was a *lot* better than full royalties from anyone else.

[14]Tony Palmer, "All You Need Is Love," (1976; rpt. New York: Penguin, 1977), p. 229.

[15]Marcus, "Mystery Train," p. 149.

[16]Robert Sheldon, "No Direction Home," (New York: William Morrow, 1986), p. 480.

[17]Lester Bangs, "Psychotic Reactions and Carburetor Dung," (New York: Knopf, 1988), p. 216.

Photo courtesy of Glenn Gass

Elvis Presley with Richard Nixon

Photo courtesy of UPI/BETTMAN

Jerry Lee Lewis in action.

[4] ROCKABILLY

Elvis Presley's 1954-55 Sun recordings, though largely unknown in the North, were a revelation to the young southerners who shared his social and musical roots and his impatience with the rigid conventions of country music. Having heard the startling news that a white boy could sing the blues, keep its energy and add his own, aspiring Elvises began springing up throughout the South, setting their sights and dreams on Sam Phillips' tiny Memphis studio.

Rockabilly and the South

"Rockabilly" was invented the night Elvis, Scotty and Bill launched into "That's All Right," and the frenzied mix of country, blues, gospel and pop that the trio perfected at Sun became, and remains, the blueprint for the style. The stripped-down production, emotional immediacy and sheer energy of Elvis' Sun recordings are rockabilly's common denominator, and the slapback echo, slapping bass, piercing twangy guitar, vocal "Elvis-isms" and other musical traits are its raw materials. It's impossible to play rockabilly and not sound a little like Elvis—most sounded a *lot* like him, and proudly so. (When Elvis' mother first heard Gene Vincent's "Be-Bop-A-Lula" on the radio, she called her son to congratulate him on his new release, or so the story goes.)

For the poor whites on the stage or on the dance floor, the unbridled energy of rockabilly offered at least a momentary escape from life's everyday drudgeries. As Carl Perkins put it, "We shook the devil loose! We bopped those blues! It's up-tempo, it's rhythm. You ain't sittin' there worrying about car payments or house notes. You're out there shakin' dust loose on those honky-tonk floors."[1] The pervasive spirit was one of youth and *fun*—of cutting loose and living for Right Now, with a hint of violence underlying it all, born of bottle-dodging nights playing roadhouses where the bands and drunken, brawling audiences had to be separated with chicken wire...

A sense of regional identity and pride also fueled the music. Rockabilly was distinctly and proudly *southern*, and its success on the national pop charts was something of a victory for all the southerners who felt shut out of the mainstream. Blues harpist Charlie Musselwhite recalls Elvis' triumphant appearance: "The Yankees had put us down for so long, I just can't express how important it was when Elvis made it. He was immediately recognizable as being southern—the minute he opened his mouth, we knew he was just like us."[2]

No longer confined to the world of country music (which watched with alarm as its young artists and audience defected to rock & roll), a new generation of Confederate rebels could now take aim at the pop world without hiding their accents or polishing their sound. Rockabilly's rough, southern edges were an exciting contrast to the group-oriented rhythm & blues produced in the North's urban centers. Unfortunately, it was also the rough and untamed quality of rockabilly that fell out of favor in the later 1950's when the major record labels tightened their grip on rock & roll and began the process of taming and sweetening it (helped along by Elvis himself). By the end of the decade rockabilly seemed primitive and archaic to the fans of the teen idols and "American Bandstand," and its greatest practitioners were again banished to the backwoods and county fair circuit (or to Europe, where a hunger for all things American kept the rock & roll flame alive).

Rockabilly's heyday may have been relatively brief, but it provided a crucial sound, image and rebellious spirit for rock's initial wave. For many it remains the "purest" form of rock & roll. The rockabilly revival in the early 1980's, led by the Stray Cats, and all the mini-revivals before and since are happy reminders of the music's timeless spirit and vitality. That spirit lives on every night in clubs where rockabilly and "roots rock" bands continue to reach back to rock's earliest years for inspiration. And it certainly lives on in the now ancient records by the original masters. In the words of rockabilly veteran Charlie Feathers, "We were young, you know, we didn't really know what we was doing. But I'll tell you, buddy, we really did do *something!*"[3]

Sun Records After Elvis

Classic rockabilly was almost entirely the product of one small record label: Sam Phillips' Sun Records. The regional success of Elvis' first recordings made Memphis the Mecca for aspiring rockabillies. Young hopefuls from across the South came to audition for Sam Phillips and his partners, Judd Phillips (Sam's brother) and Jack Clement. Most were turned away; others made records of little interest and quickly returned to their regular jobs or family farms, but many proved to have considerable talent. After all, Memphis sat at the heart of the most musical region of the country, and when Sam Phillips sold Elvis to RCA, he did so largely to finance the recording and promotion of other promising artists he had signed to Sun. First among them was Carl Perkins.

CARL PERKINS

Carl Lee Perkins was born on April 9, 1932, near Tiptonville, Tennessee, and grew up in dire poverty, the son of the only white sharecropper on a cotton plantation. Perkins developed an interest in music early on, and the family managed—just barely—to scrape up the money to buy him a three dollar guitar. He loved the Grand Ole Opry, of course: as a white southerner, country music was his native music. But he also fell in love with the blues and gospel music that pervaded the air around him, accompanying the field work in the daytime, drifting in from the surrounding shacks on hot summer nights and from the chapel on Sunday mornings. Perkins easily and naturally incorporated blues licks into his country style from the time he first learned to strum a guitar. Like Sam Phillips, he realized that country music could benefit from the vitality of black music: "Even though I enjoyed the Opry, something seemed to be lacking in the songs. One night, after a long day working the fields and listening to the blacks sing, I realized country music needed the black man's rhythm. I began to put that rhythm to every country song I learned."[4]

The Perkins family moved to Jackson, Tennessee when Carl was fourteen, and by 1950 Carl and his brothers Jay and Clayton had formed the Perkins Brothers Band and were performing regularly on a local radio show and in the honky-tonks around town. The long nights playing in rowdy clubs and dance halls further hardened Perkins' music. By the time he heard Elvis' "That's All Right" and "Blue Moon of Kentucky," Perkins had already developed his own version of rockabilly, or "country music with a black man's rhythm."

Carl Perkins made his first record for Sun, "Movie Magg," in January 1955 and began crisscrossing the South with Elvis, fellow newcomer Johnny Cash and others from the Sun roster. His first records were a mixture of country weepers and uptempo honky-tonk numbers with strong dancebeats. When Elvis left for RCA at the end of 1955, Carl was positioned to fill the void and urged to move toward more rock & roll oriented songs. He responded with nothing less than rockabilly's anthem: "Blue Suede Shoes."

Go Cat Go!

"**Blue Suede Shoes**" was released on New Year's Day 1956. The record beat "Heartbreak Hotel" to the top of the charts and left RCA wondering if they had contracted the wrong artist! It remains one of rock's all-time classics, immediately recognizable from its famous beginning, "Well it's one for the money..." "Blue Suede Shoes" captures the spirit of the rockabilly Moment with great wit and insight: in the face of a multitude of possible calamities (burn my house, steal my car," "knock me down, step on my face") the singer cares about nothing but his prized shoes and the fun he's having right now. It also captures the hint of violence in those redneck, honky-tonk nights: there's no telling *what* might happen to the poor soul who DID step on his shoes... The song had a real-life inspiration: Carl overheard a boy at a dance tell his girl not to "step on my blue suede shoes," and the line struck a chord and stuck in his mind. As he later put it, "you've got to be real poor, like I was, to know what a new pair of shoes can mean to you."[5]

"**Honey Don't**," released on the flipside of "Blue Suede Shoes," is a self-mocking plea to a straying woman ("You've been out a-paintin' the town, uh-huh baby been slippin' around...") goaded along by a loping boogie riff and a strong accent on the offbeat. Like "Blue Suede Shoes," "Honey Don't" is full of the clever rhymes and wordplays, down-home humor, hillbilly imagery, hepcat slang and excited interjections ("bop bop!," "rock!," "go cat!") that characterize most of Perkin's songs, along with Sun Records' musical trademarks: slapping bass, slapback echo, the percussive acoustic guitar, lean production, etc. Both songs are based on a 12-bar blues and feature a halting stop-start verse rhythm balanced by a more propulsive feeling in the choruses and lead breaks. The whole is shaped by Perkins' distinctive guitar playing— a blend of blues and boogie runs and jangling country licks, delivered with a mix of flat picking (using a guitar pick on the chords and on the low-string boogie riffs, such as those accompanying the "Honey Don't" refrain) and finger-picking (on the high-string leads and on the "fills" between sung lines, as in the "Blue Suede Shoes" chorus). "My guitar style is nothin' in the world but black blues speeded up. If you slowed down the guitar break on "Blue Suede Shoes" or any of my Sun records, it wouldn't be a thing but black blues."[6] Perkins' guitar playing was supremely tasteful and musical, the purest definition of rockabilly guitar playing for those who followed. (George Harrison, for one, idolized Perkins and nailed his style perfectly on "Honey Don't," "Matchbox" and "Everybody's Trying to Be My Baby," the three Perkins songs covered by the Beatles .)

For all the similarities and style traits shared by Perkins and Elvis, their music and personalities were very different. Shy, retiring Perkins, with a wife and kids at home, had little of Elvis' charismatic sensuality and burning ambition, and always seemed more comfortable with a country lifestyle than with the trappings of stardom. (It's hard to imagine Carl Perkins in Hollywood!) Similarly, his recordings lack the unrestrained abandon and overt passion of Presley's and seem, instead, more like a natural extension of his hillbilly roots than a rebellious break with tradition. Elvis' move to RCA clarified the distinction between rockabilly and rock & roll: his rendition of "Blue Suede Shoes" is propelled by a huge drum beat, full band sound, streamlined dance rhythm and polished production that makes it very different from Perkins' countrified original. With its barndance beats and twangy vocals and guitar, Perkins' music could never leave its southern accents far enough behind to pass for mainstream rock & roll.

Dixie Fried

Carl Perkins wrote his own songs, unlike Elvis and most of the other white rockers of the fifties (only Buddy Holly showed the same talent for writing), and he always stayed true to his pristine rockabilly style, unwilling or unable to bend and adapt to changing trends and styles. His music seemed to spring directly from his life and the honky-tonk world he knew best, and it always served as a reminder of the "hillbilly" roots of "rockabilly." Indeed, many of Perkins' greatest songs are anthems to the South and the freewheeling side of its culture. In "Boppin' the Blues," Perkins sings of the joys of country folk discovering the purifying powers of a big blues beat, while "**Dixie Fried**" spins a tale of a wild, brawling southern night complete with flashing razors ("he jerked out a razor but he wasn't shavin!"), a police raid and a drunken hero behind bars still exhorting his pals to "rave on" and get "Dixie Fried." Perkin's dedication to his heritage gave his music much of its charm and "authenticity," but it also limited its commercial appeal in a market that was being increasingly geared toward a younger teen and pre-teen national audience. Nonetheless, with the huge success of "Blue Suede Shoes," it seemed at first that Carl Perkins was destined to be a big star.

That dream ended abruptly in March 1956 when the band was traveling to New York for a string of major television appearances. A terrible car wreck badly injured Carl and his brother Jay (who died in 1958 from complications resulting from the crash). Instead of gaining invaluable media exposure for himself and his hit record, Carl was out of commission for nine months, watching from the sidelines as Elvis released his own version of "Blue Suede Shoes" and became more associated with the song than Perkins himself.[7] Perkins was back in form and in the studio by the end of the year, but it was too late. He kept making great records, including "**Matchbox**" (a rockabilly reworking of an old Blind Lemon Jefferson blues, featuring Jerry Lee Lewis on piano), "Everybody's Trying to Be My Baby," "Put Your Cat Clothes On" and "Glad All Over," but his moment had come and gone and the records were only regional hits.

The King of Rockabilly

Carl Perkins left Sun Records for Columbia in 1958, but the move to a major label failed to work the same type of magic that it had for Elvis. The late 1950's and the early 1960's "teen idol" era was a wasteland for Carl, who had to follow other "old-timers" to England and Europe to find the respect he deserved. Depressed by his dormant career, the death of his brother and other personal problems, Perkins drank heavily and self-destructed for many years.

Perkins joined old friend Johnny Cash's band in 1968 after the death Cash's guitarist, Luther Perkins (no relation), and spent several happy years with the Cash entourage. Perkins played on the famous prison shows that solidified Cash's "man in black" image and fame, and wrote a few hits for Cash, including "Daddy Sang Bass." He also quit drinking, got religion and straightened out his life, and completed his circle in the late seventies when he began touring on his own again with his sons, instead of his brothers, as his backup band.

The 1980's rockabilly revival brought a renewed appreciation of the King of Rockabilly. Ever humble and always grateful for his good fortune, Perkins seems genuinely touched by the admiration of his descendants and feels a bond with them that bridges the years. One crucial point separates them, however, as it separates all the "original masters" from their disciples—Perkins can remember a time *before* rock & roll: "[Rock & roll] came out of black spiritual music... We mixed that up with country music. But the new guys don't go that far back with the *music*. They go back with the *records*. We go from the record on down to the cotton patch where it came from. That's the difference."[8]

JERRY LEE LEWIS

At the outskirts of Ferriday, Louisiana, there is a sign proudly proclaiming it the home of Jimmy Swaggart, Mickey Gilley and Jerry Lee Lewis. The three are first cousins, and between them they pretty well sum up the extremes of the white South, from fire 'n' brimstone religion to good ol' boy country & western to raving madman rock & roll.

Actually, Jerry Lee Lewis pretty well sums up those extremes by himself. Religion was deeply ingrained in young Jerry Lee: raised a Pentecostal, he even attended the Southwestern Bible Institute with an eye toward becoming a preacher, before he was expelled for playing hymns over a boogie-woogie bass(!) A tape of a "theological debate" he had with Sam Phillips is a testament to the inner battles that continued to haunt him. In the Sun studio to record his second hit, "Great Balls of Fire," Jerry has a sudden attack of conscience, brought on by the hell-fire images in the song he was about to sing. As the recording session grinds to a halt, Sam and Jerry debate whether one can sing rock & roll and be a true Christian at the same time. Sam sees no contradiction, but Jerry's answer is unequivocally NO: if you choose to pursue "worldly music," you'll find heaven's gates closed to you come Judgement Day. Or as Jerry put it, "Man, I got the Devil in me!" Truer words have rarely been spoken. The irony, of course, is that Jerry Lee Lewis *did* pursue worldly music, with a vengeance and with the passion of a man possessed. For Jerry Lee, there is no middle ground and, as if to prove it, he finally tears into the first take of "Great Balls of Fire," playing with a particularly demonic intensity and sounding for all the world like a man laughing at the face of eternal damnation—like a man who believes, just as surely as Robert Johnson, that he owed the Devil Himself for his extraordinary talent.

It's certainly no coincidence that the two great piano playing wildmen of rock & roll—Jerry Lee Lewis and Little Richard—were both tormented by their religious convictions and driven to manic excess by the guilt and the exhilarating freedom of ignoring them. One extreme seemed to feed the other, passionate belief fueling an equally passionate reaction. Jerry Lee played the "Devil's music" as if a Faustian bargain had made it his alone, and the reckless spontaneity of his music and flamboyant personality were the essence of rockabilly's freewheeling spirit. While Elvis invented rockabilly and Carl Perkins gave it a defined, even dignified, form, Jerry Lee Lewis gave it its very soul—the soul he sold for rock & roll.

Ferriday to Memphis

His own religious convictions notwithstanding, Jerry Lee (born Sept. 29, 1935) was the hell-raiser of the family, a redneck Eddie Haskell continually getting his poor cousins into trouble with his penchant for going places he didn't belong. Lewis found plenty of trouble, and his own version of "country boy discovers the blues," at Haney's Big House, the black club in Ferriday where he could hide in the rafters and watch the great barrelhouse piano players who floated up-river from New Orleans, adding their influences to those of his heroes Jimmie Rodgers, Hank Williams, Moon Mullican and Al Jolson. Lewis began performing in area clubs and then, with the arrival and inspiration of Elvis Presley, set his sights on Sun Records and Sam Phillips, who signed him in 1956 on the basis of both his solo talent and his usefulness as a session piano player. Lewis' first record, a cover of Ray Price's "Crazy Arms" backed with the self-penned "End of the Road," received little attention, but he did lend his inimitable piano style to several other Sun releases while waiting for a hit of his own, including Carl Perkins' "Matchbox" and "Put Your Cat Clothes On" and Billy Lee Riley's "Red Hot." As Jerry had no band of his own, Riley's Little Green Men (named to capitalize on Riley's regional hit, "Flying Saucers Rock & Roll") became Lewis' backup band as well, with Roland Janes on guitar, Jimmy Van Eaton on drums, and Jay Brown and Riley alternating on bass.

Shake, Baby, Shake!

"**Whole Lot of Shakin' Going On**" was Jerry Lee's first hit, a rock & roll classic recorded at the end of an otherwise unproductive session in February 1957. Recorded originally and obscurely by Roy Hall, and more memorably by Big Maybelle, Lewis' rowdy version has a huge sound enhanced by Sun's trademark slap-back echo which Sam Phillips, in an inspired moment, layered onto the piano and drums as well as the voice. Jerry Lee's "pumpin' piano" trademarks also appear in all their glory: the driving boogie bass figures, high pounding chords, flashy runs, sweeping glissandi and a sprawling, confident command of the entire keyboard.

"Whole Lot of Shakin' Going On" also introduces a favorite Lewis device, a method of pacing tension and release that was particularly effective in live shows. In the extended middle section he pulls the band back ("let's get *real* low one time..."), drops to a near-whisper and nearly abandons the song itself to tell his pretty young listeners that "all you gotta do, honey, is kinda stand in one spot and wiggle around just a little bit... that's when you got somethin', ye-e-aah..." Then, almost as an aside, "... now let's go one time," and the full fury of the song kicks back in with a sweep up the keyboard and a triumphant "shake it, baby, shake!" "Whole Lot of Shakin' Going On" made everything else on the radio, save Little Richard, seem somewhat tame by comparison, and it was a shot of adrenaline for a rock market that was already starting to soften. Just as Elvis was beginning to seem like a nice guy after all, and newcomers like Buddy Holly and the Everly Brothers held out hope for decency and melodies, Jerry Lee Lewis' frenzied, leering delivery and recalcitrant redneck image were a timely reminder of rock's raucous roots.

Lewis' great follow-up hit, "**Great Balls of Fire**," seems barely able to contain itself to a mere piece of plastic. Written by Otis Blackwell, author of "Don't Be Cruel" and "All Shook Up," the song might have sounded fairly innocuous had it ended up in Elvis' hands. In Jerry Lee's it becomes a joyous surrender to temptation. Having exorcised the pangs of religious conscience that threatened to derail the recording session, he wrings out every ounce of lust and transcends the song itself with the sensual abandon of his delivery. Backed only by drums and his own piano, Lewis twists and bends the melody, glides into falsetto, trails off mischievously into thin air then dives back into song with a wonderfully elastic energy, while the piano and drums stop, start, push forward and pull back in perfect sync.

Another Otis Blackwell song, the aptly-titled "**Breathless**," followed "Great Balls of Fire" with an equally inspired performance full of sudden pauses, unexpected accents and dynamic shifts and pure, redemptive lust. The exciting spontaneity of the music owes much to the band's uncanny ability to follow the unpredictable Lewis, who never sang or played a song the same way twice. Jimmy Van Eaton's drumming was particularly important in creating the fluid feel of the records: "A lot of people try to copy Jerry Lee Lewis' sound, but they'll never copy it because they're trying to play a straight 4/4 beat when, in fact, it's a shuffle with a backbeat. That's the whole rhythm."[9] The huge, hammering rhythm section formed by Van Eaton's drums and Lewis' left-hand boogie runs was intensified still further by Sam Phillips' knack for achieving maximum effect from minimal resources.

"The Killer"

Jerry Lee Lewis was even more impressive in concert: a vintage Lewis performance was an exercise in controlled frenzy from one of rock's greatest showmen. "Controlled" may be too strong a word, however, for he often enough crossed the line into an *uncontrolled* frenzy unleashed on hapless piano benches, piano keys and piano lids, which rarely escaped intact or without a few sets of footprints as proof of their surrender. At the end of the show, after pummeling the piano into submission, he'd leap on top of it, hair flying and eyes bulging like a madman as he shouted out the final song. The television public got its first glimpse of Lewis in action on July 28, 1957, on the Steve Allen Show: "Viewers were shocked by the display—this boy appearing on national television and mistreating a fine instrument. He was out of control. And the audience loved it."[10]

Chuck Berry may have detailed rock's attack on High Culture in "Roll Over, Beethoven," but the image of Jerry Lee Lewis—the Killer, as he was called—savagely attacking a concert grand delivered a more powerful and threatening punch. The two stars had a chance to fight it out, in fact, on a memorable Alan Freed package show which Berry was chosen to close, much to Lewis' chagrin. Determined to make Berry rue the day he had to follow the Killer onstage, Jerry Lee played the show of his life, poured out his energy and soul and, when things were reaching a climax, poured a can of kerosene over the piano, lit it, and broke into "Great Balls of Fire!" As he walked away from the smoldering piano and disbelieving audience, he smiled at Freed and Berry and quietly said "Follow that..." (There has been some dispute about whether this story is actually rooted in fact, but if it's not true, it ought to be.)

The Fall

Lewis was at the peak of his formidable powers in 1958, viewed as Elvis' only serious rival—even by the recently drafted King himself. Lewis' outlandish image was a perfect foil to Elvis' increasing "respectability," and he seemed primed and eager to fill the void left by Elvis' absence. Instead, his next rock & roll hit, "High School Confidential," was his last, thanks to his marriage to his 13-year-old cousin, Myra Brown. Lewis married Myra, his third wife, in December 1957 at the ripe old age of 22.[11] While certainly odd, such a marriage was not as uncommon in the South as it might have seemed, though it *was* complicated by the fact that Jerry had neglected to divorce his second wife! At any rate, things might have been fine if Jerry Lee had kept quiet about it. Instead, unable to keep quiet about anything, he flaunted his new bride before the press and public on an important tour of England in May 1958. Outraged by Lewis and his "child-bride," newspapers savaged Lewis and angry crowds heckled and picketed his appearances until the tour was finally scrapped.

The backlash of moral indignation quickly spread to America, where the media and scandalized public seized the chance to bring down another rock & roll degenerate who was corrupting their youth. Just a year after "Whole Lot of Shakin' Going On," Lewis' career fell victim to a ruthlessly effective boycott that killed his record sales and media exposure. Fearing the public's reaction, and the loss of their advertising revenue, radio stations wouldn't play his records, stores were afraid to stock them and TV shows and concert promoters refused to book him. (Dick Clark, for one, considers bowing to the commercial pressures that fueled Lewis' blacklisting to be the biggest mistake of his career. Clark liked Lewis, who had appeared on "American Bandstand" several times, but he buckled under when the show's sponsors threatened to pull out if he booked him again. Clark says now that, if he had it to do over again, he would book Jerry Lee every week until the boycott was crushed, and he did, later, go out of his way to help Jerry get his career going again.)

Middle Age Crazy

Jerry Lee kept recording great records for Sun, but no one seemed to notice. A switch to Mercury Records in 1963 did little to improve matters, despite some excellent releases like 1964's "I'm on Fire." The early sixties were bleak years, spent drinking and playing the county fairs, but his live shows remained as exciting as ever. He was eventually able to reestablish himself as a headlining act in Europe, winning back even the British fans. And though America may have turned its back on him, Jerry Lee Lewis never lost his biggest fan and greatest admirer—himself. The stubborn, arrogant pride that precipitated his fall from grace also got him through the hard times with his dignity intact. He refused to apologize for marrying a woman he loved, and never pandered to the public with syrupy ballads or Las Vegas routines. Live recordings from the early sixties attest to the undiminished energy of an unrepentant Lewis—a man who knew he was the greatest of them all, and proved it night after night.

A mid-sixties move to the country & western market finally revived his career and established Lewis as a country star, with self-referential hits like "Another Place, Another Time," "Middle Age Crazy," "39 and Holding" and "What Made Milwaukee Famous (Made a Loser Out of Me)." It was not really a major shift for Lewis, as he had always recorded country songs along with the rock & roll at Sun, though he now abandoned the back-to-basics Sun style in favor of the slick, string and choir-laden "modern Nashville" sound. With country music and audiences as his home base, Jerry Lee continued to record new material, with no intention of living out his days as a mere oldies act. (He can, however, still fire off a mean "Whole Lot of Shakin' Going On" when so moved.)

Lewis' legacy far transcends his record sales and *Billboard* chart listings. He was one of rock's true pioneers—an original rock & roll spirit who refused to be tamed. Driven by a supreme confidence in his inexhaustible talent, he has survived through personal tragedies that would have defeated weaker souls, including the boycott and blacklisting, the death of his two sons, severe drug and alcohol problems, frequent run-ins with the police, press and IRS, and two serious illnesses that nearly killed him. Whether you love or detest his personality, his hell-bent determination to live his life and play his music the way he chooses is inspiring. As the title of one of his later country-rock hits put it, "I Am What I Am (Not What You Want Me to Be)." With so many of the original stars gone or—like rock & roll itself—creeping respectably into old age, it's somehow comforting to know that Jerry Lee Lewis is still, well, Jerry Lee Lewis: a living legacy of the original, wild-eyed spirit of rock & roll.

JOHNNY CASH

The "Man in Black" was never really a rock & roller, but he has remained surprisingly popular with younger rock audiences through the years, thanks to his craggy, enigmatic persona and to the world-weary directness of his best music. Cash was a star of the Sun roster from 1955 to 1958, though his tastes and talents led him away from rockabilly toward a storytelling country-folk style that better suited his resonant voice and adult sensibilities. Backed by guitarist Luther Perkins and bassist Marshall Grant, the **Tennessee Two**, Cash recorded several country classics at Sun, including "**Folsom Prison Blues**," "Cry, Cry, Cry" and "I Walk the Line."

Cash's music had little of rockabilly's manic energy, though his records are sparse and streamlined in classic Sun style and feature slapback echo, slapping bass and other distinctive Sun traits, along with a distinctly southern wild side (consider the singer in "Folsom Prison Blues" who "I shot a man in Reno, just to watch him die...") that formed the basis of Cash' desperado image. In contrast to the trebly, excited sound of the Sun rockers, however, Cash's voice was deep and mature, resigned rather than rebellious, while Luther Perkins presented a similarly subdued mix of choked low-string melodies and single-string solos.

Cash and Sam Phillips experimented with more pop-oriented songs and arrangements, such as "Ballad of a Teenage Queen," but Cash's heart remained rooted in country music while Phillips' attention turned more toward Jerry Lee Lewis' rock & roll career. Cash left Sun in 1958 for Columbia Records, along with his friend Carl Perkins, and promptly plummeted into a decade-long drug and alcohol binge. He became a country superstar in the 1960's nonetheless, and built upon his Memphis lessons to popularize a leaner, rawer "outlaw" alternative to the Nashville country establishment. At a time when the country establishment and the rock world seemed like polar opposites, Cash retained a kinship with rock & roll reflected in his vocal duets with friend Bob Dylan, on Dylan's *Nashville Skyline* album, and in his insistence on booking rock artists on a television program he hosted in 1969-70. (Dylan, James Taylor, Joni Mitchell, Neil Young, Derek & The Dominos, Creedence Clearwater Revival and other progressive voices received rare network exposure on the *Johnny Cash Show*.) A true survivor, forty harrowing years beyond his Sun days, Cash remains a larger-than-life hero able to transcend time, changing styles and the limits of his own talent to forge a distinctly American voice.

CHARLIE RICH

Charlie Rich recorded for Sun's subsidiary Phillips label during the late 1950's, though he never achieved the sales or success he deserved. Sam Phillips often remarked that Rich had the voice and talent to outshine Elvis, but only 1960's "Lonely Weekends" managed to make the charts. Rich largely earned his keep at Sun as a session pianist and staff songwriter. The furious **"Break Up,"** for example, was written for and recorded by Jerry Lee Lewis in 1959 and promptly assigned to the oblivion of the Lewis media boycott. Rich's demotape of the song is classic Sun rockabilly, lean and raw and driven by Rich's virtuoso piano, which outmaneuvers Jerry Lee at every turn, and a voice that does indeed top even Elvis for range and power.

Charlie Rich could never be confined to "rockabilly," however, or to any single style. His bluesy piano playing, jazzy embellishments and soulful voice defy easy labels. In **"Who Will the Next Fool Be,"** for example, Rich turns his phrases like a great soul singer while his piano mixes country honky-tonk with jazz, blues and gospel inflections set against a pop-style backing chorus and a country-soul band accompaniment. At his best, Rich is a great stylist who leaves a personal imprint on any song he touches. He seems most akin to Ray Charles, another great style-blending stylist, and his emotionally direct songs are proof of country music's claim to be "white man's soul music."

Rich signed with Smash Records in 1965 and had another run at the charts that year with the novelty song "Mohair Sam." He moved on to Epic Records in 1967, where he was teamed with Nashville producer Billy Sherrill. The pairing produced a string of successful records, climaxing in 1973 with "Behind Closed Doors" and "The Most Beautiful Girl," which helped establish the country-pop crossover style known as "countrypolitan" and paved the way for other country crossovers like Kenny Rogers and Dolly Parton. The "Silver Fox" clung tenuously to the good graces of the country establishment in the mid-seventies then fell back out of favor and into his own idiosyncratic musical world. Unfortunately, aside from the few hits, Charlie Rich remains for most a sadly neglected and undiscovered treasure.

ROY ORBISON

Roy Orbison's first Sun single, **"Ooby Dooby,"** was pure rockabilly—a rather surprising start for a singer famous for heavily orchestrated, near-operatic ballads that occupy the opposite end of the musical spectrum from Sun's sparse intensity. Like Johnny Cash, Roy Orbison was never quite comfortable as a rockabilly singer, but he certainly made a valiant effort at it. "Ooby Dooby" reached #59 on the national pop charts in 1956, and though none of his successive Sun releases came any closer to hit status, his tenure at Sun as a recording artist and house songwriter was a crucial learning experience and morale booster for the shy Texan. Orbison concentrated on songwriting after leaving Sun in 1958 (he wrote "Claudette" for the Everly Brothers) before rekindling his singing career in 1960 on Monument Records with "Only the Lonely."

The Sun Roster

Elvis Presley, Carl Perkins, Jerry Lee Lewis, Johnny Cash, Charlie Rich and Roy Orbison were joined on the Sun rockabilly roster by a host of less talented but equally enthusiastic performers. The very best of the Sun artists left a permanent mark on rock & roll, but even the lesser lights made fun, honest music and occasionally transcended their limitations through sheer exuberance. It's a tribute to Sam Phillips that his artists developed such varied and distinct individual styles while always retaining an immediately recognizable "Sun Sound."

Billy Lee Riley and The Little Green Men were the house band at Sun, available to singers (like Jerry Lewis) who had no band of their own. In the spotlight, Riley was typical of Sun's second string: not blessed with a particularly great voice or original talent, he still managed to make good, lively records like "**My Gal is Red Hot**" and the novelty hit "Flying Saucers Rock & roll" (both from 1957) that captured the infectious enthusiasm of a hot Memphis Saturday night. Warren Smith ("Ubangi Stomp"), Charlie Feathers ("Defrost Your Heart"), Sonny Burgess ("Ain't Got a Thing"), Carl Mann ("Mona Lisa"), Bill Justis ("Raunchy," one of the first rock & roll instrumental hits), Harold Jenkins (who later took the name Conway Twitty) and a small army of others had their moments at the Sun microphone and on the endless string of one-nighters across the South. While a talent like Elvis or Jerry Lee could forge a personal style that transcended rockabilly's ultimately limited form, the rowdy voices that filled out the Sun roster reflected the music's populist appeal as a southern equivalent of doo-wop, accessible to anybody with a little talent and a lot of energy and a burning desire to sing their souls and forget their troubles for a while.

Sunset

The decline of Sun Records was partly the result of Sam Phillips' knack for losing his top artists to bigger labels, but it was more a reflection of the changing popular tastes at the end of the 1950's. As rock & roll moved from the domain of independents like Sun to the bigger stakes of the major labels, the music industry tightened its grip and sent the pop charts on a downward spiral toward the watered-down pop of the early sixties "teen idol" era. The rough edges, regional flavors and spontaneous feel that made rock & roll so exciting were gradually smoothed over, and Sam Phillips, already demoralized by the

Jerry Lee Lewis boycott, simply lost interest. He quit making records in 1963 and sold the Sun catalog in 1969.

In its day, Phillips' tiny studio at 706 Union Avenue was witness to some extraordinary moments, from the transported intensity of Howlin' Wolf to the Revelation of "That's All Right," but none summed up Sun's impact better than an amazing "family" gathering in December 1956. The setting was Carl Perkins' first recording session following his car wreck and long convalescence. On hand were Johnny Cash, welcoming his buddy back to the studio, and Jerry Lee Lewis, a Sun newcomer hired to play piano on the session. The illustrious trio became the "million dollar quartet" when Elvis Presley, by then a superstar at RCA, joined the well-wishers. Sun's biggest stars—past, present and future—soon found themselves huddled around a piano singing gospel and country songs from their shared southern past. The famous picture of that incredible scene is a happy reminder of the legacy of Sun Records and its farsighted owner. Sam Phillips was in the first group of inductees to the "forefathers" division of the Rock & Roll Hall of Fame, a much deserved recognition for the man who contributed so much to the development of rock & roll.

Rockabilly Beyond Sun

THE JOHNNY BURNETTE ROCK & ROLL TRIO

Sam Phillips could only sign and record a select few from the steady stream—often approaching flood levels—of singers and groups that turned up at his door. The Johnny Burnette Rock & Roll Trio was one of the many acts Phillips auditioned and turned down, though their credentials were certainly impeccable: they were from Memphis, went to high school with Elvis and even worked at the Crown Electric Company with their old schoolmate. The Trio finally signed with Coral Records in 1956 after a winning performance on Ted Mack's *Amateur Hour* show.

Singer Johnny Burnette, bassist Dorsey Burnette and lead guitarist Paul Burlison represented the lunatic fringe of rockabilly, thanks to Johnny's high-octane vocals and a aggressively distorted guitar sound Burlison used on several recordings—a proto-"fuzz" tone he stumbled onto when a tube in his amplifier shook loose.

"Honey Hush," "Rock Therapy," "Tear It Up," "Eager Beaver Baby" and other Rock & Roll Trio recordings are now revivalist favorites, but the group received little attention at the time and disbanded within a year. They left a lasting mark, however, with **"Train Kept A-Rollin',"** an inspired set of sexual metaphors and musical madness and that has been repeatedly covered by other over-the-edge bands (most notably the Yardbirds and Aerosmith).

The song features all of the classic rockabilly traits and Elvis-isms taken to a deranged extreme, climaxing in a bizarre guitar solo played in octaves with a heavily distorted sound and a snaking modal melody that sounds as if it was transported back in time from a psychedelic raga-rock song.

The Burnette brothers moved to California n 1957 to concentrate on songwriting and wrote several hits for Ricky Nelson and others before Johnny changed styles and reemerged as a pop singer in 1960 with "You're Sixteen." Johnny drowned in a fishing accident in 1964. Dorsey was a well-respected country artist until his death in 1979, while Burlison has chosen to remain in relative seclusion. Johnny's son Rocky ("Tired of Toein' the Line") and Dorsey's son Billy have carried on the Burnette name in the rock world.

GENE VINCENT

Gene Vincent was the original fifties hood: the black-leather biker with dirty, greasy hair and a mind and singing style to match. Unlike Elvis, he seemed threatening both onstage and off, smashing up hotel rooms, scowling at the press and public and definitely *not* talking about how much he loved his mother and his country... Vincent was actually, by all accounts, a perfectly nice guy, but he played up his rock wildman role to great effect and even managed to incorporate a crippled leg into his act. After first attempting to minimize his handicap (the result of a motorcycle accident), Vincent chose instead to exaggerate it, and took to dragging his bad leg behind him to the horror and delight of his audience in an early Alice Cooper-ish bit of macabre rock theater.

Gene Vincent had Elvis Presley to thank, even more directly than most, for his style and career. In the wake of RCA's huge success with Elvis, other major record labels suddenly displayed a newfound interest in the music they had fought and condemned so vehemently (if you can't beat it, at least make a profit off it). Capitol Records held a contest to find "their Elvis," and found and promptly signed Gene Vincent and the Blue Caps, largely on the basis of his similarity to the King. (Vincent's backing band was named after President Eisenhower's golfing cap.)

Vincent scored quickly for Capitol with "**Be-Bop-a-Lula**," a Top Ten hit in the summer of 1956. Whether it really fooled Mrs. Presley or not, Vincent's voice certainly owed much to the Elvis model. Vincent took the rebel side Elvis to a dramatic extreme, exaggerating the brooding demeanor and agitated sensuality that Elvis always balanced with a playful, self-mocking response. (Buddy Holly, by contrast, took Elvis' model in an opposite, playful direction.) Vincent's panting delivery of "Be-Bop-a-Lula" has a sinister edge that transcends the song's inane lyrics, while the Blue Caps provide a darkly-lit aural backdrop, with a hushed tempo, heavy echo and brushed drums that lend an eerie jazz tinge to the proceedings.

The suggestive lyrics and lecherous delivery, heavily reverberated vocals, brushed drums and spacious, jazzy sound of "Be-Bop-a-Lula" were used to equally striking effect on "Woman Love," "Race With the Devil" and other early Vincent efforts, all featuring the searing guitar work of **Cliff Gallup**. (Gallup tired of rock & roll life and was replaced in 1957 by Johnny Meeks, who played lead guitar on "Lotta Lovin'" and "Dance to the Bop," both relatively minor hits.)

Unfortunately, Capitol Records didn't have much of a taste for rock & roll or much of a talent for promoting it. (A few years later, Capitol would drag its feet for a full year before agreeing to sign and promote the Beatles.) Repeated record bannings and fines and court battles over obscenity charges didn't help matters much, and Vincent's career quickly floundered in America. He did find a second home and wildly enthusiastic audiences in England, and did quite well there until a tragic car wreck in London killed his friend Eddie Cochran and badly re-injured Vincent's crippled leg. His life in the sixties was a depressing slide through pain killers, alcoholism and a series of unsuccessful comeback attempts. He died in 1971 at the age of 36, but his image still haunts and gives shape to rockabilly's timeless rebellion.

Rockabilly's Legacy

The rough edges of rockabilly had been effectively smoothed over by the end of the 1950's. An authentic "grass roots" music, rockabilly's influence and offshoots far outlasted its short-lived Moment as the truest rock & roll. The instrumental records by influential guitarists **Duane "Mr. Twang" Eddy** ("Rebel Rouser," "Ramrod") and fuzz-tone pioneer **Link Wray** ("Rumble," "Rawhide"), for example, had a distinct rockabilly edge to them. So, too, did Dale Hawkins' 1957 hit "Suzy Q," which featured 15-year-old **James Burton**'s stunning swamp-rock guitar.[12] Burton later added a classy rockabilly touch to many of Ricky Nelson's records and was guitarist and bandleader for Elvis' comeback bands.

Wildman **Ronnie Hawkins** had a 1959 hit with "Mary Lou" and carried the spirit of rockabilly into the early sixties with his backing band, the Hawks—later to become The Band. The Everly Brothers' country roots brought a subtle rockabilly feel to many of their records, and Buddy Holly and Eddie Cochran each began as Elvis-styled rockabilly singers before forging their own styles. Many mainstream country & western singers, such as Conway Twitty and George Jones, went through a rockabilly period; and on the other side of the Atlantic, nearly all of the English guitar heroes of the 1960's credited the rockabilly pioneers alongside the blues players in their pantheon of heroes and influences. (Rolling Stones guitarist Keith Richards, for example, once boasted that he never went on tour without a tape of Elvis' Sun Sessions and the inspiration of Scotty Moore.)

Rockabilly was a liberating music for young southern whites, who could now sing and play with an intensity and sexuality that had previously seemed reserved for blues and R&B musicians. A lucky few managed to get recording contracts and national exposure, but for every one that managed to make it there were hundreds of equally spirited singers and bands playing every night in the small clubs, bars and desolate roadhouses that dotted the landscape of the South. Rockabilly's spirit of fun, rebellion and refreshing simplicity remain eternally young, as the many revivals of its sound and spirit have shown. Like the blues, it was a uniquely American music and it remains a crucial continuing impulse for rock & roll.

---

[1]Bill Flanagan, "Written in My Soul," (Chicago: Contemporary, 1986), p. 16.

[2]Musselwhite quote from December, 1983 "Guitar Player" magazine.

[3]Peter Guralnick, "Lost Highway," (1979; rpt. New York: Random House, 1982), p. 109.

[4]Carl Perkins, "Disciple in Blue Suede Shoes," (Grand Rapids: Zondervan, 1978), p. 41.

[5]ibid.

[6]Flanagan, "Written in My Soul," p. 15.

[7] There were no hard feelings: Perkins liked his friend's version and was grateful that Elvis had held back its release until Perkin's original had run its chart course.

[8]Flanagan, p. 22.

[9]Jimmy Van Eaton, from June, 1987 *Modern Drummer* magazine interview.

[10]Myra Lewis and Murray Silver, "Great Balls of Fire," (New York: Quill, 1982), p. 79.

[11]To add further insult to injury, Myra was the daughter of Lewis' bass player, Jay Brown. Myra and Jerry Lee were divorced in 1970.

[12]Creedence Clearwater Revival had their first hit with a direct cover of Susie Q.

Photo courtesy of UPI/BETTMAN

Fats Domino

Photo courtesy of UPI/BETTMAN

Little Richard

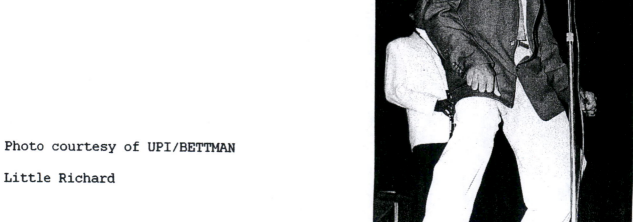

[5] NEW ORLEANS

A few hundred miles and several musical styles downriver from Memphis, the great melting pot of New Orleans made its own unique contribution to the development of rock & roll. The Crescent City's distinct musical tradition was shaped by a long history of cultural crossbreeding and a by a spirit of easygoing fun that made for a natural leap into the popular market. Famous for being one of the birthplaces of Jazz, New Orleans also had a rich heritage of rhythm & blues styles nurtured by a civically-mandated wild streak and a flourishing club scene that provided an outlet for all types of music (not to mention behavior). While the Memphis rockabillies made a screaming break from their country & western roots to create their own brand of rock & roll, the New Orleans rockers simply kept playing the R&B they'd played for years and felt little need to rebel against their proud heritage. As Fats Domino put it, "What they call 'rock & roll' now is just rhythm & blues—I've been playing it for fifteen years in New Orleans."[1] By the time Domino crossed over to the pop charts in 1955, the French Quarter clubs had long been filled with hard-driving, big beat sounds that needed little altering to be called "rock & roll."

"The Cradle of Jazz"

The rich, varied cultural textures of New Orleans were shaped by centuries of intermingling among the American Indian, Spanish, French, British, African, Caribbean, Latin American and other peoples who settled in or, in the case of the slaves, were forced to settle in the bustling port city at the mouth of the Mississippi. In contrast to other parts of the South, where slaves came predominantly from Africa, many of the slaves that came to New Orleans were brought from the West Indies and Latin America. Along with the early Spanish influence, this Latin influence established a link to South American customs, such as the Mardi Gras celebrations, and to the rhythms and flavors of Latin music which figured prominently in New Orleans rhythm & blues.

Music has always been an integral part of New Orleans life—a perpetual soundtrack for a city that loves festivals, parades and any excuse for a party. The European tradition of marching parade bands became an essential ingredient in the festivities, especially at Mardi Gras time and in the city's famous funeral processions, where a solemn march to the burial ground was followed by a spirited romp back into town. The bands were important training grounds for future jazz musicians, and the parade band tradition established the lively beat and rhythmic orientation that characterizes all New Orleans music. (As the seminal New Orleans drummer Earl Palmer recalled, "you could always tell a New Orleans drummer the minute you heard him play his bass drum because he'd have that parade beat connotation."[2])

By the end of the 19th century, marching bands made up of blacks and Creoles had equaled and surpassed the white bands in numbers and talent. Segregation laws passed in 1894 forced together the two previously distinct and antagonistic social classes of "uncultured" blacks and "Creoles of color" (people of mixed blood who had been trained in the European tradition and had enjoyed a privileged status). The interaction between the two groups wedded African-derived elements—the improvisatory melodic styles and syncopated rhythms of the black folk traditions—with the harmonies, instrumentation and regular meters (the groupings of beats against which the syncopations made themselves felt) of European tradition. This blending of traditions was gradually felt in the parade band music: the drum beats and march melodies grew less rigid and more inventive and the march melodies were embellished with bent and "blue" notes and set against improvised countermelodies and syncopated "second lines."

In a nutshell, this mixture of European and African-American elements laid the groundwork for the creation of ragtime and jazz. The piano-based ragtime style evolved in the 1890's from the marches and the from the rhythms of popular dances. As its popularity grew, instrumental "orchestrated ragtime" developed out of the parade bands and, with a healthy dose of the blues thrown in, formed the basis for classic New Orleans jazz. The music thrived in the red-light district known as "Storyville," then spilled over into the legitimate clubs and illegitimate pleasure houses after the Storyville bordellos were officially closed in 1917. And if a club owner couldn't afford an entire band, a piano player would suffice to keep the spirits up and the dancers moving. The "barrelhouse" piano players mixed jazz, ragtime, blues and boogie over a dance beat powerful enough to bring the most broken-down piano back to life. Most of all, the music—like the city—was Fun. The bleak lyrics and desolate mood of the guitar blues from the surrounding rural regions had no place in the "Big Easy," where even funerals were cause for celebration.

NEW ORLEANS RHYTHM & BLUES

While "Dixieland" and later jazz styles dominated the New Orleans music scene until World War II, club blues and barrelhouse piano styles charted a parallel course and spawned a unique style of rhythm & blues in the post-war years. The Latin flavor and rhythms, the bass-heavy boogie feel, the rhythmic variety, the piano and sax-dominated band instrumentation and the spirited ensemble playing of traditional New Orleans styles combined to give the city's R&B a distinctive sound and character.

Behind the Scenes

Jump-blues singer **Roy Brown** scored the city's first big rhythm & blues hit in 1947 with his self-penned "Good Rockin' Tonight," released on the

DeLuxe label. ("Good Rockin' Tonight" was also a hit the following year for Wynonie Harris on Cincinnati's King label. Elvis turned it into a rockabilly rave-up six years later.) DeLuxe's success with New Orleans artists inspired other record labels to take notice of the city and her abundant talent, most notably the California-based **Imperial** and **Specialty** labels, which were the recording homes of Fats Domino and Little Richard, respectively, and were the dominant presences in New Orleans through the 1950's. Unlike other musical centers, New Orleans was slow to establish hometown record labels, which forced the local artists to depend on outside labels for many years. In fact, the city had only one major recording *studio*: the tiny J&M studio run by **Cosimo Matassa** (later called simply Cosimo's), where all of the city's great R&B and rock & roll recordings were made from the forties through the sixties. Matassa's "live in the studio" approach was geared to capturing a great performance with no tricks or gimmicks, and though his studio was far from modern, even in those days, the sound he captured still sounds remarkably fresh.

Bandleader **Dave Bartholomew** was another behind-the-scenes figure who played a crucial role in the development of New Orleans R&B. Bartholomew's crack band was very popular in the city's clubs and, more importantly, formed the core group of sessionmen at Matassa's studio. The tight-knit "**Studio Band**" changed personnel only gradually over the years and always had a keen musical rapport and a gutsy sound that inspired the singers they backed and contributed much to the success of their records. Bartholomew himself achieved his greatest fame as a songwriter and arranger, working independently at first, producing sessions for Shirley and Lee, Smiley Lewis and Lloyd Price, then as the musical director of Imperial Records' New Orleans operations, where he secured his place in history with his collaboration with Fats Domino.

Fats Domino hit the R&B charts in 1950 with "The Fat Man," featuring the Bartholomew band, and was a major R&B star through the early fifties before crossing over to the pop market in 1955. Domino's success and the distinctive sound of his music further heightened interest in New Orleans. Matassa and the Studio Band found themselves in great demand, and Bartholomew's bass-propelled arrangements formed the blueprint for the next decade of New Orleans recordings. The emphasis on piano, saxophones and bass riffs set New Orleans music quite apart from the trebly, guitar-dominated sound of the rockabillies and the blues-derived guitar emphasis of Chicago's Chess Records rockers, Chuck Berry and Bo Diddley. The rhythmic inventiveness and variety of New Orleans styles also stands in sharp contrast to the more one-dimensional, repetitive rhythms of most early rock & roll.

Professor Longhair

Professor Longhair was New Orleans' most beloved musical figure and the patriarch of a line of great piano players—Fats Domino, Huey "Piano" Smith, Allen Toussaint, Art Neville, Dr. John and many others—who anchored the New Orleans R&B sound. Born Henry Roeland Byrd in 1918, the self-taught "Fess" developed a thoroughly unconventional approach that mixed jazz, ragtime, blues, boogie-woogie, calypso, rhumbas and all types of dancebeats into a carefree carnival sound and style that embodied the spirit of the city. He described his own style as a "gumbo" and a mixture of "offbeat Spanish beats and Calypso downbeats" topped by his boisterously rowdy singing.[3] Longhair's highly syncopated **boogie-rhumba** style—boogie bass lines set to a rhumba beat—influenced Dave Bartholomew's bass-driven arrangements and became a widely recognized New Orleans trademark.

Professor Longhair began playing professionally in 1949 and quickly achieved a cult status that he was never able to parlay into national recognition. "She Ain't Got No Hair" (later re-recorded as "Bald Head") and "Mardi Gras in New Orleans" were among his first recordings, released on the Texas-based Star Talent label. He recorded "**Tipitina**," one of his best-known songs, for Atlantic Records in 1953, then went on to record for a dozen other labels, only rarely producing a record that moved beyond the "local hit" category. After many obscure years of menial work and ill-health, Professor Longhair was finally rediscovered in the early seventies. He reclaimed his rightful spot with a triumphant performance at the city's Jazz and Heritage Festival, and he remained the revered elder statesman of New Orleans R&B until his death in 1980.

Smiley Lewis

Among the many Domino followers in the early fifties was Smiley Lewis, who was also on the Imperial label, produced by Bartholomew and backed by Bartholomew's band. Although he was never able to break into the rock market, Lewis had a sizable R&B hit in 1952 with "The Bells Are Ringing," and hit again in 1955 with the original version of "**I Hear You Knocking**." Lewis' songs have tended to be better known in their cover versions: Gale Storm's 1955 cover of "I Hear You Knocking," for example, made it to the Top Five on the pop charts, as did Dave Edmunds' 1971 version, while Lewis' "One Night" was covered by Elvis Presley in 1958.

Lloyd Price

Lloyd Price recorded for Specialty Records, whose owner, Art Rupe, had come to New Orleans in 1952 in search of his own Fats Domino-styled singer. Rupe discovered the 17-year-old Price at the end of an otherwise fruitless talent audition, and was struck by his intense and pleading vocal delivery. "**Lawdy Miss Clawdy**" was recorded with Bartholomew's band and features Fats himself on piano. The record was a #1 R&B hit, and was popular with young white listeners as well (Elvis was one of many who later covered the song). After a stint in the army, Price switched to ABC Records and scored a number of pop hits in the late fifties, including 1959's "**Stagger Lee**," a hard-driving update of the traditional black folk song "Stagolee." Price actually did two versions of the song, since Stagger Lee's cold-blooded murder of Billy—while the chorus chants "Go Stagger Lee!"—in the original was deemed a bit much for impressionable pop ears. Price's other hits, such as "Personality" and "I'm Gonna Get Married," were done in a pop style with syrupy choirs and slick productions that were far removed from his New Orleans roots.

Guitar Slim

Specialty Records also struck gold in New Orleans with Guitar Slim (born Eddie Jones), a blues guitarist and singer, and hence something of a rarity among New Orleans frontmen. Slim hit #1 on the R&B charts in 1954 with "**Things That I Used to Do**," an ingenious wedding of Slim's gritty voice and guitar blues to a classic New Orleans R&B band backing. The man responsible for the unique blend was none other than Ray Charles, who arranged and played piano on the record. (Charles was strongly impressed by his visits to the city in the early fifties and by his work in Matassa's studio, which inspired him to start his own band and to take his own music in a new, rootsier direction.)

Guitar Slim was a famously flashy performer and an inventive guitarist who exploited the full range of effects then available with the electric guitar. Fellow New Orleans artist Al Reed recalls Slim's live act: "...this guy had cords on his guitar that were something like 200 feet long. This guy would play on stage with his band, he would get off the stage, walk out of the door at the club, go out into the middle of the street, still playing guitar and never drop a beat, *never* drop a beat... he had an electric sound like you never heard and they would open the club doors wide so that the sound could just go in and out of the club, and he would draw people off the street."[4] Guitar Slim followed "Things That I Used to Do" with "The Story of My Life," then shifted his base to Specialty's studios in California, where he continued recording in rather spiritless fashion. Slim never regained his stride, and died of alcoholism in 1959 at the age of 32.

Larry Williams

Larry Williams was a New Orleans native with a job as Lloyd Price's valet and a singing style strongly influenced by Little Richard, both of which helped get him signed to Specialty Records. Williams launched his career with a 1957 cover of Price's "Just Because," then began writing his own Little Richard-style tunes full of rhyming nonsense lyrics and lots of energy. He had a succession of moderate hits through 1957 and 1958, including "Short Fat Fanny," "Bony Moronie," "You Bug Me, Baby" and the ever-popular "**Dizzy Miss Lizzie**." Williams was all but forgotten in America when the Beatles revived his name by covering three of his songs: "Dizzy Miss Lizzie," "Slow Down" and "Bad Boy." (All three were sung by Williams admirer John Lennon, who also recorded "Bony Moronie" on his solo *Rock 'N' Roll* album.)

Shirley and Lee

"The Sweethearts of the Blues," Shirley and Lee, recorded for the California-based Aladdin label. They began their career in 1952 with "I'm Gone," followed by "Shirley Come Back to Me," "Shirley's Back," "Lee Goofed," "Feel So Good" and various other installments of their romance. Backed by Matassa's Studio Band, the pair recorded a number of R&B hits built around their alternating declarations of love and highlighted by Shirley's endearing buzzsaw of a voice. They finally hit pop charts in 1956 with "**Let the Good Times Roll**," a New Orleans classic and a wonderful mixture of teenage innocence and breathless eroticism. As Shirley and Lee trade verses, the song alternates between a humorously stilted circus rhythm and a swinging sax riff and dance beat, then collapses into sparse repeating downbeats for the bridge section: "feel so good when you're home, come on baby, rock me all night long!" Shirley and Lee continued as a team until 1963, but their remaining hits never equaled the inspiration of "Let the Good Times Roll."[5]

Clarence "Frogman" Henry

With Clarence "Frogman" Henry, Chicago's Chess Records tapped into New Orleans via its Argo subsidiary. Henry's first hit, 1957's "**Ain't Got No Home**," was in the gimmicky novelty vein into which New Orleans records often tended to fall. Henry sings the three verses of "Ain't Got No Home" with three different voices, singing first in his normal voice, then in falsetto and finally with an inhaling, playground joke voice to illustrate the story of the lonely boy, lonely girl and lonely frog that "ain't got no home." The croaking voice gave him his nickname, which proved to be more of a hindrance than a help since he had no intention of making a career of singing like a frog. Henry hit again in 1961 with the elegant "But I Do" and "You Always Hurt the One You Love," before dropping back into the local club scene.[6]

Huey "Piano" Smith & the Clowns

Huey "Piano" Smith & the Clowns recorded for Ace Records, the first prominent local label to appear in New Orleans. Huey Smith was a veteran sessionman, songwriter and performer, and a direct piano descendent of Professor Longhair. He also inherited Longhair's playful sense of humor, and turned his "Clowns" recordings and live shows into one long party. The Clowns were one of New Orlean's most popular live acts, and though their crowd-pleasing singalongs didn't always transfer well to the studio, their records were pure fun in the best New Orleans tradition. Their one pop hit, 1959's **"Don't You Just Know It,"** is driven by Smith's piano playing and a chorus of alternating voices singing partytime gibberish (like the stirring "aah-ha-ha-ha, gooba, gooba, gooba, gooba") in shouted unisons and rowdy call-and-response.

Ironically, Huey "Piano" Smith & the Clowns' greatest record didn't even bear their name when it was released. **"Sea Cruise"** was written by Smith and recorded by the Clowns in 1959, with Huey on lead vocals. Ace sensed a massive hit and, eager to establish itself as a prominent label, increased its odds by keeping the Clowns' explosive backing tracks but replacing Smith's rather quirky vocals with white singer **Frankie Ford** (who turned in a fine performance).

"Sea Cruise" opens with the sound of ship's bells and foghorns that set a maritime mood and return periodically in a demented touch of genius. An irresistible bass & sax riff rumbles to life out of the bells and horns, joined by the kinetic energy of Huey Smith's double-time calypso piano. Although it was something of a stolen hit, "Sea Cruise" is a masterpiece of good times and great musicianship, and a high water mark for New Orleans R&B.

Fats and *Little*: Two Sides of the New Orleans Coin

"The Fat Man," "Lawdy Miss Clawdy" and "Things That I Used to Do" were a few of the R&B hits that focused attention on New Orleans and laid a groundwork for things to come. The advent of rock & roll opened new markets to the New Orleans musicians, who saw the "new" sounds as anything but new, and viewed rock & roll as more of a challenge than a threat. In 1955, the city provided rock & roll with two of its first true giants: Fats Domino and Little Richard.

Fats Domino was the homegrown hero with a solid R&B career under his belt by the time he crossed over into the pop charts with "Ain't That a Shame." Little Richard, from Georgia, was one of the many "outsiders" sent to New Orleans by their record companies to capture the sound of the city and its famous studio and sessionmen. Their styles and temperaments couldn't have been less similar: Fats' music always straddled the vague line between R&B and rock & roll while Little Richard eagerly plunged across it. But both men benefited greatly from the New Orleans sound that drives their records and makes them more closely related than it might seem. Inspired by their examples, many other New Orleans artists took aim at the rock market, but none matched the success and far-reaching influence of the two pillars of New Orleans' contribution to rock & roll.

FATS DOMINO

Antoine "Fats" Domino was born on May 10, 1929, in New Orleans, the city he still calls home. A quintessential New Orleans musician, Domino became the city's biggest homegrown star and remains a joyful ambassador of the New Orleans sound. The success of "The Fat Man" established Domino as an R&B star, and the crossover success of "Ain't It a Shame" turned him into a rock & roll headliner, though even then he made a point of calling his music "rhythm & blues" to emphasize his musical roots. Domino felt he was carrying on a tradition rather than breaking away from it, and consequently his music displayed none of the rebellious energy that sparked the rockabilly wildmen and his own polar opposite, Little Richard. Indeed, the graceful dignity and easygoing manner of his music is one of its great charms.

Fats displayed that same charm and grace as a performer and personality. He seemed like a rhythm & blues Santa Claus—jolly and kindly, without a hint of sex or rebelliousness. In other words, he seemed *safe*: he never set his pianos on fire or caused any scandals, there were no "hidden meanings" lurking behind his songs, and he didn't appear eager to lead your sons and daughters down the road to juvenile delinquency. His unthreatening image helped him avoid much of the parental suspicion and outrage that accompanied the advent of rock & roll. More importantly, it helped him overcome the racial biases and fears that kept many black performers of the fifties off the charts and in the shadows. Domino's low-key personality and image kept the focus of his appeal where it belonged—on his unique and immensely pleasurable music. Of rock's initial wave of solo performers, only Chuck Berry and Little Richard were similarly able to transcend racial prejudices and reach anything close to the wide audience they deserved: Berry by becoming the Eternal Teenager, Little Richard by being such a clownish lunatic that race became a secondary issue. Mild-mannered Fats outdid them both and ranked behind only Elvis and Pat Boone in terms of consistent sales in the 1950's.

"The Fat Man"

Antoine Domino was one of nine children, the only one to inherit his jazz violinist father's musical ambitions. A school dropout at 14, Fats nearly lost those dreams and several fingers in a factory accident, and only reclaimed them after a long and painful struggle to regain his mobility. (He never did achieve the facility of the great boogie and barrelhouse players, and stuck instead to a constant-chording style.) Domino established himself in the local clubs like the Hideaway, where he was discovered in 1949 by Dave Bartholomew and Imperial Records president Lew Chudd. Bartholomew: "We went down and Fats was singing a song the prisoners used to sing, 'Junkers Blues,' you know, a song about the junkie. In December 1949 most people didn't know what that word meant. We went down and we heard Fats and we really liked it. So I told Fats would he like to record and introduced him to Lew and we went on from there."[7]

"Junkers Blues" was rewritten as a theme song for Fats and recorded at the end of 1949. "The Fat Man" hit the national R&B Top Ten in 1950, beginning a long association between Domino and Dave Bartholomew, his co-writer, arranger and alter-ego. "The Fat Man" was recorded in Cosimo Matassa's studio with Bartholomew's stellar band, highlighted by Herb Hardesty and Alvin "Red" Tyler on riffing saxophones, and drummer Earl Palmer's aggressive swing. The focus of the record is Fats himself, wailing away in a surprisingly high and gritty voice and pounding out a mistakenly over-recorded piano part. (Bartholomew liked the resulting up-front sound of the piano and used the unbalanced mix for the record, which in turn became a model for subsequent sessions. Fats also employed a vocal gimmick on the record—an odd, trumpet-like falsetto "wah-wah" sound that he abandoned on his later recordings.)

Domino hit #1 on the R&B charts in 1952 with "Goin' Home," and scored several more R&B hits through the early fifties—including 1953's "Please Don't Leave Me," later covered by the Johnny Burnette Trio—as he honed his uptempo style. A bluesy slow number from 1950 called "Every Night About This Time" introduced the other, slower side of Fats' style and the steady piano triplets that would accompany his pop hits (and nearly every fifties rock ballad).[8] His other "trademark," his peculiar but endearing French Creole accent, came more to the fore as he began to sing in lower registers and as his overall style became smoother, calmer, less bluesy and more in keeping with Fats' even temperament. Fats was settling into a groove, fine-tuning a melodic style that turned out to be perfect for the rock market.

"Ain't That a Shame"

Domino finally broke the pop barrier in 1955 with "Ain't That a Shame," which contains all the classic Fats Domino elements.[9] A modified 12-bar blues, written by Domino and Bartholomew, "Ain't That a Shame" is a rollicking good-times number despite its broken-hearted lyrics. As always, Fats refuses to take himself or his problems too seriously: the "ain't that a shame" refrain sounds more like a shrug than a sigh. With its easy-rhyming lyrics, instantly memorable tune and strong, midtempo dance beat, "Ain't That a Shame" was a natural crossover hit.

"Ain't That a Shame" is firmly rooted in New Orleans R&B tradition: the propelling bass riffs, rhythmic variety and unlabored tightness of the ensemble playing give the record a sound that simply couldn't have come from anywhere else. The song opens with a stop/start call-and-response between Fats and the band, then glides into the refrain, where the beat straightens out and the band divides into a multi-layered accompaniment: Fats plays straight chorded triplets on the piano, the guitar and bass double on a gentle boogie-bass riff, the saxes smooth out the texture with long held notes, and Earl Palmer gels it all with a swinging shuffle on his cymbals, booming downbeats on his bass drum and crisp backbeats on his snare. The syncopated verses and full-band refrains alternate throughout the song, embellished by a sax solo that gives the band and the song a chance to stretch out. Thanks to Bartholomew's arranging skills and the band member's natural rapport, the dense accompaniment sounds as loose and lively as a New Orleans parade band.

The repeating bass riff in "Ain't That a Shame," a descendent of Professor Longhair's boogie-rhumba, was one of Dave Bartholomew's musical signatures and is a key feature of most of Domino's songs. The solos on Fats' records were always taken by a saxophone, usually played by Herb Hardesty, that mirrored Fats' voice with a languid melodic style (which became an appropriately frenzied squall when backing Little Richard). Special note should be made of Earl Palmer, rock's first great drummer and the man responsible for the rhythmic push-and-pull that makes "Ain't That a Shame" and other early New Orleans hits so exciting. His snare cracks and parade beat bass drum anchor the song while his drum fills and playful offbeat kicks drive it forward and bridge the different sections. (The equally able Charles "Hungry" Williams took over the bulk of the drumming in Matassa's studio in 1957 when Palmer moved on to California and great acclaim as a session drummer for Phil Spector, Ricky Nelson, the Beach Boys and many others.)

"Ain't That a Shame" went to #1 on the R&B charts and reached #10 on the pop charts in the summer of 1955. Released at the peak of the cover song era, "Ain't That a Shame" was quickly covered by Pat Boone, who took his pallid version to #1 on the pop charts. Fats' next big hit, 1956's "I'm In Love Again," outsold the Fontane Sisters' cover version, however, and no one tried to steal his version of "Blueberry Hill," which was also released in 1956—the biggest hit of his career.

Fats Domino, Rock & Roll Star

Released in 1956, **"Blueberry Hill"** was a time-honored standard (Louis Armstrong's 1949 version probably inspired Fats to do the song), as was "My Blue Heaven," a hit for Fats the same year. Although Fats and Bartholomew generally wrote his material, Fats' easygoing style lent itself well to popular standards and made them sound wholly original. Although his version of "Blueberry Hill" was supremely tasteful, some older critics feigned outrage at the rock "perversion" of "their" song, and even Dave Bartholomew had serious doubts about the wisdom of recording it: "It had been done a million times before and I wasn't too interested in Fats doing it. But he insisted he wanted to do 'Blueberry Hill...' Lew Chudd asked me what did I think and I said it was horrible, pull it off the streets fast, you're gonna ruin Fats. He said, 'What do you mean, we just sold two million records,' and that was in two weeks."[10]

"Blueberry Hill" opens with one of rock's classic intros—a triadic piano figure that ushers in Fats' wistful remembrance of that night on Blueberry Hill when the moon stood still and "you were my thrill." *Something* certainly happened up there, but the amiable Fats disarms the sexual overtones that other rockers might have exaggerated, just as his delight in the memory of the night overcomes the fact that the girl's gone and all of her promises "were never to be." The band arrangement of "Blueberry Hill" is similar to that of "Ain't That a Shame," though slower and calmer. The verses are shaped by a graceful boogie riff in the guitar and bass and by Earl Palmer's snare backbeat. Palmer's cymbals double Fats' piano triplets, giving the relatively slow "rock-a-ballad" a constant inner pulse. The saxophones play long held notes through the verses to create a smooth background texture, then supply a lilting countermelody to Fats' vocals in the bridge section ("the wind in the willows..."); as the saxophones come to the fore, the guitar/bass riff drops out, giving the bridge section a contrasting dreamy feel—suspended between the verses as that night is suspended in time.

"**Blue Monday,**" a 1957 hit written by Domino and Bartholomew, is a further example of the rhythmic dynamics and subtleties that were second-nature to the New Orleans bands. Here, instead of being a calm hiatus, the bridge section ("Saturday morning...") heightens the tension as the full band piles onto Fat's triplet piano rhythm before fanning back out for the return of the verse/refrain ("Sunday morning..."). The beat itself never changes, but the *articulation* of the beat—the way it is played and felt—changes dramatically, from a multi-layered arrangement to a pounding unison crescendo and back again. And as always, the Fats' voice rides above the hard-driving arrangement as if it took no special effort at all.

For the most part, Fats' style varied little from one record to the next, though there was a gradual softening of his sound. Mindful of the fact that his primary audience was now teenagers, the themes of his songs grew younger, the tunes and lyrics grew simpler and the arrangements were embellished in an attempt to change with the times. "I'm Walkin'," "Whole Lotta Loving," "I'm Ready" and other late-fifties hits were sped up to rock & roll dance speed, the size of his backing band grew larger ("Be My Guest" has an almost Big Band swing sound), sweet choirs were occasionally added, as in "Valley of Tears," and some of his more lightweight numbers, such as "The Rooster Song" and "I'm Gonna Be a Wheel Someday," had novelty-style productions that fit their nursery rhyme lyrics.

Walking to New Orleans

Fats' steady stream of releases sold well and kept him in constant demand for television, movie and live appearances. His innocent songs and uncontroversial image also helped make him one of the few rock "founding fathers" to escape the fifties unscathed, though 1960's "Walking to New

Orleans" was his last Top Ten hit, an appropriately melancholy good-bye wave. His records continued selling at a steady, if diminished, rate until 1963, when he left Imperial for ABC Records. His new label tried unsuccessfully to repeat the pop success they'd had with Ray Charles by burying Fats under glossy, middle-of-the-road material and "Modern Nashville" productions. Domino left ABC in 1965 for even deeper obscurity at Mercury Records, then ended up the decade on the Reprise label, where he had a minor hit with a cover of the Beatles' "Lady Madonna" (a song directly inspired by Domino's New Orleans style).

Although his recording career never recovered, Domino has remained a popular live performer on the "oldies shows" and the Las Vegas nightclub circuit. Fats continues to work comfortably within a tradition—including, now, his own, and he has weathered the decline of his career as gracefully as he handled his sudden leap to stardom. Fats was a calm in the center of the storm—his mere presence lent a certain dignity to rock & roll, and the ever-present smile on his face made it seem that his life was as easy and happy as the songs he sang. Pushing seventy, he sings his old songs, as always, without a hint of strain. His voice and charm remain perfectly intact and his classic hits remain true classics.

LITTLE RICHARD

It's hard to imagine what rock & roll would have been like without Little Richard, the living embodiment of rock's raucous soul. His maniacal passion and outrageous image presented the *other* extreme from the polite crooning of Pat Boone (who, nevertheless, covered a couple of Little Richard's songs to truly comic effect). In two short years he wrote some of rock's landmark songs and ripped through the remaining boundaries of "good taste" to show what rock & roll could be if you dared to take it all the way. From the opening "WopBopaLooma-beLopBomBom" of "Tutti Frutti" straight through every note he sang, Little Richard fulfilled rock's promise of liberation through sheer energy and audacity. If rock & roll was indeed "nothing but a bunch of noise," as its many critics claimed, then Little Richard showed just how joyous that noise could be.

Little Richard shared many musical traits with Fats Domino: both played piano and wrote their own beatifically childlike songs, both were backed by bass-driven and sax & piano-dominated band arrangements, both hit the pop charts in 1955, and both shared Matassa's recording studio and Studio Band, though the friendly confines became something of a padded cell during Richard's sessions. For all the similarities, Little Richard and Fats Domino were musical and temperamental opposites: where Fats was calm, refined and unassuming, Little Richard was crude, high-strung and outrageous; and where Fats never seemed to strain, Little Richard seemed to do little else. His music had none of the polish and melodicism of Fats' style, and none of its easygoing charm. In fact, Little Richard seemed always on the verge of spinning out of control—just barely able to rein in his energy—and it is that feeling of controlled chaos that made his music so exciting.

Little Richard really had more in common with Jerry Lee Lewis, the other piano wildman, than with studio mate Domino. His music is the R&B equivalent of Lewis' rockabilly: a stripped-down and manic extension of rhythm & blues that shredded R&B conventions just as Lewis bulldozed over his country roots. In addition, the two kindred spirits were both racked by religious crises and inner demons that seemed to fuel the too-late-to-stop-now intensity of their music and the transcendent madness of their live performances. Being black and gay (though that wasn't directly articulated at the time), Little Richard had two big additional strikes against him in the conservative world of Eisenhower America. But everybody loves a clown, as they say, and he demanded and got attention by exaggerating his genuine oddness to the point that the kids cheered and the adults simply stared in disbelief. His mega-watt voice, outrageous image and antics, piled-high pompadour and liberal use of lipstick, mascara and other makeup(!) created a truly bizarre and unforgettable sight—a "Bronze Liberace," as Richard liked to call himself, before he took to introducing himself as "the King of Rock & Roll... and the Queen too!"

Another favorite moniker, the "Quasar of Rock & Roll," seems particularly apt in light of the dictionary definition of quasar: "one of a number of celestial objects... that are powerful sources of radio energy."[11] From the moment the first horrified parent heard "Tutti Frutti" blasting over the airwaves in 1955, Little Richard was rock's greatest source of radio energy. He seemed to suddenly appear from the outer galaxies with a strange new message ("WopBopaLooma!?") and a crazed, alien voice shouting—in coded messages only teenagers could understand—that the Invasion had begun. And it wasn't merely another case of white ears reacting to an R&B crossover: a good many R&B fans were as surprised as the pop listeners by the ferocity of the onslaught, which owed more to deep southern gospel styles than to the comparatively polished singing styles of R&B. In fact, "Tutti Frutti" must have surprised even Little Richard: "I came from a family where my people didn't like rhythm & blues. Bing Crosby—'Pennies from Heaven'—and Ella Fitzgerald was all I heard. And I knew there was something *louder* than that, but I didn't know where to find it. And I found out it was me."[12]

Background: Macon to New Orleans

Richard Penniman was born on December 5, 1932, in Macon, Georgia, which was also home to James Brown, Otis Redding and, later, the Allman Brothers. He was one of twelve children in a devout Seventh Day Adventist family (though his father did embellish his religious beliefs by selling bootleg whiskey). Richard's earliest musical experiences were in the church, and his gospel roots are clearly evident in his singing. The harsh, frenzied vocal styles of many of the black gospel groups of the forties and fifties are the nearest equivalent to Richard's screaming delivery—much closer than any pop or R&B model. (Richard has often said that his trademark shrieking "woo" came directly from gospel giant Marion Williams, while his shrieking hiccups—like those that punctuate "Lucille"—were inspired by Ruth Brown's "Mama, He Treats Your Daughter Mean.")

Richard was a misfit from the start, and his wild streak, his love for the forbidden blues and his early awareness of his homosexuality kept him at odds with his family. He ran away from home to join a traveling "medicine show," then took to singing on the streets of Macon and finally, at 13, was kicked out of the house. He was taken in by a white couple who encouraged his music and often gave him the stage at the local nightclub they ran. In 1951, Penniman, now "Little Richard," sang in a talent contest sponsored by a radio station and won a recording contract with RCA Records.

Little Richard's RCA releases, recorded in Atlanta, showed few signs of things to come. The standard jump-blues material was sung in a restrained style heavily influenced by Roy Brown and Wynonie Harris. (Richard's own "Every Hour" is the most widely available song from this period, and is hardly recognizable as Little Richard.) He left RCA in 1952 for the Houston-based Peacock label, where his recordings proved a bit more exciting but still fairly run-of-the-mill. He had already developed a flamboyant stage routine, but his recorded music captured little of his personal extravagance and his records failed to sell. By 1955, Richard was back in Macon washing dishes at the Greyhound station and still dreaming of his big break, which finally came in a call to audition for Art Rupe's Specialty Records in Los Angeles.

"Tutti Frutti"

After Specialty's success with Guitar Slim and Lloyd Price, Rupe was anxious to do more recording in Cosimo Matassa's studio, and particularly anxious for the type of pop success recently enjoyed by Fats Domino on Imperial Records. Specialty A&R man **Bumps Blackwell** was signed on as Richard's manager and producer and plans were made for a recording session in New Orleans. Thus Little Richard, from Georgia, became linked with New Orleans through a record label based in Los Angeles. The connection was tenuous but all-important, for in New Orleans Little Richard would finally find the sound and let loose the voice that had eluded him for four years at RCA and Peacock.

It still took an inspired accident to create Little Richard's first hit. His initial Specialty session, on September 14, 1955, was largely taken up with mediocre R&B recordings similar to his RCA and Peacock material. Blackwell deemed the proceedings so unpromising that an early halt was called to the session so that everyone could retire for afternoon drinks at the Dew Drop Inn.

While Blackwell nursed his disappointment at the bar, Richard—visions of dirty dishes at the Greyhound station filling his mind—headed for the piano to vent his frustrations and screamed out some rhyming obscenities in a rowdy voice unlike anything he'd hinted at in the studio. Like Sam Phillips hearing Elvis stumble onto his true voice with "That's All Right," a startled Bumps Blackwell knew he'd just heard the real Little Richard. A local songwriter, Dorothy La Bostrie, was quickly called in to clean up the words, which an embarrassed Little Richard at first refused to sing "in front of a lady. " (He was finally coaxed into blurting them out while facing a wall.) With fifteen minutes of studio time remaining, "Tutti Frutti" was recorded and the blueprint was laid for all the Little Richard hits to come.

The rapid-fire pace and last minute recording of "Tutti Frutti" left little room for subtleties, but the record still captures the freewheeling New Orleans rhythmic drive. The record is propelled by Richard's piano and Earl Palmer's drums, which manage to swing even at ninety miles an hour, and is punctuated by sudden stops & starts and by brief saxophone answers to Richard's voice. As with most of his songs, "Tutti Frutti" is built over a 12-bar blues and features a saxophone as the solo instrument in the lead break. Lee Allen and Red Tyler played most of the solos on Richard's records, in styles far more gritty and clamorous than their work with Fats Domino and other artists. Just as Little Richard was inspired by his excellent sessionmen, they in turn responded to Richard's frenzied style by reaching outrageous heights of their own.

All of this is secondary, though, to the VOICE: a vocal fuzz box punctuated by trademark shrieks and falsetto "whooo's" that shredded microphones and any remnants of a discernible tune. Although the words were sanitized for popular consumption, "Tutti Frutti" still sounds gleefully obscene, with orgasmic whoops giving explicit meaning to the otherwise nonsensical title refrain and "wopbopalooma's." While parents bemoaned the final collapse of decency and good taste, kids bought the record in droves and sent it up to #17 on the pop charts (and #2 on the R&B charts). Although the full impact of "Tutti Frutti" was blunted somewhat by Pat Boone's tepid cover version, the success of Little Richard, Fats Domino, Chuck Berry and other black artists helped break through the racial and musical barriers that separated audiences and provided a rationale for covers. As the consciousness of the record buying public was raised, more rock fans and radio listeners began demanding the genuine article. Richard's next release, 1956's "Long Tall Sally," hit the pop Top Ten and outsold Pat Boone's cover, marking the symbolic end of the era of the cover songs.

The Specialty Years

Little Richard begins "**Long Tall Sally**" by threatening to tell Aunt Mary about straying Uncle John ("he claimed he has the misery but he havin' lotta fun") and the time he's been having with Long Tall Sally ("she's built for speed—she got everything that Uncle John need"). Before long, however, he seems to have forgotten about all of them: "I'm havin' me some fun tonight!" is the real message of the song, and by the end of the two minute cataclysm there's little doubt about it—Little Richard's having more fun than Pat Boone could imagine in his wildest dreams.

The stop-and-go band arrangement of "Long Tall Sally" mirrors "Tutti Frutti" and keeps the band thrusting forward in its race to keep up with Little Richard. All of Richard's vocal trademarks are present in abundance as well: he works falsetto "whooo's" into every refrain, announces the sax solo with a great lead-in scream and then, at its end, launches into another verse with a measure-long, glass shattering "weeeelll..." Moments like these and the sheer *sound* of his shredding vocal cords are the real "meaning" of Little Richard's songs. The words themselves don't seem to matter and tend to be oversexed utter nonsense, when they're intelligible at all, and little more than vehicles for his incredible voice.

For that matter, his *songs* seem little more than vehicles for his voice and magnificent presence. In isolation, songs like "Tutti Frutti," "Heeby-Jeebies," "Ready Teddy" and "Jenny Jenny" are a blissful noise that make about as much sense as their titles. Considered together, every crazed installment illuminates another tiny corner of the Richard's self-absorbed world. His songs and the characters that populate them—Daisy, Sue, Sally, Jenny, Lucille, Miss Ann, Miss Molly and all the other objects of his delight—seem like interchangeable parts of one long vision and one long, joyous shriek. As Arnold Shaw put it, "Little Richard represents a triumph of style over substance."[13] More than with any other artist, when you listen to Little Richard you don't hear "songs," you hear *him*. He is the crowing glory of rock & roll's subversion of pop, of the ascendance of the Singer over the Song. He never expounded much on "wopbopalooma," and never needed to: HE was the meaning of every word he sang.

It's hard and rather pointless, then, to single out individual Little Richard recordings, since they are all classics and all so similar to each other. **"Keep A-Knockin'"** merits special notice, as it was recorded in a Washington, D.C. radio station during a tour break and features his touring band, The Upsetters, instead of the New Orleans sessionmen. The furious sound of "Keep A-Knockin'" stands out even in Richard's catalog, and is a good indication of what his tumultuous live shows must have been like. **"Lucille,"** on the other hand, stands out for the elegance of its arrangement, shaped by an understated guitar/bass/sax riff, alternating with short stop-start verses and a great, growling sax solo. The piano and drums play the constant duple rhythm (1-2, 1-2) that gives Richard's songs a more assertive drive than the smooth triplets that articulated Fats Domino's slower tempos.

"Good Golly Miss Molly" ("you sure like to ball!") is Little Richard's finest moment. It is highlighted by voice-and-drum breaks and dramatic band pauses that keep the song fresh and exciting. The arrangement is driven by an aggressive guitar, bass & sax riff borrowed from "Rocket 88," and by some particularly inspired drumming, piano playing and breathless singing. "Heeby-Jeebies" takes the stop-start arrangements to a hilarious extreme, like a carrousel lurching out of control, while "The Girl Can't Help It," the title song of the 1956 movie, is one of Richard's more involved productions, with responding background vocals and a swinging sax section.

"Rip It Up" and "Ready Teddy" have a cut loose rockabilly feel that inspired Elvis, Buddy Holly, the Everly Brothers, Eddie Cochran, Jerry Lee Lewis, Bill Haley and many others to record their own versions. The raw energy of Little Richard's songs transcended any particular style and made them favorites of his fellow rockers who, Pat Boone aside, were challenged and inspired to match his exuberance with their own. When "Tutti Frutti" hit, rock & roll was brand new and just starting to build a "tradition" of its own. Along with Chuck Berry, Little Richard gave rock & roll a repertoire of its own that defined it as more than a borrowing or retooling of older styles. Although Berry would outstrip Little Richard in the following decade as rock's most covered songwriter, in the 1950's Richard had that honor all to himself.

"Ooh! My Soul"

At the height of his career, Little Richard suddenly announced that he was giving up show business to devote his life to God, or as he put it, "giving up rock & roll for the Rock of Ages." Richard's innate religious qualms about playing the Devil's music were rekindled by a fellow Specialty artist determined to convert him, and they flared into a spiritual identity crisis during a 1957 tour of Australia. Apparently, according to one of the many explanations for his change of heart, a plane that he was flying on between shows caught fire, prompting Richard (understandably!) to promise God he'd give up rock & roll if only He'd make the plane land safely. His decision was reinforced during an outdoor concert when Richard witnessed the ascent of the Russian Sputnik, the first satellite launched into space: "That night Russia sent off that very first Sputnik. It looked as though the big ball of fire came directly over the stadium about two or three hundred feet above our heads. It shook my mind. It really shook my mind. I got up from the piano and said, 'This is it. I am through. I am leaving show business to go back to God.'"[14]

Little Richard held a press conference the next day to officially announce his decision and then, in a characteristically dramatic gesture, dumped $20,000 worth of jewelry into Sydney Harbor to prove his sincerity. It was widely viewed as a publicity stunt, but he meant it: he turned his back on his fame and riches, enrolled in the Oakwood Bible College in Huntsville, Alabama, and vanished from the music scene for the next six years. (Specialty kept Little Richard on the charts as long as they could by releasing the remaining songs from their vaults: "Keep A-Knockin'," "Good Golly Miss

Molly" and his last hit, "Ooh! My Soul," appropriately enough, were all released after Richard's conversion.)

Little Richard finally agreed to perform again on a 1962-63 package tour of Europe and England, providing he sang only gospel numbers. His religious songs received an understandably lukewarm audience response, and before long his pride and fiery competitiveness overcame his convictions. Watching the other acts steal the shows was simply more than Richard could stand, and he finally raged back with "Tutti Frutti" and the rest of his magnificent catalog of classics, fueled to new heights of lunacy by the years of pent-up silence. Nik Cohn describes Richard's plunge back into the Dark Side: "The first time I saw him was in 1963, sharing a bill with the Rolling Stones, Bo Diddley and the Everly Brothers, and he cut them all to shreds. He didn't look sane. He screamed and his eyes bulged; the veins jutted out of his skull. He came down front and stripped—his jacket, tie, cuff links, his golden shirt, his huge diamond watch—right down to flesh. Then he hid inside a silk dressing gown, and all the time he roared and everyone jumped around in the aisles like it was the beginning of rock all over again... When it was through, he smiled sweetly. 'That Little Richard,' he said. 'Such a nice boy.'"[15]

With the Rolling Stones paying him homage, the Beatles covering "Long Tall Sally" and Paul McCartney borrowing his "oooh's" and shrieks every chance he got, Little Richard decided it was time for a full-scale comeback.[16]   Richard recorded "Bama Lama, Bama Loo," his last Specialty release, in classic, raving Little Richard style—a little *too* classic, unfortunately. In 1964, the year of the British Invasion, it simply sounded like an oldie and failed to make the charts. Although his live shows remained exciting, Richard never regained an audience for his recordings. He went through a series of record labels, alternating between ill-conceived new material and uninspired re-recordings of his old hits. The maniacal commitment to a single, self-defining style that made his early music so exciting also left little room for artistic growth. An early seventies stint with Reprise Records yielded some good new material, particularly the album called *The Rill Thing*, but it was still a far cry from the his glory days and the sales were poor.

As his frustration mounted Richard's personality became increasingly bizarre and his live shows lapsed into self-parody. Always something of a rock & roll Muhammad Ali, he had, in his prime, achieved an effective balance between his outrageous behavior and his music. Now, with no new music to bolster his claims to greatness, he generally made a clown of himself onstage and on the TV talk shows he seemed to appear on with alarming regularity.

Little Richard fluctuated between rock and God through the seventies and into the eighties, when the release of his autobiography prompted a return to the talk show circuit and a flurry of movie and media appearances. Today a somewhat calmer Little Richard speaks openly about his crises of religion and sexuality and about his former problems with drugs and money (like far too many of rock's early stars, Richard received only a fraction of the amount due him). He also speaks with justifiable pride about his enormous contribution to rock & roll and his vast influence on so many that have followed him. Besides "teaching Paul McCartney how to sing," Richard directly inspired and helped launch the careers of James Brown, Otis Redding, Billy Preston and Jimi Hendrix, who played guitar in one of Richard's comeback bands (and was later quoted as saying "I want to do with my guitar what Little Richard does with his voice"[17]). Creedence Clearwater Revival's "Travelin' Band" was clearly a tribute to one of their formative influences, and the list of singers influenced by Little Richard, from Elvis through Mitch Rider and Bob Seger all the way to Prince, would be endless, and would ultimately have to include everyone who's ever gotten crazy and wailed rock & roll. Still, there's only one "rill thing." Little Richard was an original's original and, for sheer energy and excitement, the inspired madness of his rock & roll has never been topped.

NEW ORLEANS IN THE SOUL ERA

New Orleans music adapted to the softening pop sounds of the early sixties with lighter beats and an emphasis on catchy hooks and novelty-styled tunes. Although softened, the music was still full of lively rhythms and ensemble work and still retained a distinctly "New Orleans" sound. In fact, the Twist and the other dance crazes that swept the country in the early sixties inspired something of an R&B revival that was right up New Orleans' alley. Huey Smith's "Pop-Eye" and Chris Kenner's "Land of 1,000 Dances" are notable New Orleans dance tunes of the era, and the Twist King himself, Philadelphian Chubby Checker, owed much—including his nickname—to Fats Domino and the New Orleans sound.

The long-overdue establishment of local record labels kept Cosimo Matassa's studio in high gear after the involvement of the outside labels began to wane at the end of the fifties. Minit, Rex, Ric, Ron, Rip, Instant, Fire, Fury, Red Bird, Watch, Dover and many other small labels came and went in the late fifties and through the sixties. Although none achieved the consistency of Chicago's Chess or Detroit's Motown labels, they provided a crucial outlet for local artists.

Minit Records, founded in 1959, pioneered the new styles, followed quickly by Instant and a rash of other labels that seemed to spring up daily. The recording was still centered around Cosimo Matassa's studio, now home to a younger group of sessionmen led by pianist/writer/arranger **Allen Toussaint**, who inherited Bartholomew's influential role. Most of New Orleans' early 1960's hits came from veteran local performers who managed to come up with a one-shot fling at the national pop charts. Toussaint and Minit Records had their first hit with Jessie Hill's "Ooh Poo Pah Doo" in 1960. Other standout

Touissaint productions included Ernie K-Doe's "Mother-in-Law," Benny Spellman's "Fortune Teller," the Showmen's rock tribute "It Will Stand," Barbara George's "I Know," Aaron Neville's "Over You," Art Neville's "All These Things" and Chris Kenner's "I Like It Like That." The few New Orleans hits from the period that were not produced by Toussaint include Lee Dorsey's "Ya Ya" and "Do-Re-Mi," Joe Jones' "You Talk Too Much," Barbara Lynn's "You'll Lose a Good Thing," and the Dixie Cups' "Chapel of Love," and guitarist Earl King's "Trick Bag" and "Come On" (later covered by Jimi Hendrix).

The arrival of the Beatles brought most New Orleans operations to a halt, and the city's music was slow to mirror black music's transition from R&B to soul music. New Orleans regained some of its stride in the mid-sixties: New Orleans native Irma Thomas made a handful of great soul records for Imperial in 1964, including "I Wish Someone Would Care" and the gospel-style "Time Is On My Side," quickly reworked by the Rolling Stones; Robert Parker's 1966 hit "Barefootin'" is a dance-soul classic, and Aaron Neville hit again that same year with the soul ballad "Tell It Like It Is." The major New Orleans soul star turned out to be "Mr. Ya Ya" **Lee Dorsey**, who hooked up with Allen Toussaint in 1965 and crafted a contemporary, funk-soul dance style. Dorsey's mid-to-late sixties hits included "Ride Your Pony," "Working In the Coal Mine," "Holy Cow," "Riverboat" and "Get Out of My Life, Woman." An ill-conceived switch to topical "message" songs and the changing audience tastes of the early seventies brought Dorsey's career to a halt. He died in 1987 after a decade of local appearances and unsuccessful comeback attempts.

Toussaint remained active as a producer, arranger and much-covered songwriter, expanding beyond his New Orleans base to work with The Band, John Mayall, Joe Cocker and many other artists. Although New Orleans' heyday was well-past by the end of the 1960's, the spirit of its music has been kept alive by "**Dr. John**" (Mac Rebennack), a piano playing veteran of New Orleans' glory days who recorded a tribute to his city's music called *Gumbo* in 1972 and had a pop hit in 1973 with "Right Place, Wrong Time." The city's musical traditions have also been sustained by the durable backup group the Meters, by "black Indian" Mardi Gras groups like the Wild Tchoupitoulas and the Wild Magnolias, by the resurgent popularity of brass band, Cajun and zydeco styles, and by the continuing appeal of the timeless **Neville Brothers**, the most visible ambassadors of the city's music, whose members have had hits that span three decades of New Orleans styles.

Although its artists rarely make the charts or break new ground, the sound of New Orleans lives on night after night in the city's clubs and festivals. Music still plays a large role in the daily life of the city, and the big beat and happy sound of New Orleans carries on like a living monument to the musical contributions of that unique city. New Orleans record man Marshall Sehorn summed up the spirit of the city this way: "You can go anywhere you want to, there's no music like New Orleans music... Nobody else has as good a time as we do, nobody else shakes their ass as much as we do, and that's everybody, everybody from young to old, black and white, Indians, jumpin', dancin', carryin' on and having a good time. And that's what it's all about, that's what this city is all about."[18]

---

[1]Fats Domino quote from "Rock abd Roll: The Early Days" videotape (Archive Films, 1984).

[2]Max Weinberg, "The Big Beat," (Chicago: Contemporary, 1984), p. 89.

[3]Arnold Shaw, "Honkers and Shouters," (New York: Macmillan, 1978), p. 492.

[4]John Broven, "Walking to New Orleans," (Sussex, England: Blues Unlimited, 1974), p. 54.

[5]Shirley made an unlikely comeback as "Shirley and Company" in 1975 with the disco hit "Shame, Shame, Shame," co-written and produced by fellow veteran Sylvia Robinson (of Mickey & Sylvia, who had a 1956 hit with "Love Is Strange").

[6]"But I Do" was written by Bobby Charles, who also wrote "Walking to New Orleans" for Fats Domino, and wrote and recorded the original "See You Later, Alligator," later a hit for Bill Haley.

[7]Broven, "Walking to New Orleans," p. 30.

[8] The piano triplets were probably inspired by Little Willie Littlefield's 1948 hit "It's Midnight."

[9]The title was originally "Ain't It a Shame," though he sings "that."

[10]Broven, p. 67.

[11]The Random House College Dictionary.

[12]Shaw, "Honkers and Shouters," p. 191.

[13]Shaw, p. 190.

[14]Charles White, "The Life and Times of Little Richard," (New York: Harmony, 1984).

[15]Nik Cohn, "Rock from the Beginning," (New York: Stein and Day, 1969), p. 33.

[16]The Beatles hooked up twice with their hero and mentor during his European tour: at the Star Club in Hamburg , Germany, and back home in Liverpool at a concert organized by Brian Epstein.

[17]White, "The Life and Times of Little Richard."

[18]Broven, "Walking to New Orleans," p. 217.

Photo courtesy of UPI/BETTMAN NEWSPHOTOS

Chuck Berry

[6] CHICAGO AND CHESS RECORDS

Chicago was the Promised Land for a vast number of southern blacks who migrated northward in the period before and immediately after World War II. The exodus from the cotton land of the Mississippi Delta included a great many rural bluesmen who joined in the search for better opportunities in the factories and steel mills of Chicago and Gary. The spontaneous flowering of talent that created the Delta blues was repeated and amplified in Chicago, where the harsh realities and alienation of the blues were set against an electrified urban landscape in one of the great musical epiphanies of the century. Chess Records, launched in the late forties by two Polish-born immigrants, Leonard and Phil Chess, was the most stable and long-lived of the Chicago blues labels and was home to the best of the tough, Delta-rooted style of urban blues played by transplanted southerners like Muddy Waters, Howlin' Wolf, Willie Dixon, Sonny Boy Williamson, Little Walter, Elmore James, Robert Nighthawk and other Chess luminaries.

Chess Crossovers

Now universally accepted as one of America's great musical gifts to the world, the blues still appealed to a very small audience in the 1950's and Chess Records was simply a tiny independent label struggling to get by. The Chess brothers realized that their releases sold to a strictly limited and racially-defined market, and that even that market was beginning to shrink as a new generation of younger blacks began listening to and playing the happier and more dance-oriented *rhythm* & blues. As R&B records began crossing over into the pop charts and the rock & roll boom approached, the Chess brothers were painfully aware that their pure blues was far too raw for pop ears, and they began looking for other ways to tap into a wider market without losing their natural base.

Chess' first inroads into the pop charts came with two vocal groups, the **Moonglows** and the **Flamingos**, who sang sentimental ballads in an early "doo-wop" style that appealed to both the pop and R&B listeners. In fact, the Moonglows' "Sincerely" was appealing enough to be covered by the McGuire Sisters in 1955, while the Flamingos' "I'll Be Home" received the inimitable Pat Boone treatment in 1956. Needless to say, both covers outsold the originals: the Moonglows' "Sincerely" made it to #20 on the pop charts, while the McGuires took the song to #1; Pat Boone's "I'll Be Home" went to #4 while the Flamingo's original version failed to make the charts at all. The Flamingos had only minor success at Chess and left the label in 1956 (they had their biggest hit in 1959 with "I Only Have Eyes for You," on George Goldner's End label.) The Moonglows stayed on, singing background vocals for other Chess artists and recording a few more hits of their own. When the original group split up in 1958, Moonglows lead singer and "Sincerely" author Harvey Fuqua assembled a new group of Moonglows and scored a final hit with "Ten Commandments of Love." Fuqua moved on to be a producer and songwriter at Motown in the 1960's, taking along one of the replacement Moonglows, a young Marvin Gaye.

Another Chess vocal group, the aptly-named Monotones, scored a Top Ten hit in 1958 with the doo-wop classic, "Book of Love." Through its Checker, Argo and Cadet subsidiaries, Chess also produced several novelty-style hits in the fifties, including Clarence "Frog Man" Henry's "Ain't Got No Home," Jimmy McCracklin's dance number "The Walk," and Dave "Baby" Cortez' instrumental "Rinky Dink." The label even scored a rockabilly hit with Dale Hawkins' "Susie-Q," and hit again with Eddie Fontaine's "Nothin' Shakin' (But the Leaves on the Trees)," a favorite live number of '60's British bands. R&B veteran Etta James recorded a string of hits on Argo and Cadet through the 1960's, including "Tell Mama," which was covered by Janis Joplin.

Two Chess rockers proved to have the depth and staying power of the label's blues giants: **Bo Diddley** and **Chuck Berry**, two of the seminal figures in rock's history (and in Berry's case, perhaps *the* seminal figure). Just as New Orleans was a natural musical home for piano players like Fats Domino and Little Richard, it is wonderfully appropriate that two of rock's greatest guitar innovators recorded for Chess Records, home of the electric blues. The signing of these two men and the brilliant records they made says much for the musical vision—and business acumen—of the Chess brothers, who, with their blues masters, had already recorded and preserved some of America's greatest music. Considering the far-reaching influence of urban blues along with the fact that Diddley and Berry both hit the pop charts a year before Elvis' first national hit, there's no disputing Chess' crucial role in the development of rock. As Bo Diddley put it, "we were the beginning of rock & roll, and Chess Records should be labeled as that—it deserves that honor."[1]

BO DIDDLEY

The distinctive rhythmic pattern called the "Bo Diddley Beat" is an immediately recognizable element of rock's shared language and legacy. Simple, hypnotic, eminently danceable and endlessly adaptable, Bo's beat is the rhythmic equivalent of the 12-bar blues. Not that Bo Diddley actually "invented" the beat. In spirit, at least, its origins trace back to the "hambone" beats and frenzied, repetitive "ring shouts" of slavery days, and from there back to the rhythms of Africa (a lot of nervous white parents heard little else in Diddley's music). In the Big Band era, bandleaders summoned up variations of the rhythm by calling for the "shave and a haircut... two bits" beat. Diddley used the beat to its fullest and greatest effect, however, and made it his trademark. He defined himself and his music in terms its rhythm, and in doing so he proclaimed the primacy of rhythm to an extent unprecedented even in the beat crazy world of rock & roll.

Background: Mississippi to Chicago

Bo Diddley was born Otha Ellis Bates on December 30, 1928, to a farm family in McComb, Mississippi. After the death of his father, Otha was taken in by the McDaniel family and given the name Ellas McDaniel, the name that appears on most of his songwriting credits. His new father died soon afterwards, and in 1934 the family moved to Chicago, where his schoolmates playfully mocked Ellas' backwoods roots by dubbing him "Bo Diddley," after a homemade single-string instrument from the South called the "diddley bow." The family scratched their way through the Depression years and even managed to buy Bo his first musical instrument—a violin, which he used to surprising effect on a few of his Chess recordings. He also studied trombone with his church's musical director, but his heart was in a different type of music, much to his family's chagrin. Like many religious black families, Bo's relations considered the blues and R&B the "devil's music" and strongly disapproved of his interest in it (which, of course, made it all the more enticing).

Diddley picked up the guitar as a teenager and taught himself to play using an open-tuning that he would employ on most of his songs.[2] By the mid-fifties, Diddley was playing around the Maxwell Street market and in the clubs on Chicago's South Side with drummer Frank Kirkland and maraca player Jerome Green, who would remain his sidekick and alter ego over the next decade. (Green is given the spotlight in "Bring It To Jerome," and trades jive-talking mock insults with Diddley in "Say Man.") The trio developed a distinctive combination of Latin-tinged maracas, pounding tom-toms and a tremolo guitar sound that Diddley set in phase with the percussive rhythms. The overall effect was startlingly new, with no direct influences or antecedents.

"Bo Diddley"

Bo approached the Chess brothers in 1955 with a song called "Uncle John." They loved the sound and made plans to record the song, but felt that the words could use a bit of work... "They told me to rewrite it. The words was a little rough. It had lyrics like 'Bowlegged rooster told a cocklegged duck/Say, you ain't good-looking but you sure can... crow.'"[3] "Uncle John" was cleaned-up and turned into "Bo Diddley," one of the first great rock & roll classics. While slightly sanitized, the song retained the slang expressions, backwoods jargon and comic yarn-spinning quality that characterized most of Diddley's lyrics.

The beat and sound, on the other hand, didn't have to be changed at all: the "Bo Diddley Beat" is there in all its savage glory from the opening note of "Bo Diddley." In fact, the entire record is really one big rhythm section, with vocal incantations and scattered guitar interludes set against a rhythmic juggernaut created by the entire band. The vocals have a chanting singsong feel, with no real "tune"; the "verses," such as they are, are chopped up and asymmetrical and seem almost a stream of consciousness; the band accompaniment never changes—there aren't even any *chord* changes; there's no flashy lead break and no catchy refrain or "hook" beyond the rhythm itself and the sheer, amazing SOUND. A record with no tune, chord changes or rhythmic variety ought rank as one of the most boring records ever made; instead, it is one of the most exciting.

Rhythm and *sound* are the focus of "Bo Diddley," as they are on all of Diddley's recordings. Even the short "solos" in "Bo Diddley" are really just a change in sound and register, but with nothing else changing or moving, the mere shift to a higher range and a single hint at a chord change—which the rest of the band ignores—become dramatic events. The sound is intensified by the reverb added to the voice and percussion and by the tremolo of Diddley's guitar, which vibrates in time with the voodoo spell of the tom-toms. There are no cymbals to brighten the sound or snare drum accents to pull a beat out of the rolling hypnotic pulse. "Bo Diddley" sounds both huge and powerful and strangely empty and spacious, and certainly unlike anything else coming out of the radio in 1955.

"Bo Diddley" alone would have secured Diddley's place in the history of rock & roll. It's flipside was the equally famous "**I'm a Man**," a single-riff blues mantra similar to "Bo Diddley" in its relentless and trance-inducing pursuit of self-glorification.[4] Diddley's signature beat, one-chord trances, strange guitar sounds and humorous jive lyrics appear in various permutations throughout his work, from the playfully sinister "Who Do You Love" to the haunting "Mona" and the Willie Dixon-penned "You Can't Judge a Book By Its Cover." Other Bo Diddley highlights include the comic calypso send-up "Cracking Up," the riff-heavy "Road Runner" and the nursery rhyme call-and-response of "Hey Bo Diddley" (a return to his favorite subject).

Diddley's records were consistent hits on the R&B charts but seldom made a dent in the pop charts. In fact, 1959's "Say Man" was the *only* Bo Diddley record to crack the pop Top Forty. His spectacular showmanship kept him in great demand on the live circuit and his records were favorites at dance parties and on jukeboxes, but his music was simply "too black" for the majority of the pop audience, or at least too black to risk buying and playing at home. He was also one of the first artists to concentrate on albums as well as singles, though teen-oriented album titles like *Bo Diddley Is a Gunslinger*, *Bo Diddley is a Twister* and *Surfin' with Bo Diddley* didn't do much to improve his sales (though they did inspire some bizarre album covers). Diddley toured and recorded steadily through the fifties and into the sixties, but his music never reached the wide audience or gained the respect it deserved.

Bo Knows: The Beat Goes On

Bo Diddley was a true original. His sound and style owed relatively little to anything that preceded him, and nearly everything that has followed has been touched, directly or indirectly, by his commitment to the primal force of rhythm in rock & roll. His approach to the guitar was equally original and ahead of its time: he was a pioneer in recognizing and taking advantage of the expanded possibilities of the *electric* guitar, experimenting with odd-shaped, custom-built guitars and new sounds and special effects long before such things were commonplace. (Diddley was a revelation to the late-sixties audiences at the rock revival shows who assumed that Jimi Hendrix had invented psychedelic guitar sounds.)

A great dance beat and an exciting change of pace from the standard rock backbeat, the "Bo Diddley Beat" was quickly felt as one of rock's primary inspirations. Bandleader Johnny Otis, for example, used the beat and Diddley's maraca-laden arrangements on several records, including the 1958 hit "Willie and the Hand Jive." Mickey and Sylvia's 1956 hit "Love Is Strange" was co-authored by Diddley, and Mickey Baker's exotic guitar work shows his influence. Diddley fan Buddy Holly recorded his own version of "Bo Diddley" and adapted many Diddley traits into his own style, as did other admiring guitarists like Duane Eddy and Link Wray. The influence of Diddley's rhythmic focus can be felt in artists ranging from James Brown to the Everly Brothers, who called him the biggest influence on their acoustic guitar style. Diddley was also an enormous influence on the British Invasion groups, particularly the blues-based bands who covered his songs and made frequent use of "his" beat. The Rolling Stones, for example, amplified the Bo Diddley feel of Buddy Holly's "Not Fade Away" and turned Muddy Waters' "I Just Want To Make Love To You" into a Diddley rave-up. The Who's "Magic Bus" is built over the Diddley beat, the Yardbirds recorded "I'm a Man" and the Animals recorded "Bo Diddley" and their own impressionistic "history" of Bo and rock & roll, "The Story of Bo Diddley."

A list of influences and "borrowings" could go on indefinitely, in all directions, up to the present day. Bo's beat, sound and style have become part of rock's Public Domain. Unfortunately, you can't copyright a beat and sound, and while his fortunes have improved of late, thanks to television commercials and the belated recognition of the music industry, he still has relatively little to show for having made such a vital contribution to the music that has made millions for others. "I don't sound like nobody else—everybody's trying to sound like me... And I haven't gotten a thing from it. Just give me credit for being the person that's sending everybody to the bank!"[5] He may not have received the financial rewards, but he can certainly take pride in the permanent mark he has made on rock & roll and the living monument he will leave behind: the distinctive rhythm that everybody knows as the "Bo Diddley Beat."

CHUCK BERRY

Chess Records' continuing search for a blues-based artist who could appeal to the rock & roll market yielded nothing less than the very *definition* of rock & roll: Chuck Berry. Berry's influence is so pervasive that simply playing rock & roll is paying him homage. While Elvis' magnetic presence embodied the stance and spirit of rock & roll, Chuck Berry, more than any other artist, defined rock's musical style and articulated the concerns and attitudes of its audience. "Roll Over Beethoven," "Johnny B. Goode," "Rock & Roll Music," "Sweet Little Sixteen," "School Days," "Back in the USA," "Memphis" and the other Chuck Berry classics helped establish rock & roll as a musical form in itself, no longer a hybrid of R&B and country styles, and formed the musical cornerstone—the musical alphabet—upon which rock & roll was built.

Performer and Poet

Chuck Berry established the guitar as *the* rock instrument: both the highlighted solo instrument and the rhythmic backbone of the music. He synthesized the diverse styles of his guitar heroes Muddy Waters, jazz guitarist Charlie Christian, electric blues pioneer T-Bone Walker, and Louis Jordan's guitarist, Carl Hogan, who Berry credits with inspiring his chiming song introductions. To these and other influences he added his rather peculiar fascination with "hillbilly" music and his interest in adapting for guitar the hard-driving solos of jump blues sax players and the pumping rhythms of boogie-woogie piano playing (an influence clearly heard in the rhythm guitar parts of songs like "Johnny B. Goode" or "Sweet Little Sixteen").

Berry was equally inventive as a songwriter and has deservedly been enshrined as the first great "rock poet." His songs display a great wit and insight, a great gift for storytelling and an eye for the tiniest details of teenage life. He was the first to celebrate the rock audience and rock & roll itself—the first to recognize adolescence as a world in itself, timeless and complete, with rock & roll as its rallying point and common language. His chants of "Hail! Hail! Rock & Roll, Deliver me from the days of old!" and "Roll Over Beethoven, and tell Tchaikovsky the news!" were good-natured but resounding battle cries for young fans eagerly defining their own private world and communal identity.

That a thirty-year-old black man proved to be the most articulate spokesman for young, largely white America is one of the great ironies of the rock era, though perhaps it was that very distance and perspective that enabled Berry to view his audience so clearly. Berry knew that the pop market of the 1950's wasn't ready to accept a black man speaking directly from his own experience, so he wrote for his audience and expressed *their* concerns instead: "Everything I wrote wasn't about me, but about the people listening to my songs.

I didn't write "School Days" in a classroom—I wrote it in the Street Hotel, one of the big, black, low-priced hotels in St. Louis."[6]

As the Eternal Teenager, Berry was able to sidestep issues of age and color. He took care to keep the sensibilities of his mixed audience in mind, and developed a clearly enunciated singing style that was expressive yet free of overtly bluesy, "black" mannerisms. As a result, many early fans—and shocked southern concert promoters—had no idea that Berry was black. He sang his rapid-fire words with a delivery that combined the humor and showmanship of Louis Jordan with the emotional urgency of Muddy Waters and the smooth clarity of his other hero, Nat "King" Cole: "Listening to my idol Nat Cole prompted me to sing sentimental songs with distinct diction. The songs of Muddy Waters impelled me to deliver the down-home blues in the language they came from, Negro dialect. When I played hillbilly songs, I stressed my diction so that it was harder and whiter. All in all it was my intention to hold both the black and the white clientele by voicing the different kinds of songs in their customary tongues."[7]

Chuck Berry broke through color barriers and played and sold to a thoroughly integrated audience. He sang for Teenagers: a race defined by age, not color. Berry's songs have hardly aged at all in four decades. He remains the Eternal Teenager, and his songs remain the quintessential anthems to what it's like to be young in America, or at least what it *ought* to be like.

St. Louis to Chicago

Chuck Berry was born on October 18, 1926, and grew up in a lower middle-class neighborhood in St. Louis, Missouri ("the best of the three colored sections of St. Louis"[8]). His early years were relatively uneventful, that is until a misguided string of small burglaries with some friends landed Berry in Reform School for three years—the first of several run-ins with the law that have plagued his life and career. Upon his release, in 1947, Berry helped out with his father's carpentry business, landed a job in an auto assembly plant and studied to become a hairdresser. Fortunately, he continued playing the guitar as well, and began developing something of a reputation around St. Louis. On New Years Eve 1952/53 (the night Hank Williams died), Berry joined the successful Sir John's Trio led by pianist **Johnny Johnson**, beginning a long association between the two men. Berry was strongly influenced by Johnson—he adapted many of his piano boogie riffs and always considered the piano an integral ingredient in his songs (which is why many of them are pitched in "piano keys" such as C and Eb).[9]

The Sir John's Trio became the house band at the popular Cosmopolitan Club in East St. Louis, and was soon renamed the Chuck Berry Combo as Berry's singing, playing and humorous stage act began to grab the spotlight. Blues numbers and Nat Cole ballads formed the core of the combo's material, but the joking "hillbilly" songs that Berry stuck into the act proved to be the real crowd pleasers: "Curiosity provoked me to lay a lot of the country stuff on our predominantly black audience and some of the clubgoers started whispering, 'who is that black hillbilly at the Cosmo?' After they laughed at me a few times, they began requesting the hillbilly stuff and enjoyed trying to dance to it. If you ever want to see something that is far out, watch a crowd of colored folk, half high, wholeheartedly doing a hoedown barefooted."[10]

Having achieved hometown hero status, Berry set his sights on a recording contract and set out for Chicago and an audition with Leonard Chess in May of 1955. Berry assumed that the blues numbers he'd written would be of greatest interest to Chess. (One of them, "Wee Wee Hours," was used as the B-side of his first single). Much to his surprise, however, it was one of the *hillbilly* numbers from his club act that caught Leonard Chess' ear. Based loosely on an old country song called "Ida Red," Berry's "Ida May" had been popular at the Cosmopolitan Club, but he never dreamed that the great blues label would be interested in a hillbilly novelty number! But Chess was looking for a way to move beyond the R&B market and felt that this "black hillbilly" just might be it. He was right: "Ida May," renamed "Maybellene," climbed to #5 on the Pop charts and #1 on the R&B charts in the summer of 1955. Chess Records had found its way into the mainstream with a curious reversal of the country-boy-plays-the-blues scenario that launched Elvis and his rockabilly followers. Coming from the opposite direction, the equation still added up to rock & roll.

"Maybellene"

"Maybellene" was recorded on May 21, 1955, with Berry and Johnny Johnson supported by Jerome Green (from Bo Diddley's band) on maracas, Chess veteran Jasper Thomas on drums and blues legend Willie Dixon on standup bass. (Berry: "Willie, stout as he was, was a sight to behold slapping his ax to the tempo of a country-western song he really seemed to have little confidence in."[11]) There had certainly never been a recording quite like it at Chess before: the country bass line, boom-chick rhythms and the witty yarn-spinning vocals sound more like a C&W or Bill Haley recording than anything one would expect from Chess. Even the bluesy vocal slides ("oh Maybelle-e-ene") during the choruses wouldn't have seemed out of place on a Carl Perkins record.

On the other hand, Berry could not sound truly "country" any more than Elvis could pass for authentic blues, and it is the mixture of elements and Berry's playful stretch beyond his normal style that made the record sound so different and exciting. Johnson's piano playing, the heavy drums and maracas, and the lead style and distorted sound of Berry's guitar give "Maybellene" a hard R&B feel that balances the country elements. The "car horn" that opens the song is the first of many signature riffs that announce Chuck Berry songs, and the guitar solo in the middle is a first taste of his supremely economical and rhythmic lead playing. The first half of the solo is simply a single, repeated note played with a biting tone and propulsive rhythm, and even when the solo branches out it stays within a relatively narrow range and emphasizes repeated phrases that push against the beat. Berry builds tension and shapes the lead much as a riffing sax player in a jump blues number might, hammering a single note then shifting to a higher register and a pair of bluesy bends for a climax before straightening out to end the solo and make way for the vocals. Like his Chess compatriot Bo Diddley, Berry always concentrated on the *feel* of his guitar playing—the sound and rhythm were as important as the notes he played.

The lyrics of "Maybellene" introduce Berry's playfully descriptive writing style. ("As I was motorvatin' over the hill, I saw Maybellene in a Coupe de Ville...") He spins an impeccably detailed story of a car chase after a straying woman, though he seems a good deal more interested in the performance of the cars than in Maybellene herself—catching that <u>Cadillac</u> is the real objective. As in many of his songs, the narrative verses alternate with a repeating chorus based on a 12-bar blues progression. (In "Maybellene," the chorus—"Maybellene, why can't you be true?"— opens the song and serves as its catchy "hook.")

On the business side of things, "Maybellene" benefited from a form of "payola" that was widespread in the fifties. Although Berry wrote the song, the songwriting credits on the record read "Berry, Freed, Fratto," meaning that the songwriting royalties would be split between Berry and powerful music industry figures Alan Freed and Russ Fratto. It was clearly in everyone's interest to make the record a hit and, not surprisingly, Freed plugged the record on his radio shows, Fratto pulled some strings and, lo and behold, "Maybellene" *was* a hit. It all came as a surprise to Berry, who knew nothing of the "deal" until he saw the record label himself, but he wasn't complaining—he had a hit! (This type of royalty sharing was common, and though it was certainly underhanded, it was at least a bit more dignified than the widespread practice of handing DJ's sacks of cash in exchange for playing a record.[12])

The Brown-eyed Handsome Man

Two other songs recorded at Berry's first Chess session were further examples of his storytelling talent: "30 Days" is "Maybellene"'s musical twin, while "You Can't Catch Me" continues the car-chase theme, this time without a woman to complicate matters. At subsequent recording sessions, Berry moved away from the overt country tinges of "Maybellene" and crystallized his pure rock & roll style, though he didn't immediately target the teen audience alone. "Too Much Monkey Business" and "Brown-Eyed Handsome Man," recorded at the same session in 1956, are examples of the more "adult" and R&B oriented side of Berry's style.

"**Brown-Eyed Handsome Man**" opens with a distinctive guitar flourish that was later borrowed by Duane Eddy (on "Moovin' & Groovin'") and the

Beach Boys (on "Surfin' USA"). The song employs Latin-tinged rhythms and guitar interludes to accompany Berry's ode to all the troubles women have gone through "ever since the world began" in search of a brown-eyed handsome man (including Venus De Milo, who "lost both her arms in a wrestling match" to win one). Given the racial climate of the fifties, "brown-eyed" was rather dangerously close to "brown-skinned," a coded implication not altogether lost on at least some segments of Berry's audience, though the humorous storylines, jumbled imagery and quick, comic asides defused the tension. (In a similar vein, the "little country boy named Johnny B. Goode" was originally the "little colored boy," until Berry decided not to push his pop listeners too far.)

The rapid-fire imagery and tongue-twisters of "**Too Much Monkey Business**" are one of Berry's most inspired sets of lyrics. The song is set to a 12-bar blues and a stop-start rhythm stripped down to a mere downbeat from the bass for the verses and punched up in the refrains by a surprisingly tough and bluesy guitar. The lyrics zoom through a catalog of everyday hassles—going to school and, with an older audience in mind, working in the mill and the filling station, fighting in the war and "fighting" with conniving women, shady salesmen and hostile pay phones. Each verse is a little tableau of "botherations" in the Real World, and each could easily have been an entire song. (The verses certainly contain more *words* than most entire songs. The flurry of syllables and images directly inspired the verbal assault of "Subterranean Homesick Blues," by the next generation's poet laureate, Bob Dylan.) Instead the hassles flash by, illuminated for a moment, and etched with dead-eye accuracy, but cut with a disarming humor and punctuated by wonderful, exasperated "aah"'s at the end of the verses.

"**Memphis**," from 1958, seems similarly aimed at an audience beyond teenagers. Berry recorded the song in his home studio, "on a $79 reel-to-reel Sears, Roebuck recorder that had provisions for sound-on-sound recording—I played the guitar and the [electric] bass track, and I added the ticky-tick drums that trot along in the background which sound so good to me."[13] "Memphis" is a lovingly detailed story of a young love thwarted by his sweetheart's disapproving mother, or so it seems at first. Like a great short story writer, Berry sets the scene with vivid, concrete imagery: he pleads with the operator to get through to Marie, who called while he was out ("my uncle took the message and he wrote it on the wall"); he describes where Marie lives ("on the South side, high up on the ridge—just a half a mile from the Mississippi bridge") and how much he's missed her since her mother "tore apart our happy home in Memphis, Tennessee." But the last verse contains a heart wrenching twist:

> The last time I saw Marie she was waving me good-bye,
> With hurry-home drops on her cheek that trickled from her eye,
> Marie is only six years old, information please,
> Try to put me through to her in Memphis, Tennessee.

Suddenly it's clear that the song is about a broken marriage and a father trying desperately to reach his daughter. Berry sings the song with an endearingly fragile voice, and embellishes the mood with one of his most tender guitar leads.

In "Memphis," as in most of his songs, Berry uses one specific character and setting to convey a universal truth, and does so with an elegance that any poet would admire. As Bruce Springsteen put it, "If you listen to one of his songs, it sounds like someone's coming in, sitting down in a chair and telling you a story about their aunt or their brother or describing some girl... it's descriptive, his eye for detail."[14] Berry's songs were truly in a class by themselves in the 1950's, when most songs attempted little more than simplistic variations on "I love you, let me carry your lunchbox" or "come on baby, you *know* what I like!" The imagery and lyrical depth of "Memphis" is a tribute to the expressive powers of rock & roll in the hands of a great writer.

Roll Over, Beethoven!

"Brown-Eyed Handsome Man" and "Too Much Monkey Business" were big sellers in the R&B market but failed to make much of a dent in the pop chart, perhaps because the teen audience couldn't easily relate to them. They certainly *could* relate to another song from the same 1956 session: rock & roll's first anthem, **"Roll Over Beethoven**." In a playful swipe at the bad old, pre-rock days Berry invites the Maestro to "dig these rhythm & blues," and tell Tchaikovsky about it while he's at it. A lot of adults viewed the song as proof of their kids' poor taste and shocking lack of respect for "good music"— Beethoven surely *must* be rolling over in his grave!

But who cares what the adults think? They have nothing to do with "Roll Over Beethoven." "Roll Over Beethoven" celebrates the young new world of rock & roll and all the DJ's and jukeboxes that keep the music playing—the medium *is* the message—for all the dancers and sweethearts inflicted with the "rockin' pneumonia" cured only by a "shot of rhythm & blues." "Roll Over Beethoven" was rock's first great monument to itself and its audience, capturing all the magical excitement of a rock & roll dance and all the fun of being young. (All this from an almost middle-aged man? "I was thirty-one years old, but I could *remember*."[15])

Berry found his rock groove with "Roll Over Beethoven": a punched-up 12-bar blues, the song glides along in an upbeat dance tempo that is a little less frantic than the rockabilly rhythms of "Maybellene." The song is propelled by Berry's guitar, Willie Dixon's standup bass (which moves in and out of walking bass figures, giving the music an elastic feeling), and Fred Below's insistent drumming, which emphasizes a sparse snare drum backbeat. The chiming, double-string guitar intro to "Roll Over Beethoven" marks the first fully realized appearance of that most recognizable Berry trademark, and the piercing, rhythmic guitar solo is classic Chuck Berry as well.[16] To fill out the sound, Johnny Johnson provides a strange but effective piano embellishment, at times seeming lost in his own world, while a barely audible saxophone and trumpet provide a wash of sound behind the verses.

Berry learned a valuable economics lesson with "Roll Over Beethoven" as well. Although his songs always had a wide appeal, he now realized that teenagers would be his biggest market and he began tailoring his songs to their specific tastes and concerns. ("I write songs to sell. Everybody does, but most people won't tell you that. I will write whatever I think is going to sell to the most people."[17]) Berry wrote for anyone who wanted to listen, but the Teenager with his hands on the wheel, his eyes on his girl and his record money in his pocket was never far from Berry's songwriting mind after "Roll Over Beethoven." Cars, girls, driving, drive-ins, dancing, rock & roll and all the other Facts of Life (including, unfortunately, school and parents) are described, celebrated or bemoaned in his teenage mini-dramas. Berry's songs were a mirror that reflected Young America's interests, concerns and idealized images of itself. For his legions of listeners on both sides of the Atlantic, they created a mythic landscape of an America full of fun, freedom, fast cars and wide-open spaces.

The Eternal Teenager

"**Sweet Little Sixteen**" is Chuck Berry's love letter to Everyfan, and was inspired by a frantic, real-life fan who was so anxious to get her prized autographs that she missed an entire show in the process. In "Sweet Little Sixteen," Berry looks on with a bemused compassion and captures the excitement and even the language of the breathless, starry-eyed fan: he describes her collection of famed autographs ("about half a million") and takes us into her home as she pleads for permission to go to the show ("Oh Daddy, Daddy, I beg of you—whisper to Mommy it's alright with you"). The last verse describes her "growin' up blues": as long as she's at the show, decked out in "tight dresses and lipstick," she's somebody special—almost an adult! For a few magic moments she can live her dreams, and she's determined to make the most of it, for tomorrow morning she'll just be "sweet sixteen, back in class again..."

In the choruses, Berry moves from the specific to the universal and makes his little heroine a symbol for *all* the young, excited fans. He takes us on a whirlwind of tour stops—Boston, Pittsburgh, Texas, San Francisco, St. Louis, New Orleans—where everybody's rockin' and "all the cats wanna dance with sweet little sixteen," and gives radio listeners around the country a chance to cheer as their city flies by (and a good reason to go out and buy the record; on top of that, the resourceful Berry virtually assured an *American Bandstand* booking by writing in a plug for the show). The stop-start rhythm in the verses, the swinging cymbals, Berry's boogie-rhythm guitar and some insanely exuberant piano playing all help to make "Sweet Little Sixteen" one of Berry's most irresistible songs.[18]

"**School Days**" opens with a guitar/alarm clock and takes us, step by step, through the Dark Side of teenage life: school, where boring classes, annoying classmates, crowded lunchrooms and mean teachers make the day drag on forever. The full band stops in between verses were an inspired bit of text painting: "Recording the song with breaks in the rhythm was intended to emphasize the jumps and changes I found in classes in high school compared to the one room and one teacher I had in elementary school."[19] Mercifully, and with brilliant economy, Berry dispenses with the school day itself in two verses, then takes us "down the hall and into the street" and right to the *real* center of teenage life: the jukebox. Free at last! In Teenage America, as defined by Chuck Berry, one puts up with teachers and parents and a world that can't remember what it's like to be young for those glorious moments when the music's playing and you're dancing with your sweetheart and all the distractions and "botherations" seem like distant memories. As the song so eloquently puts it, "Hail! Hail! Rock & Roll, Deliver me from the days of old!"

Berry provides his own call-and-response throughout "School Days," with guitar lines that answer each sung phrase, echoing the melodic contour and syllabic rhythms of the lyrics. The interplay illustrates Berry's desire to imbue his guitar playing with the expressive immediacy of the human voice. In the final verse, the band accompaniment and guitar response are stripped down to a stark, pounding drum and single guitar note for the climactic chant of "rock, rock, rock & roll," as if in tribute to Rock's defiant simplicity and liberating beat.

That liberating beat—so strong you can't lose it—is praised again in "Rock and Roll Music," where the contrast between the Latin flavor of the verses and the straight rock of the chorus underscores the message. "Reelin' & Rockin'" and "Around and Around" are a return to the dancehall, while the delightfully rough and lively "Carol" hits on all of Berry's major themes— cars, dancing, lost and found love—and makes extensive use of Berry's chiming guitar interludes and guitar/voice dialogues. The equally infectious "Little Queenie" ("she's to cute to be a minute over seventeen") features sly spoken interludes where Berry mulls over his approach to the girl, while "Back in the USA" broadens its scope and pays tribute to the land of skyscrapers, freeways and hamburgers.

The key to Berry's music is it's simplicity, in the best sense of the word, and on the surface the musical and lyrical elements of Berry's music do not seem to vary greatly from one song to the next. The consistency and sustained vision of Berry's songwriting is indeed remarkable, but the variety he creates within his rather strict, self-defined limits is equally remarkable. The Sweet Little Sixteens of "Oh Baby Doll," "Sweet Little Rock & Roller" and "Little Queenie," the runaway women of "Maybellene," "Carol" and "Nadine," the school halls of "School Days" and "Almost Grown, " and the dancehalls of

"Roll Over Beethoven" and "Around and Around" and his other characters and settings are distinct but ultimately interchangeable parts, both new and familiar. Likewise, Berry's band arrangements and guitar intros, leads and rhythm patterns are similar but never quite the same. As with the blues, the overall effect is that of variations on a theme: a knowledge of the theme enriches your understanding of the variations, but each variation stands on its own as well.

"Johnny B. Goode"

One song stands out as Chuck Berry's masterpiece: "**Johnny B. Goode**," recorded in February of 1958. All of the elements of Berry's sound are fully realized in "Johnny B. Goode," beginning with the chiming guitar intro that opens the song and the addition of a second guitar that toughens the overall sound ("Roll Over Beethoven," by comparison, has only one guitar and sounds relatively empty). A relentless dance groove drives the song, embellished by the lead guitar and rollicking piano. The song combines a repetitive 12-bar blues with a melodic pop song form of alternating verses and repeated refrains. The guitar solo before the final verse is announced by a return of the opening guitar intro and is a mini-catalog of Berry's rhythmic lead riffs; the intro returns again in the middle of the lead break, shaping both the solo and the song and giving the band a chance to make another dramatic full stop and re-acceleration back up to tempo.

"Johnny B. Goode" finds Berry in typically articulate form: in one concise verse, like a camera zooming from a wide-angle shot to a close-up, Berry presents all of the essentials about Johnny—that he lives "deep down in Louisiana" and is a poor country boy who can't read and write too well but he can "play his guitar just like ringing a bell." The second verse finds Johnny down by the tracks, playing his guitar to the rhythm of the passing trains heading for the Big World out there, while in the final verse his mother promises that someday *he'll* be out there too, a big star with his "name in lights." (In Chuck Berry's world all things are possible—even a mother encouraging her son to play guitar!) By the end of the song, there's little doubt that he will make it—his success was confirmed in the 1960 sequel, "Bye Bye Johnny"—and the refrains celebrate his impending glory as Berry exhorts Johnny to "Go!" and gives his answer with his guitar.

"Johnny B. Goode" is the quintessential rock & roll "rags to riches" story, and though it is obviously not autobiographical, there are certainly elements of Berry's own life in the saga of rock's first mythic guitar hero. On a deeper level, the song and its setting in Louisiana ("close to New Orleans") was partly inspired by a tour stop in that city and "the thrill of seeing my black name posted all over town in one of the cities they brought slaves through..."[20] Remembering that the song was originally written about a "little colored boy," it does indeed represent a sweet triumph for a man who lived to see his "name in lights" over places he couldn't even have entered in other circumstances. "I imagine most black people naturally realize but I feel safe in stating that *no* white person can conceive the feeling of obtaining Caucasian respect in the wake of a world of dark denial. 'Johnny B. Goode' was... brought out of a modern dark age."[21]

Into the Sixties: No Particular Place to Go

Chuck Berry's name was always in lights through the end of the fifties. Chess Records released a steady string of singles and albums and Berry made numerous television and movie appearances, most notably in 1959's *Go, Johnny, Go,* in which he had a substantial acting as well as performing part. Berry was also in great demand on the tour circuit, headlining on the big "package tours" that crisscrossed the country and on Alan Freed's famous Paramount Theater shows in Brooklyn. At his first Paramount show, Berry spontaneously broke into a comic crouched walk that he had used to entertain his family when he was young. The crowd went nuts, and the "duckwalk" became his most famous visual hook.

Berry *almost* made it unscathed out of the decade that had already claimed the life of Buddy Holly and the careers of Elvis, Jerry Lee Lewis and Little Richard. On December 21, 1959, however, he was arrested and charged with violation of the Mann Act: "the transportation of a minor across state lines for immoral purposes", also called the White Slave Act. After a December 1st show in Texas, Berry had visited Juarez, Mexico, where he became friendly with a young Apache girl named Janice. (Berry was happily married, but he never denied his incurable attraction to all women.) Berry offered her a job as a hat check girl at his newly purchased St. Louis nightspot, Club Bandstand, and she readily accepted, even though she was, as it turned out, all of 14. What happened next remains a bit unclear, but Janice apparently left the club while Berry was on tour and returned to her former livelihood of prostitution. She was arrested, and in short order implicated Berry.

The press had a field day with the story of the "poor unfortunate" lured into a life of sin by the degenerate, *black* rock & roller. The general public needed little convincing: as the last of the untamed original rockers, Berry was a prime target in a pop world already rocking from the highly-publicized Payola scandals and several concert riots and other proof that rock & roll was destroying the moral fabric of America's youth. He was doomed. After a first trial so blatantly racist that it had to be thrown out (the judge continually referred to Berry as "this Negro"), he was finally sentenced to three years in prison. Although he didn't actually start serving his sentence until February of 1962, the intervening two years were taken up with trials, appeals and delays, and his record sales and concert bookings all but disappeared.

Berry ended up serving about two years in prison. By the time he was released, things had changed considerably . In fact, his songs were more popular than ever and *everybody* wanted to hear "Roll Over Beethoven." The catch was, they wanted to hear George Harrison sing it (and probably thought he wrote it). At the height of the British Invasion it seemed that this most American of songwriters could have been Knighted: all of the British bands were playing his songs, singing his praise and bringing Berry's music back to its homeland. Chuck Berry's songs formed the center ground between the blues-based bands led by the Rolling Stones and the power pop of the Beatles and their followers. Both camps covered his songs convincingly and were able to use his style to inform their own, whether they viewed him as the consummate tunesmith with a big beat or the guitar hero from Chicago's blues Mecca.

Meanwhile, in America, the jail term was quickly forgotten and Berry was enshrined as rock's official Elder Statesman.[22] He resumed his recording career and found himself in great demand for live shows, though now as an "oldies act." "Promised Land," "Nadine" and "No Particular Place to Go" (a carbon copy of "School Days") were highlights of Berry's comeback recordings, but the title of the latter pretty well summed up his musical predicament in the 1960's. In a time of constant change and innovation, Berry remained true to the pristine rock & roll that he'd invented—that a new generation was now building on and leaving behind.

Berry left Chess in 1966, then returned in 1970 and released an album entitled *Back Home*, one of the high points of his later career, followed by 1973's *Bio* and 1979's *Rock It*. The "Rock Revival" shows of the late sixties and early seventies brought Berry back as a returning hero for nostalgic hippies who had grown up with his music. Ironically, Berry scored the only #1 hit of his career in 1972 with "My Ding-A-Ling," a stupid, smutty live singalong that dismayed his old fans but thrilled a new generation of teens and subteens. He hit the charts for the final time the same year with a raunchy re-recording of his 1958 hit "Reelin' & Rockin'," then disappeared back into the oldies circuit, where he always played with local pick-up bands hired for the occasion, secure in his knowledge that *any* band anywhere will know how to play "Johnny B. Goode."

Although the hits dried up, Berry's talent for legal problems never deserted him. In 1979, a mix-up with the Internal Revenue Service sent him back to prison, this time for tax evasion. His three-year sentence was reduced to 120 days in jail and four years of probation, plus the bizarre additional requirement of 1,000 hours of community service and benefit concerts. Since then he has managed to get into trouble with alarming and depressing regularity. Berry plays on, though, his place in history secure. 1986 saw his induction into the Rock Hall of Fame and a gala 60th birthday concert at the Fox Theater in St. Louis (which, Berry recalled with sweet irony, was off-limits to blacks when he was young). The concert was filmed and included in the 1987 movie *Hail! Hail! Rock & Roll*, and features an all-star cast of supporting musicians—including Eric Clapton and concert organizer Keith Richards—who are all obviously delighted to pay tribute to the original guitar hero.

Chuck Berry's music is now heading ever deeper into outer space aboard the Voyager I spacecraft on a digitally encoded copper disc of "Music from the Planet Earth." "Johnny B. Goode" was chosen as rock's representative in the musical greeting card to whoever might be Out There. In the meantime, his music lives on here in this world, and lives on in spirit every time anyone picks up a guitar and plays rock & roll.

---

[1]Bo Diddley quote from Feb. 12, 1987 Rolling Stone magazine, issue #493, p. 98.

[2]An open tuning produces a chord when the open—unfingered—strings of a guitar are strummed.

[3]*Rolling Stone* magazine #493, p. 80.

[4]A near clone of "I'm a Man," called "Mannish Boy," was recorded by Muddy Waters and credited to Willie Dixon. The true origins of the song have been a matter of some dispute, though it seems that Diddley's version was first.

[5]Bo Diddley, in conversation with author.

[6]Arnold Shaw, "The Rockin' '50's," (New York: Hawthorne, 1974), p. 146.

[7]Chuck Berry, "Chuck Berry: The Autobiography," (New York: Harmony, 1987) p. 90.

[8] ibid., pg. xxii.

[9]Johnson alternated with Lafayette Leake as pianist on Berry's classic rockers; Bo Diddley, uncredited, contributed rhythm guitar to several Berry recordings.

[10]Berry., p. 89.

[11]ibid., p. 103.

[12]Berry finally won full rights to "Maybellene" in 1986.

[13]Berry, p. 161.

[14]Springsteen quote from *Hail, Hail Rock and Roll.*

[15]Bill Flanagan, "Written In My Soul," (Chicago: Contemporary, 1986), p. 82.

[16]For an example of Berry's "stylistic continuity," notice the striking similarities between the "Too Much Monkey Business" and the "Roll Over Beethoven" guitar solos.

[17]Flanagan, p. 80.

[18]"Sweet Little Sixteen" was also, several years later, the direct model for the Beach Boys' "Surfin' USA"—only the most obvious illustration of the musical & lyrical debt that the Beach Boys and surf rock owed to Chuck Berry.

[19]Berry, p. 152.

[20]ibid., p. 127.

[21]ibid., p. 158.

[22]1965's *T.A.M.I. Show* concert film features a symbolic passing of the torch as Berry trades licks with Beatle substitutes Gerry & the Pacemakers.

Photo courtesy of THE BETTMAN ARCHIVE

The Drifters

[7] VOCAL GROUPS AND DOO-WOP

For many fans, vocal group "doo-wop" *was* rock & roll: the soundtrack of the fifties and the purest of musical forms, shaped entirely by the human voice. Unlike other styles of rock & roll, doo-wop emphasized melody above rhythm and glorified the Song above the singer—a beautiful blending of voices above a sharply defined individual personality or style. And in contrast to the southern roots of other rock styles, doo-wop was predominantly northern and urban: the sound of the city streetcorner. The classic doo-wop tableau of a group of city kids singing sweet, a cappella harmonies on a hot summer night remains one of rock's great heart-tugging images.

Doo-wop reflected the increased, though still limited, commercial possibilities for black music in the pop market. At a time when black solo artists still had to struggle for acceptance, the relatively anonymous and interchangeable doo-wop groups seemed less threatening and were better able to sidestep the racial issue. The lack of specific stars, the focus on the melody and the idyllic innocence of the lyrics helped to stave off criticism: white teens could sing along without any uncomfortable hint of worshipping the "wrong" heroes, and their parents could assure themselves that doo-wop was just harmless, idiotic fun.

The "doo-wop" label did not comer into use until the early 1970's—in its day, the music was simply called rock & roll or R&B. The term is now loosely applied to all of the vocal group styles of the rock & roll era, even though the "star" groups of the time—the Platters, Coasters and Drifters—had very little in common with the endearingly amateurish streetcorner groups. At the height of the music's popularity in the mid-to-late fifties, an untold number of doo-wop groups dotted the musical landscape of the East Coast and other urban centers, all hoping for their big break and a way out of the poverty of the inner city. Since no instruments or amplifiers were needed, doo-wop was accessible to anyone: all you needed was a voice, and even that was negotiable (if you couldn't carry a tune, you could at least groan out a bass line or sing the background "ooh-wah's," "shoo-be-doo's" and "doo-wops" that gave the music its name). Only a handful of the groups made it from the streetcorner to stardom, but a surprisingly large number managed to make a record and score at least one minor hit. While Elvis, Chuck Berry, Little Richard and the other major solo artists managed to sustain careers and create a self-defining body of work, doo-wop was largely the domain of the "one hit wonders"—a collectively created style with few giants but many enthusiastic contributors.

Background and Style Traits

Doo-wop grew out of the popular R&B vocal group styles of the early fifties, with the added emotive influence of gospel group singing. The success of the Mills Brothers and the Ink Spots in the 1930's and 1940's popularized the vocal group sound for the pre-rock era. The smooth sound of the Ink Spots, fronted by Bill Kenny's silky lead tenor, was particularly influential in establishing soft, romantic ballads as best avenue for appealing to a wide audience that was beyond the reach of more blues-based styles. The Ink Spots were the most successful black act of the 1940's (only Nat "King" Cole and Louis Jordan had a similarly wide-raging appeal), and their success inspired a flood of younger groups who took the polished pop sound of the Ink Spots in a more R&B-oriented R&B direction.

The Orioles and the Ravens were two important transitional groups: the Orioles' 1948 ballad "It's Too Soon to Know" was the first vocal group recording to clearly cross the line from Ink Spots-style pop to rhythm & blues, while the Ravens' "Count Every Star" anticipated, in 1950, the sound and style of doo-wop, with a full-ranged vocal backing highlighted by the wordless vocal bass-lines and high "soaring falsetto" that constitute a virtual definition of "doo-wop." The Orioles were also the first to break through to a pop audience in a big way, when their smooth rendition of "Crying in the Chapel," hit #11 on the pop charts in 1953. A reverent ballad, "Crying in the Chapel" was, nonetheless, unmistakably black sounding: lead singer Sonny Til's emotional singing and the wordless falsetto and other backing vocals reflected the trend towards gospel vocal styles that several groups, most notably the Dominoes, were employing to give their music a greater passion and urgency. "Crying in the Chapel" opened the door for a flood of crossover hits promoted to a young white audience as "rock & roll" by Alan Freed and other pioneering disk jockeys.

The crossover success of more dance-oriented R&B vocal groups like the Dominoes, Drifters, Clovers, Five Royales and Midnighters marked the true dawn of the rock & roll era. The raucous sound and beat of vocal group R&B contained all the excitement and sensuality that was missing in the sanitized pop music of the early fifties and was the era's most popular and accessible form of rhythm & blues. As the teen market opened up, however, the music began to change and grow younger as well. The beat stayed strong and exciting on uptempo songs, but the general trend was toward more melodic ballads with idyllic love lyrics and instrumental backings that grew ever more modest as the traditional roles of the instruments were assumed by the singers.

1954 was a pivotal year in the transition from R&B to the rock & roll version of vocal group music that was later dubbed "doo-wop" to distinguish it from the music of the earlier era and to acknowledge the riffing nonsense syllables, "blow harmonies," sung bass lines, wordless falsetto countermelodies, crooning "ooh-wee-ooh"'s and other vocal devices that gave the music its distinctive flavor and charm. Records by the Crows ("Gee"), the Chords ("Sh-Boom"), the Moonglows ("Sincerely"), the Spaniels ("Goodnight, Sweetheart, Goodnight"), the Charms ("Hearts of Stone") and other teen-oriented groups made the pop charts and presented the younger worldview of doo-wop and the lively vocal interplay between the singers that became the focus and great pleasure of the music (enhanced, in the live shows, by equally elaborate choreography and outfits). While the lead singers sang the praises of love or mourned its loss, the ever-resourceful supporting voices found new ways to make it through an entire song without ever singing a comprehensible word.

The intricacy of the vocal arrangements varied with the style and tempo of the song and the talents of the singers, but enthusiasm ultimately counted as much as talent. The singalong melodies rarely strayed beyond four or five notes, but they were clear and catchy and instantly memorable *because* of their simplicity. The melodies were usually supported by a simple, melodic chord progression (I-vi-IV(ii)-V) that became known as the "doo-wop progression" (though it was often used in popular songs of earlier eras, such as Hoagy Carmichael's "Heart and Soul"). Compared to the 12-bar blues progression favored by band-oriented R&B and most rock & roll, the doo-wop progression moves more rapidly—with chord changes every two or four beats—and allows for a more melodic style of singing while retaining a similar feeling of inevitability that keeps its constant repetition from seeming tedious.

The structure of most doo-wop songs followed the melody-derived pop model (*aaba*) shaped by recurring verses and contrasting "bridge" sections. The candid innocence of doo-wop lyrics also reflected a shift toward pop sensibilities. The records spoke to and for teenagers in teenage terms, like a love poem written on the back of a homework assignment. The joys and heartaches of love formed doo-wop's emotional landscape, though not the earthy, sensual love of "Sixty Minute Man," "Work With Me Annie" or other scandalous R&B crossovers. Doo-wop was the domain of innocent teenage love: the Dream—longed for and usually unfulfilled—of idyllic love unfettered by adult concerns and realities (or actual experience). In other words, the dream of finding a little bit of Heaven right here on Earth.

"Earth Angel"

That vision of perfect love fueled **The Penguins'** "Earth Angel," the first "pure" doo-wop record and Our Song for countless couples. "Earth Angel" blended pop's melodicism and lyrical innocence with the emotional directness of gospel and R&B. A classic "ballad with a beat," the song is sung over swaying piano triplets and a gentle I-vi-IV-V-I chord progression fleshed out by a sparse instrumental backing ("Earth Angel" popularized both the triplets rhythm and the chord progression). The yearning lead vocals and the ragged but ever-so-earnest group of background voices create a glorious mess: lead singer Cleve Duncan seems more sure about his love than the melody he's singing, and the rest of the Penguins continually bump into him and each other with a clattering mix of vocalisms. The overall sound of the record is "amateurish" in the best sense, delightfully devoid of any pretension or self-conscious artiness. Sincere emotion triumphs, happily, over vocal technique and accuracy. (A comparison of the Penguin's original with the lifeless cover by the Crew Cuts serves as a painful illustration of what can happen when those priorities are reversed.)

Free of the complexities and adult sensibilities of rhythm & blues and sophisticated pop, "Earth Angel" seems more at home in Sunday School than in the nightclubs. The simple lyrics ("earth angel, will you be mine...") have an innocence that the untrained voices and "garage" sound only serve to heighten. ("Earth Angel" was, literally, recorded in a garage—that of Dootone Records owner Dootsie Williams!) The Penguins sound like what they, in fact, were: a group of high school students singing a song written for one of their girlfriends. The great message of "Earth Angel" was "That could be *ME*," a message taken to heart by other aspiring young singers who couldn't imagine crooning like Bill Kenny or fronting a hot jump blues band, but *could* imagine writing and singing a song just like "Earth Angel."

The Penguins' manager, **Buck Ram**, took the group from tiny Dootone to Mercury Records as part of a package deal that also included another of the groups Ram managed. The Penguins weren't able to recreate their "Earth Angel" success on the new label and faded quickly from the scene. The second group, on the other hand, became one of the most successful crossover acts of the 1950's, rivaled only by Fats Domino in terms of record sales and chart appearances: the Platters.

THE PLATTERS

The Platters were at the other end of the spectrum from the garage ambiance and amateurism of the Penguins. They were the Ink Spots of the rock era, modeled on their predecessors' polished, romantic sound and their presentation of familiar pop standards alongside equally soothing new material (no 12-bar blues or blaring saxophones for the Platters). Buck Ram had been a songwriter for the Ink Spots and often declared his intention to make the Platters the "New Ink Spots," a goal he achieved partly by having the Platters record several convincing remakes of old Ink Spots hits, including "My Prayer." Ram helped to shape a group sound that could appeal to an older audience while retaining enough of a dance beat and doo-wop vocal flavor to be called "rock & roll." Between 1955 and 1960, the group placed eighteen entries in the Top Forty, including four #1 pop hits. "The Great Pretender" and "My Prayer" both hit #1 in 1956, the first-ever pop chart-toppers for a black act. They were followed in 1958 by "Twilight Time" and "Smoke Gets in Your Eyes," making the Platters responsible for half of the small total of eight recordings by black acts that managed to make it to #1 on the pop charts before 1959. (The other black #1's from this period were Johnny Mathis' "Chances Are," Sam Cooke's "You Send Me," the Silhouettes' "Get a Job," and Tommy Edwards' "It's All in the Game." With the exception of the comic doo-wop novelty number, "Get a Job," all were unthreatening ballads. Despite the greater acceptance of black music that rock & roll represented, the "rules" for success on the highest level hadn't really changed: as with the 1940's popularity of the Ink Spots, Nat "King" Cole and Louis Jordan, black artists were most successful when they were crooning like whites or being funny.)

Buck Ram met the struggling Platters in 1954 in Los Angeles, where they were working as parking lot attendants. Ram signed the group and added a female voice, that of 15-year-old Zola Taylor, to the line-up to further soften their sound. The Platters recorded "**Only You**" for Mercury in 1955 and promptly scored a Top Five hit that linked them to the exploding rock & roll movement. A sentimental ballad, written by Buck Ram in classic Ink Spots style, "Only You" was a showcase for lead singer **Tony Williams**, who built upon Bill Kenny's delicate inflections and added his own virtuosic falsetto sweeps and a choked, pleading delivery that became his trademark.

The Platters followed "Only You" with another Ram composition, "**The Great Pretender**," a rock-a-ballad with a graceful melody and an elegant set of lyrics that presents the love of "Only You" as a heartbreaking memory—alive only in a make-believe world carefully hidden under the singer's happy mask of a face. The song is driven gently by a polite New Orleans-style arrangement dominated by piano triplets, gently swinging background riffs and crisp drum backbeats. "The Great Pretender" was released in December 1955 and hit #1 on the pop charts early in 1956, making it only the second rock & roll record to reach the top spot (after Bill Haley's "Rock Around the Clock").

The remainder of the Platters' #1 hits—"My Prayer," "Twilight Time" and "Smoke Gets in Your Eyes"—were pop standards that reflected the increasingly mainstream, supperclub direction of their music. The Platters' career was nearly ruined in 1959 when the four male group members were arrested in Cincinnati for soliciting prostitutes and drug possession. The dubious charges were eventually dismissed, but the group never regained its popularity. They managed one last appearance on the Top Ten in 1960 with "Harbor Lights," a song popularized decades earlier by Rudy Vallee. Tony Williams left for an unsuccessful solo career in 1961, and was replaced by Sonny Turner, who led the group through many years of nightclub and "oldies" shows.

FRANKIE LYMON & THE TEENAGERS

Frankie Lymon & the Teenagers were the vocal group flipside of the Platters: pure streetcorner doo-wop with all eyes on the teenagers and no reverent looks backward to anything that the adults might call "music." They were the doo-wop sensation of 1956, running up a quick succession of hits powered by child star Frankie's amazing voice. Their first hit, "**Why Do Fools Fall in Love**," is the quintessential uptempo doo-wop song: the first to fully incorporate the vocal devices, the doo-wop chord progression, and the direct, unadorned sentiment of the doo-wop ballads (such as "Earth Angel"). The

Teenagers' self-penned "Why Do Fools Fall in Love" opens with a famous wordless vocal-bass intro, followed by a group chant ("ooh-wah, ooh-wah") and the title refrain. From there on it's the Frankie Lymon show: the 13-year-old sings the simple melody with an exuberant grace that seems far beyond his years, climaxing in the "tell me why"'s that float out of the bridge section and glide above the background singers in one of early rock's most majestic moments.

"Why Do Fools Fall in Love" also benefits from a good and unusually prominent band arrangement, featuring a saxophone solo that suddenly veers into jump band R&B until the voices return to reclaim the song. The lyrics express the childlike wonderment of first discovering the mysteries and heartaches of love. Coming from the mouth of an authentic "child," they sound wholly convincing.

Young Frankie was a perfect "hook" for the Teenagers, who wore high school letter-sweaters to further sanitize their image. They followed "Why Do Fools Fall in Love" with "I Want You to Be My Girl," "I Promise to Remember," "The ABC's of Love" and other teen love songs that followed a similar, melodically-focused design highlighted by Frankie's boy soprano. (At the other end of the vocal range, bass singer Sherman Garnes also deserves special mention for kicking songs off with immortal beat setters like "ooly poppa cow, poppa cow, poppa cow-cow," "comb-a laddie-sadie boom" and "doo-bopsie doo, bumba bum-bum-bum.")

None of the follow-ups matched the inspired musical heights or sales figures of "Why Do Fools Fall in Love," but all sold well enough in both the pop and R&B markets to keep Frankie Lymon & the Teenagers entrenched as the country's hottest vocal group. Their wholesome image helped them land spots on the big package tours and appearances on television and in early "rocksploitation" movies like *Rock, Rock Rock*, which featured the group singing "I'm Not a Juvenile Delinquent." Angelic Frankie was perfectly convincing with the sentiment on film, but the reality was somewhat different, as he was already involved with drugs and prostitutes and succumbing to bad career advice that fed his ballooning ego and led him to leave the group in 1957 to pursue a solo career in the pop mainstream.

Lymon's first solo recording, "Goody Goody," sold well but the stifling big band arrangement and glossy pop production of the record lacked any trace of the streetcorner charm of his Teenagers recordings. After "Goody Goody," Lymon's career went into a steep, rapid decline—his voice changed, and much of his remaining appeal disappeared along with his bell-like voice. His repeated comeback attempts proved as futile as efforts to hit the high notes of his old songs. To make matters worse, the huge "trust fund" that was supposedly waiting for him on his 21st birthday turned up empty.[1] Lymon resurfaced in the press in 1967 after a well-publicized arrest on drug charges, and became a symbol of the vagaries of the music business and the pitfalls of fleeting fame.

In 1969, a young singing sensation hit the charts fronting an updated version of Frankie Lymon & the Teenagers. But the original "boy wonder" didn't live to see Michael Jackson and the Jackson Five. 25-year-old Frankie Lymon died a junkie in Harlem in 1968.

THE "ONE-SHOTS"

The Platters' claim to the Ink Spots' legacy of pop success set them apart from most groups of the era, as did even the brief run of hits for Frankie Lymon & the Teenagers. Few doo-wop groups managed to make it onto the charts and airwaves at all; fewer still were able to sustain careers beyond a single hit, and only the Platters, Drifters and Coasters achieved the recognition and longevity of the established solo stars. Hundreds gave it their best shot, though, creating doo-wop's vast catalog of "one-shots," or "one hit wonders," who scored big and then sank without a trace.

Success was fleeting, to say the least, for the groups lucky enough to have a hit in the first place. Most, like the Penguins, spent a few frustrating years trying in vain to recapture the magic of their first hit, supporting themselves with live appearances that gradually dwindled as their hit receded further into their audience's memory. The groups quickly learned that, in the eyes of the music business, they were expendable: new groups were always in the wings and around the corner, just waiting for *their* chance.

The pop market is, by its very nature, always eager for new sounds and performers and just as eager to discard the old ones. The doo-wop groups' grip on fame was particularly tenuous. Solo stars—especially *white* solo stars—could develop an image and audience identification that guaranteed publicity and follow-up hits, but listeners rarely even knew the name of a group's *lead* singer, much less those in the background, and tended to remember doo-wop songs without giving much thought to who sang them. The very qualities that made doo-wop so successful as a "school" also made it difficult for the individual groups to distinguish themselves from all the rest, and made it difficult for them to reclaim the unspoiled innocence of their first hit even if they were lucky enough to have one.

Above all, the groups were victims of their own youth and inexperience. Nearly all were signed to small record labels that had no interest in or resources for cultivating careers. After a group "failed" a couple of times, or started questioning their royalty payments, it was simply cheaper to find a new group of kids who would gladly sign their lives away for their shot at the spotlight. The label owners knew that the naive young singers would sign contracts offering abysmally low royalties and would sign away the rights to their own songs without thinking twice if it meant that they would actually be on a record. Too often, and too late, the groups would discover that they weren't getting any money from their million-selling record or from any cover versions of their song—that they didn't even *own* the song they wrote and that it was all, technically, legal.

The songs outlived the singer in most cases, ingrained in the hearts of a generation and passed along to posterity. A complete list of great "one-shots" would be nearly endless, but several stand out as particularly good representatives of the spirit and styles that made doo-wop the soundtrack of an era (though it's still painful to neglect great songs like the Dells' "Oh What a Night," the Dubs' "Could This Be Magic," the Heartbeats' "A Thousand Miles Away," the El Dorados' "At My Front Door," the Mystics' "Hushabye" and so many others).

DOO-WOP BALLADS

"Story Untold"

"Earth Angel" established lovelorn ballads as the first pure doo-wop style and the natural terrain for such a young and melodic music. **The Nutmegs'** "Story Untold" was 1955's great "ballad with a beat" successor to "Earth Angel," with a similar dreamy, longing feel and swaying beat articulated by the piano's "rock & roll triplets," the constant piano figures that provided an inner pulse for slow songs and served—to the point of monotony—as the standard accompaniment for fifties rock ballads. The doo-wop chord progression also returns, as does the pop (verse/bridge) song form. The lead melody of "Story Untold" has a greater range than most doo-wop songs, highlighted by the octave leap that opens each verse and the elegant downward descent that follows. Not that there is anything remotely sophisticated about the record: Leroy Griffin's unadorned lead singing is backed by a jumble of voices dominated by a classic "walrus bass," the distinctive feature of the most gloriously artless doo-wop songs. The feel is light and innocent as Griffin pours out his love for the girl who left him "standing in the cold," and left his love a "story untold."

"In the Still of the Night"

The memory of an unforgettable romantic evening fills the dreamy sound of **The Five Satins'** 1956 hit, "In the Still of the Night," one of the great, devotional doo-wop ballads—recorded, appropriately enough, in the basement of a church (it certainly *sounds* like it was recorded in a basement, which is part of its charm). Songwriter and lead singer Fred Parris' plaintive vocals recalls that "night in May" so vividly that the song seems a shared memory, palpably real to everyone who's ever been in love. Built around the familiar doo-wop chord progression and piano triplets, "In the Still of the Night" is as notable for its background vocals as for its lead: Parris is surrounded by a mesmerizing chorus of "shoo-doot-'n-shoo-be-doo," supplemented by a chant of "I'll remember" that repeats like a mantra during the bridge section. The feel of the song is complemented by a wistful sax solo and, finally, summed up by dreamy falsetto sighs as the song and that night fade into memory.

"In the Still of the Night" was filed away in the collective consciousness of an entire generation (the mere mention of the song can still bring a faraway look to people of the right age), but Parris was unable to follow-up on its success. He was in the army by the time the record was released, stationed in Japan while the remaining Satins and replacement lead Bill Baker toured America without a mention of Parris in their live shows or publicity packets. The group returned to the charts with "To the Aisle" in 1957, while Parris watched from a distance, unable to convince even his army friends that he had written and sung their favorite ballad. (When he tried to prove it, they even told him he was singing the wrong words!) He eventually regained his proper recognition, though none of the royalty money, for "In the Still of the Night" and built a marginal performing career around nightly renditions of his classic oldie, enduring a love-hate relationship—familiar to all "one-shots"—with the hit that kept him both in demand and chained to the past: "It never ceases to amaze me how popular the song has remained. Sometimes I get sick of it, but it beats digging a ditch."[2]

"Silhouettes"

The Rays' "Silhouettes," from 1957, was one of the first doo-wop songs to feature a relatively sophisticated production and song structure, hinting at the Uptown R&B to come. The song was recorded in high-tech style with a band arrangement that is an integral part of the song, not merely a backing for the voices. The voices abandon the doo-wop nonsense syllables in favor of more elaborate vocal trade-offs, while the backing band weaves among the voices and takes off on its own for a New Orleans-style interlude. The lyrics are rather "sophisticated" as well: the detailed and humorous plot follows a man who goes to visit his girlfriend but finds an embracing couple silhouetted against her window shade. The heartbroken hero pounds on the door, only to discover a pair of strangers—he's on the wrong block! As the band makes a dramatic modulation to a new key, he rushes to the right house and embraces his girl, leaving their own "silhouettes on the shade."

"For Your Precious Love"

"For Your Precious Love," from 1958, was the only hit for the original incarnation of the Chicago-based **Impressions**, which featured the talents of Curtis Mayfield and lead singer **Jerry Butler**. "For Your Precious Love" is a beautifully haunting, dirge-like pledge of love, highlighted by the eyes-lifted gospel feel of Butler's emotional baritone and an ethereal wordless falsetto that seems suspended above the song's hushed accompaniment and the snail's paced arpeggiated guitar chords. Butler left the group and began a long and successful solo career in 1960 with "He Will Break Your Heart," while the Impressions veered toward a gospel-based sound with Mayfield in the lead on a string of great sixties soul classics, including "Gypsy Woman," "It's All Right" and "People Get Ready."

"Ten Commandments of Love"

Arpeggiated triplets (played one note at a time rather than as full chords) became the ballad backing of choice toward the end of the fifties, lending a more dignified and soulful feel to the proceedings. The guitar pattern of "For Your Precious Love" was echoed later in 1958 in "Try Me," a gospel-edged ballad from newcomer James Brown, and in the arpeggiated piano of "Ten Commandments of Love," which brought the Moonglows back to the charts three years after their crossover success with "Sincerely." The group was now called **Harvey & the Moonglows** and included a young Marvin Gaye, who would follow leader Harvey Fuqua to Motown a few years later. With a spoken Preacher Voice reciting love's Ten Commandments ("Thou Shalt Never Love Another," "Stand By Me All the While"...) in a solemn call-and-response with Fuqua's lead vocal, "Ten Commandments of Love" sounds like a Bible School lesson in teenage love—the final chapter of the book of "Earth Angel."

"Come Softly to Me"

The Fleetwoods created some of the most memorable slow-dance records of the fifties—records that seem forever suspended in the high school gym on Prom night. The white trio from Olympia, Washington, hit the charts in 1959 with "Come Softly to Me" and "Mr. Blue," featuring lead singer Gary Troxel backed by two angelic female voices. The self-penned "Come Softly to Me" begins with Troxel's clear-voiced tenor singing an impossibly polite set of doo-wop nonsense syllables, quickly joined by the sweetly chanted angelic refrain. The close-miked intimacy and tame but catchy rhythmic backing create an unpretentious charm that eluded the more contrived efforts of the "teen idol" era. "Mr. Blue" and other Fleetwoods efforts, such as "Graduation's Here" and "He's the Great Imposter," have a similar innocent sincerity that tempers the sickly-sweet wholesomeness of the voices and lyrics.

"16 Candles"

More and more white groups embraced the doo-wop sound and turned the music in a more pop direction at the end of the fifties. Most came from Philadelphia or the New York area and most were of Italian-American descent: Danny & the Juniors, Dion & the Belmonts, the Four Seasons and other "Italo-American" rockers kept the streetcorner alive in the early sixties in both their ballad and uptempo styles. **The Crests'** "16 Candles," a hit in 1958, speaks directly to the era's longing innocence and has been one of the more durable and oft-revived ballads of the doo-wop era. The Crests' were an integrated group of New Yorkers— blacks and Puerto Ricans—fronted by lead singer Johnny Maestro (Mastrangelo). Maestro led the Crests through another hit, "Step By Step," in 1960, and later fronted the Brooklyn Bridge on their 1969 hit, "The Worst That Could Happen."

"Where or When"

While "16 Candles" retained the freshness and immediacy of doo-wop, other recordings by both white and black artists were leaving the streetcorner behind and moving in a more mainstream direction. After a string of great uptempo hits, **Dion & the Belmonts** had the biggest hit of their career in 1960 with an earnest reading of Rodgers & Hart's "Where or When," one of many pop ballads of the late fifties that didn't seem far removed from the type of music rock & roll had originally rebelled against. Others included the Platters' "Smoke Gets in Your Eyes" and "Twilight Time," and Tommy Edwards' "It's All in the Game," which was originally recorded in 1951. That a pop song from 1951 could become a "rock & roll" hit seven years later says much about the direction rock was heading as the 1960's approached. As the "threat" of rock & roll receded, old songs were revived and most new ones were cleansed of the sensuality that had been the undercurrent of doo-wop's romantic yearning. Songs like the Tempos' "See You in September" wouldn't raise your parents' eyebrows, much less ire, though they surely made old Little Richard fans reel in horror.

"Since I Don't Have You"

While some pop ballads looked backward for inspiration, others reacted to the changing times and tastes with a forward-looking sophistication that moved away from the amateurism of early doo-wop without sacrificing its heart and vitality. Little Anthony & the Imperials' 1958 hit, "Tears on My Pillow," was a signpost of the new direction, but it was **The Skyliners**, a group of white teenagers from Pittsburgh, who officially ushered in a new era in 1959 with "Since I Don't Have You," which featured the first orchestral arrangement on a "doo-wop" record (if that term could still apply to a record this lush). "Since I Don't Have You" also featured one of the blackest sounding records to come from a white group: lead singer Jimmy Beaumont turned in a nicely polished version of a streetcorner lead that soars into falsetto for the final verse and avoids the vibratoed crooning style one might have expected over such a glossy arrangement. Written by the group, the song is drenched in echo and embellished with soaring string and woodwind lines that play against the piano triplets and walrus bass and manage, somehow, to sound entirely appropriate.

"I Only Have Eyes for You"

The Flamingos' version of "I Only Have Eyes for You," a timelessly romantic pop standard, was an even more advanced production. A lush, heavily-echoed vocal arrangement and a smoky nightclub accompaniment heightens the sensual urgency of the song's lyrics and achingly slow tempo. Even the piano triplets and the rapid-fire "doowopshabop"'s from the background singers sound classy in this context. The familiar tune and Nate Nelson's silky-smooth lead singing helped to make the unmistakably "black" recording accessible to pop ears in a manner reminiscent of the Orioles' "Crying in the Chapel." "I Only Have Eyes for You" was a hauntingly romantic masterpiece for the car radio that, in 1959, seemed both rooted in a pop's past and stunningly modern. (The Flamingos actually had a history of eerie productions dating back to their first R&B hit, "I'll Be Home," which was a strange mix of pop, R&B and country blended with a dramatically reverberated lead vocal. The record was covered by Pat Boone, who didn't sound strange at all.)

"I Only Have Eyes for You" was produced by Richard Barrett for George Goldner's End label. The Goldner/Barrett team was directly responsible for many of the seminal doo-wop hits of the fifties, including hits by the Crows, Harptones, Cleftones, Frankie Lymon & the Teenagers, the Dubs, Little Anthony & the Imperials, the Flamingos, and the Chantels—records that helped usher in, define and finally expand doo-wop's boundaries. With the Chantels' "Maybe," they helped lay the foundations for "girl group" pop, while "Tears on My Pillow" and "I Only Have Eyes for You" looked ahead to "Uptown R&B"—the sophisticated doo-wop offshoot, perfected in Leiber & Stoller's Drifters productions, that reshaped rhythm & blues and formed a bridge between fifties R&B and sixties soul.

UPTEMPO DOO-WOP

"Speedo"

The uptempo, dance-driven "Speedo," a 1955 hit for **The Cadillacs**, was the stylistic flipside of the doo-wop ballads, including the Cadillacs' own 1954 R&B hit "Gloria," which features lead singer Earl Carroll in a dramatically different and equally effective setting. (Once the bird names had been exhausted, cars became the inspiration of choice for group names, and the Cadillacs quickly grabbed the best.) Fronted by Carroll, the Cadillacs were actually closer to the older R&B group tradition than to "doo-wop," with sexier lyrics, a bluesier singing style, a more integrated mix of voices and instruments and a jazzier arrangement with a prominent saxophone solo. Urged on by a frantic backbeat and an elaborate vocal accompaniment, "Mr. Earl" brags of his exploits and his unfailing ability to get pretty women to "change their minds." (While Carroll struts in the spotlight, the record is really driven by an active and agile bass voice, doubled effectively by the string bass and piano.) The Cadillacs were one of the flashiest and most visually-oriented groups of the fifties, always dressed to kill and ready with a perfectly-synced dance routine. Although they never equaled the success of "Speedo," and lost Earl Carroll to the Coasters in 1961, the group continued performing and recording into the sixties and was a major influence on the choreographed style of other groups, most notably the Temptations and their fellow Motown acts.

"Come and Go With Me"

Formed by group of servicemen when all were stationed in a Pittsburgh Air Force base, **The Dell-Vikings** were the first racially integrated doo-wop group to make the charts. After the group won a local talent contest in 1957, they recorded "Come and Go With Me" in a hotel room—with the singers standing in a closet(!) The song's lively party atmosphere captures the spirit of carefree fun at the core of fifties rock & roll: it's easy to imagine a group of singers and players crammed into a hotel room with a single microphone set up to record the festivities. "Come and Go With Me" captures the streetcorner feel of earlier doo-wop records, but the ever-so-earnest presentation of "Earth Angel" and the vocal virtuosity of Frankie Lymon is discarded in favor of a ragged but infectious singalong pop sound and a slightly tongue-in-cheek delivery that tosses off nonsense syllables and the song's lyrics with equal nonchalance. The Dell-Vikings followed "Come and Go With Me" with "Whispering Bells," another Top Ten hit which features a similarly memorable melody and a sparkling arrangement propelled by an appropriately bell-like guitar line. The group then moved up to the Mercury label, scored a hit with "Cool Shake" and promptly vanished into the rock's Bermuda Triangle, resurfacing years later with their fellow doo-wop ghosts at rock revival shows.

"Get a Job"

Two of the all-time great "streetcorner" one-shots were released in 1958: "Get a Job," a surprise #1 hit for **The Silhouettes** (a group name inspired by the Rays' hit song) and "Book of Love" by the Monotones—an apt name inspired by the groups' formidable lack of vocal talent. "Get a Job" details a man's exasperation with his nagging woman, who's always "preachin' and a-cryin'" about him finding a job. While the subject itself is rather "adult," the record is pure artless rock: the lyrics are treated humorously and the lead vocals are surrounded and rendered all but incidental by great, whacked-out background "vocals"—"yip yip yip yip yip yip yip yip, bom bom bom bom bom bom get a job, *Sha*-na na na, *Sha*-na na-na nah..."—that render the title line and the woman's demands as nonsensical as the rest of the clatter. The backing band sounds as pleasantly drunk and ragged as the singers: they barely hang together through the sax solo and drop out altogether for the drums-and-voices break ("I better go back to the house...") that snaps the song back into focus before it starts to crumble into an inspired mess again. The Silhouettes followed "Get a Job" with "Heading for the Poor House" a minor and prophetic hit.

"Book of Love"

The Monotones' "Book of Love" has an aggravatingly catchy refrain that is repeated seven times in the course of the short song, interrupted every time by a thud that makes no sense and seems perfect. The memorable "thud" from the bass drum was actually the result of a happy accident: while the group was rehearsing the song, a kid playing outside threw a ball at the window of the rehearsal room at just the right moment. Monotone Charles Patrick: "That ball hit the window, 'BOOM,' and we played back the tape and we heard this here sound, so we kept it and wrote it in as the drum part. That's what sold the record!" Thus inspired, the group built the song around the refrain and a bridge section that uses drum beats as the sole accompaniment ("chapter one says you love her..."), both punctuated by stops and starts that are balanced in brief verses that let the band stretch out. The loose, wax-party feel of "Book of Love," highlighted by bass singer John Raynes' comically nasal voice, made it a fun and funny hit, and one of the last of the original breed of no-frills streetcorner doo-wop.

"Little Darlin'"

The Diamonds, from Toronto, were the first successful all-white doo-wop group. They recorded for a major label, Mercury Records, and followed the established major label pattern of covering black artists. In contrast to earlier cover artists, though, the Diamonds remained faithful to the music and spirit of the originals and added their own happy, slightly loopy enthusiasm. Their good-natured refusal to take themselves or their music too seriously put them squarely in the best of doo-wop tradition. Their first successful venture was a cover of "Why Do Fools Fall in Love" in 1956, but the following year's cover of The Gladiolas' "Little Darling" was their biggest and most enduring hit.

"Little Darlin'" cashed in on a craze for Caribbean-flavored **calypso** music that swept the nation in 1957, to the delight of music industry heads who saw it as a long-overdue replacement for the more unwieldy rock & roll "fad." Popularized by Harry Belafonte's "Banana Boat (Day-O)," calypso never managed to replace rock & roll, though it did echo in the "islands" feel of songs like Mickey & Sylvia's "Love is Strange," Chuck Berry's "Havana Moon," Bo Diddley's comic "Cracking Up" and the Diamonds' "Little Darling."

"Little Darlin'" was written by 15-year-old Maurice Williams and recorded by his group, the Gladiolas, with chopped lyrics, castanets, cowbells and a rhumba beat, all aimed at cashing in on the calypso boom. The Diamonds' playful, self-mocking cover plays up the calypso beat and exaggerates the melodrama of the lyrics and spoken bass soliloquy to disarmingly comic effect—poking fun, it seems, at the very notion of a white group singing doo-wop. The record also exaggerated and popularized the shrill falsetto style that would dominate early sixties pop. (Maurice Williams & the Gladiolas, renamed the "Zodiacs," popularized it still further with "Stay," a #1 hit in 1960.)

"At the Hop"

In contrast to the fun, winking approach of the Diamonds, the music of the other leading white group of 1957-58, **Danny & the Juniors**, sounds a bit glossy and contrived. The Philadelphia natives were at the top of the charts as 1957 ended with "At the Hop," a spirited but formulized version of doo-wop that was carefully crafted in the studio and written with self-consciously "teen" lyrics. The record helped establish the style of pre-processed pop that made Philadelphia the "teen idol" capitol of the music industry. Originally entitled "Do the Bop," after a local dance step, the title was changed at the suggestion of Dick Clark, who received partial songwriting credits (and royalties) for his efforts. Not surprisingly, Clark plugged the record and booked Danny & the Juniors on his Philadelphia-based *American Bandstand* television show, virtually guaranteeing that it would be a hit. The group hit again in 1958 with "Rock & Roll Is Here to Stay," a curiously flat celebration of rock & roll (and an ironic one at that, since it came from the Philadelphia "production line" that would nearly kill the music off in the early sixties). Danny & the Juniors continued performing and recording into the early sixties, then regrouped a decade later on the revival circuit. Lead singer Danny Rapp committed suicide in 1983. The group's saxophonist, Lenny Baker, was a founding member of Sha Na Na, the cartoonish group formed in the late sixties that was based on the Danny & the Juniors style and did much to advance the unfortunate stereotype of fifties rock & roll as mindless "greaser" music.

"Teenager in Love"

The best of the white groups retained rock & roll's spirited directness, if not its hard beat and rebellious tone. **Dion & the Belmonts**, the premier white group of the late fifties, emerged from the Bronx and launched their career in 1958 with "I Wonder Why," a blast of pure streetcorner bliss that presents a full-ranged layer of voices—walrus bass to falsetto shriek—officially claiming doo-wop for the Italian-American neighborhoods. The group hit full stride the following year with "Teenager in Love," written by the prolific team of Doc Pomus and Mort Schuman and brought to life by Dion

Demucci's distinctive, piercing voice. The midtempo teen-love lament was originally conceived as "It's Great To Be Young and in Love." Pomus and Schuman changed the title and lyrics to better reflect the true experience of a love-struck teenager ("Why must I be a teenager in love...?"), and achieved an effective balance between melodrama and streetcorner realism. The balance shifted away from the streets in Dion & the Belmonts' next hit, "Where or When," and in their further travels down the old chestnut road in their renditions of "When You Wish Upon a Star" and the Five Satins' "In the Still of the Night" (now an "old chestnut" itself).   Dion left the Belmonts and revived his rock & roll energies in 1960, though "Runaround Sue," "The Wanderer" and "Lovers Who Wander" and his other solo hits remained rooted in the streetcorner group style.

The Early Sixties and "Neo-Doo-Wop"

Although classic doo-wop, like classic rock & roll, disappeared with the 1950's, vocal group styles continued to play a large role in shaping popular music in the new decade. Many new groups, like the Impressions and the Isley Brothers ("Shout," "Twist & Shout"), infused their sound with a heavy dose of gospel styles that linked them to the "soul" movement that was shaping a new era in black popular music. In Detroit, Motown Records perfected a pop-oriented brand of soul built largely around the vocal group interaction, while on the West Coast Phil Spector perfected his pop vision and turned girl group rock—a doo-wop sibling — into one of the high points of the pre-Beatles era. White pop-rock styles of the early sixties continued to incorporate many doo-wop elements as well: the Beach Boys, Jan & Dean and other "surf" rockers layered elaborate group harmonies on top of Chuck Berry guitar rock, while the Four Seasons, Del Shannon, Neil Sedaka, Dion, Jay & the Americans and other early sixties stars built on doo-wop vocal styles—particularly falsetto singing—to create their own brand of streetcorner pop. Even the Beatles could count doo-wop among their many influences: they performed three Coasters songs at their first recording audition and often looked to fifties vocal groups and early sixties girl groups as models for utilizing several voices rather than a single lead singer.

While the influence of group styles was helping to shape a new era, the early sixties also saw a "neo-doo-wop" revival of the sound of the Good Old Days. **Little Caesar & the Romans** tapped into rock's first nostalgia craze with 1961's **"Those Oldies but Goodies (Remind Me of You),"** a sentimental ballad with a deliberately "fifties" sound invoked by the doo-wop chord progression, piano triplets and doo-wop vocal styles, complete with a spoken interlude, walrus bass and falsetto ending. The wistful lyrics summon up the innocence of those younger, "simpler" times and forever link the special songs—now "oldies"—with the memory of that special Girl.

Most neo-doo-wop was uptempo and fun, paralleling the dance crazes launched by the "The Twist." **The Marcels** hit the top of the charts in 1961 with a rapid-fire assault on "**Blue Moon**" that would have left composers Rodgers & Hart gasping in disbelief. ("Bom-baba-bom, da-Dang-a-dang-dang, da-Ding-a-dong-ding Blue Moon, Blue Moon, Blue Moon, dip-a-doot-a-doo..."), while **The Tokens** followed the same year with "**The Lion Sleeps Tonight**," a rewrite of a South African folk song, "Wimoweh," that had been popularized by the folk group the Weavers. The record's lilting falsetto lead appealed to pop listeners while the romanticized "native" sound and lyrics tapped into folk music's resurgent popularity and a fad for "exotic" music reminiscent of the Calypso boom.

Other "neo-doo-wop" highlights included Maurice Williams & the Zodiacs' "Stay," the Edsels' "Rama Lama Ding Dong," the Dovells' "Bristol Stomp," the Cleftones' version of "Heart and Soul," the Jive Five's "My True Story," the cartoon character novelty number "Alley-Oop" by the Hollywood Argyles, and "Denise" by Randy & the Romantics, the most blissfully mindless and irresistible love pledge of the era. Brill Building writer Barry Mann recorded his own tribute to romantic power of doo-wop in "Who Put the Bomp (in the Bomp, Bomp, Bomp)," and the Regents' "Barbara Ann" replaced Buddy Holly's Peggy Sue as the ideal rock & roll woman. The elegant Gene Chandler, working with Chicago producer Carl Davis, proclaimed himself the "Duke of Earl" in a inspired mixture of fifties doo-wop and sixties pop, while the Rivingtons brought nonsense syllables to breathtakingly absurd heights in "Papa-Oom-Mow-Mow," "Mama-Oom-Mow-Mow" and "The Bird's the Word."

The Trashmen, a landlocked surf band from Minneapolis, combined all of the Rivingtons' hits and came up with the wonderfully outrageous "Surfin' Bird." Released at the end of 1963, "Surfin' Bird" peaked at #4 on the charts on February 2, 1964. The number one spot that week was held down by "I Want to Hold Your Hand," the first American hit for an entirely new type of "group." A new era had begun, and doo-wop, like nearly all else that had gone before, was officially pronounced dead, though the best of the records and many of the musical aspects of the style lived on and influenced later artists. Periodic "revival" concerts began in the late sixties and continue to bring old and new fans together to celebrate the joys of the music where human voices reigned supreme, and to give many of the old—but ageless—"one-shots" another brief moment in the spotlight.

LEIBER & STOLLER AT ATLANTIC RECORDS

Jerry Leiber and Mike Stoller formed the great songwriting and production team of the fifties: a Rodgers and Hart for the rock & roll era who updated Tin Pan Alley and paved the way for the Brill Building writers and Phil Spector productions of the early sixties. Leiber and Stoller wrote hits for a wide range of artists in a wide range of styles, but are best known for their songs for Elvis Presley ("Hound Dog," "Jailhouse Rock," "Loving You," "Love Me," "Treat Me Nice") and their songwriting and production efforts for two Atlantic groups: the Coasters and the Drifters, Atlantic Record's biggest selling acts of the fifties and early sixties. While their Presley hits naturally took on the star's aura and personality, their work at Atlantic bore a more personal stamp and were more a reflection of *their* artistic vision than of that of the singers. Their recordings with the **Coasters** and the **Drifters** can hardly be called "doo-wop" in any strict sense of the term: the carefully crafted arrangements and productions placed the Coasters on a wholly different level from the streetcorner "one-shots" and made a new term—"Uptown R&B"—necessary for describing the Drifters' music.

Leiber and Stoller (both born in 1933) began writing together as teenagers in Los Angeles and had a string of R&B successes to their credit by the time they were 21, including Little Willie Littlefield's "K. C. Lovin'" (later famous as "Kansas City") and Willie Mae "Big Mama" Thornton's original recording of "Hound Dog," a song they wrote and produced with Johnny Otis. The pair shared a love for rhythm & blues and a streetwise knowledge of black culture that set them apart from their peers. They were among the first white writers to compose "authentic" rhythm & blues and, in the process, they helped expand R&B's range by incorporating a pop-style emphasis on melody and song construction.

Leiber and Stoller combined the songwriting (Leiber wrote the words, Stoller the music), arranging, producing and A&R roles usually assigned to different people within the traditional Tin Pan Alley hierarchy. They further revolutionized the music business by establishing themselves as independent producers not tied to a single record label and fully in command of their material from the original song conception to the completed recording, a move they felt was necessary after several frustrating experiences with producers who did not share their vision or talent. (Mike Stoller: "We found that if we wrote a piece that was to be played as a Texas shuffle, for example, it would more than likely end up sounding like some Mickey Mouse swing record if we weren't there to supervise. And so we became record producers in self-defense."[3])

THE COASTERS

After recording "Hound Dog," Leiber and Stoller launched their own Spark record label with industry veteran Lester Sill, and began focusing their attention on a Los Angeles group called the Robins who had been working under the tutelage of bandleader Johnny Otis. Their 1954 recording of "**Riot in Cell Block #9**" introduced Leiber and Stoller's story-song style of writing they called "**playlets**": tongue-in-cheek mini-dramas full of wit and insight, in this case revolving around a prison riot, complete with police sirens and tommy guns, a mock-menacing lead vocal and a gleefully anarchic chorus of "there's a riot goin' on!"[4] The music sounds like a *Dragnet* send-up and the lyrics read like a TV crime thriller told through the eyes of a hard-boiled narrator, rife with details and condensed to two-and-a-half minutes. The wailing saxophone and hard-driving R&B band accompaniment lifts the song out of the realm of "mere novelty," while the jive talk and prison setting give it a hint of social realism.

The Robins' Spark recordings caught the attention of Atlantic Records' Jerry Wexler: "They were making great R&B records, very idiomatic records. Not only did the records have intelligent production, they were in tune, had a good beat and were properly balanced. And the songs also had great penetration, social understanding—their music had real roots."[5] Atlantic bought the Spark masters, signed the Robins to their Atco subsidiary in 1956 and offered Leiber and Stoller a generous contract that left them free to work with other labels and groups. Atlantic re-released one of the last Spark recordings, "Smokey Joe's Cafe," and the Robins had a national hit on the R&B charts.

The move to Atlantic caused some dissension within the band, which ended with two members and the group manager leaving, taking the "Robins" name with them. Lead tenor Carl Gardner remained, along with bass singer Bobby Nunn; second tenor Leon Hughes and baritone Billy Guy were added and the group christened themselves "the Coasters" in tribute to their West Coast home. The Coasters scored a succession of R&B hits before finally breaking into the pop charts in 1957 with "Searchin'" and "Young Blood." "Young Blood" is a slice of urban life that mixes streetcorner R&B and pop tunefulness and utilizes the full range of contrasting voices and the comic touches that made the Coasters the clown princes of rock & roll.

In "**Searchin'**," lead singer Billy Guy is bent on pursuing his dream girl with the tenacity of Sherlock Holmes, Sam Spade, Sgt. Friday, Charlie Chan, Boston Blackie, a Northwest Mountie and Bulldog Drummond all put together, even if he has to swim a river or climb a mountain—even if she's "hiding up on Blueberry Hill." The song lopes along with a novelty-esque honky-tonk feel from the instrumental backing and a constant refrain of "gonna find her" that clashes incessantly against Guy's lyrics and adds to the comically plodding feel of the song. With the inclusion of figures from popular novels, television and radio shows, Leiber and Stoller placed rock & roll firmly in the noble tradition of American popular culture. Indeed, the Coasters' playlets were like regular installments of a situation comedy, with entertaining plots and a colorful cast of characters.

"**Along Came Jones**" is a comic send-up of the predictability of TV Westerns, starring a generic hero who always arrives in the nick of time to save the damsel in distress from the evil villain. The innocuous novelty number was first conceived with a more satirical subtext, though the original lyrics were rewritten with the sensibilities of pop radio stations in mind. Jerry Leiber: "It *was* a satire on Western movies on television, and there was a picture with Gary Cooper called "Along Came Jones." But originally it was written much more heavy-handed than it came out. The original joke in it was that here are four black cats singing about a hero—a white cowboy—who keeps saving people. Originally, the refrain was different: it had to do with 'Ain't he some kind of special cat/He was wearin' white boots/And he was a-wearin' a white hat, riding a white horse.' Everything was white."[6]

"Yakety Yak"

With the arrival of rock & roll and the emergence of the "teenager" as a distinct social class, the subtext of most of Leiber and Stoller's material—the "us" against "them"— changed from a racial to a generational conflict, still set in a disarmingly humorous vein. The Coasters and Leiber and Stoller kicked off their teen vignettes with 1958's **"Yakety Yak,"** the group's only #1 pop hit and the first pop #1 for Atlantic Records. "Yakety Yak" chronicles the endless struggle with nagging parents in terms that any teenager can understand:

> Take out the papers and the trash
> Or you don't get no spendin' cash
> If you don't scrub that kitchen floor
> You ain't gonna rock & roll no more
> Yakety Yak—Don't talk back!
>
> Just finish cleanin' up your room
> Let's see that dust fly with that broom
> Get all that garbage out of sight
> Or you don't go out Friday night
> Yakety Yak—Don't talk back!
>
> You just put on your coat and hat
> And walk yourself to the laundromat
> And when you finish doin' that
> Bring in the dog and put out the cat
> Yakety Yak—Don't Talk Back!
>
> Don't you give me no dirty looks
> Your father's hip, he knows what cooks
> Just tell your hoodlum friends outside
> You ain't got time to take a ride
> Yakety Yak—Don't Talk Back![7]

"Yakety Yak" is a great illustration of Jerry Leiber's wit, eye for detail and deceptively simple lyrics. His laundry list of teenage complaints transcends social and racial barriers and focuses on the true enemy: parents. Mike Stoller's piano, banjo and brushed drum accompaniment gives "Yakety

Yak" a comic, novelty tone and Dixieland flavor. Stops and starts break up the beat and the stern "don't talk back" from the Voice of Authority (an effect echoed a few months later in Eddie Cochran's "Summertime Blues"). The stop-starts and nagging title refrain, embellished by a clucking saxophone solo, form an effective musical picture of badgering parents and the frustrated quest for a good time.

"Why is Everybody Always Picking On Me?"

With "Yakety Yak" the Coasters and Leiber and Stoller moved their operations from Los Angeles to Atlantic's New York studios, where they could take advantage of Atlantic's stellar house band, most notably saxophonist **King Curtis**, whose stuttering "yakety sax" solos became a regular feature of the Coasters' songs. The move to New York also brought about another change in the group line-up, with Cornell Gunter replacing Leon Hughes and Will "Dub" Jones taking over the comic bass role, which he used to great effect on "Yakety Yak" and its sequel, **"Charlie Brown,"** where he supplies poor Charlie's bewildered refrain of "Why is everybody always pickin' on me?" Here we follow the victimized teenager to school, where his problems with authority continue unabated. A well-meaning but chronic troublemaker, Charlie Brown does manage to gain his classmates' grudging admiration along the way to his Fall. After all, it's hard to not admire a guy who smokes in the auditorium, gambles in the gym, writes on the walls and calls the English teacher "Daddy-o."

Leiber and Stoller's work as producers was as important as their contributions as songwriters. The comic flavor of the Coasters' recordings inspired sound effects, studio "tricks" (such as the sped-up "chipmunk" voices and exaggerated echo on "Charlie Brown") and clever arrangements that were an integral part of the song, rather than a mere backing for the voices. The voices, too, were arranged in a unique way, with lots of unison singing juxtaposed with elaborate harmonies, and with a distinct style and range assigned to each voice to emphasize the different "characters" in the playlets. Leiber and Stoller's inventive productions were far ahead of their time and, along with Buddy Holly's studio experiments, pointed toward the sixties view of the studio itself as a creative tool. Atlantic Record's open atmosphere, first-rate musicians and commitment to quality records made it an ideal working environment for the creative pair.

Leiber and Stoller kept turning out pop and R&B hits for the Coasters through the late fifties, including the wonderful Latin-tinged **"Poison Ivy,"** which pivots around a band halt and a single, inexplicably perfect guitar note. The lyrics have a delightful, teasing sexuality: "Poison Ivy" is a woman who comes creepin' while you're sleepin', though the Coasters warn that "you can look but you'd better not touch." (The song inspired some creative interpretations—does she really have VD?) In any case, Leiber and Stoller offer a remedy in one of rock's greatest couplets: "You're gonna need an ocean of Calamine lotion."

The Coasters scored their last pop hit in 1961 with "Little Egypt." The group went through an unending series of personnel shifts (former Cadillacs frontman Earl Carroll joined in 1961) and continued working sporadically with Leiber and Stoller through the sixties and into the seventies. They made a minor comeback in 1971 with a revival of the Clover's 1959 hit, "Love Potion #9" (which was also written by Leiber and Stoller). Various incarnations of the Coasters remain popular attractions on the rock revival circuit, where the fun and humor of their songs and stage act epitomize the spirit of vocal group rock & roll.

THE DRIFTERS AND "UPTOWN R&B"

"Uptown R&B" was the most inventive and significant manifestation of the trend at the end of the fifties toward softened beats and elaborate arrangements. The highly-produced and polished sound of "Since I Don't Have You," "I Only Have Eyes for You" and other sophisticated vocal group recordings took doo-wop's emphasis on the Song over the Singer a step further and emphasized the *Record* above the Song—declared the Record an entity in itself (not merely a recorded performance), and established the producers as the true creative forces in the studio. As perfected in Leiber and Stoller's productions for the Drifters, Uptown R&B embraced the new trends towards elaborate productions without sacrificing R&B's direct emotion and rhythmic vitality. Leiber and Stoller's productions reflected their "voice" more than that of the artists whose names appeared on the record label, beginning a process that climaxed with the early sixties recordings of Phil Spector, who served an "apprenticeship" with Leiber and Stoller before heading off on his own and completing the picture of the all-powerful Producer.

Through their work with the Coasters, Leiber and Stoller established the concept of songwriters and producers as "auteurs" who left their personal stamp on a body of work and created a sustained musical vision over a period of time and a series of record releases. The comic style of the Coasters recordings lent itself to novel productions that enhanced the plot and narrative of the songs. When Leiber and Stoller turned their attention to more "serious" productions for the Drifters, they crafted a high-tech production style that enhanced the drama, romance and urban realism of the Drifters' songs. (It is interesting to note that Leiber and Stoller didn't feel comfortable writing in the sweeping, romantic style that best fit the Drifters; the songs they produced for the group were written by others and were very different from Leiber and Stoller's humorous "playlet" style.)

The Drifters at Atlantic

The "Drifters" who produced sixteen Top Forty pop hits between 1959 and 1964 were a completely different group from the original Drifters fronted by ex-Dominoes lead **Clyde McPhatter**. After McPhatter's induction into the army in 1954, the group went through a series of personnel changes and a number of lead singers—the most notable of which was **Johnny Moore**, who sang lead on "Ruby Baby," "Fools Fall in Love" and other R&B hits from the mid-fifties, then returned again as lead singer nearly a decade later. In 1958, personal frictions and declining popularity led manager George Treadwell to fire the entire group and replace them with a new set of "Drifters" pulled from a local New York group called the Five Crowns. The new group featured lead singer Benjamin Nelson, who adopted the name Ben E. King and revived the gospel influences that had been Clyde McPhatter's trademark. The "new" Drifters also picked up the old group's habit of changing members periodically: along with a constantly shifting group of background singers, the 1959-64 era Drifters featured the talents of three great lead singers: Ben E. King, Rudy Lewis and Johnny Moore.

The Ben E. King Era

"There Goes My Baby" was the first hit for the new incarnation of the Drifters. Written by Ben E. King and recorded in March 1959, "There Goes My Baby" is often referred to as "the first rock record with strings," though it was actually preceded by string-laden recordings by Buddy Holly, the Skyliners, the Moonglows and others. It *was*, however, the first to lift the strings beyond the syrupy, generic "heavenly violins" sound and treat them as a vital part of an integrated arrangement, rather than merely as "sweetener." "Integrated arrangement" is stretching things a bit in this case, though: "There Goes My Baby" is a confused mess of clashing notes and rhythms that somehow holds together in spite of itself. (Jerry Leiber has often remarked that it sounds like two radio stations playing at once.) The doo-wopish walrus bass and chanted syllables that open the song sound familiar enough, but the rest of the record is a bizarre and mesmerizing free-for-all.

Leiber and Stoller used a distinctive stop-start Brazilian rhythm called a **"baion"** for the basic beat of "There Goes My Baby" and many subsequent Drifters productions. The baion is articulated by the bass and "drums" (timpani) and forms a murky, rhythmic rumbling beneath the more regular, on-the-beat rhythmic feel of the strings. While the strings' rhythm fights it out with the baion, their notes seem to clash with the voices, as if no one can quite agree on what key or tempo the song is in or where it's supposed to be going. To make matters even more interesting, the tympani are out of tune, clashing with everyone. The song is based on the standard I-vi-IV-V doo-wop progression, though no one seems too clear about that either, and the mind-numbing amount of echo added to everything creates an impressionistic atmosphere in which chords, notes and rhythms seem merely evoked or implied.

The lyrics seem impressionistic as well: Ben E. King's plaintive lead vocal rides atop the glorious musical mess, pining for his woman and reeling from the shock of her leaving, too upset to try to rhyme his words or follow any kind of logical song form. All he can do is grieve and wonder: "Where is she bound?" "What can I do?" "Why did she leave me?" "Did she really love me?" "Where is my baby? I want my baby." "There Goes My baby" is a free-form expression of anguish that the confused musical background serves to intensify: like the music, the self-tormenting singer seems ready to come unglued. His sorrow is unrelieved as the song fades and the mantra-like title refrain returns, behind King's moans, to freeze the moment in time like a snapshot of his woman walking away.

"This Magic Moment" was written for the Drifters in 1960 by the team of Doc Pomus and Mort Schuman. The song opens with a flamboyant flourish from the violins (quite a contrast to the raucous saxophones of traditional R&B) and features a now thoroughly integrated mix of instruments and voices and a cohesive baion rhythmic undercurrent. In the song's most dramatic moment, the orchestra and other auxiliary instruments and voices drop out, leaving Ben E. King suddenly alone ("sweeter than wine...") with a simple guitar and bass accompaniment that seems to transport the song into a folk music coffee house until the background voices return and the music swells upward again. Pomus and Schuman also wrote the Drifters' biggest hit, "Save the Last Dance for Me," for which Pomus wrote an intentional awkwardness into the words in order to create the effect of a literal English translation of a Spanish song, in tribute to the pervading Latin flavor of the Drifters' records.

"Save the Last Dance for Me" was the last Drifters record to feature Ben E. King. He embarked on a successful solo career in 1960 with "Spanish Harlem," written by Jerry Leiber and Phil Spector and produced by Leiber and Stoller in a style very similar to their Drifters work, with a baion rhythm and a Latin feel appropriate for the song's setting. King had his biggest hit in 1961 with the ever-popular **"Stand By Me,"** a secular re-write of the Soul Stirrers' "Stand By Me Father." The immediately recognizable bass figure that opens the song is doubled by the strings to form a stark backdrop to King's "testifying" lead vocal. In the tradition of the Clyde McPhatter and Ray Charles' gospel borrowings, King sings to the Woman with the same devotional feel reserved for the Lord in the gospel original (and the line between "R&B" and gospel-based "soul" is effectively crossed).

The Rudy Lewis Era

The Drifters continued on as Atlantic's biggest selling act with new lead singer Rudy Lewis, who proved himself an able replacement for King with "Some Kind of Wonderful" and "Up on the Roof," which were both written by

Brill Building luminaries Gerry Goffin and Carole King. Like most of the group's hits, "**Up on the Roof**" is set in the city and reflects an urban sensibility in its lyrics and in the classy sound of its high-tech "uptown" production. Recorded in 1962, "Up On the Roof" takes a romantic view of a plain city rooftop and transforms it into a private paradise far removed from the troubles of the world below. The song's elegant lyrics are complemented by an equally elegant production that blends strings, brass, marimbas, various percussion instruments and a full battery of guitars, bass and drums into a seamless orchestral arrangement.

The Drifters moved further uptown in 1963 with "**On Broadway**," a more mainstream production featuring Rudy Lewis lamenting the tough times and broken dreams on Broadway, then defiantly reaffirming the dream anyway ("I won't quit till I'm a star"). The syncopated beat, the hypnotic, seesawing chords and the intricate melody of the song created a jazzy feel that reached beyond the teen audience and inspired numerous cover versions in a wide range of styles. The Drifters' original features a very strange guitar solo, played by Phil Spector, that cuts through the lush string sound to keep the song rooted in rock & roll.

Johnny Moore Returns

The Drifters had their last hit in 1964 with "**Under the Boardwalk**." By that time, Leiber and Stoller were devoting themselves to their new Red Bird record label and the production duties for the Drifters were handled by veteran producer and songwriter **Bert Berns**. Berns continued the Drifters' tradition of sophisticated productions with an undercurrent of Latin rhythms and a soulful feel.[8] The Drifters gave one of their most moving and emotional performances on "Under the Boardwalk," inspired and heartbroken by the sudden death of Rudy Lewis on the morning of the recording session. Group veteran Johnny Moore stepped in to sing lead in Lewis' place and delivered a supremely melancholy performance that belies the song's upbeat lyrics.

Moore continued as the lead singer through a series of minor hits in the mid-sixties before the group settled into the nightclub and oldies circuit. The 1964 British Invasion and Atlantic's shift to gritty, southern soul music brought an end to the era of Uptown R&B, though not before the Drifters' influence was felt on Motown, "Philly Soul" and other northern, pop-oriented soul styles.

Leiber and Stoller concentrated on girl groups (particularly the Shangri-Las and the Dixie Cups) with their Red Bird label, then gradually lost interest as a new type of sixties rock and soul took over. They sold their shares of the labels in 1966 and charted a more mainstream direction with "Is That All There Is," a hit for Peggy Lee. They remained at least casually connected to the rock world for some time, though, producing records for Stealer's Wheel ("Stuck in the Middle With You"), Procol Harum and others.

The witty songs and inventive productions of Leiber and Stoller's glory days lent an artful dignity to the process of recording and helped turn a piece of wax into something noble. As they were fond of saying, "We didn't write songs, we wrote *records*."

[1]Lymon's shoddy treatment continued long after his death as well. It took a quarter century for the surviving group members to receive any songwriting royalties for "Why Do Fools Fall in Love."

[2] Shannon and Javna, "Behind the Hits," (New York: Warner, 1986), p. 168.

[3]Robert Palmer, "Baby That Was Rock & Roll," (New York: Harvest, 1978)

[4]The lead vocals were sung by Richard Berry, who did not join in the group's Coasters incarnation , but did later write and record the original "Louie Louie."

[5]Palmer, p. 23.

[6]Shannon and Javna, "Behind the Hits," p. 121.

[7]"Yakety Yak," by Leiber and Stoller, Copyright c 1958 by Tiger Music, Inc.

[8] Berns was already a Latin music aficionado, albeit with a decidedly "garage band" slant: several of the songs he wrote, including "Twist and Shout" and "Hang On Sloopy," used and popularized what he called a "Latin American" or "La Bamba" chord progression.

Photo courtesy of UPI/BETTMAN NEWSPHOTOS

Ray Charles

[8] RHYTHM & BLUES AND THE PUSH TOWARD SOUL

"Rock & roll" was, at first, just another name for the rhythm & blues that was starting to reach a young white audience. The new name was used to obscure the music's black origins, but it became something of a self-fulfilling prophesy as the music itself began to change in recognition of that new audience. To varying degrees and in varying manners, R&B artists began tailoring their music and lyrics to the ears, dance steps and wallets of American teenagers while striving, at the same time, to maintain their core audience of older and more world-wise R&B fans.

Rhythm & blues" was as vague as most musical labels, broad enough to encompass soft Ink Spots ballads, jazzy jump-blues numbers and raucous rock precursors like "Rocket 88" and "Shake, Rattle and Roll." Ultimately it had little specific meaning beyond "music made by black artists for a black audience," and even that generalization was rendered inoperative by the new rock & roll fans (though the label "rhythm & blues" continued to be applied exclusively to black artists). The arrival of Elvis and the crossover success of black artists made the distinction between "rhythm & blues" and "rock & roll" difficult to define in terms of either audience or musical style. The most successful artists crafted personal styles that transcended musical boundaries, though the issue of "labeling" remained. Some, like Little Richard and Bo Diddley, felt that "rhythm & blues" had become a demeaning term and preferred the even racial footing of "rock & roll." Others, such as Fats Domino, proudly affirmed their musical and cultural roots by continuing to call their music "rhythm & blues," while still others echoed Chuck Berry's attitude of "Who cares as long as it sells?"

Records by black artists *did* sell in unprecedented numbers, though for all the doors that rock & roll helped open, it was still difficult for black artists to achieve the type of success that so many white acts enjoyed. Most recorded for small, independent labels (even established "indies" like Atlantic, Chess, Specialty, Imperial and King were dwarfed by the economic clout of the major labels) and depended on a core following in the R&B market to sustain their careers between scattered pop hits. As a whole, the doo-wop groups were most successful at making inroads into the rock & roll market, since the relative anonymity of the groups helped them overcome the racial barriers that made personal identification with a single black artist difficult (though few groups were able to sustain careers beyond a hit or two, since that type of identification was a central ingredient in rock's appeal).

Chuck Berry, Fats Domino and Little Richard were the only three black solo artists who gained a mass acceptance on a par with the era's white stars. All three projected images—Eternal Teenager, jolly fat man, raving lunatic—that helped to shift the focus and make their race a secondary issue. While none could rival that trio in terms of sustained popularity in the rock market, a steady stream of black singers and performers kept R&B in the pop charts through the 1950's.

Johnny Ace

Johnny Ace is better-known for his dramatic death than for his music, though his smooth and sensual style made him something of a heartthrob for his legions of female fans and would have served him well in the pop market had he survived into the rock & roll era. Ace came from Memphis and was a member of the "Beale Streeters," a loose band of Memphis blues luminaries that included Bobby "Blue" Bland, Junior Parker and B. B. King. After moving to Houston, Ace signed with Duke Records and launched an impressive string of R&B successes with 1952's "My Song." Despite his strong blues background, Ace specialized in romantic ballads in the Nat "King" Cole vein and was one of the last of the "sepia Sinatras" descended from Cole and Charles Brown's club blues style. The sensual Ace was something of a heartthrob for his legions of female fans. His rich baritone was used to best effect on "**Pledging My Love**," a straightforward pronouncement of love in a slow-dance tempo backed by a smooth supperclub sax & vibes accompaniment from the Johnny Otis Orchestra. "Pledging My Love" was a Top Twenty crossover hit in 1955, but Ace did not live to see the record's success. Intent on impressing a female friend, Ace shot himself in a game of Russian roulette and died backstage at the Houston City Auditorium on Christmas Eve 1954.

Wilbert Harrison

Wilbert Harrison had recorded since the early fifties without much success before his recording of Leiber and Stoller's "**Kansas City**" ambled its way to #1 in 1959, beating out five other simultaneously released versions of the same song. Originally recorded as "K. C. Lovin'" by Little Willie Littlefield in 1952, Harrison's definitive version is a "melodic blues" with a distinctive shuffle rhythm, a gentle boogie bass, a rock & roll guitar solo and an easygoing melody that glides between pop, blues and R&B. Harrison toured as a one-man band, playing guitar, piano, drums and harmonica, and remained a "one-hit wonder" for over a decade before returning to the charts in 1970 with his own "Let's Work Together," which was covered the same year by Canned Heat.

Etta James

Immortalized at 16 with "Roll With Me Henry," a 1955 "answer" to Hank Ballard & the Midnighters' "Work With Me Annie," Etta James made an easy transition from R&B to soul and developed a deeply personal singing and songwriting voice. James never caught on in a big way with the pop market, but she did score nine Top Forty hits that capped a twenty-year string of R&B hits. She worked with bandleader Johnny Otis on the Modern label in the fifties, then moved to Chicago in 1959 and signed with Chess Records, where she developed her gospel-inflected mature style. Her early sixties hits included "Something's Got a Hold On Me," "All I Could Do Was Cry" and "Pushover." After a fallow period in the mid-sixties, and a debilitating battle with heroin, James reemerged in 1967 in the southern soul capital, Muscle Shoals, Alabama, where she recorded the soul classic "I'd Rather Go Blind" and her biggest pop hit, **"Tell Mama."** "Tell Mama" was covered by Janis Joplin, who looked to Etta James as an influence and a contemporary link in the chain of strong black female voices dating back to Bessie Smith.

Screamin' Jay Hawkins

Screamin' Jay Hawkins earned a place among rock immortals with the strangest record of the fifties, his 1956 hit **"I Put a Spell On You,"** and with a bizarre stage act that featured human skulls, snakes, ghoulish vampire costumes and dramatic entrances in flaming coffins that sent the youngest fans fleeing in terror while, from the balcony, his stage crew dropped rubber bands on their heads and chanted "worms, worms." Hawkins recorded a string of flops on various small labels, including a restrained original version of "I Put a Spell On You," written when Hawkins' girlfriend left him in 1954, that caught the ear of Columbia Records head Arnold Matson, who signed Hawkins to Okeh Records, Columbia's R&B subsidiary.

A stellar backup band was assembled for a remake of "I Put a Spell on You" that could capture that frenzy of Hawkins' stage act. The session was disappointing and strangely subdued, however, until Hawkins finally admitted that his unhinged live style owed much to the fact that he was rarely sober onstage. A case of muscatel soon remedied the problem and inspired a truly demented performance from a blind-drunk Hawkins and an equally inebriated group of professional sessionmen now reduced to struggling to stay in tune, in time and out of fits of convulsive laughter.

The screams and groans that punctuate and finally consume "I Put a Spell on You" add up to a fit of recorded psychosis that is truer to the painful inspiration for the song than any "straight" reading could have been. The screams, the ominous minor key, the drunken simplicity of the arrangement and the sick, death-waltz tempo might have added up to a mere novelty record if Hawkins' lunacy hadn't seemed so disturbingly real. As it is, it stands as a testament to maniacal, possessive jealousy—and to the uninhibited expression inspired by recording on the edge of an alcohol blackout (Hawkins couldn't remember recording the song, and was surprised and horrified when he finally heard it).

"I Put a Spell on You" was too much for many radio stations, even with the sexual moans edited out of the end of the song. The record failed to crack the Top Forty, but it was an instant cult classic and kept Hawkins' vampirish stage act in hot demand. Hawkins eventually came to resent the freakish typecasting that locked him into the role of monstrous comic relief. Still, for an artist with only one hit, Screamin' Jay Hawkins has had quite an impact: he virtually invented the black comedy "rock theater" that inspired Arthur Brown, Screaming Lord Sutch, Alice Cooper, David Bowie and many others, though for sheer high-camp horror, the old master has never been equaled. As Hawkins himself put it, "I just torment a song—frighten it half to death."[1]

Little Willie John

Little Willie John was an important "proto-soul" singer who incorporated gospel's emotional delivery and helped expand R&B's musical vocabulary, though he never achieved the fame that his great voice and talent warranted. John's recordings for the Cincinnati-based King label had a profound influence on Sam Cooke, Jackie Wilson and many others, especially his King labelmate James Brown, who served as John's opening act on several tours. John had his first R&B hits in 1955 with "All Around the World," a jump blues dance number, and "Need Your Love So Bad," a sensuous, longing ballad that revealed the quiet intensity of John's softer style. The pained, pleading feel of "Need Your Love So Bad" was echoed in "Let Them Talk," "Person to Person," the great "Talk To Me, Talk To Me" and other songs that formed a virtual blueprint for later soul ballads.

John's best-known song and first crossover success was 1956's **"Fever,"** which was written by the ubiquitous Otis Blackwell (though he sold the copyright for $50). The smoky jazz arrangement and urgent sensuality of John's original "Fever" was rekindled two year's later in a hit version for Peggy Lee. John managed a final pair of pop hits in 1960 with "Heartbreak" and the Tin Pan Alley standard, "Sleep." His rock-styled "Leave My Kitten Alone" wasn't a hit but was a favorite of sixties British groups (including the Beatles, who recorded a great version that was never officially released).

Little Willie John shot and killed a man during a drunken argument in a Seattle bar in 1965, and died of pneumonia in prison in 1968. James Brown, who recorded a tribute album called *Thinking of Little Willie John and Other Nice Things*, recalls his friend and mentor: "Little Willie John was a soul singer before anyone thought to call it that... the man died young, died in prison. But the man left his mark. On my music, on lots of singers who understand how to sing with feelin'."[2]

ATLANTIC RECORDS

Atlantic Records was the premier R&B label of the 1950's and continued its preeminence in black music as the great soul music label the 1960's. Headed by Ahmet Ertegun, Atlantic set the standard for all other indies: they actually paid their performers fairly and took the time to craft creative, polished and well-recorded productions, drawing on the talents of a pool of seasoned New York session players and an inspired staff that included producers Jerry Wexler, engineer Tom Dowd and arranger Jesse Stone. Atlantic turned out some of the best R&B of the 1950's: Leiber & Stoller's productions for the Coasters and the Drifters and the seminal recordings of Ray Charles were only the most successful of the label's deep and talented roster.

Chuck Willis

Chuck Willis recorded several R&B hits for Okeh Records in the early fifties before signing with Atlantic Records in 1956. Willis' first Atlantic session yielded "**It's Too Late**," a slow, lost-love blues written by Willis and later covered by Buddy Holly, Derek and the Dominos and many others. The almost painfully personal lyrics read like a tormented blues but are set to a typically creative Atlantic arrangement featuring female background vocals and the surprise appearance of a celesta that adds an aura of childlike sincerity. (The backing vocals were supplied by an Atlantic group called the Cookies, who later, as the "Raeletts," became an integral part of Ray Charles' sound; the celesta on "It's Too Late" inspired Buddy Holly's better-known use of the instrument on "Everyday.")

Willis' 1957 reworking of the blues standard "**C. C. Rider**" earned him the "King of the Stroll" title, since the song happened to be paced just right for the new dance. The record opens with a marimba melody then floats into a gentle boogie pattern embellished by constant piano triplets, a chorus of background voices chanting the title refrain, and a plaintive tenor saxophone that forms a duet with Willis' vocals. "C.C. Rider" was followed by a similar update of a blues standard called "Betty and Dupree." Willis then returned to original songs for a final pair of hits that were released together on a single in 1958: "What Am I Living For" and "(I Don't Want to) Hang Up My Rock & Roll Shoes." He died during emergency abdominal surgery before the songs reached the charts, giving a sadly ironic twist to their titles.

LaVern Baker

LaVern Baker was a consistent pop chartmaker, scoring seven Top Forty hits for Atlantic in addition to her string of R&B hits. After singing in her teens as "Little Miss Sharecropper," dressed in demeaning rags and "backwoods" sack dresses, Baker became a featured soloist with the Todd Rhodes Orchestra in the post-swing days of touring R&B troupes. Baker signed with Atlantic in 1953, late enough to have her music aimed at the teenage crossover market that eluded labelmate Ruth Brown. Her first Atlantic hit, 1954's "**Tweedlee Dee**," was a clever pop song with a samba beat and a classy Atlantic production (even though it was actually recorded in an office rather than a studio). The song one of the big hits of the crossover era, though in keeping with the pattern of the times, it was outsold by Georgia Gibbs' saccharine cover, which drained the energy of the original and rendered the song merely "cute."

"Tweedlee Dee" inspired similar follow-ups like "Bop-Ting-A-Ling," "Fee-Fee-Fi-Fo-Fum" and "Tra La La." She broke away from the nursery rhyme model, fortunately, with "**Jim Dandy**," a 1956 hit that set Baker's growling blues voice against a gentle boogie bass and playful pop-style arrangement similar to the sound of "Don't Be Cruel" and other Elvis Presley hits for RCA. Baker's biggest pop hit, the 1958 torch-ballad "I Cried a Tear," employed a more subdued, soulful sound highlighted by a plaintive call-and-response between Baker and saxophonist King Curtis. Baker's "Saved," from 1961, is an upbeat gospel-pop celebration of redemption sung with a worldwise wink ("I used to smoke, I used to drink... now I'm saved"). Her last pop chart appearance came in 1963 with "See See Rider," her version of the blues standard popularized by Chuck Willis.

Ivory Joe Hunter

Ivory Joe Hunter was forty-two years old and a well-established performer when he landed on the pop charts in 1956 with "**Since I Met You Baby**." Hunter was one of the first black artists to adapt elements of country music, foreshadowing Ray Charles' celebrated C&W recordings and the country-soul of Solomon Burke. The country flavor of "Since I Met You Baby" mixes easily with club blues and pop shadings, creating a broad appeal that inspired cover versions by a range of disparate artists, including Freddy Fender, B. B. King and Dean Martin. Hunter's "Empty Arms" evoked a similar mood and achieved a similar success in all three—Pop, C&W and R&B—markets. Although his songs continued to be widely covered (Elvis Presley and Pat Boone both covered his songs), Hunter was unable to sustain his own recording success. He joined the Grand Ole Opry in the late sixties, and was attempting a comeback when he died of lung cancer in 1974.

Other Atlantic artists who achieved a significant measure of pop success included white pop idol Bobby Darin and two ex-Drifters—original lead singer Clyde McPhatter and Ben E. King. Blues legend Joe Turner helped launch rock & roll with "Shake, Rattle & Roll," but his own style remained a bit too raw for the pop market. While Turner looked back to the era of the great blues shouters, another big, burly singer named Solomon Burke looked forward with the country-soul of 1960's "Just Out of Reach (Of My Two Empty Arms)" and the emotional gospel delivery of 1962's "Cry to Me," a landmark release that reflected a shift to a new, southern style of R&B that was beginning to be called "soul."

SOUL PIONEERS

The difficulties faced by black performers in the rock & roll era grew worse with the coming of the pop-oriented Teen Idol era. Like rockabilly and the raucous sound of classic rock & roll, rhythm & blues fell largely out of favor in the early sixties, though the popularity of the Twist and other dance crazes did inspire a mini-revival and hits for Twist King Chubby Checker and other "neo-R&B" artists like Gary "U.S." Bonds ("New Orleans," "Quarter to Three"), Jimmy Jones ("Handy Man," "Good Timin'"), Joe Jones ("You Talk Too Much"), Bobby Lewis ("Tossin' and Turnin'"), Ernie K-Doe ("Mother-In-Law") and Jimmy Soul ("If You Wanna Be Happy").

The most significant development in black music in the early sixties was the advent of **soul music**. "Soul" is as hard to define as "rhythm & blues," and came to mean as much or as little as the previous label (i.e., "black music"). The key ingredient in soul music, and the element that defined it as a new style, was the influence of gospel music. The vocal styles, musical devices, emotional intensity and the spirit of community central to soul music came largely from the gospel tradition. The gospel elements blended with and influenced the dance grooves, musical arrangements and secular, sensual subject matter of R&B and created a new style for a new and rapidly changing era. The soul movement closely mirrored the growing civil rights movement in America, and functioned as a unifying "secular church." Soul music's success on the pop charts and influence on all other styles marked the second great wave of musical crossovers and airwave integration, and was a happy reflection of the changing racial attitudes and the buoyant optimism that, at least for a time, seemed justified.

Gospel styles had been creeping into R&B for many years in a natural and largely spontaneous progression that only seemed shocking because of the clash of subject matters. The Dominoes, Drifters, Midnighters, Little Willie John, Bobby "Blue" Bland and many others helped lay the foundations for soul music (including, of course, James Brown, "the Godfather of Soul," who began recording in 1956 but reached the peak of his powers and influence in the 1960's). Gospel styles and devices were a common feature of doo-wop songs, and gospel music itself enjoyed a steady, if limited, popularity through the fifties.

Three artists were of particular importance to the development of soul music: Ray Charles, Sam Cooke and Jackie Wilson. The three were very different—their styles ranged from hard driving R&B to teen pop to adult popular standards—but they shared a gospel background that helped shape their music. Ray Charles ignited his jazz combo R&B with the impassioned testifying of a southern, Holy Roller revival meeting; Sam Cooke brought his melodic style of gospel to pop songs with graceful ease; and Jackie Wilson used the expressive range of all styles of gospel singing to fuel his spectacular vocal gymnastics. Above all, the three vocal giants sang with an emotion that united their music and artistic vision, and they remain three of the Great Voices of all time.

RAY CHARLES

It would be stretching things quite a bit to call Ray Charles' music "rock & roll," even in the broadest sense of the term. Charles' sophisticated music and world-wise lyrics have always appealed to an older audience and seemed more at home in nightclubs and concert halls than on *American Bandstand*. In his autobiography, *Brother Ray*, Charles recalled, "I never considered myself part of rock & roll... My stuff was more adult, filled with more despair than anything you'd associate with rock & roll."[3] Nonetheless, his rise to popularity coincided with the rise of rock & roll, and he was *the* seminal figure in the development of soul music and a profound influence on singers and artists in nearly every field.

Once called "the only genius in the business" by no less an authority than Frank Sinatra, Charles made a career of ignoring musical and cultural boundaries. As a singer, songwriter, arranger, pianist and bandleader, he drew from the entire spectrum of popular music—rhythm & blues, gospel, jazz, swing, country & western, mainstream pop, romantic ballads, showtunes, easy-listening music and patriotic anthems—to create wholly new possibilities and lend them an immediate authenticity with the conviction of his voice and vision.

Charles was and remains one of the truly great musical stylists of our time: the only label that really fits Ray Charles' music is "Ray Charles' music." In his prime, he made every song he sang his own—imbued each with the fascinating blend of icy cool detachment and intense emotion that characterizes both his music and his personality. And though his later career has been marked by a move toward rather bland, middle-of-the-road material, he can still summon an unexpected depth and meaning from even the most mundane song, and lift it into realms undreamed of by its composer and previous interpreters.

Background: The South to Seattle

Ray Charles was born Ray Charles Robinson in Albany, Georgia on September 23, 1930, and moved to Greenville, Florida with his family while he was still an infant. (He later dropped his surname to avoid confusion with boxer Sugar Ray Robinson.) Desperately poor, his early life was marked by heart wrenching traumas. At five he watched his brother drown in a large washtub: "I was trying to pull him out and he had all his clothes on and they were too heavy... it took me a long time to get over that."[4] A short time later, Charles began losing his sight to glaucoma. His family couldn't afford the available treatments and the disease progressed, leaving him totally blind by the time he was seven. He was sent to a state school for the blind in St. Augustine, Florida, where he remained until his mother's death in 1945.

With the onset of his blindness, music became the center of Charles' private world and his link to the larger one. The greatest early influence on his singing came from the Baptist church he attended regularly; his early piano style, on the other hand, was based on jazz and barrelhouse boogie-woogie, while his musical heart was firmly rooted in the blues. Charles also developed a rather surprising fondness for country music—the other end of the southern musical spectrum—and was particularly drawn to the Grand Ole Opry radio broadcasts: "Every Saturday night, I never did miss it. Although I was bred in and around the blues, I always did have an interest in other music, and I felt like it was the closest music, really, to the blues. They'd make those steel guitars cry and whine, and it really attracted me."[5]

Charles learned to "read" music at St. Augustine and began writing his own songs and big band arrangements by dictating the notes, one line at a time, to anyone willing to write them down for him. He also received some classical piano instruction, though his access to the school's pianos was hampered by the fact that they were on the "white side" of the segregated school. (The segregated <u>BLIND</u> school!) Orphaned at 15, Charles left school and played in clubs around Jacksonville until he saved enough to move to Seattle—"as far away from Florida as I could get." He played for a time with 15-year-old trumpeter Quincy Jones, then formed a piano, guitar and bass trio modeled after that of his idol, Nat "King" Cole. Charles patterned his sound, to the point of imitation, on the smooth West Coast club blues of Cole and Charles Brown and, on the uptempo dance numbers, the jump blues of Louis Jordan. After four years of moderate success on the small Swing Time label, Charles signed with Atlantic Records in 1952 and began the search for his true voice.

The Atlantic Years (1952-1960)

Charles was, from the start, given great artistic license at Atlantic and encouraged to experiment. "Mess Around," a boogie-woogie dance number written by Ahmet Ertegun, is a standout from his first Atlantic sessions. Backed by an all-star Atlantic house band, including Sam "The Man" Taylor on tenor sax, Mickey Baker on guitar and Connie Kay on drums, Charles blasts through "Mess Around" in classic barrelhouse style, displaying his formidable piano technique and a new-found vocal confidence.

The crucial turning point for Charles proved to be an extended stay in 1953 in the musical hotbed of New Orleans, where he recorded his next hit, "Don't You Know," in Cosimo Matassa's J&M Studio and worked with the legendary Studio Band. He also served as arranger and pianist on the recording sessions that yielded Guitar Slim's "The Things That I Used to Do." The whole experience confirmed Charles' own yearning for his musical roots and inspired him to form his own band and make the final leap to—or back to—the emotional gospel style that was his most natural voice. "Nothing was more familiar to me, nothing more natural. Imitating Nat Cole had required a certain calculation on my part... I loved doing it, but it certainly wasn't effortless. This new combination of blues and gospel was. It required nothing of me but being true to my very first music."[6] His next recording session, hastily arranged at an Atlanta radio station, yielded "I Got a Woman" and revealed the fully-formed "new Ray."

Hallelujah!

Based on the gospel song "My Jesus Is All the World to Me," "**I Got a Woman**" combined the musical structure, celebratory spirit and emotional delivery of gospel with the instrumentation, dancebeats and earthy sexuality of rhythm & blues. Charles took the tune, feel and 16-bar structure of the gospel song and added "profane" lyrics, a sax break, jump blues stop-time sections and dance band that answers the Charles' calls. The integration of gospel and R&B that had been hinted at by earlier singers and groups was now made explicit: backed by a jazz-laced R&B septet (two trumpets, 2 saxophones, bass, drums and Charles' own piano), Charles embellished his shouting blues with falsetto shrieks, "oh yeah!"'s and other expressive devices lifted from the unrestrained vocal style of the Southern Baptist church, and sang the praises of his Woman in a style and with a passion that was previously reserved for praises of the Lord.

"I Got a Woman" provoked a considerable outcry within the black community from people who felt that the blues and gospel, the Devil and the Lord, should never mix. "Many folks saw my music as sacrilegious. They said I was taking church songs and making people dance to 'em in bars and nightclubs."[7] Charles was unmoved by the criticism—the record sales spoke a lot more—and remained convinced that the two styles had musical and emotional links that made some sort of fusion inevitable. (Elvis Presley covered "I Got a Woman" on his first television appearance, adding a further strand to the song's fabric of styles.)

Charles followed the model of "I Got a Woman" and based a number of his Atlantic recordings on a gospel songs: "Nobody but You, Lord" was transformed into "Nobody But You," "I've Got a New Home" into "Lonely Avenue," "This Little Light of Mine" into "This Little Girl of Mine," and so on. Even when they weren't based on a specific models, his songs were always informed by the liberating union of gospel and R&B that "I Got a Woman" had announced.   Highlights of Ray Charles' Atlantic years include the delightfully playful mood of "This Little Girl of Mine," which introduced the Latin rhythms and flavor that became another key ingredient of his style, the brassy strut of "Hallelujah, I Love Her So," and the tortured, bluesy reading of "Drown In My Own Tears," which featured the first appearance of the female backing group, the Raeletts, who became a prominent part of his sound and live show.

"What'd I Say"

Charles was an R&B star through the late fifties but did not reach the pop charts until 1959, his last year at Atlantic. "What'd I Say" fleshed out the baptized abandon hinted at in "I Got a Woman." Ironically, Charles' biggest fifties hit began life as an improvised keyboard riff and a call-and-response singalong "written" merely to kill time at the end of a show. "I had about fifteen more minutes to go and I couldn't think of nothing else to play, so I just told the guys, 'you guys just get a groove going when I tell you to come in,' and I told the girls, 'whatever I say, you all repeat after me,' and we started to do it and the people started really dancing and going crazy over it. So we tried it in a few other towns, and finally somebody asked me, 'Do you have a record of that?' So we went in and did the song, and today it's kind of like our anthem."[8]

"What'd I Say" is a righteous blend of gospel, boogie, blues, Latin rhythms and jazz band R&B. The song begins with a simple 12-bar blues outline from Charles' electric piano—the inspiration for many rock riffs to come—and expands until the entire band has joined the festivities, with the horns punctuating the rhythm and answering the vocals. At what appears to be the song's end, the "live" genesis of "What'd I Say" is recalled as the backing band and Raeletts turn into a crowd of dancing partygoers urging a reluctant Ray to keep the music going. Sufficiently inspired, Charles plunges back into the song and into a lascivious call-and-response with the Raeletts that is filled with enough grunts, groans and ecstatic moans to drive radio programmers completely crazy. The extended climax of "What'd I Say" sounds like a Pentecostal revival meeting gone berserk—the frenzied worshippers suddenly gripped by the Devil (in the form of a 12-bar blues) and plunged into an orgy of earthly desire, with the "Right Reverend Ray Charles" (as Aretha Franklin liked to call him) presiding over the High Church of Sexuality. As Charles later recalled, "They said it was suggestive. Well, I agreed. I'm not one to interpret my own songs, but if you can't figure out "What'd I Say," then something's wrong. Either that, or you're not accustomed to the sweet sounds of love."[9]

Movin' On

Ray Charles enjoyed a remarkable degree of creative freedom at Atlantic and was encouraged to follow his muse in any direction it led. He concentrated on albums as well as singles and surrounded himself with excellent musicians, most notably tenor saxophonist Dave "Fathead" Newman, who took most of the solos in Charles' songs. He made a triumphant appearance at the Newport Jazz Festival and recorded two jazz albums—*Soul Meeting* and *Soul Brothers*—with Modern Jazz Quartet vibraphonist Milt Jackson. (The musical connotation of the term "soul" originated in the '50's jazz community, where it signified a rootsy, blues and gospel-derived authenticity and a reaction against the West Coast "cool" jazz style.)

Three songs recorded in 1959, the year of "What'd I Say," reflected the range of his talents and the direction of things to come: "I'm Movin' On," "Let the Good Times Roll" and "Just for a Thrill." All three were old standards from distinct musical traditions—C&W, R&B and Popular—and together they signaled a shift of focus away from songwriting towards song interpretation. "I'm Movin' On," a 1950 hit for country star Hank Snow, added a pedal steel guitar to his blues-gospel mix and was a foreshadowing of the "country soul" that would later earn Charles the biggest success of his career. Charles recorded "Let the Good Times Roll" in classic big band style, building on Louis Jordan's famous 1946 recording of the song and supplementing his own band with the large Quincy Jones Orchestra (Charles also shared arranging chores with his old friend from the Seattle days). "Just for a Thrill," on the other hand, was a move to the middle-of-the-road, with a lush string arrangement inspired by Nelson Riddle's arrangements for Frank Sinatra. "Let the Good Times Roll" and "Just for a Thrill" were released as singles and included on an album, *The Genius of Ray Charles*, that paired a side of big band arrangements with a side of string-laden ballads and showed Charles clearly moving away from the dancehall fervor that inspired "What'd I Say."

ABC Records (1960-1973)

Charles left Atlantic at the end of 1959 and moved to ABC Records, drawn by a lucrative offer and the promise of continued artistic freedom. Although his biggest popular successes were still ahead of him, he would only fitfully achieve the type of innovative brilliance that marked his Atlantic tenure. Nonetheless, Charles' association with ABC started on a high note with his definitive version of the Hoagy Carmichael's **Georgia On My Mind**." Charles delivered the ode to his home state with a melancholy longing that is as good a definition of "soul" as any, though sweetened a choir of voices and soaring violins that helped make "Georgia On My Mind" the first Ray Charles release to do better on the Pop than on the R&B charts. The record sold mainly to an adult audience and set the tone for the soulful reinterpretations of old and new classics that enabled this wider and whiter audience to appreciate his expressive twists within a familiar context. Charles' increasingly middle-of-the-road output came to include songs like "Old Man River," "Over the Rainbow," "Sentimental Journey," "Yesterday" and "America the Beautiful," but even the blandest material was sung with great dignity and with a emotion that remained rooted in gospel and the blues.

I Can't Stop Loving You

Charles balanced his mainstream arrangements at ABC with R&B and jazz-laced uptempo songs, the best of which—"Hit the Road Jack," "Unchain

My Heart," "Don't Set Me Free," "Busted" and "Let's Go Get Stoned"—rank with his Atlantic output. The biggest hits of his career, however, came from a rather surprising direction—country & western. His cover of Don Gibson's "I Can't Stop Loving You" and his album of country songs, *Modern Sounds in Country and Western Music*, both went to #1 in 1962, and were followed by other renditions of C&W favorites, including "Born to Lose," "You Are My Sunshine," Buck Owens' "Crying Time" and Hank Williams' "Take These Chains from My Heart." In contrast to the stripped-down R&B version of "I'm Movin' On," the ABC country recordings received the complete "modern Nashville" treatment, full of heavenly strings and choirs and slick productions that appealed to listeners who had never liked country music before. His incorporation of C&W, like his blend of gospel and R&B, seemed bizarre at first (a black man singing country?), then made perfect sense. Growing up surrounded by both the blues and the Grand Ole Opry, he'd always felt the close kinship between the two styles. Both were, above all, *real*: "I think the words to country songs are very earthy like the blues, see, very *down*. They're not dressed up, and the people are very honest and say, 'Look, I miss you darling, so I went out and got drunk in this bar.' That's the way you say it. Wherein Tin Pan Alley will say, 'Oh, I missed you darling, so I went to this restaurant and I sat down and I had dinner for one.' That's cleaned up, you see? But country songs and the blues is like it is."[10]

Charles' country recordings obliterated the lines between Country, Pop and R&B and made him the most popular singer in the country in 1962 and 1963. The rough edges of Charles' sound were further smoothed over as his audience and concert venues grew more and more "respectable" (though he continues to anchor his concerts with a well-placed blues or two). He has been firmly entrenched on the black tie circuit since the end of the sixties, and seems content in the role of National Treasure. In a sense he has returned to his first professional style, playing sophisticated, jazz-laced pop music for a largely white audience, much as his first mentor Nat "King" Cole had done. His style and his success are all his own, however, and the story of his ascension into the pantheon of popular music is as inspiring as any before or since. Charles overcame his blindness and his country's racism to win a love and respect that even a well-publicized drug bust and battle with heroin addiction failed to tarnish (he kicked a nearly twenty-year habit in 1965).

Ray Charles' impact on popular music has been immeasurable: he has been a direct influence on generations of singers and pianists, of whom Joe Cocker, Stevie Winwood, Van Morrison, Eric Burdon, the Band's Richard Manuel, Charlie Rich are only the most obvious. More to the point, Charles he virtually invented soul music with his integration of R&B and gospel, and he laid the foundations for the church-based music of Aretha Franklin, James Brown, the Stax/Memphis singers and the Motown hit machine. When he is so moved, the old master can still erase all other versions of a song from memory and stamp it with his inimitable style: "That style requires pure heart singing.

Later on they'd call it soul music. But the names don't matter. It's the same mixture of gospel and blues with maybe a sweet melody thrown in for good measure. It's the sort of music where you can't fake the feeling."[11]

SAM COOKE

Sam Cooke possessed one of the greatest voices ever to grace a record. "Grace," in fact, is the key word for Cooke's voice and his sublime sense of pitch, tone and phrasing. He could fill a dance floor and whip a crowd into a frenzy, but he was at his best when gently bending a delicate pop melody or reverent gospel tune. Although his northern and urban gospel roots and resulting pop style were very different from those of Ray Charles, Cooke's beautifully arched melodies and quiet intensity were just as revelatory and important to the development of soul music.

Sam Cooke was a true pioneer: a supremely gifted singer and songwriter and a successful businessman with a firm grip on his own career at a time when few black artists even dreamed that such a thing was possible. Cooke was a great inspiration to those who followed him, and it is a great tragedy that he died just as the soul movement that he helped found was flowering. His voice remains a standard against which all others can be measured; as Keith Richards put it, "Sam Cooke is somebody other singers have to measure themselves against, and most of them go back to pumping gas."[12]

With the Soul Stirrers (1951-57)

Sam Cooke was born on January 2, 1931, in Clarksdale, Mississippi, but grew up in Chicago, Illinois. One of eight children of Baptist minister Charles Cook (Sam added the "e" later), he grew up immersed in the church and gospel music and spent his teens in a gospel group called the Highway QC's and gradually developed a reputation as a surprisingly mature and facile young singer. The Highway QC's were patterned after the renowned **Soul Stirrers**, and had the good fortune to be coached by Soul Stirrers baritone R. B. Robinson.

Founded in 1934, the Soul Stirrers were one of the most popular gospel groups of the day, thanks largely to lead singer and guiding spirit R. H. Harris. Harris revolutionized the group dynamics of gospel quartet singing, emphasizing a steady, chanted background against a freely improvised lead vocal. His pious sincerity and florid singing had a strong influence on Sam's style (as well as that of Jackie Wilson and a host of other young singers). When Harris left the group at the end of 1950, R. B. Robinson brought Sam, barely twenty years old, into the group as his idol's successor. Understandably nervous at first, Sam quickly gained confidence and stopped trying to imitate Harris' powerful voice, singing instead in a sweetly longing natural style, embellished with an expressive rasp, that stood in sharp contrast to the frenzied lead vocals of other groups and prompted the Soul Stirrers to soften their overall sound and move toward more delicate, pop sounding arrangements. Cooke also proved himself a skilled songwriter, writing "Touch the Hem of His Garment," "That's Heaven to Me" and other gospel hits the Soul Stirrers, and he always seemed more concerned with the meaning and message of the songs he sang that with showing off his voice or personality.

Cooke's recordings with the Soul Stirrers, on Specialty Records, stand with and perhaps even surpass the best of his pop output. All of the musical traits that he would bring to his pop recordings are in fully-formed evidence in his gospel music: the sweet, gentle tone, the lighter-than-air phrasing, the impeccable melodies and diction, the sincere sentiment, the quasi-yodeled "whoa-o-o-o-oh"s and lilting melismas that became his most recognizable vocal trademark. Cooke's unforced ease and genuine conviction won him the respect of older gospel artists and fans, while his charismatic personality and sensual look and sound gained him a large young following, as Soul Stirrer Jesse Farley recalls: "In the old days young people took seats six rows from the back, the old folks stayed up front. When Sam came on the scene, it reversed itself. The young people took over."[13]

By the mid-fifties Cooke was something of a matinee idol: "the sexiest man in gospel music." His appearances inspired a frenzied reaction from the female fans that seemed more appropriate for a pop idol than for a troubadour for the Lord. The response did not go unnoticed: Cooke was already eyeing the pop market and couldn't help but wonder what type of reaction he could get from a pop audience if he could make girls swoon at a *gospel* show. Cooke made his first, tentative steps away from gospel music and recorded a few secular pop songs in 1956 with Specialty producer **Bumps Blackwell**, who was also producing the label's rock & roll star, Little Richard. Specialty was doing well in the crossover market, but owner Art Rupe felt that the gospel and secular wings of his label should remain separate—that any intermingling would offend the gospel audience and that Sam Cooke, in particular, would destroy his credibility by recording pop music. It took some prodding, then, to persuade Rupe to release Cooke's first pop venture, "Lovable," in 1957. The record was released under the name "Dale Cook," but the pseudonym could hardly disguise Sam's distinctive voice and there was, indeed, an immediate backlash from his gospel fans and fellow Soul Stirrers.

Rupe ruled out any further pop recordings, only to discover Cooke and Blackwell in the studio one night recording more syrupy pop material behind his back. Rupe sold Cooke's contract to Blackwell, who became his manager as well as producer, and promptly fired them both, along with gospel singer and A&R man **J. W. Alexander**, who remained a close friend and business partner until Cooke's death. Cooke, Blackwell and Alexander took the tapes from that fateful night to the newly formed Keen label, which signed Cooke and gave Rupe reason to regret his rash move when one of the songs that so angered him, "You Send Me," went to #1 on both the Pop and R&B charts in the Fall of 1957.

Keen Records (1957-60)

"**You Send Me**" was the perfect record to launch Cooke's pop career—the soft, self-penned love song had broad appeal and was a marvelous vehicle for his voice. Backed by a sweet pop choir and an understated band accompaniment, Cooke glides through the song suspended above the beat, gently pushing the melody then soaring up to his exhilarating "who-o-oas" and floating back down into the sighing lyrics. Like Ray Charles, though in a completely different manner, Cooke sings to the Woman just as he had sung to the Lord, with the same yearning devotion and eyes-lifted reverence. Filled with the joys of love, "You Send Me" is the very best accompaniment for a romantic night by the fireplace.

"You Send Me" established Cooke as a "romantic lead" with a sensuous, intimate voice to match his wholesomely seductive looks and image. The record also sparked the anticipated wave of resentment among Cooke's gospel following. While his younger fans followed eagerly, many of Cooke's devout, older fans were upset by his "sell out" to the commercial world. Cooke was quickly ostracized from the gospel community, a painful loss but irrelevant compared to the huge number of new fans he gained as millions of pop listeners heard his voice for the first time. (Cooke's role in the gospel world and his switch to pop was mirrored in the next decade by Bob Dylan, who drew huge numbers of young listeners to folk music in the early sixties, then raised the ire of the traditionalists—and gained a much broader audience—when he plugged in an electric guitar and switched from folk to rock.)

"Wonderful World"

Cooke's Keen recordings featured a variety of pop shadings, ranging from crooners like "(I Love You) For Sentimental Reasons" to the calypso-tinged "Everybody Likes to Cha Cha Cha" and the teen pop of "Only Sixteen" and 1960's "Wonderful World," his last hit for Keen. "Wonderful World" is a featherweight gem of a song, with a delicate, childlike melody and a gushing adolescent sentiment that surely horrified Cooke's gospel fans. It certainly is a far cry from the weight and depth of his songs to the Lord, but it is sung with the same ennobling grace and devotion. Backed by a softly rocking band arrangement and pulsing background harmonies, Cooke sings in the first-person as a teenager experiencing love for the first time. Sure of his love, if not his homework, he admits that he doesn't know much about his schoolwork, but he knows he's in love and he's even willing to make the ultimate sacrifice and work to become an "A student" if it might win his girl's heart. Cooke's songwriting style (he wrote most of the songs he recorded throughout his career) was as graceful as his singing, as evidenced by the twist this verse takes into the final couplet:

Don't know much about geography,
Don't know much trigonometry,
Don't know much about algebra,
Don't know what a slide rule is for,
But I do know one and one is two,
And if this one could be with you,
What a wonderful world this would be.

Cooke's problems at Specialty Records made him determined to keep full control over both the musical and the business aspects of his career. With J. W. Alexander as his partner, Cooke launched his own publishing company, Kags Music, and his own record label, Sar Records, established as an outlet for his production work with other artists. In an era marked by a shameless exploitation of young and inexperienced performers, and a particularly unconscionable treatment of black artists, Cooke's success and self-reliance was extraordinary and helped pave the way for Motown Records and the greater inclusion of blacks on all levels in the music industry. Cooke also helped launch the careers of Billy Preston, Lou Rawls, Bobby Womack and other former gospel singers who decided to try their luck in the pop world (including Johnnie Taylor, Cooke's replacement in the Soul Stirrers).[14] Cooke's business acumen eventually led to his departure from Keen Records in 1960, when he demanded an audit of his recording royalties and found that, like most artists, he'd been grossly underpaid. Cooke won a series of lawsuits, split from Bumps Blackwell and signed with RCA, leaving Keen Records bankrupt and permanently out of business.

RCA (1960-64)

Cooke's move to RCA was a personal triumph and a confirmation of his star status. Although RCA had little experience with any type of black music, it did have the resources and industry clout to broaden Cooke's appeal and expand his base further into the pop market. As his music and image "matured," Cooke found himself increasingly torn between opposing musical directions—between the gospel roots of the burgeoning soul scene, the teen-oriented pop of his Keen days, and the lure of the big money and respectability that the mainstream adult market offered. He recorded in a wide variety of styles at RCA, ranging from the most soulful and affecting music of his career to the middle-of-the-road glitz of his *Live at the Copa* album and other attempts at establishing Cooke as an "all-around entertainer."

The best of Cooke's RCA output took on a more personal depth than his Keen recordings. The teen love songs like "Cupid" and "When a Boy Falls in Love" were given lusher treatments and strike a deeper chord than his similar Keen material, while his brass-driven dance numbers like "Shake" and "Twistin' the Night Away" (the best of the flood of early sixties "twist" songs) showed a tougher uptempo side of Cooke's style. His best and most enduring recordings were the slow and mid-tempo songs tinged with a weary realism and sung with Cooke's most personal voice. Working with RCA staff producers Hugo Peretti and Luigi Creatore, and with Keen veterans arranger Rene Hall and guitarist Cliff White, Cooke wrote new songs that fully accommodated his emotion and forged a soft soul style that fully integrated his gospel roots.

"Chain Gang"

Sam Cooke's first RCA hit was the biggest seller of his career: "Chain Gang." Released in the summer of 1960, the song also marked a shift away from the teen love songs and lightweight productions that characterized most of his Keen output. The hardships of prisoners chained together in a work crew was an odd subject for a pop song, made even odder by the extended introduction featuring a clanging anvil and syncopated grunts and groans from the "chain gang." The groans give way to a plaintive violin melody for the first verse, then return to accompany the second and continue through the third, where the violins return and all of the backing figures join together to witness Sam's lament and the sounds of the work crew as they fade, unrelieved, into the distance.

Inspired by his images of men "moaning their lives away," missing their women and yearning for deliverance, Cooke sings "Chain Gang" with the longing spirit of his religious songs. His verse melodies float freely above the background, bending and pleading without ever playing for cheap sentiment. At the end of the song Cooke breaks out of the arrangement altogether and testifies in pure gospel style, with elaborate melismas ("my-y-y-y-y-y work is so hard") and a perfect, sighing "whoa-o-o-o-oh" as the song fades.[15]

"Chain Gang" set the tone, musically and emotionally, for Cooke's best work at RCA. His next release, "Sad Mood," was another melancholy masterpiece, sung by the real Sam Cooke (not Sam playing a moonstruck teenager) in a heartrending expression of sorrow and penance that was universal enough to appeal to both teenagers who fantasize about the heartaches of love and adults who know it only too well. A similarly sorrowful quality colors all of Cooke's greatest recordings, even the songs that "ought" to sound happy. "Good Times," for example, is an invitation to "get in the groove and let the good times roll," but the tired 3:00 a.m. tempo and Cooke's wistful singing make it sound less like a celebration than a desperate attempt to escape his blues. "Meet Me at Mary's Place" has a similar, 'come on and party' storyline, and the same troubling feeling that it won't do any good. "Having a Party" was the highlight of Cooke's set of "gotta dance to keep from crying" songs. Frequently covered as a bar-band party song, the original sounds almost mournful, like a funeral wake—a feeling that the singalong at the end only seems to heighten. Cooke addresses the song to the radio DJ, pleading with him to keep the music playing, and even puts in requests for "Soul Twist," "I

Know" and "Mashed Potatoes," a tip of the hat to contemporary hits by King Curtis, Barbara George and James Brown. Cooke's yearning, double-edged emotion gave his songs a depth that lifted them beyond their surface "meanings" (and beyond the expressive grasp of most of the singers who try to cover them).

"Bring It On Home to Me"

Cooke's melancholy feel and pleading gospel delivery were used to fullest effect in the "country soul" ballads that reflected the influence of Ray Charles and the southern soul movement. "Bring It On Home to Me," from 1962, is his most integrated arrangement: a seamless blend of piano, strings, saxophone, guitar and bass, gently pushed along by a steady snare drum backbeat and cymbal triplets, all supporting a set of lyrics and lonesome melody so perfectly in sync that it's impossible to imagine one without the other. "Bring It On Home to Me" opens with a piano line straight out of an afterhours Nashville honky-tonk, then gains momentum through a church-like call & response between Cooke and Lou Rawls. Nothing is allowed to get in the way of the direct emotion: there is no lead break and no bridge section or isolated chorus, just the plaintive refrain of "bring it on home to me" at the end of every verse and the insistent, anthemic passion of the voices and feel of the music. "Bring It On Home to Me" simply *says* it, as directly and sincerely as possible, and shows Cooke's debt—repaid in full—to his gospel roots.

"A Change is Gonna Come"

"Shake" and "A Change Is Gonna Come," released as a single a month after Cooke's death, show the two extremes of Cooke's big production numbers. A brassy horn section and strong dancebeat give "Shake" more of a straightforward R&B sound than most of Cooke's output. The tougher, louder arrangement let Cooke sing full-voiced and show the raw energy that inspired a revival meeting frenzy at his live performances in black clubs, where he was free to let the "real" Sam Cooke show. (Cooke's *Live at the Harlem Square Club* album shows a completely different singer from the Sam Cooke singing "supperclub soul" for the white crowd at the Copacabana.)

"A Change is Gonna Come" is one of Cooke's greatest achievements and represents, in light of his untimely death, the end of a homeward musical journey. In spite of its overblown orchestral setting, it is a gospel song in the purest sense—an eyes-lifted reaffirmation of faith and redemption, though the object of faith is not the Lord or the Woman but the promise of long overdue justice for his race. Cooke's growing involvement with the civil rights movement deepened his sense of musical and personal identity. "A Change is Gonna Come" is sung with a passionate conviction that soars above the production and lends a supreme dignity to Cooke's most important and heartfelt lyrics. Few singers can ever achieve such heights and truly sing with the "voice of millions" as Cooke does here. "A Change Is Gonna Come" stands as one of the great monuments to the struggle for human dignity, and ample evidence of why Cooke's death was a terrible loss felt far beyond the confines of the music world.

Cooke was at the peak of his success and artistry when, on December 10, 1964, it all ended suddenly in a seamy motel in South Los Angeles. According to testimony at subsequent hearings, Cooke attacked a woman at the Hacienda Motel and, when she fled, assaulted the motel's manager, who shot and killed Cooke in the motel office. Despite attempts, led by Cooke's new personal manager, Allen Klein, to find sinister, racial and even mob-related explanations for Cooke's unbelievable death, the true facts were apparently as simple and stupid as first reported.

The sordid circumstances of Cooke's death did nothing to blunt the outpouring of grief that accompanied his funeral services in Los Angeles and Chicago, where over 200,000 people turned out to pay respects, or the sorrow felt by his admirers across the nation. Few artists have inspired such intense love and devotion, and few have been so sorely missed. Sam Cooke had a profound influence on all soul singers, particularly the sweet soul sound of artists like Marvin Gaye, Curtis Mayfield, Jerry Butler, Smokey Robinson, Percy Sledge, Al Green and Otis Redding, who idolized Cooke and always performed "Shake" at his shows as a tribute. His songs have been covered by Aretha Franklin, Sam and Dave, Eddie Floyd, Diana Ross & the Supremes, Van Morrison, the Rolling Stones, the Animals, the Band, John Lennon, Steve Miller, Cat Stevens, Mickey Gilley, Southside Johnny, Rod Stewart and many others, and his voice has inspired singers of all styles. Jerry Wexler, the Atlantic producer who recorded many of the greatest soul singers, summed it up this simply: "Sam was the best singer who ever lived, no contest."[16]

JACKIE WILSON

Jackie Wilson was another important link between the R&B of the fifties and the soul music of the sixties. Unlike Sam Cooke, Wilson lived to be a part of soul's triumph, though not the vital part that his spectacular gifts should have warranted. The enormous range and sheer, facile power of Wilson's voice made it one of the great "instruments" of the rock era; unfortunately, it was also one of the most misdirected and squandered.

Wilson was an incredibly energetic and agile showman, able to reel off a series of perfectly executed flips, cartwheels, "moonwalks" and handstands without a missed note or dropped beat. His acrobatic performances were more than matched by his vocal gymnastics—the soaring falsettos, cascading melismas and other tradmarks of his distinctive and much-copied singing style (the Isley Brothers' "Shout" is one of the more obvious appropriations of Wilson's gospel-swoon style). Unfortunately, his recorded material was only rarely able to do justice to the raw talent on display at his live shows, thanks to Wilson's own schizophrenic musical personality and to the appallingly bad career guidance and musical management he received. Wilson was eager to apply his talent and voice to all types of music, and was particularly drawn to the schmaltzy ballads and novelty numbers that highlighted his voice and left plenty of room for his impressive arsenal of vocal tricks. His inspired oversinging helped to create some revelatory surprises, such as his breathtaking version of "Danny Boy," but his operatic range and power were all-too-often placed in the service of mundane material that even Wilson couldn't salvage, or nearly buried beneath corny Las Vegas productions in a misguided attempt to sell Wilson to the mainstream pop market. But if his recording career was not all it could have been, a talent like Wilson's can still shine through any material, and a *voice* like Wilson's is always a joy to hear.

With the Dominoes (1953-57)

Jackie Wilson was born on June 9, 1934 in Detroit, where he grew up singing in church and soaking up gospel stylings. He was also an avid fan of the pop polish of the Ink Spots and Mills Brothers, the entertaining jump blues of Louis Jordan and the showbiz theatrics of Al Jolson—influences that can all be felt in his music. After a brief fling at boxing in the late 1940's, Wilson, with much coaxing from his mother, set his sights on a less injurious musical career. He was discovered in 1951 by bandleader and talent scout Johnny Otis, who circulated Wilson's name and stirred up interest in the young singer. (Otis discovered Jackie Wilson, Little Willie John and Hank Ballard & the Midnighters all at the same Detroit talent show.) Two years later, in an echo of young Sam Cooke's surprise leap to the front of the Soul Stirrers, nineteen-year-old Jackie was hired as lead singer Clyde McPhatter's replacement in Billy Ward and The Dominoes.

Led by McPhatter's emotionally charged voice, the Dominoes were ground breakers in the incorporation of gospel styles into R&B and one of the country's premiere vocal groups in the early 1950's. Billy Ward hired Wilson in 1953, confident that he had the voice, talent and necessary gospel inflections to step in when McPhatter left to front the newly-formed Drifters. The Dominoes never regained their full stride after McPhatter's departure, but they remained a popular live act and gave Wilson a chance to find his voice and establish his reputation. His predecessor's unrestrained theatrics inspired Wilson to expand and exaggerate his own range of vocal and dramatic effects. (His most obvious tip of the hat to McPhatter's influence were the sobs and shrieks—McPhatter's trademark—that began to punctuate his own singing.)

The sweeping register leaps, the rich vibrato, the impassioned falsetto breaks and other hallmarks of Wilson's style are all in evidence in his Dominoes recordings, as are, unfortunately, the contradictory directions and ill-advised choices of material that would plague the rest of his career. After some good initial efforts in the Dominoes' classic gospel-meets-jump style, such as "You Can't Keep a Good Man Down," the group changed their approach and began concentrating on lighter jazz, pop and novelty styles in hopes of reaching a wider audience. Instead, they lost much of their R&B following without gaining many new fans. They finally made their way into the pop charts in 1956 with the syrupy "St. Theresa of the Roses," an alarming taste of things to come that sold well enough to convince Wilson that it was time to launch a solo career. In 1957 he signed with Brunswick Records, where he remained for the rest of his troubled career.

The Solo Career and Brunswick Records

Wilson launched his solo career, and began his peculiar seesaw between styles and audiences, in the Fall of 1957 with **"Reet Petite"** a minor pop hit that failed to place at all on the R&B charts. Musically, "Reet Petite" set the pattern for his Brunswick output, with blaring horns and a bland big band arrangement that always threatens to suffocate the song and singer. Wilson's powerful voice cuts through, though, and reels off an impressive display of his range, depth and signature "devices," such as the rolled "r"'s on "r-r-r-reet," the grinding "she's a-w-w-l-right"'s and the falsetto leap at the end of the song. ("Reet Petite" is also peppered with low, sensuous vibratos and stuttered syllables that reminded many listeners of Elvis Presley. His new label encouraged Wilson to add some "Elvis-isms" to his naturally flamboyant style—an ironic twist, since Elvis counted Jackie Wilson among *his* influences.)

Most of Wilson's early hits, including "Reet Petite," were written by an old friend from Wilson's boxing days, **Berry Gordy, Jr.**, the future founder of Motown Records.[17] Gordy wrote several hits for Wilson over the next two years, including "To Be Loved," "That's Why (I Love You So)," "I'll Be Satisfied" and **"Lonely Teardrops,"** Wilson's biggest fifties hit. "Lonely Teardrops" walks a middle line between Wilson's schmaltzy ballads and his more uptempo dance style. The song is part dancetune, part operatic ballad, part novelty number, and an equal mix of pop, R&B and gospel vocal styles. The baby-come-home lyrics were custom-made for Jackie's pleading vocal style ("My heart is crying, crying" became his signature line), and the stops and starts of the backing arrangement provided an effective vehicle for Wilson's dramatics. His falsetto explosion in the gospel-style fadeout of the song feels like a joyous release from the confines of pop convention—he even manages to coax the ever-present K-Mart choir into a downhome call-and-response.

Wilson maintained his musical balancing act into the sixties, bouncing between the pop and R&B charts and audiences, hemmed in by the questionable taste of his manager Nat Tarnopol and producer Milton DeLugg.[18] His attempts to reconcile himself to some of the pure schmaltz he was given to sing led to some rather incongruous but oddly successful results. His 1960 hits "Alone At Last" and "Night," for example, were based on melodies pulled from a

Tchaikovsky piano concerto and the opera "Pagliacci" (truly an "operatic ballad"). Wilson fared better on uptempo and bluesy recordings, such as "Baby Workout," "Please Tell Me Why," "You Don't Know What It Means," and the great "**Doggin' Around**," which features one of his most soulful vocal performances, supported by a "country soul" piano and churchy organ (and marred by a syrupy and completely inappropriate choir of voices). A few songs from the early sixties, such as "I Just Can't Help It" and "Am I the Man," stand out as relatively integrated productions, though they still only hint at the type of music Wilson was capable of making when he was given a backing arrangement that he could work *with* instead of against.

Higher and Higher

Wilson's music was out of step with the times by the mid-sixties, when his career was unexpectedly revitalized by his collaboration with Chicago producer **Carl Davis**, who brought Wilson's music into the modern soul era. The team began a string of hits in 1966 with "**Whispers (Gettin' Louder),**" a thoroughly contemporary urban soul record with a bass-heavy, Motownish production featuring a tightly compressed string and horn arrangement and a background chorus that, for a change, actually enhances the song. Wilson's pleading, emotional voice is used here to full effect without sounding the least bit melodramatic, as if the music and times had finally caught up with his voice.

With a sympathetic producer and good new material, Wilson finally made records that matched his talent. He followed "Whispers" with "**(Your Love Keeps Lifting Me) Higher and Higher,**" his most popular song. The record begins with a distinctive bass figure, then gradually unfolds with the addition of bongos, tambourine, guitar, vibraphone, drums and piano, with the further layering of strings, brass and background singers for the title refrain. The relentless backing groove—supplied by moonlighting Motown musicians—propels the song through an exultant solo from the trumpets before climaxing with the final chorus and ending fadeout. Wilson sang "Higher and Higher" with joyous abandon, heightening the celebratory spirit of the words and music and turning the song into an almost religious testimony to the redeeming power of love. Wilson's career renaissance continued with "Since You Showed Me How to Be Happy" and "I Get the Sweetest Feeling," pop hits in 1967 and 1968, and several other songs that placed in the upper reaches of the R&B charts. As black music took on a harder edge in the early seventies, however, Wilson's pop-soul was again out of step with times, and Wilson found himself confined to the oldies circuit—where his old hits lived on and where, in a final, helpless twist of irony, he died.

Ill-fortune plagued Wilson's life: two of his children were gunned down on the streets of Detroit and Wilson himself was shot and nearly killed by a crazed fan in 1961. The end for Wilson finally came at an oldies concert in 1975 in Cherry Hill, New Jersey, where he suffered a stroke and collapsed onstage. At first it seemed merely a part of his flamboyant act, as Wilson devotee Tom Jones recalls: "he clutched his chest and went down his knees and [the audience] thought, you know, 'this is Jackie doing a thing.' And he was dying."[19]

Wilson lapsed into a coma and a tortuous decade-long struggle for life in a New Jersey hospital, where he was horribly neglected and even, according to many reports, abused. Wilson's family had no money to pay for the kind of treatment that could have helped him, and Brunswick and his manager were, characteristically, unwilling to help. Wilson's chronic destitution is one of the most tragic examples of rock era rip-offs (and a distinct contrast to the enlightened self-determination of Sam Cooke and Ray Charles). Wilson's finances apparently weren't handled any better than his talent—it is alleged that he never received a royalty payment from Brunswick and was forced to tour constantly to pay his bills and support his family. It seems that Wilson's big heart suffered all the indignities the music industry could dish out, and finally just gave up.[20]

Wilson went in and out of a coma for nine years, and died a ward of the State of New Jersey in 1984. Money was finally raised to buy a headstone for his grave in 1987. That an artist of Wilson's stature could suffer such a horrible fate is a sad indictment of the music industry at its very worst.

---

[1]N. Cohn, "Rock From the Beginning" (New York: Stein & Day, 1969), p. 36.

[2]Gerri Hirshey, "Nowhere to Run" (New York: Penguin, 1885), p. 59.

[3]Peter Guralnick, "Sweet Soul Music," p. 51

[4]Dotson Rader, "Ray Charles Sees the Beauty," in *Parade* Magazine, Aug. 7, 1988, p. 4.

[5]Ben Fong-Torres, "Ray Charles," in "The Rolling Stone Book of Interviews, 1967-1980," by the Editors of Rolling Stone, (New York: St. Martins, 1981), pg. 264.

[6]ibid., p. 165.

[7]Ray Charles, "Brother Ray," p. 167.

[8]from *Ray Charles* BBC documentary (Omnibus Films, 1988).

[9]Ray Charles, "Brother Ray," 211.

[10]ibid.

[11]Ray Charles, "Brother Ray," (New York: Warner, 1978), p. 196.

[12]ibid.

[13]Peter Guralnick, "Sweet Soul Music," p. 34

[14]Cooke and Alexander even recorded the Soul Stirrers after Art Rupe disbanded Specialty Records, and wrote "Stand By Me Father" for the group to record. (Ben E. King turned "Stand By Me Father" into "Stand By Me" in 1960.)

[15]A "melisma" is a single syllable stretched out over several notes.

[16]ibid.

[17]In an industry full of if-only's and what-could-have-been's, few are more tantalizing than the prospect of Jackie Wilson joining Motown as the standard-bearer of his friend's new label. Having an established name like Wilson on the label's roster would have gotten Motown off to a running start, and Gordy's aesthetic guidance—and quality material from Motown's great staff songwriters—could have made Wilson one of the great stars of the sixties. In any case, it wasn't to be. Speculation about the reason for Wilson's decision to remain at Brunswick has ranged from simple loyalty to the label to bizarre charges of Mafia involvement and gangland pressure on Wilson to stay put. For his part, Gordy felt compelled to form his own independent production company—his first step toward Motown—by the frustration of hearing his songs for Wilson buried under schmaltzy productions over which he had no control.

[18]DeLugg was later the band leader for the *Tonight Show* and musical director for the *Gong Show*.

[19]Interview from Jan. 1989 "Entertainment Tonight" television program.

[20] There have also been more sinister allegations about Wilson's death that are hard to dismiss, given the way he was handled in life.

Photo courtesy of UPI/BETTMAN NEWSPHOTOS

Buddy Holly

[9] ROCK STYLES EXPAND: THE PUSH TOWARD POP

A second wave of rock performers appeared in 1957, the year after Elvis' triumphant assault on the mainstream. Jerry Lee Lewis, Buddy Holly, Eddie Cochran, the Everly Brothers and Ricky Nelson were the most prominent of the year's new rock arrivals. (Sam Cooke and Jackie Wilson also had their first pop hits in 1957, reflecting the push from R&B towards soul.) Jerry Lee was the final defiant shout of rock's rebellious origins, all those months ago, while the others pointed toward a more innocent and melodic brand of rock & roll—toward a new definition of "pop."

The late fifties were a transitional period between the initial explosion of rock & roll and the rather dismal "teen idol" era of the early sixties. The success of Elvis at RCA brought rock & roll to a much wider audience and increased its profitability to a point where even the music industry leaders had to take notice. (Not that they ever developed a taste for rock & roll: the kindest thing Mitch Miller, A&R man for Columbia Records, could say was "it's not music, it's a disease.") The cautious and conservative music industry approached rock & roll as a product to be sold to the largest possible audience while offending as few people as possible. The days of the Jerry Lee Lewises—and Lewis himself—were numbered.

The other newcomers, by contrast, had clean-cut images that blunted criticism and broadened their appeal. They appeared to be the kind of boys you could bring home for dinner without unduly alarming your parents (though Eddie Cochran could be rather sullen, in good Elvis fashion). They even made *records* you could play for your parents with little embarrassment: they'd still hate them, of course, but at least the overtly rebellious and sexual overtones were fading, replaced by innocent lyrics and a new emphasis on melodic "hooks" and hummable tunes. The beat, excitement and vitality weren't gone, however—not yet. To varying degrees, the Everly Brothers, Ricky Nelson, Eddie Cochran and, especially, Buddy Holly combined the beat and energy of rock & roll with the lyricism and inventiveness of pop in the last creative surge of rock & roll's Golden Era.

Class of '57

In contrast to the career flameout of Jerry Lee Lewis and the short-lived success of most other early rockers, the Everly Brothers and Ricky Nelson managed to survive the change of decades, and the shifts in their sound and style roughly paralleled the overall shift from fifties rock & roll to early sixties pop. Although neither had ever been particularly wild or threatening, by the time they were crushed by the British Invasion their music had become, for the most part, overproduced and overly sentimental, lacking the focus and rock & roll grounding of their earlier work. (Much the same could be said of

Fats Domino, the only other original rock voice whose career weathered the change of decades intact.)

Eddie Cochran and Buddy Holly both started as genuine rockabillies before crafting their own unique songwriting, guitar and production styles. They were certainly two of the most inventive and adaptable of the early rockers, and could well have given the pop world of the early sixties some much needed depth and energy. Instead, both died young and tragically—Holly at 22, Cochran at 21.

Paul Anka and **Bobby Darin** also hit in 1957 and, as two of the first pop "teen idols," were definitely harbingers of the future. Anka and Darin were never really committed to rock & roll, but they were talented singers and songwriters and were the most gifted of the teen idols. Anka's "Diana" went to #1 in 1957, when he was fifteen; his other Young Love ballads included "Puppy Love" (his ode to Mouseketeer Annette Funicello), "Lonely Boy" and "Put Your Head On My Shoulder." Darin scored teen hits like "Splish Splash," "Queen of the Hop" and "Dream Lover" before hitting the mainstream in 1959 with "Mack the Knife." Anka and Darin were both able to parlay their success in the rock market into careers as nightclub singers and "all-around entertainers," abandoning the teen audience in favor of the adult market that better reflected their tastes and talent. Their move "uptown" came to represent the ultimate success for the teen idols, who generally viewed their pop fame as a stepping stone to "respectable" careers in the nightclubs, variety shows, Vegas and Hollywood.[1]

RICKY NELSON

Ricky Nelson grew up in front of the entire nation as "little Ricky" on *The Adventures of Ozzie and Harriet*, television's longest running sitcom, which starred Ricky and his real-life parents Ozzie and Harriet and brother David. As a recording artist, Nelson has too often been written off as simply another "teen idol." He certainly was good-looking and safe as milk—a wholesome member of America's most wholesome family. And the fact that he was already "America's darling" before he ever sang a note *did* make his career seem cynically calculated in typical teen idol fashion. He had a pleasant voice, though, and a genuine talent, and he had the good sense and taste to surround himself with excellent songwriters and backup musicians. His producer, Jimmie Haskell, recalls: "Ricky knew what he wanted. He couldn't analyze it, but he knew. He had a good ear and was a good musician. Most people aren't aware of that."[2] Nelson made consistently good, if polite, records and was a major figure on the pop charts from 1957 to 1963.

The Adventures of Ozzie and Harriet was even, in its small way, a victory for rock & roll. Once Ricky began making records, his songs were routinely worked into the plots of the show. There was Ricky, every week, playing his latest hit at the ice cream social, church picnic, high school mixer or fraternity dance. The exposure obviously helped sell his records, but it also put rock & roll in America's living room—right there in front of Mom and Dad. As with Pat Boone, though with infinitely more conviction, the unthreatening "little Ricky" was able to get a reasonable facsimile of rock & roll to a general audience that would never have given it a chance otherwise.

Ricky Nelson—again like Pat Boone—had his first hit with a cover of a Fats Domino song: "I'm Walking," a 1957 hit for the seventeen-year-old Ricky on the Verve label. (He later switched to Domino's label, Imperial Records.) Nelson was prodded into a singing career to counter his girlfriend's infatuation with Elvis: Ricky bragged that he could sing rock & roll too, then had to back it up! Nelson's own infatuation with Presley is clear in his versions of Elvis' "Milcow Blues" and "Tryin' To Get To You," and in the rockabilly slant of many of his other recordings. But the world Nelson grew up in was far removed from the rural South, and his smooth voice and temperament really weren't suited for the rock & roll rave-ups he attempted. The hopped-up singing and manly stance in "Milcow Blues," "Down the Line" and "My Babe," for example, seem beyond his range and a bit contrived.

The "L. A. Rockabilly"

Nelson was at his best in the songs written for him, where no existing model made him feel compelled to alter his natural style. His most effective songs combined a hot but controlled band accompaniment with his smooth pop singing and polished state-of-the-art productions. **"Stood Up"** (1957) and **"Hello Mary Lou"** (1961) are good examples of Nelson's "L. A. Rockabilly" style of cool vocals over a hot band. They also feature the guitar work of the two lead players that highlighted Nelson's stellar backup bands: Joe Maphis and rockabilly legend James Burton. Maphis' aggressive style can be heard on "Stood Up" and Nelson's other early records. Burton's hard-driving but exquisitely polished playing lights up the majority of Nelson's hits. Burton could always make a good song great, as he did with "Hello Mary Lou," "Believe What You Say" and "Travelin' Man," and even Nelson's more lightweight outings are punctuated with classy guitar breaks.

Nelson had his biggest hits with midtempo pop songs that left plenty of room for his sensitive voice and personality. His singing is especially graceful on 1958's "Poor Little Fool" and 1961's "Travelin' Man," his biggest hits, and on 1962's "Teenage Idol." His voice was also well-suited for ballads—"Lonesome Town" and "Young Emotions" are particularly lovely—and he sang his songs of young love, heartache and the trials of growing up with an unaffected sincerity. He was, after all, growing up. Nelson's music generally steered clear of the melodramatic excesses and stylized mannerisms that marred most "teen idol" music. His songs were as good-natured and pleasant as the young man who sang them.

After seven successful years, Nelson joined most of his peers in the "overnight has-been" category created by the British Invasion. *The Adventures of Ozzie and Harriet* went off the air in 1966 and, no longer a "teenage idol," or even a teenager, Nelson spent the late sixties searching for a musical direction. In 1969 he formed a pioneering country-rock group, the Stone Canyon Band, and officially became "Rick" to emphasize his new maturity. The success of a 1969 cover of Bob Dylan's "She Belongs to Me" fueled his determination to remain a contemporary artist and not a mere "oldies" act.

His resolve to avoid relic status was strengthened in 1972 by a traumatic appearance at a "rock revival" show at New York's Madison Square Garden. After a quick swing through his old hits, Nelson launched into his newer songs only to be jeered by the oldies crowd who wanted to hear "little Ricky." Hurt and enraged, Nelson wrote his response in "Garden Party" ("if memories were all I sang, I'd rather drive a truck"). It was Nelson's last Top Ten hit. He continued performing through the rest of his life, playing a mix of old songs and new, stuck in limbo between past and present. Rick Nelson died in a plane crash on December 31, 1985. His twin sons Gunnar and Matthew now perform as "Nelson," negotiating a rather similar balance between rock and pop, image and substance.

THE EVERLY BROTHERS

Nashville finally found an inroad to the rock market with the Everly Brothers. Don and Phil Everly's sweet harmonies were a calming and reassuring alternative to the frenzied rhythms coming out of Memphis. Their music was a break from country & western tradition, but not the screaming repudiation of it that rockabilly seemed to be. The Everly Brothers updated the country duo harmonies of acts like the Delmore Brothers, Louvin Brothers and Blue Sky Boys, then integrated them with rock and pop arrangements and lyrics clearly aimed at the young rock audience. Their best records brought a soft, melodic beauty to rock & roll while remaining true to rock's direct and unadorned appeal. Like the best country music, their songs seemed *real*: they sang of young love and high school heartaches with a genuine longing and hurt that any young person could relate to. Their safe sound and image helped broaden their appeal, but the Everly's wistful melodies and sublime harmonies could always melt the heart of the most hardened rocker.

In an era dominated by solo stars and vocal groups that always featured a single lead singer, the Everly Brothers' two-part harmonies were a refreshing novelty to pop listeners. Their influence on later generations can be clearly heard in the close John/Paul harmonies of early Beatle songs and the melodic harmonies of the Byrds and the Beach Boys, as well as in the music of direct descendants like Simon & Garfunkel, Peter & Gordon and Chad & Jeremy. Along with Buddy Holly, the Everly Brothers were also the ancestors of the

California "country rock" sound of Linda Ronstadt, the Eagles and other seventies superstars.

The Road to Nashville

Don Everly was born on February 1, 1937, his brother Phil on January 19, 1939. Like Ricky Nelson, though on a much smaller scale, the Everly Brothers grew up in a show business family. Their parents, country singers Ike and Margaret Everly, worked Don and Phil into their act as soon as they could carry a tune. (Ike Everly was also a fairly well-known and influential guitarist from the Kentucky "school" that included Merle Travis and Bill Monroe.) The boys grew up in front of a microphone, singing together on live radio broadcasts, at barn dances and anywhere else the Everly Family could get a booking. In the early fifties, after several years in Shenandoah, Iowa, the family settled in Knoxville, Tennessee, and the brothers set their sights on Nashville—coming, appropriately, from the opposite direction of Memphis.

With the help of family friend Chet Atkins, young Don landed a job as a songwriter for the Hill & Range publishing house in 1955. The following year, both Don and Phil were hired as songwriters for the other Nashville giant, the Acuff-Rose publishing house, headed by Wesley Rose. Rose became the Everly Brothers' manager and negotiated a recording contract with Cadence Records, a New York label headed by Archie Bleyer. He also hooked them up with two other Acuff-Rose songwriters, the husband and wife team who would write most of their Cadence hits, **Boudleaux and Felice Bryant**. In March, 1957, the Everly Brothers recorded the Bryant's "Bye Bye Love," after the song had been turned down by 29 other acts. "Bye Bye Love" was the first of 26 Top Forty hits for the Everly Brothers, including fourteen Top Ten's and four #1's.

"Bye Bye Love"

"Bye Bye Love" introduced all of the distinctive elements of the Everly Brothers' sound. The song is sung in close, parallel harmony—the two voices separated by the interval of a third, moving up and down together—with slightly nasal country accents, supported by the twin attack of the two jumbo acoustic guitars that became the Everly's instrumental and visual trademark. The twin acoustics underline the rock feel of the song, while the rest of the backing remains tastefully understated, with the drummer using brushes and nothing competing with the voices for attention.

"Bye Bye Love" captures the End-of-the-World feeling of losing your love and reason for living. (20-year-old Don, the older and wiser of the pair, takes the lead on the lovelorn verses: "I'm through with romance, I'm through with love...") It was an appropriate opening sentiment for their career: nearly all of the Everly Brothers' songs are about young love, either the innocent dream of an idyllic love or the crushing disappointment and hurt of a love lost. In either case, the Everly Brother's image of love was never of the suggestive "behind the barn" variety that the wilder rockabillies hungered for. The decorous morality of the C&W tradition was kept intact in the Everly's songs, which helped them appeal to the kids without offending the parents.

"Bye Bye Love" was recorded in the Nashville RCA studios, where the Everly Brothers were backed by a pool of Nashville "super-sessionmen," including Chet Atkins and Hank Garland on guitars, Floyd Cramer on piano and Buddy Harmon on drums. With such all-star talent behind them, the Everly Brothers' Cadence recordings had a tight and polished sound with at least a hint of country flavor, though great care was always taken to see that Don and Phil's voices and guitars were never overshadowed and, with the pop audience in mind, to make sure that overtly country elements were avoided. With Wesley Rose and Archie Bleyer overseeing their career and Boudleaux and Felice Bryant supplying most of their hits, the Everly Brothers were the center of a thoroughly professional team effort that kept them near the top of the charts throughout their three-year association with Cadence.

When "Bye Bye Love" was released, however, the Everly Brothers still considered themselves country artists and viewed an appearance on the Grand Ole Opry as the very pinnacle of success (and they did, in fact, make frequent appearances on the Grand Ole Opry for about a year after "Bye Bye Love" hit). They toured in 1957 as part of Bill Monroe's troupe, performing at "tent shows" throughout the South and alternating straight country sets with rock & roll shows for the younger crowd. While on tour they received the awful news that country superstar Webb Pierce had covered "Bye Bye Love," a potentially fatal blow for the struggling newcomers. Don Everly: "Disaster! I almost fainted. I called Archie Bleyer up in New York. I said, 'Something terrible's happened.' He said, 'What?' I said, 'Webb Pierce has covered our record.' And he said—I never will forget this—he said, 'Webb who?' He didn't even know who Webb Pierce was! He said 'Forget about that—the record's hitting pop.' I didn't have a clue what he was talking about."[3]

The Cadence Years: 1957-1960

The Everly Brothers became country *and* rock & roll stars in one fell swoop. "Bye Bye Love" climbed to #2 by May of 1957, denied the #1 spot by Elvis' "All Shook Up." Their next release did make it all the way to #1 in September, 1957, though not before causing some unexpected controversy along the way. **"Wake Up Little Susie,"** written by the Bryants, tells the tale of a young couple who innocently fall asleep at a drive-in movie, only to wake to the horrifying realization that it's four in the morning(!) They know, too well, that their parents will be furious and that, even worse, their friends won't believe that it really *was* all very innocent: "Our goose is cooked, our reputation is shot!" Now Jerry Lee Lewis would have worried about his reputation if he ever brought a girl home *before* four in the morning, and the moral values expressed in "Wake Up Little Susie" are certainly of the highest order. Nonetheless, the suggestion that a boy and girl had been sleeping together in *any* circumstances caused the song to be banned by many radio stations—which, needless to say, increased its sales.

The music of "Wake Up Little Susie" follows the pattern set by "Bye Bye Love." Don again takes the lead on the brief solo sections; otherwise the song is sung in close parallel harmony. The background arrangement carries the song along unobtrusively, with the Everly's jumbo acoustics again up front in the mix and given an integral part in the structure of the song. Boudleaux Bryant: "After 'Bye Bye Love' was a hit, we realized that the [guitar] intro... was a valuable piece of business. So on "Wake Up Little Susie" we wrote all these little riffs into the song. The holes were left for the guitars to be featured. It was similar to "Bye Bye Love," but at the same time a modification."[4]

The remainder of the Everly Brothers' uptempo hits at Cadence used similar vocal and instrumental arrangements. In 1958, the Bryants supplied the light-hearted "Bird Dog" and "Problems," two of their most specifically "teenage" songs, while Roy Orbison contributed "Claudette," a good example of the Everly Brothers as "choir boy rockabillies." Don and Phil wrote their own hits as well, including Don's "Till I Kissed You" (backed by Buddy Holly's band, the Crickets, shortly after Holly's death in 1959) and Phil's "When Will I Be Loved," a particularly superb effort with soaring harmonies and elegantly crafted lyrics. (A laconic 1975 cover of "When Will I Be Loved" helped launch Linda Ronstadt's career.) While convincing in uptempo songs written by or especially for them, the Everly Brothers' natural charm and restraint made their attempts at straight rock & roll seem a bit tentative. Their honky-tonk version of Gene Vincent's "Be-Bop-A-Lula" and their several Little Richard covers lack the excitement and bold sexuality of the original versions.

On the other hand, the Everly Brothers were the greatest teen ballad singers of the 1950's. Their sad, yearning slow songs were the best vehicles for their voices and keen melodic sense. The Bryants' **"All I Have to Do Is Dream"** hit #1 in 1958 and went a long way toward erasing any ethical doubts still lingering from the "Wake Up Little Susie" controversy. It is a beautiful, longing teenage love song—the melodies are gorgeous, the harmonies impeccable, Chet Atkins plays a wonderfully understated tremolo guitar accompaniment and the lyrics capture both the dream of idyllic love and the shattering of the illusion in the most tender and uncontrived manner. The equally and achingly beautiful **"Let It Be Me"** was recorded in New York in 1960, near the end of their tenure with Cadence, and was their first recording outside of Nashville. The syrupy strings were a sign of things to come, but the beautiful singing and sentiment more than made up for the Hollywood-ish production.

The Everly Brother's own ballads were just as convincing: the country-waltz "I Wonder If I Care As Much" and the beautifully written "Oh What a Feeling," for example, were ample proof of their songwriting talents and delivered a more personal message than the songs written for them by others.

As always, though, the sentiments were shared and the messages were delivered by a set of identical musical twins, with an unearthly tightness that can only come from a lifetime of playing and singing together. As Philip Norman put it, they sang "as one voice, one guitar, suitors for the hand of one girl..."[5]

The Everly Brothers on Warner Brothers

The Everly Brothers left Cadence in 1960 after disputes with Archie Bleyer and Wesley Rose over royalty payments, moved to California and signed with Warner Brothers Records for a guarantee of $1,000,000 over ten years. In the process, they lost the songwriting services of the Bryants, who were still under contract to Acuff-Rose, and had to abandon their recording base and superstar sessionmen. Their voices remained as sweet as ever, but the inspired Nashville team that had created their best records was history.

Nonetheless, their first Warner Brothers release proved to be the biggest hit of their career, holding the #1 spot for five weeks in the Spring of 1960. **"Cathy's Clown,"** written together by Don and Phil, finds the singer(s) despairing at being such a sucker for a girl ("I gotta stand tall, you know a man can't crawl") but still longing for her return. As if to reflect his (their) ambivalence, the rhythm of the song alternates between a swing feel for the verses and a quasi-march for the choruses, which also feature a clever twist in the harmonies, with Phil—the Everly's high voice—holding a single note while Don descends with the melody. (A similar high held-note harmony shapes the Beatles' "Please Please Me"; the Beatles used the relative complexity of "Cathy's Clown" to test prospective drummers as well.)

The Everly Brothers followed "Cathy's Clown" with another original, the beautiful ballad "So Sad (To Watch Good Love Go Bad)." While off to a great start at their new label, Don and Phil were not prolific songwriters and soon had to search out songs by other writers. Given a good song they could still make a great record, such as 1962's eloquent **"Crying in the Rain,"** written by Brill Building writers Carole King and Howie Greenfield. Here the wounded lover cries in the rain so no one will see his tears: "I've got my pride and I know how to hide all my sorrow and pain—I'll do my cryin' in the rain."

Unfortunately, most of their Warner Brothers material lacked the inspired lyricism of "Crying in the Rain," and leaned instead toward bland pop that took them further away from their country and rock roots. Their uptempo material lost much of its transparent buoyancy and was often bogged down by novelty productions, as in the vaudevillian arrangement of "Walk Right Back" and the overblown settings of "Temptation" and "Muskrat," while their ballads, such as "Ebony Eyes" and "Don't Blame Me," fell victim to the musical and sentimental excesses they had managed to avoid at Cadence.

Thicker than Water

The Everly Brother's last big hit was 1962's "That's Old Fashioned," appropriately enough. To avoid being drafted, the brothers enlisted in the Marine Corps Reserves that same year and spent six months on active duty. They had barely resurfaced when the Beatles, with all their echoes of the Everly's style, signaled the end of their chart-topping days. The Everly Brothers limped along rootlessly through the sixties with a disorienting schedule of nightclub, Las Vegas, country & western, hippie and "oldies" shows. As adults, they remained trapped in the world of their teenage songs, and their musical identity crisis was mirrored by drug, marital and other personal problems.

After a lifetime of doing everything *together*, the Everly Brothers finally snapped in 1973. As with everything else in their lives and careers, their breakup took place in public and onstage, during the second of three performances at Knott's Berry Farm near Los Angeles. In the midst of their ever-sweet harmonies, Phil slammed his guitar to the ground and stormed offstage, leaving Don to finish the shows solo, explaining only that "the Everly Brothers died ten years ago."

The next ten years were barren times for the two brothers. Both released solo albums with little success and seemed to spend most of their energy on avoiding each other and any associations with their past. (They only met once—at their father's funeral.) The ice was finally broken in 1983 with an emotional reunion concert in London that was filmed for TV and released as an album. Old fan Paul McCartney wrote "On the Wings of a Nightingale" for their comeback single in 1984, and the Everly Brothers have remained on good terms since then, recording periodically, touring often and still sounding as pure and harmonious as ever. There is a reassuring sense of completeness to the Everly Brothers' saga: their reunion, renewed career and brotherly reconciliation are as heartwarming as the best of their music.

EDDIE COCHRAN

Eddie Cochran was born in Oklahoma on October 3, 1938, and grew up in Albert Lea, Minnesota, just a half-hour drive from Clear Lake, Iowa, where his friend Buddy Holly died in 1959. Cochran's family moved to the Los Angeles area in 1953, making Cochran another "L. A. Rockabilly" (he was even engaged to one of Ricky Nelson's songwriters, Sharon Sheely, at the time of his death). Although he was a big star in England and a major influence on a generation of British guitar players, Cochran's fame in America was short-lived and based largely on the eternal popularity of one song: "Summertime Blues."

Eddie Cochran's musical and vocal style—and clothes and hair style and moody look—were strongly influenced by Elvis. After discovering Elvis'

Sun recordings, Cochran switched from country to rockabilly and hooked up with **Jerry Capehart**, who would be the co-writer and co-producer for all of his recordings. Cochran's first break came in 1956, when he signed with Liberty Records and landed an appearance in *The Girl Can't Help It*, one of the first big-budget "rocksploitation" films. The movie featured Cochran singing his own "**Twenty Flight Rock**," a great rockabilly number that seemed destined to be a hit until Liberty inexplicably chose instead to release a much weaker song, "Sittin' in the Balcony." Although "Sittin' in the Balcony" did hit the Top Twenty in 1957, the far superior "Twenty Flight Rock" was lost in the shuffle.

The record and the movie appearance landed Cochran on the national package tours in 1957, but it was another year before he returned to the record charts. In the meantime he recorded steadily, having worked out a deal with Liberty and his publishing company that allowed him generous access to the recording studio. Capehart and Cochran used the opportunity to refine their studio technique, and in the summer of 1958 they came up with a classic.

"Summertime Blues"

"Summertime Blues" has been covered by countless bands—most notably by the Who and the San Francisco band Blue Cheer, who recorded a ponderously thundering version in 1968 that is often pegged as the "first heavy metal record." "Summertime Blues" was the first "power chord" classic, with a signature guitar riff played out in strong chords that obliterate the line between "rhythm" and "lead." Of course, power chords are custom-made for the electric guitar, where sheer volume can create a riveting effect and turn the hammered chords into an act of primitive defiance (as in later power chord classics like the Kinks' "You Really Got Me" and "All Day and All of the Night" and the Who's "My Generation" and "Baba O'Riley"). It is something of a shock, then, to notice that Cochran's original version is played on *acoustic* guitars, yet it still manages to sound full and exciting. Cochran close-miked his acoustic and used the still novel technique of overdubbing to create a layer of several acoustic guitars all playing the same part, giving the record a strong sound while retaining the airy quality of the acoustic guitar.

The rhythm track of "Summertime Blues" mirrors the understated power of the guitars, dispensing with the expected drum beats in favor of overdubbed hand claps and light percussion (also supplied by Cochran, who played virtually everything on the record and provided the deep, echoing voice of the boss, father and congressman as well). The prominent bass line which begins the song and provides much of its rhythmic drive is played on a six-string electric bass—an uncommon instrument, especially at a time when *any* type of electric bass was still a rarity. The overall effect of the record is unique: full yet light, simple yet intricately crafted, "Summertime Blues" is a masterpiece of production work from one of rock's first studio visionaries. Cochran and Capehart purposefully crafted an "artificial" sound that couldn't be recreated live—created a *record* rather than simply a recorded performance. The Beatles later popularized this conception of recording as an art in itself, but in the fifties only Cochran and Buddy Holly had such a clear vision of the studio as a creative tool.

The lyrics of "Summertime Blues" are as ageless as the music: any teenager can relate to the song's restless boredom and frustration. Like Chuck Berry, Cochran and Capehart recognized and wrote to the concerns of teenagers, focusing on the annoying parents and despotic bosses and all the other hassles from the adult world that are the real truths of summer. (Capehart: "I knew that there had been a lot of songs about summer, but none about the *hardships* of summer."[6]) Cochran highlights the frustration and its cause in dramatic stops and starts that punctuate the song, half filled by the lamenting refrain ("there ain't no cure for the summertime blues") and half overtaken by the Voices of Authority that form the immovable objects of teenage life, all the way up to the Halls of Congress: "I'd like to help you, son, but you're too young to vote!"

"C'mon Everybody"

Cochran's next release, "C'mon Everybody," followed the "Summertime Blues" blueprint: layers of acoustic guitar power chords, light percussion (in this case tambourines), a prominent six-string bass and lyrics aimed right at teenage life—this time the *fun* side of teenage life. Like its predecessor, "C'mon Everybody" is punctuated with stops and starts that highlight the title refrain, which is now a call for everyone to come on over and party: the house is empty, the folks are gone... and if they come home early? "Who *cares*? C'mon Everybody!"

"C'mon Everybody," released at the end of 1958, was a big hit in England but barely reached the Top Forty in America. The power chords and stop-and-start arrangement appeared again in "Nervous Breakdown," a great song but a dismal chart failure. Cochran responded with a variety of country, R&B and pop styles that hint at the range of his talent but did little to reverse his fortunes in his homeland.[7] When the excellent "Something Else" failed to hit, Cochran headed for England, where packed houses greeted him as a conquering hero. Cochran's records and live performances had a profound and direct influence on the power chord guitar style of the Who's Pete Townshend and the Kinks' Dave Davies, and on other stars of rock's second generation.

Then, suddenly, it was over. On April 17, 1960, Cochran died in a car crash while on his way to the airport for a trip back to the States. The same crash badly injured his friend Gene Vincent and shocked fans still mourning the loss of Buddy Holly. Only 21 at the time of his death, Eddie Cochran had already proven himself a formidable creative talent. He left behind one of rock's all-time classics, but it's safe and sad to say that his potential remained largely untapped.

BUDDY HOLLY

The last of the true giants to emerge in the 1950's, Buddy Holly remains one of rock's most enduring and inspiring artists. He was a good friend and touring companion of the Everly Brothers and Eddie Cochran, and had a similar interest in combining his country roots and the melodies of pop with the harder edges of rock & roll, and a penchant for innovations in the studio that pre-dated and surpassed Cochran's. His tragic death in a plane crash on February 3, 1959—immortalized in Don McLean's "American Pie" as The Day the Music Died—was one of rock's greatest losses. While the crash catapulted Holly to Rock Legend status, it extinguished a musical vision that was uniquely capable of pointing the young music toward the next decade—toward a new model of a rock "band" and a new synthesis of rock and pop that, with his death, would not be fully realized until the arrival of the Beatles.

Buddy Holly & the Crickets

Buddy Holly was the most eclectically creative of rock's Founding Fathers. In less than two years, beginning in 1957 with "That'll Be the Day," Holly turned out "Peggy Sue," "Maybe Baby," "Words of Love," "Everyday," "Not Fade Away," "It's So Easy," "Rave On" and other rock classics that run the gamut from ballads and mid-tempo pop songs to hard rockers and rockabilly rave-ups. Holly was the first major white artist to write and produce his own songs, and the first to fully appreciate the recording studio as a creative "instrument" and to explore its possibilities, experimenting with new sounds, instruments and production techniques. Holly was an inventive singer—his stretched syllables and playful hiccups are rock trademarks—and an influential guitarist who popularized the Fender Stratocaster and, with Chuck Berry, pretty well defined rock & roll guitar playing.

Holly was also a member of a true band, **The Crickets**—the prototype for the self-contained rock band we now take for granted. While Holly was clearly the focus, the Crickets were a band of equals, often co-writing and always working out the song arrangements together, so that the "arrangement" and the "song" were inseparable. Holly, guitarist **Niki Sullivan**, bassist **Joe B. Mauldin** and drummer **Jerry "J. I." Allison** established the two guitars, bass and drums attack that fueled the British Invasion. Holly was revered in England, where the Crickets model became the norm and Holly's songs became staples of every band's act. (The Beatles and the Hollies even took their band names from the Crickets' inspiration. In fact, the first song the Beatles ever recorded, in a makeshift Liverpool studio in 1958, was Holly's "That'll Be the Day," and their first official release, "Love Me Do," was clearly influenced by Holly's inventive simplicity. The big beat and arching melodies of "She Loves You," too, seem straight out of the Buddy Holly songbook—the playful twist on "well I saw her yester*da-ee-aay*" only confirms the debt. The Rolling Stones, meanwhile, made their first dent on the American charts with their cover of Holly's "Not Fade Away.")

It's a good thing the Crickets *didn't* depend on the personal magnetism of a star frontman... Gangly, bespectacled and supremely ordinary, Buddy Holly looked more like a class nerd than a rock star, and he certainly didn't look *anything* like that paragon of sexuality, Elvis Presley, against whom all rock stars were supposed to be measured. Holly's endearing "boy next door" image turned out to be an asset, however. While it was painfully unrealistic to imagine ever being like *Elvis*, Holly's message to all guys with glasses and shy personalities was: "That could be ME!" Buddy seemed reachable—an attainable goal, and one could almost hear a collective sigh of relief and the sound of guitar sales skyrocketing when average guys everywhere caught their first glimpse of the kid singing "That'll Be the Day." Holly's utter lack of sex appeal also helped keep the focus on the music, where it belonged. As Jerry Allison recalled, "compared to Frankie Avalon and all those slick dudes, we were just a bunch of ugly pickers who just picked. But really, that made it all seem better, because we felt like everybody that liked us, liked us because of what we *could* pick. They were fans because of the music, not just because of the emotions or the good looks or whatever."[8]

The simple purity of Holly's songs—the chords, melodies and lyrics all seem immediately familiar—link him the other great "rock poet" of the era, Chuck Berry. Like Berry, he chronicled life in Young America with great wit and insight. Unlike Berry, however, Buddy always sang in the first person—not as an objective observer, but as an active participant very much in the fray, going through and giving voice to all the joys and heartaches his audience felt. Holly figured in the transition from the brazen sexuality of the rockabillies and Little Richard to the more innocent "holding hands" love of the early '60's pop era, but his view of love was never simple-minded and his songs have an emotional resonance that was sorely lacking in the music of his "teen idol" descendants. Holly's music still rings true. As Bruce Springsteen once said, "I play Buddy Holly every night before I go on—it keeps me honest."[9]

Background: Lubbock and Nashville

Charles Hardin Holley was born on September 7, 1936 in Lubbock, Texas, a conservative West Texas Bible Belt city known as the "Hub of the South Plains." The youngest of four children, he was given the affectionate nickname "Buddy" at birth. (He decided to drop the "e" from Holley after his name was misspelled on his first recording contract; he often used his middle name for songwriting credits.) The Holleys were something of a musical family, and Buddy developed an early love for the country & western and western swing that filled the dancehalls and radio airwaves of the Southwest. Holly was also influenced by black music, though Lubbock's geographic isolation and the Holley's middle class, urban sensibilities meant that Buddy did not have the direct contact with black music and culture that his rockabilly compatriots in the Deep South experienced. The radio was his link, and he was particularly fond of "Stan's Record Review," a late night rhythm & blues show from Shreveport, Louisiana. (Guitarist Sonny Curtis, who played with Holly in 1955-56, recalls the many nights he "fell asleep in Holly's old Oldsmobile listening to Shreveport at 1 o'clock in the morning."[10])

The arrival of Elvis Presley in Lubbock in 1955 was the turning point for Holly, who was already playing in a "Western and Bop" combo that had a regular booking on a local radio station. Holly had been a fan of Elvis since "That's All Right" hit the South, but the records were one thing—*seeing* Elvis in action was quite another, as Curtis recalls: "Elvis just blew Buddy away. None of us had ever seen anything like Elvis, the way he could get the girls jumping up and down, and that definitely impressed Holly. But it was the music that really turned Buddy around. He loved Presley's rhythm—it wasn't country and it wasn't blues, it was somewhere in the middle, and it suited Buddy just fine. After seeing Elvis, Buddy had only one way to go."[11]

Buddy embraced rockabilly and imitated Elvis as best he could. The growing popularity of rockabilly brought his band steady work around Lubbock and, sooner than he'd dreamed possible, in short order won a recording contract with Decca Records. Holly left for Nashville in January 1956, confident that he was on his way to stardom. Instead, his association with Decca and producer Owen Bradley was uncomfortable for all concerned. The Nashville establishment was searching for an answer to Elvis, though with little taste or feel for the rockabilly that seemed so natural in Memphis. Only two poorly promoted singles, "Blue Days, Black Nights" and "Modern Don Juan," were released before Decca decided to drop its option on Holly's contract at the end of 1956. Owen Bradley: "I think we gave him the best shot we knew how to give him, at the time. But it just wasn't the right combination; the chemistry wasn't right. It just wasn't meant to be. We didn't understand, and he didn't know how to tell us."[12] (Nashville remained clueless about rock until the Everly Brothers came along a year later.)

The Crickets and Norman Petty

A disheartened Buddy Holly returned to Lubbock and assimilated the lessons—good and bad—he'd learned in Nashville. In February, 1957, Holly, drummer Jerry Allison and bassist Larry Wellborn traveled the hundred miles from Lubbock to Norman Petty's studio in Clovis, New Mexico to record some demotapes to send out to other record companies. For the occasion he revamped a song that he had already recorded for Decca: "That'll Be The Day."

Norman Petty built his studio in 1955 to record his own group, the Norman Petty Trio, then began recording other acts to finance his operations. As the owner of the best-equipped studio for many hundreds of miles around, his services were in great and constant demand. Petty was one of the independent producers so crucial to the development of rock & roll: a Southwestern Sam Phillips, though unlike Phillips he did not start his own record label and chose instead to lease his recordings to established labels. Petty worked briefly with a young Roy Orbison in 1956 and recorded the 1957 hits "Party Doll" and "I'm Sticking With You" for Buddy Knox and Jimmy Bowen, but his place in rock history was assured by his association with Buddy Holly and the Crickets.

As the Crickets' manager and producer, Petty has been a much-maligned figure among Buddy Holly fans. Shortly before he died, Holly split angrily with Petty over his failure to account properly for the group's earnings, and Buddy's widow claims that, because of Petty, Holly was virtually forced to go on his fatal final tour, a backbreaking mid-winter marathon that he would never have considered unless he was in desperate need of money. (Maria was pregnant at the time, which heightened Holly's financial anxiety. She miscarried after his death.)

Petty was clearly guilty of the common practice of adding his name to the songwriting credits of songs he had little or nothing to do with, thereby gaining a share of the publishing royalties. (Petty is listed as co-author on nearly all of Holly's songs, including "That'll Be The Day," which Holly had recorded a year earlier for Decca!) Petty was also largely responsible for the syrupy background vocals that mar some of Holly's greatest songs. With the exception of "That'll Be the Day" and "Not Fade Away," in which the background vocals were actually sung by the Crickets, all of the background vocals were added later by Petty using Clovis singing groups. (Unfortunately, the Jordanaires' backing vocals on Elvis' RCA records seem to have been Petty's model for achieving an accessible pop sound—one Elvis influence too many, perhaps.)

Nonetheless, without Petty's creative support and valuable connections within the music industry, Holly might never have had a hit or tapped his true potential as an artist. Petty's state-of-the-art studio, relaxed manner and technical and musical knowledge provided a perfect environment for Holly's creative growth. Petty was as eager to experiment as Holly and was willing to give him free reign in the studio and a control over his own music that was rare for any artist in those days, and a far cry from the frustrations Holly had experienced in Nashville. In Petty, Buddy found his catalyst—an independent producer, free from any direct pressure to conform to a record company's idea of a "hit" and willing to let his artist develop his own style.

"That'll Be the Day"

A comparison of the stilted Decca version of "That'll Be The Day" with the hit version recorded in Clovis offers a clear example of the benefits of artistic freedom. The Clovis version is remarkably self-assured and original—no longer "rockabilly" and no longer an imitation of anyone. It is the real

Buddy Holly: a fully realized synthesis of pop, country, rockabilly and rock & roll.

"That'll Be The Day" glides along with a spacious sound and a mid-tempo, shuffling swing feel that accents every beat (in contrast to the frantic backbeats of rockabilly). The well-honed interplay between Holly's guitar and Allison's drums is particularly striking in the fills between the verses and choruses and the sudden, surprising shift to triplets in the final chorus (which the Beatles lifted for the ending of "I Want to Hold Your Hand"). Holly was essentially a *rhythm* guitar player, concerned primarily with creating a good blend with the band and a good feel for the song. Even his solos were, for the most part, merely sped-up and embellished rhythm figures, played with a jangling, trebly tone but otherwise very different from the single-string country picking and blues licks of rockabilly.

Holly shared Bo Diddley's love for sheer sound—for tone and timbre as shaping elements—and Chuck Berry's style of repetitive, rhythmic solos. In "That'll Be The Day," he takes the idea of a "rhythm lead" to an extreme: after launching the lead break with a brief double-string figure repeated in rapid succession, he locks onto one chord, hammers out a furious beat and builds up to... nothing! At the height of the solo, the guitar plummets to a simple, low-string boogie/rhythm pattern as Allison drops to an equally plain drum beat, leaving a huge hole in the middle of the song. The high register filigree then returns, along with Allison's cymbals, and dovetails into a repeat of the song's opening guitar figure to round out the lead break and usher the vocals back in.[13] This type of juxtaposition of low and high, dark and bright, and simple and embellished guitar styles was a central feature of Holly's playing (for which the wide range of tone settings and bright, chiming sound of the Fender Stratocaster was perfectly suited).

"That'll Be The Day" also features the sudden leaps, dramatic swoops, clipped words, playful hiccups, stretched syllables ("a-all your hugs," "we-ell-uh") and other trademarks of Holly's singing. While Gene Vincent exaggerated the dark and sexual overtones of Elvis' mannerisms, Buddy took Elvis' example in the opposite direction and sounded enthusiastic and playful rather than rebellious and sexual. Holly was always happy to pull back and poke fun at himself and his macho posturing in his songs, which, in this case, came from an appropriate source—John Wayne's sardonic refrain of *That'll* be the day" in the 1956 movie, *The Searchers*. The phrase became faddishly popular with teenagers, so Holly and Jerry Allison wrote the song around it, juxtaposing their hero's smug assurance that his girl could never leave him ("*That'll* be the day...") with his sheer terror that she actually might ("...when I *die*").

"That'll Be the Day" was picked up and issued, direct from the Clovis demotape, by Brunswick Records—a Decca subsidiary, of all things.[14] The record broke first in regional markets, then climbed up the national charts through the summer of 1957 and ended up at #1, still a rare feat for a rock & roll singer. The record was issued under the name "Crickets," a name Holly, Allison and new members bassist Joe B. Mauldin and rhythm guitarist Niki Sullivan had decided upon while looking through bug names in an encyclopedia. Niki Sullivan: "We did consider the name 'Beetles,' but Jerry said, 'aw, that's just a bug you'd want to step on,' so we immediately dropped that. Then Jerry came up with the idea of the Crickets... I remember him saying, 'they make music by rubbing their legs together,' and that cracked us up."[15]

The success of "That'll Be the Day" landed the Crickets on the package tours promoted by Dick Clark and Alan Freed, which brought rock fan Holly into close contact with personal heroes like Bo Diddley, Little Richard and Chuck Berry (who became his favorite crap-shooting partner during the endless hours on the tour buses), and fellow newcomers like Jerry Lee Lewis, Eddie Cochran and the Everly Brothers. While touring in the fifties wasn't the high-powered operation it is today, it did have its moments: the image of the two great "rock poets" shooting craps is certainly compelling, and Holly's widow Maria recalls times when Buddy had to calm down a naked, out of control Little Richard on the tour bus and throw a drunken Jerry Lee into a shower to sober him up for his set. Above all, a spirit of camaraderie and fun prevailed, which was especially important when the tours headed South into the land of racial hatred and segregation, where the black performers were forced to eat on the bus and stay at separate hotels, and where many city ordinances would not allow whites and blacks to appear on the same stage, forcing either the white or the black performers to temporarily leave the tour. Unfortunately, the happy unity that characterized the best aspects of rock & roll was far ahead of the general state of race relations in the real world.

NOT FADE AWAY: THE CRICKETS' MUSIC

The Crickets continued recording in Clovis (and, occasionally, New York) through 1957 and most of 1958. In that relatively brief period they produced a body of work that illustrates the formidable range of Buddy Holly's talent and his unique ability to combine the energy of rock & roll with the melodicism of pop. Although the Crickets' music gained much of its resonance from Holly's knack for transcending musical labels, it can still be loosely divided into three categories: the rockers, the ballads and the midtempo fusions of pop and rock.

Rockers

Songs like "Rave On," "Oh, Boy!," "I'm Lookin' for Someone to Love," "Rock Around with Ollie Vee" and "Not Fade Away" show Holly's love for straight rock & roll, which remained his stylistic home base through his brief career. "**Not Fade Away**" is one of Holly's strongest set of lyrics (and his greatest song title), sung with a swaggering confidence and backed by an astoundingly tight rhythm section. The song is built around a skeletal Bo Diddley beat, punctuated by constant stops and starts and fused together by Jerry Allison's truly inspired drumming—on a cardboard box! The exultant lead break of "Not Fade Away" is really just a fuller, higher and brighter version of the basic rhythm pattern—once again the *sound* and *feel* matter most to Holly, who had a true gift for knowing what to leave out, as the airy open space of "Not Fade Away" attests.

Inspired by the recurring "rave on!" refrain in Carl Perkins' "Dixie Fried," **"Rave On"** opens with a six syllable(!) "well," then plunges through two 12-bar blues verses that illustrate Holly's gift for finding a perfect melody for any mood or set of chords. The 16-bar chorus ("rave on, it's a crazy feelin'...") features a syncopated stop-start rhythm that dominates the rest of the song (in fact, the verses simply disappear, giving the song a rather strange aabbb form). Norman Petty's piano doubles Holly's rhythm guitar and takes the solo in the lead break. Although he is often called a "rockabilly," the relaxed feel, syncopated rhythms and tunefulness of "Rave On" point to why the label really isn't appropriate, even in his uptempo rockers.

Ballads

At the other extreme are the "true love" ballads, such as "Words of Love," "Listen To Me," "Everyday" and "True Love Ways," that highlight Holly's gift for melody and inventive studio work. **"Words of Love"** is endearingly direct and unaffected, with harmony hums and chiming guitars that take over when mere words fail: "Words of love you whisper soft and true, darling I love you, hmmmm..." Holly captures the wondrous promise of pure love without cloying or exaggerating the sentiment. "Words of Love" was also Holly's first experiment with overdubbing—he added extra guitar tracks and his own harmony vocals—and marked the first time any rock artist used the technique.[16] Overdubbing was a still painstaking and chancy process in those days of mono recorders: the original tracks (guitar, bass and drums) were recorded on one tape recorder, then re-recorded onto another while a new part was added, and so on, with the vocals added last. With no "final mixdowns" possible, the vocal and instrumental balances had to be right each time, though every pass between machines resulted in a loss of sound quality on the original tracks. On "Words of Love," even the deterioration of the original tracks worked to the song's advantage, creating a strange blend of distant, muffled drums and bass and close, intimate voices, with a lovely wash of guitars chiming in the middle.

The ethereal **"Everyday"** features Buddy's best moonstruck teen vocals and a delicate arrangement highlighted by Norman Petty's wife, Vi, on celesta, a distinctly non-rock instrument (it's inclusion was probably inspired by the celesta on Chuck Willis' "It's Too Late," which Buddy covered). The ever-inventive Jerry Allison abandoned the drums and simply slapped his knees to create a constant rhythm without disturbing the hushed intimacy of the music and sentiment. "Well All Right" has a similarly private tone, and an equally distinctive production dominated by a powerful acoustic guitar set against a galloping rhythm tapped out on the bell of a cymbal. The sophisticated strings, harp and saxophone arrangement of "True Love Ways," recorded in New York at Holly's last session, was a dramatic departure from his earlier work and was meant to reflect his deepening vision of love (he had just been married) and his "maturing" as an artist. But if "True Love Ways" would fit fairly comfortably within the pre-rock tradition of popular music, "Words of Love" and "Everyday" helped stake out a new, younger definition of "pop," redefined within the context of rock & roll, aimed at the young rock audience and rooted in the emotional and musical immediacy of rock & roll.

Midtempo pop-rock

Holly's best-known songs—"Peggy Sue," "It's So Easy," "Maybe Baby," "That'll Be the Day"—occupy a middle ground between rock and pop, fast and slow, hard and soft, and between the confident stance of his rockers and the idyllic innocence of his love songs. Implied just beneath the hopeful sentiment of **"Maybe Baby,"** for example, is "maybe *not*." The song is full of the clever rhymes and wordplays and playful singing of Holly's "Everyteen" persona. The Crickets give "Maybe Baby" a rock & roll grounding, but the song's melody-driven formal structure (built around clear refrains and contrasting "bridge" sections) owes more to pop and country models than to the beat-driven 12-bar blues structure of most rock & roll.

"Peggy Sue"

"Peggy Sue" was recorded in June, 1957, just as "That'll Be the Day" was beginning its chart ascent. Like it's spiritual mate, Chuck Berry's "Johnny B. Goode," the song sums up nearly every aspect of Holly's style. The words are simple and direct and the singing is a virtual textbook of Holly-isms: "Sue" is stretched from one syllable to nine in the course of the song and is sung with every possible inflection, sometimes growling and manly, other times pleading and childlike, as if he is determined to try every approach to win Peggy Sue back. Like any lovestruck teenager, all he can really think to do is repeat her name, which he does—30 times!

"Peggy Sue" was originally entitled "Cindy Lou," after Holly's niece, and was conceived as a calypso-styled rhumba. Jerry Allison convinced Buddy to change the name to "Peggy Sue," after Allison's current girlfriend and future bride, and contributed the quasi-roll "paradiddles" that erased the rhumba feel and gave the song a *pulse*, rather than a beat. Allison had a hard time keeping the paradiddles steady on the initial takes, though, prompting Holly to threaten to "change it back to Cindy Lou." Allison nailed the next take. The rolling drums—all tom-toms rather than the usual snare and cymbals—give

"Peggy Sue" a very unique and original feel, reminiscent only of the hypnotic beat of "Bo Diddley."

The lead break in "Peggy Sue" is a further example of Holly's rhythmically oriented lead guitar style. The high, chiming embellishment of the song's 12-bar blues outline contrasts with the darker tone used in the verses and provides an emotional release without upsetting the flow of the song the way a more intricate solo would have. Holly's constant, rapid downstrokes also add a percussive element to the verses, thanks to Petty's idea of placing a microphone by Holly's right hand to pick up the sound of his pick hitting the strings (which seems to occupy an entirely different aural space from the droning chords coming from Holly's amp). Niki Sullivan was recruited to flick the pickup switch on Holly's guitar at the beginning and end of the lead break, so that Holly could jump directly to the bright sound of the lead without disturbing his rhythm. As a result, the lead explodes suddenly out of Holly's guitar rhythm and then, just as suddenly, implodes back into the mix when the singing returns—a great effect.

To add a further dimension to the sound of "Peggy Sue," Petty isolated Allison in a separate room, fed the drums through an echo chamber and then phased the drums in and out—from "up close" to far away—through the course of the song by varying the volume and amount of echo. (The contrast is most noticeable at the beginning of the song, where the drums alternate every two beats between a full echo and a completely "dry" sound.) It is a genuinely weird and striking effect: drums are "supposed" to keep a beat, not pulse in and out and echo around in the distance (just as guitar *picks* aren't supposed to be heard at all, and lead breaks should have *leads*). Petty and the Crickets transformed a simple nursery-rhyme of a song into a ritual lovecall unlike anything surrounding it in the pop charts.

"Buddy Holly Lives"

Buddy Holly's life had changed considerably by the end of 1958. He married Maria Elena Santiago in August, 1958, and left Clovis to live in an apartment in New York's Greenwich Village. The marriage wasn't exactly the product of a long, drawn-out romance: "We met and he took me out to dinner and proposed to me that same night. I said 'yeah, sure—why not?' I thought he was just being friendly, but the next morning he was at my door..."[17]

Meanwhile, his financial disputes with Petty brought their partnership to an unpleasant end. Holly remained close friends with the Crickets, but that partnership also ended with their decision to remain in Lubbock and continue working with Petty. Holly found himself truly a solo artist for the first time, and began to explore new possibilities. Home tapes from his last months show him experimenting with a wide range of styles, and his last recording session, produced by Dick Jacobs in New York in October 1958, yielded "True Love Ways," "It Doesn't Matter Anymore," "Moondreams" and

"Raining In My Heart," all backed by a lush string section.[18] At the time of his death, Holly was planning to open a studio of his own to produce new talent, and hoping to record duets with Ray Charles and continue his recent collaborations with the Everly Brothers and young Lubbock singer Waylon Jennings. Under pressure from his record label, however, and in desperate need of money, he put his plans on hold and agreed to go on a grueling midwinter tour of the upper Midwest.

Holly assembled Tommy Allsup, Waylon Jennings and drummer Charlie Bunch to accompany him on his tour with fellow headliners **Ritchie Valens**, a young Latin-American rocker whose "Donna" and "La Bamba" were currently climbing the charts, **J. P. "The Big Bopper" Richardson**, a Texas disc jockey who had recently hit with "Chantilly Lace," and newcomers Dion & the Belmonts. Holly never referred to his new group as "the Crickets," and always hoped for a Crickets reunion. Jerry Allison and Joe Mauldin were thinking the same thing, as Maria recalls: "They called me the night of the accident to find out where Buddy was going to be the next night so they could fly there and join him. I gave them the number where I talked to Buddy for the last time and they called him, but he had just left..."[19]

Buddy Holly gave his last performance at the Surf Ballroom in Clear Lake, Iowa, on the night of February 2, 1959. After the show, Holly, Valens and the Big Bopper boarded a small chartered plane to fly to Fargo, North Dakota, the site of the next night's show. Tired of the rickety and freezing-cold tour bus (drummer Bunch had to quit the tour when his feet became frostbitten while riding the bus!), Holly had chartered the plane for himself and his band; but while the Crickets were trying unsuccessfully to reach Holly by phone, his new band was being saved by further twists of ironic fate. Allsup recalls: "He'd chartered this plane to take three people—me, him and Waylon were gonna fly. Well the Big Bopper had caught the flu that afternoon, so somehow that night Waylon gave up his seat to the Bopper. When I went back in Ritchie was in there signing autographs, and he said 'you gonna let me fly, guy?,' and I said 'No,' and he said 'come on—flip?' He had half-a-dollar and he said, 'let's flip a coin—heads I go, tails you go.' I said 'OK, if you want to go that bad.' Well, he won the toss..."[20] Sometime in the early morning hours of February 3, 1959, the plane went down, killing the three stars and their pilot.

Buddy Holly held out the promise of being one of the few fifties stars adaptable enough to survive and thrive through the changing tastes of the early sixties, and he may well have been a creative bridge between the rock & roll era and the British Invasion. Instead, he died at 22, less than two years after "That'll Be The Day" was recorded, but he still managed to leave a lasting mark on rock & roll. His music transcends generational lines, musical boundaries and the deadly confines of mere nostalgia. His songs have never needed any updating to sound vital or ring true: the Beatles' note-for-note cover of "Words of Love," the Rolling Stones' version of "Not Fade Away," Linda Ronstadt's "That'll Be The Day" and "It's So Easy," James Taylor's

"Everyday" and the many other Holly covers that have been hits over the years never really *sound* like covers, just as Holly's timeless originals never really sound like "oldies." As with Chuck Berry, his influence as one of the true Originators has been so pervasive that it's no exaggeration to say that anyone who has picked up a guitar or written a rock song since 1959 is somehow descended from Buddy Holly. As Sonny Curtis put it, in a song about his old friend, "Buddy Holly lives every time we play rock & roll."

---

[1]Anka returned to the charts (and enraged feminists) in 1974 with "(You're) Having My Baby," and also wrote many hits for others, including "It Doesn't Matter Anymore" for Buddy Holly, "My Way" for Frank Sinatra and Johnny Carson's *Tonight Show* theme music. Bobby Darin surfaced as a quasi-folksinger after a mid-sixties career slump and a severe identity crisis. His hit version of Tim Hardin's "If I Were a Carpenter" revived his career, but Darin died during heart surgery in 1973 at the age of 37.

[2]Joe Smith, "Off the Record," (New York: Warner, 1988), p. 138.

[3]May 8, 1986 *Rolling Stone* magazine, issue #473, p. 86.

[4]ibid., pg. 56.

[5]Philip Norman, "The Road Goes On Forever," (New York: Fireside, 1982).

[6]From album liner notes for "Eddie Cochran: Legendary Masters Series," (United Artists Records - UAS-9959, 1971).

[7]The country-style "Cut Across Shorty" was recorded at Cochran's last session, in January 1960, and featured Buddy Holly's old band, the Crickets--less than a year after Holly's death, and only three months before Cochran's.

[8]John Goldrosen, "The Buddy Holly Story," (1975; rpt. New York: Quick Fox, 1979), p. 113.

[9]Goldrosen, "The Buddy Holly Story."

[10]June, 1982 *Guitar Player* Magazine, Vol. 16, N0. 6, p. 78.

[11]ibid. Buddy and Elvis became friends on that first visit to Lubbock, and when Elvis returned to Lubbock later in the year, Buddy showed him around town and took him home to meet his parents!

[12]Goldrosen, p. 47.

[13]The opening guitar flourish was borrowed from the piano intro to Fats Domino's "Blue Monday")

[14]The fact that Holly ended up back under the Decca umbrella was a complete and, for Holly, amusing coincidence; it also neatly solved the potentially sticky problem of releasing "That'll Be The Day" on a different label, since Decca was unlikely to sue its own subsidiary. In a unique arrangement, Holly was given a separate recording contract with another Decca subsidiary, Coral Records, which credited their releases simply to "Buddy Holly." This left the group in the rather confusing but advantageous position of being able to have two records out simultaneously (and of often finding themselves double-billed

on concert marquees as both "The Crickets" and "Buddy Holly") In any case, the crediting was an afterthought based on the timing of the releases and the decision of whether or not to add background vocals to the songs.

[15]Goldrosen, "The Buddy Holly Story." Contrary to legend, the name was not inspired by the unscheduled appearance of a chirping cricket during one of their recording sessions, though that did happen later--you can hear it at the end of "I'm Gonna Love You Too."

[16]Holly and Petty didn't "invent" overdubbing: it was pioneered by Les Paul in the early fifties and used previously on a few pop records, such as Patti Page's 1953 hit, "Doggie in the Window."

[17]Maria Holly, in conversation with author.

[18]The middle-of-the-road sound of "True Love Ways" may indeed have been a sign of things to come, though it seems more likely that Holly was simply experimenting to fill the empty space left by his split with the Crickets. In any case, the impression left by the lush strings in his final recordings and in the last concert scene of the otherwise excellent movie, *The Buddy Holly Story*, left many with the unfortunate impression that Holly was moving to the mainstream. He certainly wasn't touring the north plains in the middle of the winter with an orchestra! The last tour was straight rock & roll.

[19]In conversation with author.

[20]Tommy Allsup quote from *The Real Buddy Holly Story* (video).

Photo courtesy of UPI/BETTMAN

Phil Spector with George Harrison, 1971.

[10] EARLY SIXTIES POP: WORST OF TIMES, BEST OF TIMES

The crash in Clear Lake came to symbolize the end of rock & roll's Golden Era. By the early sixties, *pop* ruled the airwaves and rock & roll seemed to belong to an era already past: a brief, exciting moment in the history of popular music and the hearts of a single generation of teenagers. 1959 saw the release of *Oldies But Goodies*, the first rock "oldies" album and the surest sign that an era had passed. As a new generation of teenyboppers emerged, their older brothers and sisters grew up and entered the adult world of steady jobs, families and folk music, and began talking about the "good old days" of Elvis and Jerry Lee. It seemed that "rock & roll," like Dixieland and Big Band music, was just a passing trend in the end. (Indeed, the term "rock & roll," in the strictest sense, is applied exclusively to the music of the fifties.)

A few years earlier, Pat Boone had lamented that teenagers would not have the type of "good music" that earlier generations could reminisce to: "... when I listen to the swinging music of the 30's and 40's, to Tex Beneke, Glenn Miller, the Dorsey Brothers, I wonder how we're going to feel in ten years when we say, 'Listen dear, they're playing our song,' and in the background we hear 'Hound Dog' or 'Tutti Frutti'!"[1] But it *was* happening: rock & roll was already slipping into a nostalgia haze, with its own nostalgic "classics" that could turn rapidly aging young adults into misty-eyed teenagers once again. Pat Boone's always-questionable tastes aside, "In the Mood" and "Stardust" had nothing on "Earth Angel," or "Tutti Frutti," for that matter!

Whatever the fate of rock's past, it suddenly looked a lot better than its present. The early sixties were populated by an alarming number of cleancut entertainers singing odes to "Puppy Love," lunchboxes and good citizenship. The Melody replaced the Beat as the focus of the music, and the liberating energy of rock & roll all but disappeared into the bland conformity of wholesome entertainment. Although there was actually plenty of good music still being made, it was getting harder to find. In terms of sales and exposure, the early sixties were dominated by teen-oriented fluff, written in assembly line fashion by professional songwriters, sung by handsome "teen idols" with little discernible talent, and plugged mercilessly by the music industry on Top Forty radio and *American Bandstand*. Rebellious rock & roll had become harmless pop.

The "Death" of Rock & Roll

Rock's "death" happened as gradually, and then seemed as sudden, as its explosive birth. Of the many factors that contributed to rock's decline, the loss of the Founding Fathers was the most dramatic: Buddy Holly dead, Eddie Cochran dead, Elvis in the Army (then, even worse, Hollywood), Little Richard in Bible school, Jerry Lee Lewis blacklisted, Chuck Berry on his way to jail... A wholesale massacre. Aside from the newly respectable Elvis, only the

Everly Brothers and, to a lesser extent, Fats Domino were still recording hits in the early sixties, and they had *always* been harmless and respectable.

Rock & roll needed unifying leaders who could challenge the established order and keep things exciting, but no such figures emerged again until the Beatles launched rock's Renaissance in 1964. Jerry Lee Lewis offered the best diagnosis of the disease and its eventual cure: "All you could hear was Bobby: Bobby Vee, Bobby Vinton, Bobby Denton, Bobby Rydell, Bobby Darin... There was nothing but Bobbies on the radio. Thank God for the Beatles... Cut them down like wheat before the sickle."[2] In the meantime, however, the void left by the departed giants was filled by tepid, industry-approved entertainers and the charts became as predictable as the movies the former King of Rock & Roll was churning out. The status quo was back in force and the lessons of Jerry Lee, Chuck Berry and other victims of the backlash against rock & roll inspired career-conscious artists to adopt more wholesome images and record songs that couldn't possibly offend anyone. With any luck, you could end up like Bobby Darin, an "all-around entertainer" playing Caesar's Palace, the Copacabana and other respectable venues that wouldn't let Little Richard wash their dishes. As Bobby Rydell put it, "if you ask me my ambition, careerwise, that's easy—I want to grow up to be an all-round entertainer, like Sinatra."[3]

The rock & roll explosion had forced the music industry, which treasures nothing above a profitable predictability, into the uncomfortable position of *responding* to rather than dictating popular taste. Originally the product of Outsiders (blacks and "hillbillies") recording in renegade studios for small independent record labels, rock & roll moved into the mainstream with the huge success of Elvis at RCA. Once it was clear that rock & roll wasn't going to be a "passing fad," and that there was a *lot* of money to be made from it, the music industry swooped down with a vengeance and began smoothing over rock's big beat, rough edges and regional accents. The process was completed in the early sixties, when rock & roll was finally forced to make sense within the tradition and commercial framework of popular music.

The top selling songs for the years 1955 through 1960 chronicle the return to normalcy with depressing clarity: 1955/"Rock Around the Clock" (Bill Haley); 1956/"Don't Be Cruel" (Elvis); 1957/"All Shook Up" (Elvis); 1958/"Volare" (Domenico Modungo); 1959/"Mack the Knife" (Bobby Darin); 1960/"Theme from *A Summer Place*" (The Percy Faith Orchestra). Bobby Lewis' dance classic "Tossin' and Turnin'" topped 1961, but it was closely followed by the Highwaymen's "Michael Row the Boat Ashore" and Lawrence Welk's(!) "Calcutta." Things really were looking bleak.

Rock had come full circle back to the bland pop that it had originally rebelled against, though with one major difference: rock & roll had demonstrated the enormous buying power of American teenager, and most of the music was still crafted with that audience in mind. The beat was softened but still danceable, the lyrics were pasteurized but still aimed specifically at the "youngsters," and the arrangements still used "traditional" rock instruments (though now often sweetened by strings and background choirs). In fact, the audience was growing even younger. Impressionable pubescent girls became the target audience, and the nation of juvenile delinquents that rock haters predicted seemed to have vanished with Elvis' sideburns on the floor of the Army Induction Center. For the most part, Young America bought what it was sold: polite music by dreamy singers who looked sort of like Elvis but *never* moved their hips when they sang...

The "Teen Idols" & the Payola Scandal

The night after the Clear Lake crash, a local teenager named Bobby Velline was chosen to sing a tribute to Buddy Holly in Fargo, North Dakota, the tour's next stop. Velline used his Holly-esque voice as a springboard to stardom as Bobby Vee, one of the more talented of teen idols ("Take Good Care of My Baby," "Run to Him," "The Night Has a Thousand Eyes"). Frankie Avalon and Fabian were then called in to replace the fallen stars and finish the tour. It was truly a crossing of the times: these and other "teen idols" dominated the pop charts in the early sixties with a watered-down version of Holly's melodic pop that lacked his sense of irony and his link to rock & roll's country and R&B roots.[4]

The most successful of the teen idols was Bobby Vinton, who had three pre-Beatle #1 hits with "Roses Are Red (My Love)," "Blue Velvet," and "There! I've Said It Again," which was, in fact, the *last* pre-Beatle #1, knocked off by "I Want to Hold Your Hand." Vinton scored a final chart-topper in 1964 with "Mr. Lonely," but managed to keep his career alive longer than most of the ex-idols, stretching his string of hits all the way to 1975's "Beer Barrel Polka"(!) Vinton had a good, smooth voice and picked material that suited it well and appealed to a wide audience. In fact, a lot of parents found that they could now, for the first time in ages, actually *enjoy* some of their kids' records, as sound of rock & roll was submerged further into the mainstream pop stylings anticipated by Pat Boone, Paul Anka, Bobby Darin... and Perry Como. For better or worse, "Venus" and "Blue Velvet" were a *long* way from "Not Fade Away."

Philadelphia and *American Bandstand*

Philadelphia was the most successful teen idol "machine." The city that had turned doo-wop into a formula with Danny & the Juniors now spawned Frankie Avalon ("Venus," "Why"), Fabian ("Turn Me Loose," "Tiger"), Bobby Rydell ("We Got Love," "Wild One") and the once promising Freddy Cannon, who reflected the changing times with his shift from rockabilly of 1959's "Tallahassie Lassie" to pop of 1962's "Palisades Park." The Philadelphia idols created the stereotype of the neatly packaged pretty face, pulled from a streetcorner and groomed for instant success. The hub of the Philadelphia scene, and the engine of the idol machine, was the *American Bandstand* television show, which gave the singers—and new dance crazes like the Twist—a weekly showcase and national audience.

American Bandstand began as a locally televised Philadelphia dance party in 1952 and was picked up nationally by ABC in 1957. An appearance on *American Bandstand* virtually guaranteed a hit record, and **Dick Clark**, the show's host, soon eclipsed Alan Freed as rock's most powerful career-maker. Clark loved rock & roll and booked most of the original rockers on his shows, but he was also mindful of the sensibilities of the advertisers who kept *Bandstand* on the air and the parents who allowed their kids to watch it. As rock & roll's audience widened and the pressure to "clean it up" increased, Clark leaned toward wholesome singers who would appeal to the greatest number and broadest age range of viewers. The television format was well-suited for entertainers more handsome than talented, and was ideal for the teen idols, who could lip-synch their hits and worry about smiling rather than singing. In the late fifties and early sixties, Clark opened the *Bandstand* stage to a succession of teen idols, making overnight stars out of several local Philadelphia teenagers.

American Bandstand gave the singers invaluable exposure and they, in turn, were good for the show's wholesome image—and good for Dick Clark's personal finances as well, since he had a financial interest in many of the record labels and publishing houses connected to the singers he plugged on his show. It was simply a matter of good business sense on Clark's part, and he was certainly not alone: such arrangements were common amidst the intricate web of business partnerships and career brokering that formed the heart of the music business. This type of conflict of interest was the high-tech end of the widespread practice known as "payola," which ranged from giving paper bags full of cash to DJ's in exchange for airplay (often the only way a small record label could compete with the media giants) to awarding songwriting credits to people who hadn't written a word or note (as in the case of Alan Freed's "co-authorship" of Chuck Berry's "Maybellene"). It was no secret that payola in its many forms was firmly entrenched in the music business. Indeed, many adults simply assumed that payola-grabbing DJ's and corrupt businessmen were the only possible explanation for anyone playing or buying "this junk."

In the wake of a scandal involving rigged TV quiz shows, the practice of payola in the music business came under scrutiny as a further example of rock & roll's corrupting influence. The **payola scandal** climaxed in a series of Congressional Hearings in 1960, fueled by the media-whipped outrage of the general public and by the indignation of music industry leaders tired of seeing their profits siphoned off by the indie record labels and other "fringe" elements responsible for most rock & roll. Dick Clark and Alan Freed, were singled out for special attention as rock's most visible frontmen. Clark managed to charm his way through the hearings by admitting to an unintentional conflict of interest and agreeing to divest his outside interests. He received a slap on the wrist (committee chairman Rep. Oren Harris called him a "fine young man") and resumed his successful career and played an important role in keeping rock on television in the pre-video sixties. Alan Freed, on the other hand, lacked Clark's boyish charm and wholesome image. His role in championing black music was not forgotten (nor kindly remembered), and his reputation had been recently clouded further by a few well-publicized "riots" at the racially mixed concerts he promoted. Freed refused to attempt a whitewash or deny that he participated in what was simply standard practice in the recording industry. His career was ruined by the payola scandal: he was forced off the air and died a bitter, broken 43-year-old man in 1965, a last casualty of the war against the music he loved—the music he named "rock & roll."

ROLL OVER COLE PORTER: "BRILL BUILDING POP"

After the payola scandal, the always conservative music industry was more anxious than ever to avoid any hint of controversy in the music and image of its stars. Radio stations across the country turned increasingly to "Top Forty" formats meant to assure the public that their inoffensive playlists were dictated by popular demand, not bags of cash.

All of that said, some great music was made in the early sixties: rock & roll may have been smothered as a vital force, but reports of its death have often been, as they say, greatly exaggerated. The many great songs and creative artists of the era belie the myth that the spirit rock & roll simply died with Buddy Holly and reappeared with the Beatles. The best music of the early sixties retained rock's immediacy and playful spirit and expanded its range with innovative productions and exquisitely crafted songs and melodies. It's certainly hard to write off an era that produced songs like "Be My Baby," "He's a Rebel," "The Loco-Motion," "One Fine Day," "Runaround Sue," "Runaway," "Up On the Roof," "Stand By Me," "Walk Like a Man," "Breaking Up Is Hard to Do," "Only the Lonely," "Heatwave" and so many other classics.

The fact that favorite Songs tend to spring to mind before Singers points to a shift in the early sixties away from the strongly individual voices of fifties rock & roll and back to the pop's pre-rock emphasis on songs and melody and on songwriting and production (an aesthetic also kept alive tin fifties doo-wop). At its worst, this meant a return to the cynical commercialism and cliché-ridden formulas of Tin Pan Alley, now couched in the guise of "teenage music." At its best, however, it meant a new level of sophistication and a new brand of "pop" shaped by young songwriters raised on rock & roll and determined to force Tin Pan Alley to make sense within the context of rock & roll rather than the other way around. The new pop spoke to a new generation with their own romantic landscape: Moon/June and gossamer wings were out, Da Doo Ron Ron and drive-ins were in. And for all the talented singers whose names appeared on the record labels, the true stars of the industry-dominated early sixties were the songwriters and producers, most notably producer Phil Spector and the writers centered around New York's Brill Building.

Aldon Music

The "Brill Building" was both a real place (1619 Broadway in New York City) and the symbolic center of New York's popular music industry in the early sixties: the new "Tin Pan Alley." The Brill Building itself was the most successful center of activity, thanks largely to the presence of **Aldon Music**, a music publishing company formed in 1958 by Al Nevins and Don Kirshner. Inspired by the high standards set by Leiber and Stoller in the 1950's, Nevins and Kirshner assembled a group of young songwriting teams who were responsible for an amazing number of the era's most memorable songs. Until the Beatles and the self-contained Motown juggernaut re-wrote the rules, the Aldon/Brill Building network was the most successful pop enterprise in the country, both commercially and artistically.

The importance of Aldon Music and other songwriting and publishing houses—of any era—stemmed from the fact that pop singers rarely wrote their own material and were always in need of new songs. Rock & roll had upset the existing order, and the Beatles would render it obsolete, but the early sixties were a comforting return to business-as-usual for the songwriters, publishers, song-pluggers, A&R men, producers, promoters, arrangers and studio session musicians who wrote, recorded and marketed popular music. Like their counterparts in Philadelphia, Los Angeles and other music centers, the Brill Building writers churned out made-to-order songs with the requisite teen themes, catchy "hooks" and bouncy beat, but they did so with a love and artistry that set them apart from their competitors. The result was "pop" in the best sense: soaring, unforgettable melodies, inventive harmonies and chord progressions, inventive arrangements and clever lyrics that captured the innocence of the era without resorting to cloying sentiment.

The Aldon Music songwriters were usually grouped in pairs, one concentrating on the music, the other on the lyrics (following the Rodgers & Hart, or Leiber & Stoller, model). Howie Greenfield & Neil Sedaka and the husband-and-wife teams of Gerry Goffin & Carole King and Barry Mann & Cynthia Weil were the most successful of the Kirshner pairings. Like their Tin Pan Alley predecessors, they were literate lyricists and trained musicians, notating their work on musical staff paper that would have looked like hieroglyphics to Little Richard. But the Aldon writers also felt a close connection to their young audience (the writers themselves were barely out of their teens) that inspired their best work and kept their music attuned to the latest dance steps and street slang. The teams spent their days huddled around pianos searching for that perfect turn of a phrase or melodic twist: the perfect pop Hook that could lift a song out of the ordinary and into the hearts of American teenagers.

Goffin & King

Gerry Goffin and Carole King were the most prolific hitmakers at Aldon. Their songs set teen romance against an urban landscape and blended pop innocence with a world-wise realism and heartfelt emotion. In an era dominated by cliché-ridden formulas and "product," Goffin & King glorified the art of songwriting and created a personal voice within the songs-for-hire pop system. Goffin's graceful lyrics and King's irresistible hooks and shimmering melodies defined the best of the new pop.

Carole King (originally Carol Klein) was born in Brooklyn in 1942. She began writing with Gerry Goffin in 1958 and toyed with a singing career of her own, beginning with "Oh! Neil," her 1959 "answer" to Neil Sedaka's "Oh! Carol." When her own singing ventures proved unsuccessful, the pair concentrated on writing for others. Their first big hit came in 1960 with the Shirelles' recording of "Will You Love Me Tomorrow," an intimate and surprisingly honest look at the fears and realities of teenage love. They followed with "Some Kind of Wonderful" and "Up on the Roof" for the Drifters, the Everly Brothers' "Crying in the Rain," Bobby Vee's "Take Good Care of My Baby," Gene Pitney's "Every Breath I Take," Darlene Love's "Long Way to Be Happy," the Cookies' "Chains" (covered by the Beatles), the Chiffons' exultant "One Fine Day," and "The Loco-Motion," which started a new dance craze and propelled Goffin & King's baby-sitter, Eva Boyd, to instant, short-lived stardom as Little Eva.

Goffin & King's long lists of great songs was not confined to the pre-Beatles era. Their ability to change with the times and write convincingly in a variety of styles kept them in demand and gave some marginally talented groups (like Herman's Hermits and the Monkees) some of their best moments. They managed to stay on the charts in the wake of the British Invasion, selling songs to the Animals ("Don't Bring Me Down"), Herman's Hermits ("I'm Into Something Good") and other British groups, and remained a force through the sixties with the Righteous Brothers' "Just Once in My Life," the Monkees' "Pleasant Valley Sunday," the Byrds' "Wasn't Born to Follow," Blood, Sweat and Tears' "Hi-De-Ho," Aretha Franklin's "A Natural Woman," and a string of middle-of-the-road hits for Steve Lawrence and Eydie Gorme, including "Go Away Little Girl," a #1 hit for Steve Lawrence in 1963 and again for Donny Osmond in 1971. (On a brighter note, "The Loco-Motion" also hit #1 twice: for Little Eva in 1962 and for Grand Funk in 1974.)

Goffin and King both stayed in the music business after divorcing in 1968. Goffin continued writing for others with moderate success, while King decided to revive her singing career and worked to improve her lyric writing and overcome her stage fright. After a few false starts, King found her voice and again proved her ability to change and grow with the times. Her 1971 *Tapestry* was the largest selling album ever to that point and introduced her to a huge audience amazed to learn that the same woman had written some of their favorite "oldies." (No *wonder* those songs were so good!)

Mann & Weil

Barry Mann & Cynthia Weil were nearly as prolific and versatile as Goffin & King. Between 1961 and 1963, they wrote hits for James Darren, Tony Orlando, Eydie Gorme, Shelley Fabares and a wide range of other artists, including the Drifters' classic "On Broadway" and Mann's own recording of "Who Put the Bomp (In the Bomp, Bomp, Bomp)," a delightfully tongue-in-cheek tribute to their profession and the Great Man who wrote the tender words ("bomp, bomp, bomp, rama-lama ding-dong") that "made my baby fall in love with me."

Mann & Weil did their best and most creative work in connection with producer Phil Spector. Their songs for the Crystals ("Uptown," "He's Sure the Boy I Love"), the Ronettes ("Walking in the Rain"), the Righteous Brothers ("You've Lost That Lovin' Feelin'," "Soul and Inspiration") and other Spector artists had a genuine emotional depth and a realism that often bordered on social commentary. In the Crystals' "Uptown," for example, the singer's boyfriend toils unnoticed and unappreciated in the downtown workaday world, but when she welcomes him "each evening to my tenement" he's the most important man in the world—the man she loves. The frank references to class boundaries ("Uptown" is clearly Harlem) was strikingly honest for 1962, and the song itself remains a moving testimony to the power of love.

Mann & Weil were the last of the original gang to leave the Brill Building—they stayed until 1970 and responded to the changing times by toughening their lyrics and amplifying their undercurrent of social commentary. Their later hits included the Animals' "We Gotta Get Out of This Place," Jody Miller's "Home of the Brave," the Vogues' "Magic Town" and Paul Revere and the Raiders' "Hungry" and "Kicks," a hard-rocking anti-drug anthem. Barry Mann took another stab at a solo recording career in the 1970's, but remained more successful at writing hits for others, including "Sometimes When We Touch" (co-written with singer Dan Hill) and Dolly Parton's crossover hit, "Here You Come Again."

Sedaka & Greenfield

Neil Sedaka & Howie Greenfield wrote songs for Sedaka's own successful solo career (which was the envy of King, Mann and the other frustrated singers at Aldon). Sedaka & Greenfield signed on as Aldon songwriters and scored their first hit in 1958 with Connie Francis' recording of their "Stupid Cupid." Their focus shifted to Sedaka's own recordings later that year when he signed a recording contract with RCA and released the doo-wopish "The Diary," launching a string of thirteen hits that kept Sedaka on the charts through 1963, including the peerless pop of "Breaking Up Is Hard to

Do," "Calendar Girl," "Happy Birthday Sweet Sixteen," "Next Door to an Angel." Since Sedaka was writing for his own voice and style, the teams' songs were less varied than those of their fellow Brill writers. They strove instead to perfect their own pop formula, combining Greenfield's clever metaphors and Sedaka's impeccable melodies with a technical polish that the great tunesmiths of old would have admired. Of all the Brill writers, Sedaka & Greenfield fit most easily into the grand tradition of popular music as a blissful escape from the mundane realities of real life and love: a rarefied world where a perfect melody can create its own meaning and yield its own inexpressibly sublime reward.

Barry & Greenwich

Jeff Barry & Ellie Greenwich, yet another husband-and-wife team, were not directly connected to Aldon Music but were part of the Brill Building scene and shared their peers' creative empathy for teenage life and love. In contrast to the rather crafty sophistication of the Aldon writers, though, they wrote in an unadorned style based on simple chord progressions, singalong melodies and "teen poetry" lyrics that reflected the way teenagers really sang and spoke. Their melodies may have lacked the finesse of a Carole King or Neil Sedaka tune, but their simple structure and roughness served to heighten their sincerity. Likewise, their lyrics may have lacked Gerry Goffin's poetic elegance or Howie Greenfield's formal purity, but they only sounded more real because of it. True Love reigned supreme in their songs: no heartaches, breakups or doubts to cloud the horizon, just idyllic love the way it ought to be (and never really is, but that's what pop songs are *for*).

Like Mann & Weil, Barry & Greenwich were at their best when working with Phil Spector, with whom they shared songwriting credits for a string of 1963 songs that formed the foundation of Spector's "Wall of Sound": the Ronettes' "Be My Baby" and "Baby, I Love You," the Crystals' "Da Doo Ron Ron" and "Then He Kissed Me," and Darlene Love's "A Fine, Fine Boy," "(Today I Met) The Boy I'm Gonna Marry" and "Wait 'til My Bobby Gets Home."

Barry & Greenwich often opened their songs with a scene-setter ("He walked up to me and he asked me if I wanted to dance"; "There she was just walking down the street"; "I met him on a Monday and my heart stood still") and went on to tell a story or extol the virtues of the singer's guy—and when He was simply too good for words, a breathless "Da doo ron ron" or "Do wah diddy diddy" could make the point even better. Other songs were addressed directly to "you" and read like love letters ("The night we met I knew I needed you so," "Have I ever told, how good it feels to hold you?") and climaxed in memorable refrains ("Be my baby," "Baby, I love you") that turned a single, direct sentiment into a joyous declaration of love. "Simple" in the best sense, their sparkling gems were perfect vehicles for Spector mega-productions that would have buried songs with more intricate lyrics and fragile melodies.

Barry & Greenwich signed on as writers and producers with Leiber & Stoller's Red Bird Records in 1964, where they presided over the last days of the girl group era. They collaborated with George "Shadow" Morton on two epic melodramas by the Shangri-Las, "Remember (Walking in the Sand)" and "Leader of the Pack," and wrote and produced the Dixie Cup's "Chapel of Love" and the Jelly Beans' "I Wanna Love Him So Bad." They scored #1 hits with the British group Manfred Mann's version of "Do Wah Diddy Diddy" and Tommy James & the Shondells' "Hanky Panky," gave Lesley Gore "Maybe I Know" and "Look of Love," and returned to Phil Spector with Ike & Tina Turner's "River Deep, Mountain High." They both remained active in the music world after their mid-sixties divorce, but turned their attention to "bubblegum" groups and the Monkees, a Don Kirshner "invention," since few other outlets remained for professional songwriters once the example of the Beatles forced any self-respecting group to write their own songs. Barry produced several Monkees recordings and wrote "Sugar, Sugar" for the "Archies," and descended still further in the next decade with Olivia Newton-John's "I Honestly Love You" and the theme song for TV's *The Jeffersons*.

Doc Pomus & Mort Shuman

The archetypes for the songwriter era, Jerry Leiber & Mike Stoller, often looked to the veteran writing team of Doc Pomus & Mort Shuman to provide songs for their Drifters productions. Pomus & Shuman were nearly as versatile and far-flung as their mentors, with a songbook that included "This Magic Moment" and "Save the Last Dance for Me," their standout contributions to the Drifters, along with hits for Dion & the Belmonts ("Teenager in Love"), Ray Charles ("Lonely Avenue"), Bobby Darin ("Plain Jane") and Fabian ("I'm a Man"). Pomus & Shuman also provided Elvis Presley with some of his finest sixties moments, including "A Mess of Blues," "Surrender," "Little Sister," "(Marie's the Name) His Latest Flame" and "Viva Las Vegas."

Burt Bacharach & Hal David

The Bacharach & David team was the Rodgers & Hart of the 1960's. Although they wrote pop hits in the early sixties for the Shirelles, the Drifters, Gene Pitney and Jerry Butler, they achieved more success later with their songs for Dionne Warwick ("I Say a Little Prayer," "Do You Know the Way to San Jose," "Promises Promises"), the Fifth Dimension ("One Less Bell to Answer"), the Carpenters ("Close to You"), B. J. Thomas ("Raindrops keep Falling on My Head") and other middle-of-the-road hits.

Bert Berns

Bert Berns was an incredibly versatile producer, songwriter and talent scout. Working with various writing partners, most notably Jerry Ragavoy, Berns came up with a truly impressive catalog of pop, soul and garage-rock classics: "Twist and Shout" (Isley Brothers), "Time Is on My Side" (Irma Thomas, the Rolling Stones), "Piece of My Heart" (Erma Franklin, Janis Joplin), "Hang On Sloopy" (the McCoys), "Cry to Me" and "Everybody Needs Somebody to Love" (Solomon Burke), "Up in the Streets of Harlem" (the Drifters), "Here Comes the Night" (Them), "Brown-Eyed Girl" (Van Morrison) and many others. Berns also served as a producer for Atlantic Records before starting his own Bang Records in 1965, where he launched the careers of Van Morrison and Brill Building alumnus Neil Diamond before dying of a heart attack in 1967.

End of an Era

The Brill era ended with the British Invasion, which rendered rock's Tin Pan Alley obsolete and forced its practitioners to find a way to fit into the changing rock scene or simply abandon it altogether for the security of middle-of-the-road pop, movie soundtracks or television jingles. Don Kirshner sold Aldon Music to Screen Gems and became head of that entertainment giant's music division. He brought much of his Aldon staff along with him, added new writers (most notably Harry Nilsson and the team of Tommy Boyce & Bobby Hart) and helped launch the Monkees in 1966.

In true teen idol fashion, the Monkees were manufactured for television and hired for their looks and appeal rather than their talent. Only the model had changed: instead of watered-down Elvises, they were watered-down Beatles. The Monkees proved that there was still a market for pop—that even though the old Fabian fans were starting to freak out, wear love beads and listen to strange psychedelic music, their younger siblings still longed for safe and accessible idols and music. But even the Monkees eventually freaked out and demanded artistic control of their music, so Kirshner went a step further and created the Archies, a "group" of comic book characters who, presumably, couldn't complain or harbor secret artistic ambitions. (The Archies were actually a group of sessionmen assembled by Kirshner to provide music for a TV cartoon show.)

Kirshner's "bubblegum music" was despised by "real" rock fans and artists in the late sixties. Considered alongside Jimi Hendrix and *Sgt. Pepper*, Kirshner's contrived "product" only served to illustrate the radical changes that had taken place in a few short years. While Carole King and other old Kirshner protégés responded to rock's changes with a deepened sense of artistic commitment, Kirshner continued to market pop as a commodity, earning and alienating millions through the 1970's with projects like *In Concert*, the *Rock Music Awards* and *Don Kirshner's Rock Concert*. In many ways, Kirshner came to represent "pop" in the worst, mass-marketed sense, but for a few golden years his music machine breathed new life into pop and made the radio worth listening to during the long gap between Elvis and the Beatles.

THE GIRL GROUPS

With the rough, R&B edges of rock & roll fading into pop, "girl groups" were the most successful avenue for young black singers in the early sixties. Like their doo-wop predecessors, the groups were essentially interchangeable parts—a sound and style rather than an individual voice or image. The groups' relative anonymity meant that the focus stayed on the Song rather than singers (or their skin color). It also meant that their role in the creation of their music was limited: the girl groups were firmly entrenched in the pop "system," and the sound and success of the top groups was largely the result of their link to a specific producer: the Chantels to George Goldner, the Shirelles to Luther Dixon, the Shangri-Las to Shadow Morton, the Marvelettes to the Berry Gordy/Motown team, and the Ronettes and Crystals to Phil Spector. The producer wrote or picked the group's songs, shaped their sound and created records that projected *his* sound and vision, rather than that of the singers. Within this artistically stifling system, the girl groups flourished and made, quite simply, the best records of the early sixties.

Free from any pressure to be "all-around entertainers" (young black women certainly weren't going to make it to Vegas), the girl groups made records with all the excitement and passion that their male counterparts seemed to have lost. Although female singers hadn't made much of an impact during the rebellious days of rock & roll, the girl groups were perfect for an era that valued sweet melodies and apparent innocence above all else. For a start, they were *girls*, and in the pre-liberated days of the early sixties female singers weren't considered a potential threat to decency the way even a relatively tame male singer might be. They could be sweetly innocent without alienating the rockers (any guy would *love* to be sung to like that), and be slightly rebellious without offending the adults: after all, they only sang *about* the rebels—their boyfriends may have been contemptible hoods, but the noble girls who sang "He's a Rebel" or "Leader of the Pack" were only staying true to their guys. And though there was often an underlying current of sexuality behind the "innocence," they were shielded from criticism by sexual stereotypes that were still firmly in place: guys wanted sex, girls dreamed of love... And to extend this a bit further, rock & roll was about sex, but *pop* was all about Love.

The roots of girl group pop stretch back to the idyllic lyrics and group singing of doo-wop (nearly all of the girl groups were from the New York area, doo-wop's home base), but it was not simply doo-wop sung by women. The nature of the voices dictated a simpler vocal interplay, since female voices have a narrower range (compared to the male groups, who could fill the entire spectrum from low bass to high falsettos) and a fragile quality easily smothered by aggressive background vocals. Instead, the background singers sang unobtrusive "ooh's" and "aah's" during the verses, if they sang at all, and saved a full-voiced attack for unison refrains and call-and-response sections. The focus remained on a single lead voice and bright pop melody, and on a heightened aura of romantic yearning that inspired both a sweet innocence and a gospel-style intensity from the lead singers.

The streamlined vocal dynamics left room for bigger instrumental arrangements and larger roles for the producers and arrangers. Consequently, the musical arrangements were always an integral feature of girl group recordings (it's hard to imagine them sung a cappella). The productions grew larger and the beat stronger, but the songs and sentiment remained simple and direct ("I love you" or "get lost"). Girl group pop reached its peak in Phil Spector's productions, but the basic elements of the sound and style were anticipated in the first true girl group records: the Chantels' "Maybe," and the Shirelles' "I Met Him on a Sunday," both recorded in 1958.

The Chantels

The Chantels were basically a one-shot group, but their sound and brief success formed an important model for the groups who followed. Their producer, **George Goldner**, and arranger, Richard Barrett, helped to pioneer the "Uptown R&B" style with their sophisticated productions for the Flamingos ("I Only Have Eyes for You") and Little Anthony & the Imperials ("Tears On My Pillow"). The Chantels' "**Maybe**," on the other hand, hearkens back to the simplicity of earlier doo-wop. Backed by a simple accompaniment dominated by drums and rock-a-ballad piano triplets, Smith delivers a yearning plea for a lover's return: "May-ay-y-be if I pray every night, you'll come back to me..." He does return, but only in her dreams, night after night. The *wish* itself is everything, though: it fills the song and Smith's plaintive voice with an eyes-lifted emotion that is half-prayer and half-passion.

Written by sixteen-year-old lead singer Arlene Smith, "Maybe" captures the tension between innocent romantic dreams and the hint of longing sexuality that fuels them: the underlying tension all of the girl group classics. Smith's singing also illustrates the gospel intensity and urgency that the girl groups brought to their sweet pop melodies. Her desire simply overwhelms the melody, and her disregard for "proper" phrasing and precise intonation gives the record exactly the type of heartfelt immediacy that the girl groups kept alive while the guys polished their act and sang *about*—rather than with—love and emotion.

The Shirelles

The Shirelles were a group of high school students from Passaic, New Jersey, who patterned themselves after the Chantels and began recording shortly after their cross-river heroes. They wrote "**I Met Him on a Sunday**" for a school talent show and later, after some coaxing, auditioned the song for Florence Greenburg, a friend's mother who just happened to run the small Tiara record label. (Greenburg later started Scepter Records as a showcase for the Shirelles). "I Met Him on a Sunday" presents the *other* side of girl group pop— the emotional and musical flipside of "Maybe." Here the singers are anything but moonstruck and compliant: they're tough and they're mad. The song traces a week's romance with the guy who seems OK on Sunday and gets more interesting as the week progresses. But when the jerk doesn't show up on Friday, the Shirelles don't plead or pray for his return. And when he dares to show his face on Saturday, they greet him with a flippant "bye, bye baby" and a defiant chorus of "doo ronde ronDE ronde ronde papa..." (That's telling him!)

The tough sound of "I Met Him on a Sunday" matches the singers' indignation: the pounding drums and tambourines, layers of keyboards, guitars, grinding saxes and heavy echo create an enormous beat and sound that anticipated the Phil Spector's monolithic Wall of Sound. The singers balanced the dense production by singing in unison—a strength-in-numbers approach that became an integral part of the girl group sound. The contrasting styles of "Maybe" and "I Met Him on a Sunday"—sweetness vs. toughness, melodic solo singing vs. group chanting, sparse vs. heavy backing arrangements—defined the musical and emotional range of girl group pop.

The Shirelles moved to the lighter and sweeter side with 1959's "**Dedicated to the One I Love,**" a cover of a 1958 R&B hit by the Five Royales. The switch from male to female, from worldwise adult to innocent teenage voices and from an R&B band to a pop arrangement gave the song an entirely new feeling and shifted the context from hard reality to a yearning dreamworld more familiar to the seventeen-year-old singers and their young audience. The song remained a timeless ode to devotion in the face of separation, but the singer and her beloved now seemed separated less by physical distance than by their youth and the social conventions that keep them from truly sharing their love (or spoiling it by actually being together).

The Shirelles' first releases were not big hits at the time, and it looked like the Shirelles were joining the Chantels on the road to oblivion. Instead, they became the most successful of the early sixties girl groups, thanks largely to the songwriting and keen ear of their producer, **Luther Dixon**. Dixon's transparent productions focused on the voices and emphasized the Shirelles' endearingly amateurish style. Shirley Owens, who assumed the lead singer role after "Dedicated to the One I Love," often sounded willfully out-of-tune, and all of their songs sounded like they were written for a high school talent show. But Dixon also recognized and responded to the changes in the youth market and embellished their sound with subtle string arrangements and other touches that would appeal to pop tastes: "I wanted to have strings because R&B records weren't getting played on pop stations. I said, 'If I put in strings maybe it'll match the pop sound.'"[5]

The Shirelles' first big national hit, 1960's **"Tonight's the Night,"** written by Dixon and Shirley Owens, features a subdued string arrangement and a staggered West Indies beat that heightens the sexually-charged anticipation of the night to come. In the Shirelles' next release, Goffin & King's **"Will You Love Me Tomorrow,"** that night of romance becomes a reality full of fears and doubts. The musical variation on an age-old question—"will you respect me in the morning?"—shocked many adults and amused many others, but spoke directly to the teenagers who were living such dilemmas. It shot to #1 in 1961, becoming the first #1 pop hit for any black female singer or group, and pulled the re-released "Dedicated to the One I Love" into the Top Ten along with it.

"Mama Said," "Big John," "Soldier Boy" and other hits followed quickly. "Soldier Boy" sent the group back to #1, even though it was a lightweight piece of fluff that Dixon wrote on the spot when he realized the group had a few minutes of studio time left—the Shirelles simply sang in nursery rhyme unison over a simple band backing. Other, more fully realized Dixon songs like "Mama Said" and "Boys" kept a strongly rhythmic R&B edge and emphasized the "tough" side of the Shirelles; and when he decided to look elsewhere for songs, the group's popularity gave him his pick from the top songwriters of the day. Goffin & King followed "Will You Love Me Tomorrow" with "What a Sweet Thing That Was," and Burt Bacharach & Hal David contributed "Baby It's You." (For the latter song, Owens simply dubbed her lead vocals over a Bacharach/David demo, creating a strangely haunting blend of intimate vocals over a distant backing.)

The Shirelles' career went into a steep decline after Dixon left Scepter Records in 1962. They squeezed out a few more hits before the British Invasion sent them packing for the oldies circuit (even though the Beatles covered "Boys" and "Baby It's You" on their first album). They then discovered, like so many of others, that the small fortune in record royalties that was supposed to be waiting for them when they turned 21 had mysteriously "disappeared," prompting a bitter legal battle with Florence Greenburg. Scepter continued to thrive through the sixties, thanks to the Bacharach/David productions for Dionne Warwick and hits for the Isley Brothers ("Twist and Shout"), Chuck Jackson ("Any Day Now") and the Kingsmen ("Louie Louie") on Scepter's Wand subsidiary.

The Girls and THE BOY

In the wake of the Shirelles' success, girl groups began proliferating just as doo-wop groups had in the fifties, with a second wave of white groups on the heels of the originals. The Shirelles, Ronettes, Crystals, Marvelettes, Chiffons and Shangri-Las were among the most successful of the groups, along with solo singer Lesley Gore, who echoed the groups with her power-pop style. (Connie Francis and Brenda Lee, the top-selling female artists of the period, had more traditional pop styles and adult-oriented appeal.) As with doo-wop, though, many of the most memorable songs of the era came from "one-shots" who struck gold with a song or two and then vanished: the Cookies ("Chains"), the Dixie Cups ("Chapel of Love"), the Angels ("My Boyfriend's Back"), the Exciters ("Tell Him"), Kathy Young & the Innocents ("A Thousand Stars"), the Paris Sisters ("I Love How You Love Me"), Cathy Jean & the Roommates ("Please Love Me Forever"), Rosie & the Originals ("Angel Baby") and many other groups left a brief but indelible mark on the early sixties, along with solo singers such as Little Eva ("The Loco-Motion"), Claudine Clark ("Party Lights"), Shelly Fabares ("Johnny Angel") and Little Peggy March ("I Will Follow Him").

The songs varied between noisy celebrations of and tender ballads to THE BOY, with a few defiant rejections thrown in to keep him on his toes. After years of male yearnings and fantasies in rock & roll songs, boys suddenly joined girls as objects of desire and adoration. Like Peggy Sue, Donna, Diana, Venus and other female teen dreams, the guys were idealized images of adolescent romanticism. HE was, variously, So Fine, a Fine Fine Boy, an Angel, My Dreamboat, My One True Love, Sure the Boy I Love, a Picture of Heaven, the Kind of Boy You Can't Forget, the Boy I'm Gonna Marry... Even the misunderstood rebel had a heart of gold and a sensitive side that only his devoted girlfriend could see. Needless to say, her parents missed it altogether (the eternal enemies of youth never did understand). But love and hope flourished in spite of disapproving parents, inspiring enough heart-tugging declarations to melt the coldest heart. Two of the most memorable came from the Chiffons: "He's So Fine" and "One Fine Day."

The Chiffons

A group of high school friends from the Bronx formed a group in 1960 when a young songwriter named Ronnie Mack asked them to sing on a demotape of some of his songs, including "**He's So Fine**." They dubbed themselves the Chiffons and scored a local hit that same year with a cover of the Shirelle's "Tonight's the Night," then graduated to jobs as telephone operators while Mack kept trying to interest someone in his songs. After hearing nearly every industry figure in New York dismiss "He's So Fine" as "too trite and too simple," he finally found a sympathetic ear at tiny Laurie Records who realized that the record's unabashed simplicity was its great charm. "He's So Fine" was finally released in 1963, nearly three years after the original demotape was recorded.

"He's So Fine" is a simple wish, stated plainly and set to music. The signature "doo-lang" refrain that opens the song continues—changing to "oh yeah" for the bridge—to form a reassuring call-and-response behind lead singer Judy Craig's musings on the handsome, wavy-haired, soft-spoken and kinda shy guy she doesn't quite have yet, but *will*: "it's just a matter of time." Her strong-but-warm voice anchors the song and brings its delightfully asymmetric phrases to life, as in her fluid delivery of "I'd do anything that he asked, anything to make him my own." Why? Because, as the jubilant fade-out declares, over and over, "He's so fine."

"He's So Fine" went to #1 and established the Chiffons as a national act. In a stroke of cruel irony, Ronnie Mack contracted Hodgkin's Disease just as the hit he'd worked so hard for was finally taking off. He was awarded a gold record for the song in his hospital room, and died soon afterward. (A decade later, the song's long journey took another twisted turn into rock's most celebrated copyright infringement lawsuit, which ended with ex-Beatles George Harrison judged guilty of "subconsciously plagiarizing" "He's So Fine" in his own "My Sweet Lord.")

The Chiffons' talent for attracting good songs continued with Goffin & King's "**One Fine Day**," which featured the Chiffon's voices overdubbed onto Carole King's fully-produced demotape. Like its predecessor, "One Fine Day" exists in hope, this time the hope that the singer's wandering boyfriend will come back when he wants to settle down. In the meantime, the hope itself becomes a celebration—a self-fulfilling prophesy driven by King's bell-like piano riff and Judy Craig's confident delivery. The Chiffon's career stumbled when yet another "fine" song from 1963, "A Love So Fine," failed to follow its predecessors up the charts. The Chiffons scored a last hit in 1966 with "Sweet Talkin' Guy," a final celebration of The Boy who filled their hearts and hits.

The Marvelettes

Motown Records began as a small independent label founded in Detroit by Berry Gordy, Jr., and grew through the early and middle sixties to become America's greatest hit-making machine. Although the label reached its peak (rather amazingly) during and after the British Invasion, Motown was going strong in the early 1960's. It was particularly successful with its female singers, though the Marvelettes were Motown's only true pop "girl group," since the soulful Vandellas and classy Supremes quickly outgrew the girl group image and sound, while the Marvelettes seemed directly descended from the Shirelles. Their first release, 1961's "**Please Mr. Postman**," was the first Motown single to hit #1 on the pop charts. (The Carpenters brought the song back to the top spot in 1975; the Beatles also covered the song, much more convincingly.) "Twistin' Postman," "Playboy," "Beechwood 4-5789" and other Marvelettes hits from 1962 were among the first to bring the Motown Sound to the national audience.

The Angels

White groups tended to occupy the extremes of girl group pop, from the ultra-innocence of 15-year-old Kathy Young & the Innocents' "A Thousand Stars" to the Angels' revenge anthem, "My Boyfriend's Back," and the Shangri-Las' "Leader of the Pack," an ode to a martyred motorcycle hood. For the most part, the white singers lacked the gospel-derived emotional resonance of the black groups and relied heavily on melodramatic spoken interludes, unison group chants and breathy, half-spoken singing styles.   Their greater acceptance also made them freer to challenge the sugary girl group image: the brazen, "tough girls" attack of the Angels and, especially, the Shangri-Las formed the girl group equivalent of Dion's street-tough pop style.

The Angels' "My Boyfriend's Back" was released in 1963 and was the first #1 hit for a white girl group.   Their piece of rock immortality came courtesy of songwriter Bob Feldman and an unknown group of kids he overheard at a Brooklyn hangout.   Feldman recalls: "An altercation started between a young girl and a hoody-looking young man with a leather jacket...   She was pointing a finger at him and screaming, 'My boyfriend's back and you're gonna be in trouble.   You've been spreading lies about me all over school and when he gets a hold of you, you're gonna be sorry you were ever born!'"[6] **"My Boyfriend's Back"** had practically written itself, with a few more threats added for good measure.   ("He knows I wasn't cheatin', now you're gonna get a beatin'").   The Angels gave the song a scolding, finger-shaking reading punctuated by an exuberant refrain of "hey-la, hey-la, my boyfriend's back" and a band backing that alternates between drums & handclaps and a full band accompaniment. The teenage morality play ends with her White Knight rounding the bend to save the singer's besmirched reputation.   The Angels gratefully sang his praises in their next and last hit, "I Adore Him."

The Shangri-Las

The Shangri-Las capped the girl group era with a series of teen angst epics recorded for Red Bird Records.   Red Bird was launched in 1964 by Leiber and Stoller, with George Goldner as co-owner and veteran songwriters Jeff Barry and Ellie Greenwich as creative partners.   The label was founded just in time for the British Invasion, yet still managed a #1 hit with the Dixie Cups' "Chapel of Love," which knocked the Beatles' "Love Me Do" off the top spot in June, 1964, and several hits for the Shangri-Las.   Given the illustrious track record of its founders, it's not surprising that the Red Bird releases boasted the grandest productions outside of Phil Spector's Wall of Sound.   What is surprising is that much of the credit belongs to a brash newcomer, **George "Shadow" Morton**.

Shadow Morton had gone to high school with Ellie Greenwich and was shocked to find her name on so many of the hit records he was hearing. Determined to get in on the action, he contacted his old friend in 1964 and boasted that he too could write and produce a hit, though he'd actually never written a song or been in a studio in his life.   Greenwich called his bluff and Morton went to work: he assembled a backup band and found the Shangri-Las— two pairs of sisters from "the bad part of Queens"—to sing on his demotape. There was still one small detail missing, though, as Morton recalls: "On the way over to the studio that day it dawns on me that I have everything going except a song. I don't have a song. So I pull the car over on South Oyster Bay Road and I start to write."[7]

The seaside road inspired "**Remember (Walking in the Sand)**," the song Morton pulled out of his hat on his way to the session. The Red Bird heads were duly impressed and turned Morton loose to record the song for real. Morton responded with every trick he could conjure up to make his first production unforgettable. He layered the tale of obsessive woe with shrieking seagulls, crashing waves and enough echo to make the booming minor chords and despairing voices sound like the end of the world. Jilted by her boyfriend, lead singer Mary Weiss wails her lament on the verge of tears while the rest of the Shangri-Las cry along atop the dirge-like backing band. And just when the pain seems almost unbearable, it gets worse: the band halts, leaving poor Mary alone in her shock and anguish, repeating "oh no" until the background singers return, whispering "remember" over and over like a voice in her head that won't let her forget that magic night by the sea with her guy, or the fact that he's now gone for good. Reality and another verse crash back in, then the whispered "remember"'s and *that night* return to haunt her as the record fades, leaving Mary trapped in her memories and despair.

Morton went straight for the throat with his songs, exaggerating emotions and cramming epic teen dramas into densely-packed records that sound like aural versions of those gaudy Sunday newspaper love-and-drama comics. Similarly, the Shangri-Las were one of the few girl groups that consciously developed an "image": they played the role of the "bad girls" to the hilt, decked out in tight black pants and boots, leather suits, heavy make-up and beehive hairdos. They looked like the type who hang out with motorcycle gangs, and they became just that in "**Leader of the Pack**," a #1 hit in 1964 that tested the limits of good taste to become the last and greatest in a flood of early sixties car crash and death-rock songs (Jan & Dean's "Dead Man's Curve," also from 1964, was a close second). Hot rods, drag races and motorcycles were all the rage in the early sixties and were a favorite topic for songs, along with misunderstood, sensitive tough guys, ill-fated love, parents who don't understand, fiery death and eternal devotion. Morton and company packed it all into "Leader of the Pack," an epic, modern-day Romeo and Juliet tragedy played out in a two minute record.

A spoken, post-crash exchange between the bereaved heroine and her pals introduces "Leader of the Pack": "...is he picking you up after school today?" "Mmm-mmm" (in other words, "no, he's dead"). Then a sudden burst of plaintive singing evokes the memory of the tragic events, all accompanied by appropriately ominous music and mock-solemn interjections from the backup singers as she recalls telling her guy that her parents will not let her see him any longer. His reason for living suddenly gone, the Leader promptly races off into eternity as the singer looks on, shouting in horror. Morton's trademark sound effects high-camp realism with a wonderfully sickening, drawn out crash. As the dust clears, the widowed girlfriend vows she'll never forget her Leader of the Pack (at least not until Study Hall, anyway).

Shadow Morton and the Shangri-Las continued turning out oversized teen angst hits through 1965, returning to a celebration of the greaser in "Give Him a Great Big Kiss," and to the ever-faithful theme of untimely death caused by the generation gap in "Give Us Your Blessings" and "I Can Never Go Home Anymore." After a final hit in 1966, "Long Live Our Love," Red Bird folded and the Shangri-Las, the last of the classic girl groups, went with it. Shadow Morton went on to produce in an eclectic range of styles, including the Vanilla Fudge's hard rock version of "You Keep Me Hanging On," Janis Ian's social commentary, "Society's Child," and the New York Dolls' 1974 album *Too Much Too Soon.*

Lesley Gore

Lesley Gore was just seventeen when her first record, **"It's My Party,"** zoomed to #1 in 1963, and for the next two years her story-songs chronicled the ups and downs of teenage life from the point of view of the "average teenager" (the average white suburban teenager, anyway). Excruciatingly wholesome and rather plain looking in an "average teenager" sort of way, Lesley was a frequent guest on *American Bandstand*, *The Ed Sullivan Show* and other television showcases, and was a favorite of radio stations and concert promoters. Girls and boys alike found her Everyteen songs and "girl next door" image easy to relate to and refreshingly normal. Rather than pine for a dream lover or extol the hidden virtues of a hoodlum, her songs told specific stories that now sound like installments of a quaintly old-fashioned television rerun, with Lesley playing the perky daughter who discovers "That's the Way Boys Are" and declares "I Don't Want to Be a Loser." In real life, the dutiful Lesley stayed in school, working her singing career around her studies at prep school and Sarah Lawrence University. It wasn't a contrived image or act: she really *was* an All-American gal. Fortunately, she had a terrific voice and a keen melodic sense that equaled the era's best for pure, blissful pop.

Gore also had the good fortune of being discovered and produced by **Quincy Jones**. Jones was the A&R man and, a bit later, a vice-president of Mercury Records—the first black man to achieve such a position at a major record company. He made the most of Gore's talents, showcasing her voice in clever, if somewhat formulaic, arrangements that employed state-of-the-art recording techniques such as double-tracked vocals that gave the melodies an extra punch (and inspired the Beatles to do the same). Jones also made sure she had songs that fit her style, audience, musical range and emotional temperament. He and Gore chose **"It's My Party"** for her first release, after sifting through over 250 demotapes looking for a suitable song.

"It's My Party" was Gore's biggest hit, but not her best. The stiff production and lollipop sound of the record are painfully cute. Still, the strong, double-tracked vocals and the 'sticks in your head whether you like it or not' refrain ("It's my party and I'll cry if I want to") made the song a natural hit with her teen and pre-teen audience. The story about Lesley's guy Johnny leaving with that two-faced Judy (at poor Lesley's own party) apparently packed enough of an emotional wallop to warrant a sequel, "Judy's Turn to Cry," where Johnny comes back and Judy gets what she deserves.

Gore finally turned the tables on the guy and capped a string of four consecutive Top Five singles with "**You Don't Own Me**." Often called an "early feminist manifesto," "You Don't Own Me" is certainly a change from the compliant stance of her earlier songs and those of most other "girl" singers and groups. Lesley declares her independence with strong, defiant lyrics —"You don't own me, don't tie me down 'cause I'd never stay"—and a bravado vocal performance that seals the victory. Backed by a dense blend of instruments and echo, a weighty anthem tempo and a dramatic minor key setting that opens triumphantly to major, Gore soars to one powerful climax after another, bending, straining and twisting the melody as if the she had indeed been set free.

"You Don't Own Me" peaked at #2 in February, 1964, denied the top spot by "I Want to Hold Your Hand," the opening shot of the British Invasion. Her chart-topping glory days were over, but Gore continued turning out classy, if less feisty, recordings through 1964, including "That's the Way Boys Are" and a pair of Barry & Greenwich songs, "Maybe I Know" and "Look of Love" (not to be confused with the Bacharach-David song with the same title).

"**Look of Love**" is a true gem and a fond farewell to the heyday of perfectly crafted pop. Gore's voice—perfectly double-tracked—never sounded purer, and is supported by a thoroughly integrated arrangement highlighted by riffing background voices, an understated brass section and a Spector-ish percussion battery of sleigh bells, timpani and handclaps. The setting of "Look of Love" is a return to the classic theme (Lesley watches her ex-boyfriend with his new girl) from a more real and hurtful stance. Certainly no one could render the song's crushed innocence better than Gore. Within the context of her songs and suburban world, "Look of Love" is as tortured as any blues:

> I remember his warm embrace
> And the tender look on his face
> Yes, look at the way he looks at her now
> Isn't that the look of love?

PHIL SPECTOR AND THE "WALL OF SOUND"

Phil Spector made the grandest pop records of all: "little symphonies for the kids" he called them, and it was an apt description. His Wall of Sound was built on layer upon layer of instruments and voices that combined the heart-tugging melodies and romance of pop with the big beat of rock & roll and the sound of a symphony orchestra. His work with the Ronettes, Darlene Love and the Crystals represents both the peak of girl group pop and the rock world's first self-conscious foray into the realm of Art.

Spector virtually invented the role of the modern "Producer." While others before him had begun expanding the producer's role, most notably Leiber and Stoller, with whom Spector served his "apprenticeship," Spector completed the producer's transition from knob-turner and musician contractor to Artistic Director. And while many of his predecessors were well-known within the music industry, Spector was the first producer to become a star in his own right—a bigger star, in fact, than the singers and groups he recorded.[8] Spector challenged the notion of disposable hits and created mini-masterpieces that were built for the ages as well as the charts, and he did it without ever losing sight of pop's sentimental immediacy and the spirit of fun.

The "producer's producer" is equally famous for being a true eccentric— an iconoclastic, long-haired, outrageously dressed "freak" years before it became fashionable. His fits of weirdness, in and out of the studio, are legendary and add to his enigmatic persona. He earned his right to be weird by becoming pop's boy-wonder: the "First Tycoon of Teen," as Tom Wolfe dubbed him, who mastered the commercial as well as the artistic intricacies of popular music and beat the music establishment at its own game. The industry-dominated early sixties needed a rebel *within* the industry who could shake things up the way the outsiders had in the fifties. With maverick genius Phil Spector, they got just that.

Background and "Apprenticeship"

Phil Spector was born in the Bronx on December 26, 1940, then moved to Hollywood at the age of thirteen, after his father's death. Scrawny and rather sickly, Spector was very much a loner, out of place in the sunny paradise that surrounded him—the paradise he would reshape in his own image, as if in revenge. He formed a trio, the Teddy Bears, after high school and wrote, produced and supplied the guitar and background harmonies for "To Know Him Is to Love Him," a line lifted from his father's tombstone. The record promptly hit #1 on the pop charts and Spector was on his way, though the hushed gentle sound of "To Know Him is to Love Him" gave little hint of the cataclysms to come.

Spector was all over both coasts for the next few years, producing or co-producing, arranging, writing or engineering—usually uncredited—many hits for a variety of labels. He plunged into New York's Brill Building scene after a brief stint in teen idol capitol Philadelphia, and worked closely with Leiber & Stoller on several releases by the Drifters and Ben E. King. Spector soon established himself as a freelance producer, earning full production credit for records by Ray Peterson ("Corrina, Corrina"), Curtis Lee ("Pretty Little Angel

Eyes"), the Paris Sisters ("I Love How You Love Me") and Gene Pitney, whose "Every Breath I Take" pointed toward the aural drama to come.

Philles Records

Spector formed a partnership with industry veteran Lester Sill and launched Philles Records in 1961, then bought out Sill's share a year later to become sole owner—a record company president at the age of 21. Spector wanted to launch his label with new artists that he could mold into his production style, and looked to the girl group sound was the best avenue for his ideas. He launched his new label with the Crystals, a group of Brooklyn teenagers he discovered at an audition.

The first Philles release was the Crystals' "There's No Other Like My Baby," a wistful ode to Him that hit the Top Twenty Hit at the end of 1961. The Crystals repeated their success with "**Uptown**," the Mann & Weil rumination on the harsh realities of life and the redeeming power of love. The song's social commentary subtext is underlined in the music, which evokes Spanish Harlem with a flamenco guitar introduction (played by Spector) and a Spanish-flavored melody punctuated by castanets and Latin rhythms. The string-laden production shows Spector's debt to Leiber & Stoller's as well as his own evolving production voice. After a bizarre follow-up, "He Hit Me (and It Felt like a Kiss)"—a monumental lapse of taste from Goffin & King—Spector moved his operations to California and made the final leap to the pure Spector sound with 1962's "He's a Rebel," which gave Philles Records its first #1 hit and unveiled the Wall of Sound in all its glory.

"He's a Rebel"

"He's a Rebel" was written by Gene Pitney and submitted as a demo to Liberty Records, where Spector still served as a staff producer Actually, he did very little for Liberty beyond raiding their demotapes in search of songs for his own label. Spector grabbed "He's a Rebel" and, mission accomplished, bolted from the label, even though Liberty was already planning it for Vicki Carr's next release. Carr's version never had a chance. Spector loved the song's blend of rebellion and romanticism, and lavished his full range of production resources on the simple ode to pure devotion.

"He's a Rebel" was credited to the Crystals, even though none of the Crystals actually sang on it. Spector left the group in New York and hired a Los Angeles group called the Blossoms to sing on the record instead. The move was perfectly in keeping with Spector's view of singers as basically interchangeable parts and the *sound* of his records as the true star: "I used voices as just another instrument... singers are instruments—they're tools to be worked with."[9] (To emphasize the point, the Blossoms were paid union scale and offered no royalties for the "He's a Rebel" session, just like the piano and brass players.) Still, he couldn't have found a better "tool to work with" than lead singer Darlene Love, who belted out "He's a Rebel" and many subsequent Spector productions with a power-soul voice perfect for Spector's vision of delicate pop melodies imbedded in huge arrangements.

The Wall of Sound

Spector's productions grew larger and more spacious with each song and each added layer of instruments, voices and echo. Instead of the usual basic band backing and occasional string "sweetening," a typical Spector session used up to six guitarists, all strumming in unison, four pianos, two bass players, a large complement of brass and saxophones and a deep, full drum sound augmented by castanets, sleigh bells, tambourines, timpani, cowbells, maracas, marimbas, glockenspiels and any number of other percussion instruments that studio workers, invited guests and surprised visitors could be corralled into banging or shaking. All of this—Phil Spector's idea of "basic tracks"—was recorded live, in take after take until the perfect blend and feel were achieved. When Spector was finally satisfied, the overdubbing began, often with a string section added to the already orchestral sound, along with more percussion to make sure the beat always remained prominent. Finally it was time for the singers: a small army of voices chanting refrains and background ooh's and aah's behind a single, soaring lead singer who put the whole lovingly-crafted cacophony in the service of pretty pop melody and a simple love song.

Spector based his operations at Hollywood's Gold Star studio, which had a uniquely designed echo chamber that added just the right resonance to his mass of instruments and voices. The festive atmosphere of Spector's sessions and his reputation for artistry and hit-making gave him his pick of the best young arrangers, engineers and session musicians on the West Coast. The seasoned professionals sat side-by-side, patiently strumming the same chords, banging out the same patterns and blowing the same simple notes all night long as Spector searched for the perfect sound. This apparent exercise in overkill was the key to Spector's approach, as engineer Larry Levine recounts: "The horn section quietly blew sustained chords in droning unison behind the rhythm section. He never wanted to hear horns as horns which was, I thought, so great 'cause all it would do is modulate the chords—you'd hear the chords changing but there weren't any instruments to say 'I'm changing,' so it would be in the mind of the listener that these moving parts were moving. It was beautifully done. The guitars, like the horns, were merely suggested... a solitary guitar submerged in the pulsating morass of [arranger Jack] Nitzsche's arrangements would have contributed very little to the sound, but three or four added a definite if intangible texture. He would have the pianos playing so that they interlocked in making everything cohesive... not having individual instruments heard. Of all the musicians playing in obedient unison, only the drummer was allowed any sort of freedom. Not for Spector the inflexible metronome-like drumming of early sixties pop. He dictated round-the-kit fills to emphasize chord changes or bridge pauses between lines."[10]

Among the more notable members of Spector's "Wrecking Crew" were arranger Jack Nitzsche (who later worked with the Rolling Stones, Neil Young and many others), engineers Larry Levine and Stan Ross, pianist Leon Russell, guitarist Glen Campbell, sax players Steve Douglas and Jim Horn, backup singer/percussionist Sonny Bono and stellar drummers Hal Blaine and Earl Palmer (the New Orleans legend). These and many other talented sessionmen conspired, under Spector's watchful ear, to make the biggest sound ever blasted out of transistor radio. To further blend it all to his liking, Spector added extra echo and equalized the sound to emphasize the highs and lows—treble and bass—to a much greater degree than had been done before, and insisted on recording in mono rather than stereo to add to the monolithic Wall effect.

Spector spent days and weeks perfecting his "little symphonies." In the time it took most record companies to record ten songs in hopes that one of them would hit, Spector recorded a single gem that he *knew* would hit. "I imagined a sound—a sound so strong that if the material wasn't the greatest, the sound would carry the record."[11] The sound did carry a few songs, like "Zip-A-Dee Doo-Dah," that he seemed to pick for the sole purpose of testing his theory. For the most part, though, his reputation guaranteed him his pick of the best songs from the best of the Brill Building writers—his mission was to turn great Songs into great Records.

Darlene Love

Darlene Love reprised her role as an honorary "Crystal" for Mann & Weil's "He's Sure the Boy I Love," then joined Bob B. Soxx & the Blue Jeans on "Zip-A-De Doo-Dah," "Why Do Lovers Break Each Other's Heart" and "Not Too Young to Get Married. Love finally had hits under her own name in 1963 with "Today I Met the Boy I'm Going to Marry" and "Wait 'til My Bobby Gets Home," a bouncy affirmation of fidelity ("sure do need some lovin' and some kissin' and a-huggin' but I'll wait until my Bobby gets home"). For some reason, though, her greatest songs weren't hits: "A Fine Fine Boy" only managed to make it to #59, while "Long Way to Be Happy" failed to chart at all. Her crowning moment came on Barry & Greenwich's "**Christmas (Baby Please Come Home)**," an unbelievably impassioned plea couched as a Christmas song and buried on Spector's 1963 *Christmas Album*, a sentimental collection of new songs and Christmas standards sung by Spector's roster of stars that was itself buried by the national gloom following the Kennedy assassination.

The Crystals

After sitting out two of "their" biggest hits, the Crystals regained their rightful place with 1963's "**Da Doo Ron Ron**," singing in full-voiced unison atop a typically Spectorian cast of thousands. Only Steve Douglas' sax solo and Hal Blaine's drumming stand out from the dense mass of voices and instruments: Blaine drives the song along in magnificent fashion, with deep, echoed drum fills that punctuate each line of the chorus and long quasi-rolls that bridge the verses. The Crystals followed with "**Then He Kissed Me**," another classic monolith highlighted by soaring strings, steamrolling castanets and an opening signature riff that rings ethereally throughout the song. The gradual addition of new layers of instruments through the first verses provides a good glimpse of the Wall going up, growing from huge to devastating. "Then He Kissed Me" was the Crystal's final moment of glory. A pair of 1964 releases failed to hit and Spector lost interest in the group, having found another group to lavish his attention and best material on: the Ronettes.

The Ronettes

The Ronettes inspired Spector's greatest work. During their two-year run at the charts they were a vehicle for "Do I Love You," "Walking in the Rain," "(The Best Part of) Breaking Up" and many other great records, including Spector's crowning masterpieces: "Baby My Baby" and "Baby, I Love You." Before signing with Spector, the Ronettes—sisters Ronnie and Estelle Bennett and cousin Nedra Talley—were featured vocalists at New York's Peppermint Lounge, the home of the Twist, where they polished their dance routines and developed a sultry "bad girls" image that balanced the innocence of their songs and the Frankie Lymon-esque sound of their lead singer, **Ronnie Bennett**. Spector saw their act, signed them to Philles and promptly recorded "Be My Baby," a million seller in the summer of 1963.

Spector fell in love with and eventually married Ronnie Bennett, whose presence assured that the Ronettes were much more than another "interchangeable part" in his eyes. The Barry & Greenwich songs he picked (and helped write) for Ronnie to sing were achingly beautiful declarations of love phrased as simply and directly as possible. While the rest of the world heard the songs and fantasized that they were sung for them, Spector was able to live the fantasy: to really hear his girl sing "have I ever told you, how good it feels to hold you?" directly to him. He returned the sentiment in the magnificent palaces of sound he built to house Ronnie's earnest little voice.

"**Be My Baby**" opens with rock's most famous drum line, a heavily-echoed hook-line (boom-ba-boom-WHACK) that forms the underlying rhythm for the verses, where it is transformed into a gentle bass riff as the Wrecking Crew rumbles in beneath Ronnie's opening lines. A choir of voices and sustained brass is added as the verse begins winding its way to the jubilant chorus, where the beat straightens out into a giant sledgehammer and everyone joins Ronnie for the title refrain. The brass and voices stay with her through the second verse, bolstered by the subtle entrance of a string section that further enlivens the second chorus and takes a brief melodic solo before a final refrain. "Be My

Baby" is capped off by a sudden halt for a surprise return of the opening drum line, followed by a triumphant reentry and a joyous fade-out that turns into a lavishly accompanied drum solo.

"**Baby, I Love You**" is very similar to "Be My Baby," and even better. The arrangement is larger and more seamless, Ronnie's singing is more assured and Hal Blaine's drum extravaganza is even more aggressive, joined by sleigh bells, castanets, tambourines, cow bells and a full battery of other percussion instruments. The song itself is a love letter set to a long, gentle melody that flows into the simplest and purest of all pop refrains: "Baby I love you, baby I love you, baby I love only you."

The Ronettes followed with "(The Best Part of) Breaking Up," "Do I Love You," a forgotten classic on a par with their first hits, and Mann & Weil's great "**Walking in the Rain**." "Walking in the Rain" is all about the *dream* of love: "I want him, and I need him, and someday, someway, I'll meet him." The song's brooding melody and atmospheric production—complete with thunderclaps and rain showers—create a truly melancholy mood: the singer's feelings are so close and real, but the reality of a true love remains far away as the song ends with a wistful "where can he be?"[12] Unfortunately, "Walking in the Rain" was lost in the chart chaos of the British Invasion and the Ronettes were unable to regain their stride with their remaining releases. Pop's fairy tale romance lasted a bit longer, but ended with Phil and Ronnie Spector's divorce in 1974.

The Righteous Brothers

Phil Spector's recordings of the Righteous Brothers were his last great successes. With the arrival of the Beatles and the declining popularity of the girl groups, Spector looked for a new vehicle for his sound and found Bill Medley and Bobby Hatfield, a white singing duo from Southern California who had a local hit in 1963 with "Little Latin Lupe Lu." The duo was dubbed the "Righteous Brothers" by black fans who liked their soulful singing style. Spector was likewise drawn to their soulful two-part harmonies and their flair for vocal theatrics, pitting Medley's rich baritone against Hatfield's wailing falsettos. He signed them to Philles in 1964 and commissioned Mann & Weil to write "something different" for their first release.

"**You've Lost That Lovin' Feelin'**" was certainly "different." The record opens at a funeral march tempo with Bill Medley singing in a low, smoky voice that sent more than a few listeners running to check the speed on their record player. The spacious death-knell sound that surrounds him is as desolate as the song's opening line: "You never close your eyes anymore when I kiss your lips." The slow torture heightens with Medley's rise to full-voiced pleading and the dramatic entrance of Hatfield's harmonies and the full backing Wall for the title refrain. The chorus dissolves into a sighing bass line and a deep drum fill that rumbles into the second verse, where the introverted sorrow continues. After another gut-wrenching chorus the song implodes to stark near-silence to introduce the extended "bridge" section, where Medley and Hatfield trade lines then join in a call-and-response that builds to a high shrieking climax before collapsing into another desperate chorus. For a final dramatic flourish, Spector tacked on a false ending and a sudden full-fury return for an ending fade-out.

"You've Lost That Lovin' Feelin'" evokes the feeling of love lost with chilling force, surging from one climax to another within an emotional range bounded by quiet sorrow and unadulterated grief that seems too much for a mere record. It was, in any case, too long: at 3:50, Spector knew that radio stations would balk at playing it (even though the false ending helped disguise the length). In typically bold fashion, he solved the problem by simply stamping "3:05" on the record label. The record received massive airplay and Spector had his last #1 hit of the 1960's. ("You've Lost That Lovin' Feelin'" also hit #3 on the R&B charts and virtually invented "blue-eyed soul"; Righteous Brothers disciples Hall & Oates also had a hit with the song in 1980.)

Spector recorded a near sound-alike for a follow-up, Goffin & King's "Just Once in My Life," that managed to match its predecessor's emotional and orchestral density. Their next hit was a remake of the pop standard, "Unchained Melody," even though the song was actually released as the B-side of another Goffin & King original, "Hung On You." Spector was less than thrilled about the public's preference for the old song and, in a typically twisted stroke of vengeance, he decided to record *only* pop standards for their next releases. "Ebb Tide" followed "Unchained melody" into the Top Ten, but "White Cliffs of Dover" failed to chart and the Righteous Brothers bolted for the saner confines of the Verve label. They promptly returned to #1 with "(You're My) Soul and Inspiration," written by Mann & Weil and produced by Bill Medley in grand Spector fashion.

Ike & Tina Turner

Suddenly hitless and out-of-step with the times, Spector staked his reputation on Ike & Tina Turner's **"River Deep-Mountain High,"** recorded in 1966. Spector smothered the rather slight Barry & Greenwich composition under the most bombastic production of his career, knowing that Tina Turner's powerhouse voice could blast its way through anything. The joyously maniacal exercise in excess capped the Wall of Sound years and was a big hit in England, but it climbed only up to #88 on the American charts. Meant to re-establish Spector's preeminence, it became his grand farewell instead. Devastated by the song's inexplicable failure, Spector retreated into semi-retirement. He was 25 years old.

Let It Be

Spector returned to the charts in 1969 with Sonny Charles & the Checkmates' "Black Pearl," a great song and effective production that recalled his past triumphs but added a new element of social conscious. Spector's tenure as *the* rock producer was well in the past, however, Still, it's hard to say his career was "over" when the next group he worked with was **The Beatles**(!) He was actually an old acquaintance of the group, having met them during a Ronettes tour of England. (He even flew with them on their first triumphant visit to America. Spector visited and contributed ideas to several of the Rolling Stones' early recording sessions as well.) Spector never really "produced" the Beatles, but was called in after the fact to assemble a coherent album out of the hours and hours of tape left over from the Beatles' *Let It Be* sessions. He then produced the first solo albums for John Lennon and George Harrison, including the hit singles "Imagine" and "My Sweet Lord." Needless to say, no one was calling them "Phil Spector records": for the first time in his career, Spector was working with artists more famous and strong-willed than he was. While Spector's production touches certainly added much to the records, particularly the spacious quasi-Wall of Harrison's *All Things Must Pass* and the heavily-echoed pop sound of Lennon's "Instant Karma," he was, finally, a "normal" producer, forced to accommodate his artists' ideas and bend to their sound and style.

Spector's behavior grew increasingly bizarre as the hits that had justified his eccentricities faded. He produced sporadically through the late seventies and eighties (including the Ramones' 1980 *End of the Century* album) and ended up something of a rock & roll Howard Hughes, secluded in his mansion and memories of past glories. He has been more visible—and visibly calmer—in recent years, and he continues to be an icon and influence.

Phil Spector single-handedly changed the sound and shape of popular music and crafted some of its finest and most exhilarating moments. The Wall of Sound still stands as his monument.

---

[1]Pat Boone, "Between You, Me and the Gatepost," (Englewood Cliffs: Prentice-Hall, 1960), p. 135.

[2]Tony Palmer, "All You Need Is Love," (1976; rpt. New York: Penguin, 1977).

[3]Ian Whitcomb, "Whole Lotta Shakin'," (London: Arrow, 1982).

[4]For two of the more blatant examples (ripoffs) of Holly's influence, listen to Bobby Vee's "Rubber Ball" or Tommy Roe's "Sheila." Roe returned later in the decade with a series of hits ("Sweet Pea," "Hooray for Hazel," "Dizzy") that were derisively labeled "bubblegum music." Although the term wasn't around at the time, the early 1960's could certainly be called the "bubblegum era."

[5]Bruce Pollack, "When Rock Was Young" (New York: Holt, Rinehart & Winston, 1981), p. 39.

[6]ibid., p. 131.

[7]Joe Smith, "Off the Record" (New York: Warner, 1988), p.148.

[8]One rarely sees a "Ronettes Greatest Hits" package, for example;. You'll find your favorite Ronettes song on a "*Phil Spector's* Greatest Hits" collection.

[9]Album liner notes for "Phil Spector's Greatest Hits," Warner/Spector Records (WB 2SP 9104, 1977).

[10]ibid., quoted from Rob Finnis, "The Phil Spector Story."

[11]Shannon and Javna, p. 108.

[12] The rather run-of-the-mill sound effects won Spector his only Grammy Award, a good example of how little the Grammy Awards mean.

Photo courtesy of UPI/BETTMAN

Roy Orbison

[11] EARLY SIXTIES POP: MALE SINGERS AND GROUPS

While the girl groups were making consistently great records, their male counterparts were having a harder time defining their style and place in the early sixties. In contrast to the relatively unified musical front presented by the girl groups, the male singers and groups were scattered widely across the stylistic spectrum between the extremes of teen idol pop and mainstream respectability and artless garage band thrashing. Only a handful of pop singers and groups stood out from the pack with distinctive personal styles and voices, most notably Roy Orbison, Frankie Valli & the Four Seasons, Dion, Neil Sedaka, Del Shannon and Gene Pitney —a great collection of pop voices that covered the gamut from the resonant depth of Roy Orbison to the blissful shriek of Frankie Valli's falsetto.

ROY ORBISON

In an era filled with good voices, Roy Orbison was The Voice: a stark, solitary presence wracked with pain that seemed a bit too real for the age of puppy love and teenage crushes. He seemed equally out of place as a "pop star": he looked like a moonish pumpkin, lacked any charisma or sex appeal and, in fact, seemed to have no discernible personality beyond his songs or beneath the dark glasses and black suits that made him seem like a funeral director—which, in a sense, he was. Night after night, Orbison stood dead still before a microphone and thrilled audiences with his amazing voice and his apocalyptic visions of the death of love and hope. He was universally admired by other musicians both as a singular talent and one of the nicest people you'd ever want to meet, and only Elvis could match the fanatical devotion Orbison received from his fans.

The Shy Rockabilly

Roy Orbison was born in 1936 and grew up in Wink, Texas. He fronted a country band in high school, then attended North Texas State University with an eye toward becoming a geologist. His ears were tuned elsewhere, though. Impressed by fellow North Texas student Pat Boone's success, he decided to devote himself to music and the rockabilly that was transforming C&W into rock & roll. He formed his own band, the Teen Kings, hosted his own local television show and recorded a regional hit, "Ooby Dooby," at Norman Petty's studio in Clovis, New Mexico. Then, realizing the dream of every young southern rocker, he signed with Sun Records in the last days of Elvis Presley's reign at the label.

The Sun magic didn't rub off on Orbison, however. A new version of "Ooby Dooby" made it to #59 on the national charts in 1956, but that was the closest he came to having a hit at Sun. The experience and confidence he gained from recording for Sam Phillips and touring with Carl Perkins, Jerry Lee Lewis, Johnny Cash and the rest of the Sun roster was invaluable, however, and "Ooby Dooby," "Rockhouse," "Go Go Go" and other Orbison Sun recordings are ample proof of his rockabilly credentials, though they also betray an uneasiness with the style. Signed to the greatest rockabilly label at the height of the rock & roll explosion, Orbison wanted to be, of all things, a *ballad* singer. He loved rock & roll but felt, rightly, that his true voice and songwriting talents lay elsewhere.

After a few tentative ballads proved unsuccessful, Orbison concentrated on writing songs for others (including "Down the Line" for Jerry Lee Lewis), then moved to RCA after the Everly Brothers had a 1958 hit with his tribute to his wife, "Claudette." Working with producer Chet Atkins, Orbison recorded a couple of flops for RCA and then, having once again failed in Elvis' footsteps, signed with tiny Monument Records, a Nashville-based label primarily devoted to country music.

Monument Records

Orbison's luck, or lack of it, held at Monument as well until 1960, when he crawled up to #72 on the charts with "Up Town" (Orbison's own composition, not the Mann & Weil hit for the Crystals). The record's strings, choir and sax arrangement and the rich, full singing anticipated the hits to come and presented an entirely different Roy Orbison from the hesitant rockabilly of his Sun days. "Up Town" also inaugurated a songwriting partnership between Orbison and Texas friend Joe Melson that lasted through most of his hits, and a co-producing partnership with Monument owner Fred Foster. Few resumes could boast of having failed with three of the era's top producers: Norman Petty, Sam Phillips and Chet Atkins. In Foster, however, Orbison found a kindred spirit willing to go out on a limb and risk alienating both the country and teen pop audiences to craft a symphonic sound big enough to contain Orbison's voice and vision.

"Only the Lonely"

Orbison nearly gave his breakthrough hit away. Still considering himself primarily a songwriter, he offered "Only the Lonely" to the Everly Brothers and tried to get it to Elvis Presley before he finally recorded it himself.[1] It's hard to imagine anyone else singing "Only the Lonely," the first installment of Orbison's string of anthems to epic heartache. The song opens innocuously enough with a polite set of nonsense syllables ("dum dum dum dum-by doo-wah...") and a gentle country-ish backing that gives no hint of the emotional torrent to come. Then, suddenly, the band stops for a moment and The Voice appears, staking out its desolate emotional turf: "Only the lonely know the way I feel tonight..." Another sudden stop interrupts the first verse: the subdued backing just isn't enough to contain his grief, so a vibraphone and huge string section chime in to punctuate his vision of his girl walking away. Trapped in his sorrow, Orbison reaffirms the fact that "only the lonely" can understand how he feels, then looks to the only solace he can offer himself — the dream of a new romance, someday... risky, perhaps, but that's the "chance you gotta take."

A less powerful voice and presence would have been buried under the arrangement and the maudlin sentiment of the lyrics. Instead, Orbison triumphs over each: he strains his voice to its upper limits and then soars, all alone, into a stratospheric falsetto in a moment of pure grief at the song's climax. The long descent that follows and ends the song shows the full range of the voice Elvis Presley called the "best in the world."

"Only the Lonely" climbed to #2 on the pop charts in the summer of 1960, the first of twenty-seven Orbison records in a row to make the charts. Orbison remained resolutely committed to his inner muse and impervious to the rapidly changing styles and trends of the early sixties. He was one of the few exceptions to the "Song not the Singer" pop aesthetic that dominated the times—a singular and self-defining voice who brought the same personal intensity to the pop era that his old friends at Sun brought to rock & roll. Along with Phil Spector's pop symphonies, Orbison's majestic voice made everything else on the radio—all the teen crushes and breakups—seem trivial by comparison. (There's no accounting for taste, however: "Only the Lonely" was denied the top spot by Brian Hyland's "Itsy Bitsy Teenie Weenie Yellow Polka Dot Bikini"!)

The unrelieved sorrow of "Only the Lonely" colored most of Orbison's output, as did the song's symphonic arrangement and continually building, free-form structure, with no bridges sections, refrains or instrumental solos to break the tension as Orbison builds from a conversational tone to full-voiced anguish. Although he recorded many uptempo songs, he was most effective in the operatic ballads that fully employed his vocal and emotional range. The titles tell much of the story: "Running Scared," "Crying," "I'm Hurtin'," "It's Over"... In Orbison's world, LOVE is nothing less than a matter of life and death, and breaking up isn't just "hard to do," it's a catastrophe that lays his entire world to waste. Unlike most pop love or heartache songs, which focus on the Beloved, Orbison's songs dwell on the singer's own tormented inner landscape—the women he sings of are rarely more than fleeting images, made real only through the filter of his dreams and fears.

"Running Scared"

"Running Scared" is Orbison's monument to pathological paranoia: the singer has the girl, for now, but lives in mortal fear that her old flame will return and steal her back, that his grip on her love is so tenuous that he will lose her at any moment. He sees HIM everywhere, expects him all the time and then, suddenly... HE'S THERE, standing right in front of them like a warden nodding, "it's time." An insistent Bolero rhythm underpins the song's relentless build-up, and new layers of instruments are added for each stanza as the song swells from a simple confession of few doubts and insecurities to Orbison's final hour on emotional death row. At the peak of the orchestral and emotional tumult, however, an amazing thing happens: the woman turns away from her old flame and walks off with Orbison, who surges up to a triumphant high note as the song cadences and the struggle ends—for now. Orbison's moment of triumph seems filled more with astonishment than with joy, and the conviction that she spared him this time in order to completely crush him the next.

Orbison's romantic death wish came true in song after song, from the desolate opening of "It's Over" ("Your baby doesn't love you anymore") to the stranglehold of his memories in "Crying," where his ex-love reappears for just long enough to remind him that he still hasn't gotten over her, and never will. The melody of "Crying" stretches out endlessly like a love that won't die, while the pain in the lyrics seems to come from a deep, painful corner of the soul that should never see the light of day.

"In Dreams"

When reality got a little painful, dream worlds were the great refuge of the early sixties, the place where the girl groups and teen idols could find their true love and spend a few rapturous minutes or hours enjoying the dream itself, firm in the belief that it could someday come true. That type of naive hope was beyond the reach Orbison's romantic fatalism—he knew that dreams were the *only* place he would ever enjoy the love that reality never offered. Sometimes they even seemed to help: his dream of another love sees him through "Only the Lonely" and fills "Dream Baby" with an almost cheerful optimism. In "Blue Bayou," his wistful dream of returning to his love and the idyllic bayou help to stave off his current misery, though its hard to believe he'll ever make it back. Usually, though, the dreams only serve to remind him of how truly awful his real life has become, and that Love, like a dream, never lasts.

While "Running Scared" was an impressive portrait of extreme paranoia, "In Dreams" depicts an obsessive psychosis of clinical proportions. The song starts off innocently enough: Orbison tells how a "candy-colored clown they call the sandman" visits him every night, sprinkling stardust and telling him, "Go to sleep, everything is all right." The singer longs, a little too much, for the escape of sleep: he says a nightly prayer for his girl's return, then plunges desperately into the only world where he can pretend she's still his. The sweet, Spanish-flavored melody and orchestral arrangement lend an ironic normalcy to the torture of a man unable to let go of his love. Night after night he dreams that she's still there, *feels* her presence, then awakens time and time again to the crushing reality that she's gone. As Orbison swells to a high, half-screamed refrain at the end of the song, you know that the daily nightmare of his waking hours is just beginning.[2]

"Oh, Pretty Woman"

Orbison never really abandoned his rock roots. He regularly paired slow songs with fast ones, and even his Big Ballads were supported with a strong beat and had an emotional directness more indebted to rock than to previous pop styles. As a whole, though, his attempts at uptempo songs were less convincing than the mini-dramas better suited to his voice and style. What a surprise, then, that Orbison should come up with one of the great riff-rockers of all time: "Oh, Pretty Woman."

"Oh, Pretty Woman," a #1 hit in 1964, opens with a hard, pounding beat that shows that Orbison was keeping an ear on the British bands that were invading the charts (he even tips his hat to the Beatles at one point and sings "Pretty woman yeah, yeah, yeah"). After building the tension through two false starts, the classic guitar-and-bass riff appears in all its glory. The riff disappears for the verses then returns to frame the each section, while the beat stays hard and constant up until the bridge section ("pretty woman stop a while..."), which stretches out and nearly turns the song into a ballad before the riff returns to tip the balance back to rock & roll. Through it all Roy pleads, demands, seduces and gives his trademark growl, and the woman just keeps walking away—one more in a long line of rejections. Then, to his utter amazement, she turns around and walks back toward him! The riff hesitates again, unable to believe the change of events, then triumphantly draws the song to a close.

Alone in the Dark

"Oh, Pretty Woman" was Orbison's last major hit. Lured by the promise of bigger money and a film career, he switched to the MGM label in 1965. Instead, the hits dried up and Orbison entered the one period of his life that was actually as dark and tragic as the songs he sang. In 1966, his wife, Claudette, was killed in a motorcycle accident while Orbison was riding just a few yards ahead of her. Two years later, a fire destroyed his home and killed two of his three children. The stoic Orbison kept touring, though he didn't perform in the United States again until 1977 and adamantly refused to participate in "oldies" shows. Cover versions of Orbison classics by Linda Ronstadt ("Blue Bayou"), Don McLean ("Crying") and Van Halen ("Oh, Pretty Woman") introduced his songs to a new audience and sparked a revitalized interest in the originals. Orbison resumed his recording career, won a Grammy award for a 1980 duet with Emmylou Harris, "That Lovin' You Feelin' Again," and returned in 1988 as a full-fledged star in a tongue-in-cheek supergroup called the Traveling Willburys. His work with fellow "Willburys" Bob Dylan, George Harrison, Tom Petty and Jeff Lynne, and a new solo album,

Mystery Girl, marked Orbison's full-scale comeback as a vital artist and showed his incredible voice still in peak form after all the years and heartaches. Orbison savored his return to the spotlight, but only briefly. In a final cruel stroke, worthy of inclusion in one of his songs, Roy Orbison died on December 6, 1988.

Like the greatest country singers—such as Charlie Rich and George Jones, the only white singers who could rival Orbison's vocal power—Orbison cut through the surface and straight to the heart with such overwhelming conviction that you can *feel* his songs rather than simply "relate to them." As ardent fan Bruce Springsteen put it: "Some rock & roll reinforces friendship and community. But for me, Roy's ballads were always the best when you were alone and in the dark."[3] He gave a voice and a dignity to an inner sorrow that most pop songs try to escape or gloss over. If "only the lonely" can know how he felt, then sooner or later there comes a point when only a Roy Orbison song can express how you really feel.

NEIL SEDAKA

Shifting from Roy Orbison to Neil Sedaka is like a moving from a dimly-lit room into bright sunshine, and from a brooding melancholy to a giddy, weightless cheeeriness that occupies the opposite end of the pop spectrum from the grandoise inner tumult of Orbison's world. Sedaka offered what great pop had always offered: well-crafted songs with appealing melodies and clever lyrics that provided a pleasant little escape from reality. Within that context, there was no one better. The sugar-coated cuteness can mask the charms of Sedaka's music, but the subtle joy of his purest of pop is a taste well worth acquiring.

Neil Sedaka earned and displayed his pop credentials as one of the shining lights at Don Kirshner's Aldon Music and as the only "Brill Building" writer of the time who was able to use his songwriting skills to fuel his own successful career. Sedaka's clear, reedy voice and catchy songs were enough to make him a star of the early sixties—which was fortunate, since he certainly couldn't have depended on his looks or sex appeal. The smiling, round-faced Sedaka looked more like a science club president than a teen idol, and his nice-guy image extended to his songs as well: the girls he sang to were "sweet sixteens" and "angels" living right next door or up a "Stairway to Heaven." His intentions with them were painfully honorable and he expressed his devotion with enough corny "I love you'"s, "I'll be true'"s and "sad and blue's" to fill a rhyming dictionary of pop clichés. There was no hint of sex or rebellion—the Philadelphia teen idols seemed almost dangerous by comparison, but they couldn't touch his musical mastery and sheer exuberance, or his ability to bring a cliché back to life.

Neil Sedaka was born in Brooklyn in 1939, and began writing music for his friend **Howie Greenfield**'s lyrics while both were still in their early teens. Sedaka was also a promising classical pianist and the winner of a "best young pianist in New York" contest, though by 1958 he was balancing his lessons at the Julliard School of Music with the infinitely more thrilling experience of fronting his own doo-wop group, the Tokens (who later, minus Sedaka, had a hit with "The Lion Sleeps Tonight"). Sedaka abandoned classical music, but he retained its lessons in formal structure and finely-crafted melodies and added that influence to his abiding love for doo-wop, the melodically-driven sound of the New York streets.

Sedaka signed a recording contract with RCA in 1958 and scored a moderate hit with the doo-wopish "The Diary." He hit again in 1959 with "Oh! Carol," written for his friend Carol King, launching a run of hits that lasted through 1963. **"Oh! Carol"** opens with a soaring falsetto melody and layering of calypso rhythms that is reminiscent of the Diamond's version of "Little Darling," as is the comically melodramatic spoken interlude in the middle of the song ("Oh Carol, I am but a fool..."). Like his white doo-wop predecessors, Sedaka adopted the vocal and musical devices of doo-wop— the "doo-wop chord progression," the idyllic love lyrics, the layered background voices, falsetto countermelodies and chanted nonsense syllables—but focused it all with a clear pop melody. Sedaka also added his own over-dubbed harmony part to many of his, including "Oh! Carol," creating a tight two-part, "two-Neils" harmony that became one of his trademarks.

Sedaka & Greenfield fine-tuned their work for every release, but they rarely strayed from the "formula" they perfected with "Oh! Carol": Greenfield's clever rhymes and metaphors set to bright melodies backed by lively dance rhythms, inventive arrangements and layers of overdubbed harmonies and background voices. "Calendar Girl" and "Happy Birthday Sweet Sixteen" were notable follow-ups full of irresistible hooks and melodies, but **"Breaking Up Is Hard to Do,"** a #1 hit in 1962, was Sedaka's tour de force. The song opens with a classic set of chanted nonsense syllables (all sung by Sedaka) that weave throughout the arrangement, doubled by a piano and classical guitar, while Sedaka sings the song's beatific melody in two-part harmony over a crisp backing arrangement punctuated by stops and starts. The contrasting bridge sections ("they say that breaking up...") feature a more fluid and sentimental melody, a nicely understated orchestral flourish and, the second time around, a group of female voices that join Sedaka for a gentle call-and-response. "Breaking Up Is Hard to Do" is certainly a *happy* break-up song—quite a distance from Roy Orbison! Rather than moaning about his lost girlfriend he celebrates their love and all the great reasons for getting back together (and all the great rhymes that can go with the word "do").

The next release, the equally infectious "Next Door to an Angel," stuck closely to the "Breaking Up Is Hard to Do" blueprint—perhaps too closely. Sedaka's popularity was already on the wane by the time the British Invasion finished him off. He did, however, make a surprising comeback over a decade later. Backed by Elton John's Rocket Records, Sedaka enjoyed a second run of stardom through the mid-seventies before falling back out of the limelight and into the middle-of-the-road. His seventies hits included "Laughter in the Rain" and "Bad Blood," which were both #1 hits (as was "Love Will Keep Us Together," a Sedaka-penned hit for The Captain & Tennille). Sedaka also recorded a maudlin new version of "Breaking Up Is Hard to Do" that attempted to show a "maturing" along the lines of Carole King's remakes of her old songs, but served instead to illustrate how hard it was to recreate the fragile innocence of early sixties pop.

GENE PITNEY

Part teen idol, part sentimental balladeer, part schmaltzy crooner, part business tycoon and a key figure in the New York pop scene, Gene Pitney managed to occupy much of the ground between Roy Orbison and Neil Sedaka, and a good chunk of Frank Sinatra's turf as well. He was a sought-after songwriter (the Crystals' "He's a Rebel" and Ricky Nelson's "Hello Mary Lou" were his biggest hits for others) who more often than not turned to outside writers for his own recordings, most often Burt Bacharach & Hal David. His eclectic style encompassed adult ballads, teen pop, rock & roll, Italian love songs, exotic production numbers, schlocky showtunes and straight Country and Western, and he seemed to be able to change his versatile voice at will to fit the various styles.

Already a successful songwriter, Pitney recorded his first hit, "**(I Wanna) Love My Life Away**," in 1961 as a demotape for his publisher, Aaron Schroeder, who was so taken with it that he released the "demo" on his Musicor Records label. Pitney played all of the instruments and sang all of the record's lead, harmony and background vocal parts—the first example of the "one man band" approach employed much later by Stevie Wonder, Paul McCartney and others. Pitney's second record, 1961's "**Every Breath I Take**," was written by Goffin & King and was produced by Phil Spector, who viewed it as a turning point in his transition from Leiber & Stoller's Uptown R&B style to his own distinctive sound. The elaborate production and ornate, bathetic delivery of "Every Breath I Take" (very different from the Buddy Holly style pop vocals of "Love My Life Away") anticipated the tone of most of Pitney's later hits.

Pitney's wide-ranging talent and business acumen gave him a uniquely free hand in shaping his recordings and career. He developed a curious mixture of old and new "pop," vacillating between great Brill Building style pop-rock ("It Hurts to Be in Love") and cabaret showtunes with exotic productions ("Mecca"). He was best known for expansive ballads and exaggerated mini-dramas like "Last Chance to Turn Around," "Half Heaven - Half Heartache,"

"Twenty Four Hours From Tulsa," "Only Love Can Break a Heart" and two movie themes: "Town Without Pity" and "The Man Who Shot Liberty Valance."

Like an updated Johnny Ray, Pitney specialized in melodramatic self-pity, singing with an exaggerated, showbiz emotion that appealed to an older, more mainstream audience. He developed a large adult following in America and an even bigger one in Europe—especially England and in Italy, where he remains a revered star (he has recorded several albums in Italian). Pitney's keen ear for all pop styles also made him popular with the teen idol and *American Bandstand* audiences, though, and his musical brilliance and hip New York aura made him appealing to even harder rockers (Mick Jagger and Keith Richards wrote "That Girl Belongs to Yesterday" for Pitney and invited him to play piano on a Rolling Stones session). He even scored a soul-style dance hit in 1968 with "She's a Heartbreaker," though the majority of his releases were tied to the rock market more by attitude than by musical traits.

DEL SHANNON

Del Shannon apparently longed for the type of broad audience that Gene Pitney attracted. When asked if he would like to become that dreaded scourge of true rockers, the "all-around entertainer," Shannon didn't even flinch: "I sure would! I'd like to be able to prove my worth as a *supperclub performer*."[4] A noble ambition, perhaps, but well beyond the reach of his blue collar talents and voice. Instead, he had to be content with being one of the purest rockers of his day.

"**Runaway**" was a #1 hit for the 21-year-old Shannon in 1961, and a blast of fresh air for the teen idol era. Shannon sang "Runaway" with a rough, rock & roll urgency, backed by a big beat, strong bass, lively piano line and his own raucous electric guitar. The band is embellished with a saxophone and a memorably bizarre roller-rink "organ from Hell" (actually a proto-synthesizer called a "musitron," invented by Shannon's organ player), but there are no strings, choirs or clever nonsense syllables in sight—it really sounds like a *band* playing. A dramatic strummed minor chord opens the song, setting the scene for a brooding Shannon, walking through the rain, haunted by his memories and wondering what went wrong and why his girl ran away. In his way, Shannon rivaled Gene Pitney and even Roy Orbison for self torment, though like a true rocker he fought and railed against his cruel fate. For the chorus ("I'm a-walkin' in the rain...") the song suddenly shifts from minor to major and Shannon slams into a full-power vocal that turns his expression of sorrow into an act of defiance. He leaps to his trademark falsetto shriek ("I wa-wa-wa wa-onder, why—whywhywhywhy*why* she ran away") then crash-lands into his normal voice and wrings out the end of the refrain with a mixture of wounded rage and concern for his little runaway.

Supperclub ambitions aside, "Runaway" defined the range of Shannon's limited but effective style. The song's drama, instrumental line-up, falsetto hooks, minor key/major key shift and spotlighted "musitron" appear, with slight variations, in most of his songs and returned verbatim in the follow-up hit, **"Hats Off to Larry."** Here Shannon gets his revenge and pays tribute to the man who crushed his runaway like she crushed him: "Hats off to Larry, he broke your heart!" Del will take her back, of course, but for now it's her turn to "cry cry cr-y-y," and he's loving every minute of it.

That vengeful sentiment was echoed a couple of years later—from the other direction—in Lesley Gore's "Judy's Turn to Cry." Although Shannon's garage band sound was far removed from Gore's elaborate Quincy Jones productions, the two were very similar as singers—each had an ornate and soulful power-pop style that set them apart from most white pop singers of the time. (In addition, both Gore and Shannon enhanced the power of their voice with frequent double-tracking.) Unlike Gore, however, Shannon wrote his own songs, shaped his own band arrangements, and based his songs around his own hard-strumming guitar.

Shannon produced a handful of other hits, including two further installments of restless paranoia, "Keep Searchin' (We'll Follow the Sun)" and "Stranger in Town." "Little Town Flirt," from 1963, warned everyone about the local heartbreaker (the runaway again?) and featured some of his strongest singing, double-tracked throughout, and an inspired, melismatic pop melody that directly influenced Shannon fan John Lennon.

Shannon met the Beatles in England in 1963 and recorded their "From Me to You." His version wasn't a big hit—it peaked at #77—but it marked the first entry of a Lennon-McCartney song on the U.S. charts, nearly a year before the Beatles came to America. Shannon's British admirers effectively ended his career (nothing personal), though he did make a modest return nearly two decades and several failed comeback attempts later with an album and hit single, 1983's "Sea of Love," produced by old fan Tom Petty. After another decade of painful obscurity, Del Shannon committed suicide in 1990.

The Changing Streetcorner

Vocal group styles remained popular in the early sixties, and the "neo-doo-wop" groups did more than most to keep the airwaves fun and filled with voices of all sorts, from the odd dignity of Maurice Williams & the Zodiacs' "Stay," which opened the era in 1960, to the beatific inanity of "Surfin' Bird" by the aptly-named Trashmen, who ended it when their oh-so-promising career was cut short by the Beatles in 1964. Streetcorner groups still flourished in the East Coast urban centers, though the streetcorner itself was changing as Americans of Italian descent came to dominate the style and take it in a more carefully crafted pop direction. Danny & the Juniors, the Crests and Dion & the

Belmonts led the way in the late fifties; the greatest exponents of the New York group sound in the early sixties were the Four Seasons and Dion, who left the Belmonts in 1960 but never strayed too far from the streetcorner or the vocal group style.

DION

Dion DiMucci was the quintessential "Italo-American" rocker: part sentimental romantic and part streetwise tough guy who could charm his way through a macho manifesto like "The Wanderer" or make a simple declaration of love sound like a threat. His singing style, similarly, was a mix of florid, Italianate "bel canto" pop and growling street hood toughness. Dion's self-assured cool cut through the teen pop facade of glossy innocence and gave a voice to hardened city kids who liked their pop cut with a solid dance beat and a strong dose of rock & roll earthiness. In a 1988 speech inducting Dion to the Rock & Roll Hall of Fame, Lou Reed hailed his hero as "a voice that stood on its own, remarkable and unmistakably from New York."

Dion's first solo effort, "Lonely Teenager," hearkened back to the vulnerable, teen idolish image of "A Teenager in Love" and other earlier Belmonts recordings. (Dion continued to use the familiar setting of vocal group harmonies after leaving the Belmonts—a group called the Del Satins sang backup on most of his early sixties hits.) His next hit, 1961's **"Runaround Sue,"** presented a tougher image and sound for the singer's lash-back at the girl who dumped him and his warning to all the other guys to "keep away from Runaround Sue." Like many of his releases, and countless other early sixties pop songs, "Runaround Sue" opens with a slow, teasing, mock-dramatic introduction ("Here's my story, it's sad but it's true"), then launches into a classic nonsense syllable riff behind Dion's gritty lead vocals and bel canto "whoah's." Dion's description of the song's genesis illustrates the inspirational power of a good doo-wop riff and the festive, singalong spirit that his records sought to capture: "'Runaround Sue' was the type of song that you sing on streetcorners or on the rooftops or in the hallways or on the subway just banging on cardboard boxes and hitting beer bottles, just making a racket and getting a kind of a mantra going. We had a party one night in the school yard and that riff affected us so much we had it goin' for about three hours. The following week I wrote some lyrics to it, we did a session with it and tried recapture that same feeling. Of course we didn't, because when we took the record back to the neighborhood all our friends said, 'aw you loused it up—it was so much better the night we did it in the schoolyard.' But, it worked."[5]

"Runaround Sue" defined Dion's "pop-with-a-knife" sound and became an almost generic model for "neo-doo-wop" pop styles in the early sixties. (The vocal arrangement and party feel were echoed in many recordings, most notably Gary "U.S." Bonds' "Quarter to Three," a dense, glorious mess that sounds like it was recorded *in* the schoolyard.) Dion acted out his revenge on "Sue" in "**The Wanderer**," a boasting, tongue-in-cheek self-promotion sung by the ultimate seducer: "I kiss and I love 'em 'cause to me they're all the same, I hug 'em and I squeeze 'em, they don't even know my name." The roguish hero has the names of various conquests tattooed on his body ("There's Flo on left arm and there's Mary on right") and when a poor girl asks who he loves the best... "I tear open my shirt and I show her Rosie on chest." Dion's vocal bravado matches the swagger of the lyrics, supported by an equally tough sax solo and a strong shuffle beat based on the rhythms of an Italian dance.

Dion's subsequent releases stuck closely to the basic sound and style established by "Runaround Sue" and "The Wanderer." Both songs were co-written with Ernie Maresca, who supplied Dion with several other hits, including "Lovers Who Wander" and "Donna the Prima Donna." In 1962, Dion switched from the small Laurie label to Columbia Records, where his output was highlighted by three thoroughly revamped covers of old Drifters records ("Ruby Baby," "Drip Drop" and "This Little Girl") that retained the rough grace and confidence of his earlier hits. In general, though, his style grew more formulaic at Columbia and the spontaneity and fun too often seemed forced. The situation was certainly not helped by Dion's long-standing and rapidly escalating drug problem. When the British Invasion ended his chart run, Dion sank into a long battle with heroin addiction.

A cleaned-up and completely different Dion reemerged as a singer-songwriter in 1968 with one of the biggest hits of the year, "Abraham, Martin and John," a tribute to the assassinated Lincoln, King and Kennedys. Dion released an autobiographical anti-drug song called "Clean Up Your Own Back Yard" in 1969 and recorded a few bluesy folk albums before reuniting with the Belmonts for a well-publicized concert at Madison Square Garden. Several subsequent comeback attempts failed to attract a large audience but won him renewed critical acclaim and the continued devotion of his longtime fans. A few of his more celebrated fans came together in a late-eighties concert and fulfilled a life-long dream: Bruce Springsteen, Lou Reed, Paul Simon, Billy Joel and James Taylor became Belmonts for a night, taking their place behind the man who had sparked their own musical dreams. Like any New Yorker of their generation, they knew every "ooh," "ah" and background riff by heart.

THE FOUR SEASONS

The greatest falsetto of the Age of Falsettos belonged to **Frankie Valli**, the lead singer of the Four Seasons. While most singers used falsetto passages sparingly and for dramatic effect (such as Roy Orbison's soaring climaxes or Del Shannon's hook lines), Valli hovered in the stratosphere for long passages and entire choruses and used his "normal" voice for dramatic contrast. The glass-shattering power of his voice and its continually changing shadings, from the shredding vocal chords of "Big Girls Don't Cry-ee-i-ee-i" to the graceful register leaps of "Candy Girl," made it one of the great pop instruments, perfect for the tiny car speakers and transistor radios that supplied the soundtrack for teenage America.

The Four Seasons were the most popular male group of the early sixties, and ranked third behind only the Beatles and the Beach Boys for the entire decade. Their string of twenty-six hit singles began in 1962 with three #1's in a row—"Sherry," "Big Girls Don't Cry" and "Walk Like a Man"—and continued through 1967. The Four Seasons attracted a wide range of fans: their dancefloor beats and neo-doo-wop harmonies appealed equally to white and black audiences, and their infectious pop lyrics and melodies walked a line between sugary innocence and streetcorner toughness, attracting both teen pop fans and hard core rockers. These days, most listeners tend to either love or, too often, hate the Four Seasons. From this distance the tough edge of Valli's falsetto can sound merely grating or cute, and their songs can seem like lightweight nursery rhymes. In their time, though, the Four Seasons were the epitome of East Coast hipness on the pop charts, and their records are still the best at evoking the spirit and flavor of those distant days.

Frankie Valli's voice defined the Four Season's sound and gave their records their distinct character, but the group's consistent popularity in the age of random hits and changing fads was largely due to the great team effort behind their records. Producer Bob Crewe and group member Bob Gaudio wrote most of the group's hook-laden singalongs, and had a knack for melodies and refrains that were irritatingly simple and impossible to forget, especially when delivered by Valli's police siren voice. The other Seasons complemented Valli's lead with lower and smoother singing that mixed sophisticated nightclub harmonies with playful walrus basses and other doo-wop devices. Working with arranger Charles Calello, Crewe supported Valli's voice with inventive instrumental and vocal arrangements that blended all shadings of pop, Latin and light jazz backings. The end result was a creative whole that kept the Four Seasons supplied with hit songs and a consistent, unmistakable sound (that was lovingly reprised two decades later in Billy Joel's "Uptown Girl").

Frankie Valli, born Francis Castelluccio in Newark, New Jersey, began singing professionally in the early fifties and joined a local group called the Varietones in 1955. Rechristened the Four Lovers, the group had a minor hit in 1956 with "You're the Apple of My Eye," appeared on the *Ed Sullivan Show*, then settled back into years of obscurity on the New Jersey club circuit. Several years later the group landed a recording contract with Vee Jay Records and, now dubbed the Four Seasons, recorded "**Sherry**," a simple one-hook song written by Gaudio ("in about fifteen minutes") that shot to #1 in the summer of 1962.

"Sherry" opens with a polite but catchy Latin-tinged beat (a common feature of the Four Seasons sound) and seems like a cross between the Diamonds and the Crew Cuts until Valli soars into his elegant opening phrase: "She-e-

ER-e-r-ery-y ba-ya-by... She-ER-ur-ry can you come out tonight?"   Valli launches the line like a rocket with a quick leap up to his high falsetto balanced by a gentle glide back down; he then interrupts the second "Sherry" with a gorgeous octave drop in the middle of the word before completing the line in his tenor voice. The Four Season's appeal is pretty well summed up in the melody's graceful arc and in the range of vocal inflections—loud and soft, harsh and smooth, playful and serious, piercing and intimate—that Valli employs for the single phrase.

The Four Seasons followed quickly with the aural cotton candy of "Big Girls Don't Cry," then took a tougher turn with "**Walk Like a Man**" in 1963. "Walk Like a Man" was a nice switch from the usual pop pleading and remorse: here a jilted Valli refuses to beg his girl's return, and receives some timely advice from his father: "No one is worth crawling on the earth, so walk like a man my son." The song opens with a triumphant wordless falsetto melody that recurs throughout the song, bridging the chorus and verses and lending a defiant edge to Valli's determination to walk away with his head held high. Valli sings the verses in a strong, full normal voice, leaps to an equally "manly" falsetto for the singalong chorus then slams back down to earth to end the chorus alone and undaunted.

The remainder of the Four Seasons' Vee Jay output was highlighted by "Candy Girl," "Marlena" and the best-ever version of "Stay." The group switched to the Philips label in 1964 and promptly placed "Dawn (Go Away)" at #3, just behind the Beatles' "I Want To Hold Your Hand" and "She Loves You." Meanwhile, Vee Jay Records acquired the rights to the first American Beatles releases and pitted them against the best of their Four Seasons catalog on an album called *The Beatles vs. the Four Seasons: The International Battle of the Century.*

It wasn't much of a contest in the long run, but the Four Seasons fared remarkably well through the first waves of the British Invasion and consistently recorded hits through 1966. They retained their basic, hook-oriented pop style, but changed and modernized their overall sound, drawing heavily on the inspiration of Phil Spector and the Motown Sound. "**Let's Hang On**," released in the Fall of 1965, opens with a tongue-in-cheek slow introduction ("There ain't no good in our goodbyin'...") that reaches back to the early sixties, then abruptly drops the melodrama and enters the "Satisfaction" age with a hard rock, fuzz-tone guitar riff and a beat and arrangement that practically screams "Motown." Crewe and Calello's "Rolling Stones meet the Four Tops" production was a brilliant synthesis of mid-sixties pop, rock and soul styles, and created a fresh contemporary context for Valli's familiar—now almost nostalgic—falsetto. The Four Seasons hit a final peak at the beginning of 1966 with "Working My Way Back to You," a big production number with a strong, rhythmic refrain and another Motown-ish arrangement augmented by a brassy big band.

The Four Seaons' 1966 recording of Cole Porter's "I've Got You Under My Skin," along with Valli's first solo hit, "Can't Take My Eyes Off You," from the following year, signaled a shift to a more mainstream pop style, though the group also made some bizarre forays in other directions, including a cover of Bob Dylan's "Don't Think Twice" (credited to the Wonder Who) and a psychedelic album called *Genuine Imitation Life Gazette*. As such efforts proved, the Four Seasons were a pop singles band with little affinity for the progressive and album-oriented rock of the late sixties. After a final pair of Top Ten hits in 1967, "Tell It to the Rain" and "C'mon Marianne," the Four Season's popularity faded.

A switch to the Motown label in the early seventies came too late to do much for the group's sound or sales. Valli, however, made an unlikely comeback in 1975 as both a solo act ("My Eyes Adored You" and "Swearin' to God") and as the leader of a new "Four Seasons" line-up ("Who Loves You"). The new Four Seasons charted their last hit with "December, 1963 (Oh, What a Night)" in 1976, while Valli, solo, went out with a bang two years later with "Grease," the title song from the John Travolta/Olivia Newton-John movie. To many of his old fans, Valli seemed a little too comfortable in the glitzy surroundings of the disco era. In any case, it seems appropriate that both of his last hits were bits of calculated nostalgia for the innocent era that the Four Season's early hits so fully embodied.

Soul in the Wings

There were many other bright spots competing with at least some success for airplay against the teen idols and novelty songs. The popularity of "The Twist" kept the beat and some of the rough-edged spirit of R&B alive, while a new type of R&B, laced heavily with gospel and labeled "soul," was changing the shape and direction of black music. Although soul music hit its peak later in the decade, the changes were already apparent in the Uptown R&B of the Drifters and Ben E. King, in the country-soul of Atlantic's Solomon Burke, in the gritty Memphis Sound of Rufus and Carla Thomas, the Mar-keys and Booker T. & the MG's, and in the early sixties recordings by soul pioneers Ray Charles, Sam Cooke, James Brown and Jackie Wilson. Meanwhile, in Detroit, Berry Gordy was assembling his great Motown pop-soul roster and had his hit machine running at full speed by the time the Beatles arrived. Motown climbed to cruising altitude in the mid-to-late sixties, but Motown acts like the Miracles, Martha & the Vandellas, the Marvelettes, Mary Wells, Little Stevie Wonder, the Contours and Marvin Gaye were regularly scoring pop and R&B hits in 1962 and 1963.

As in the 1950's, black artists were responsible for much of the energy on the charts and airwaves, though they were having a harder time *reaching* the charts and airwaves in the face of pop's thorough whitewashing. R&B and early soul were popular as dance music, but the gleaming white faces of the teen idols were a constant reminder to the black artists of the difficulty they faced in finding a place in the pop world or in maintaining a style and identity outside of it. In fact, even the charts themselves reflected the changing attitudes: *Billboard* magazine discontinued its "R&B" chart in 1963, feeling that R&B had been, for all intents and purposes, been absorbed into "Pop." The sudden explosion of the popularity of the Motown and the soul acts caused the magazine to reinstate the R&B charts just a year later.

Soul music defied all logic and actually thrived and expanded through the British Invasion, much as R&B had flourished with the new excitement and increased acceptance of black styles that rock & roll had initially represented. All other living pop life seemed to be rendered extinct by the change of atmosphere in 1964: most of the early sixties pop singers and groups simply disappeared like a slate wiped clean. Two other exceptional survivors of the British onslaught were Bob Dylan and the Beach Boys, the leaders of two "subcultures"—folk music and surf rock—that occupied opposite fringes of the early sixties spectrum before they were pulled into the swirling center of the sixties.

THE FOLK MUSIC REVIVAL

The folk music boom of the early sixties was partly a reaction to the perceived "death" of rock & roll that sent "old," college-aged rock fans searching for a music that had the type of commitment that rock & roll seemed to have lost. The wide interest in folk styles began in 1958 with the pop success of "Tom Dooley" by the **Kingston Trio**, which thrilled rock-haters with its sweet melodies and literate, story-telling lyrics. *Life* magazine described a 1959 Kingston Trio album as "the brightest new sounds heard through all the racket of rock & roll—despite the surprising fact that every chord is in tune and every lyric in good taste, *The Kingston Trio at Large* is now the best-selling L.P. in the country." The Kingston Trio's cleancut collegiate image had a wide appeal, and their casual singing style was accessible to anyone who could strum an acoustic guitar and hum a tune. Singalong "Hootenannies" were the rage at campuses across the country, drawing people who had always scoffed at rock & roll as well as new converts dismayed by the teen pop that had replaced Little Richard.

The folk boom also revived interest in traditional folk, blues and other "authentic" music and its practitioners, such as Woody Guthrie, Leadbelly, Pete Seeger and the great rural and urban bluesmen. The Kingston Trio and other entertainment-oriented groups were eventually dismissed as folk's version of commercial pop and were replaced by a new wave of urban folksingers, centered in New York's Greenwich Village, who updated folk's tradition of social consciousness and political activism. **Peter, Paul and Mary** claimed the Kingston Trio's position as the link between the left-wing coffee houses and mainstream America. They popularized folk standards like "This Land Is Your Land," "Go Tell It On the Mountain" and "If I Had a Hammer," and made an instant classic out of "Blowing in the Wind" and an instant hero out of its young author, Bob Dylan.

Bob Dylan

Bob Dylan became the reigning King of the new folk movement, presiding over the folk kingdom with Joan Baez as his Queenly counterpart. Dylan's songs were rooted in folk's past but addressed contemporary topics, particularly the struggle against war and for civil rights, with a youthful commitment and depth of insight that drew legions of young listeners away from the "wasteland of commercial pop." Although the full weight of Bob Dylan's impact was felt in rock's next era, his acoustic folk songs and protest anthems were an important part of the early sixties landscape and a stark contrast to the era's teen pop.

Comparing "The Times They Are A-Changin'" and "Blowing in the Wind" with "Big Girls Don't Cry" and "Breaking Up Is Hard to Do" certainly did seem like comparing a great poetry with a comic book; and who could do the *Twist* with a straight face when the world was just a push of The Button away from nuclear war? The pop and folk worlds seemed light-years apart: the folk audience prized lyrics with a message and music with a sense of tradition, and there was certainly little of *that* to be found on *American Bandstand*. Most pop fans, on the other hand, prized a good dancebeat and pop hook and had little use for the smug intellectualism they sensed in folk music, if they had any exposure to it at all.

The Beatles were viewed as just another teenybopper craze by most folk music lovers in 1964. A few, like Bob Dylan, knew otherwise and saw in the Beatles a rebirth of rock's vitality and validity. The two worlds weren't so far apart after all, as it turned out: the Beatles' example prompted Dylan to go "electric," while Dylan's example shamed everyone else into actually thinking about their songs and lyrics. Dylan's "defection" to rock styles and the pop world in 1965 shocked ardent folkies and, in effect, rendered their world obsolete, assuring that folk music would find its biggest audience and have its biggest impact as the last great American traditional style to add its influence to rock & roll.

SURF ROCK

Surf Rock was the sound of Southern California, the "Promised Land" that offered endless summers, endless beaches, endless blondes and endless fun without an adult in sight. The dream of the teenage utopia depicted in surf music appealed to landlocked listeners (who responded with their own "sidewalk surfin'" skateboard and craze) as well as to the Southern California teens who knew it was largely a myth but shared it anyway. As the Twist and other dances crazes swept the country in the early sixties, the West Coast developed a scene and sound of its own and began California's transformation from a rather minor rock outpost to the center of sixties youth culture.

Instrumental Bands

Although the Beach Boys and Jan & Dean were the style's biggest stars, surf music was, at first, primarily an instrumental style that accompanied dances and beach parties along the Pacific coast. Led by the Ventures and Dick Dale, instrumental bands crafted a distinctive group sound fronted by piercing guitar melodies and driven by aggressive drumming and a spirit of carefree fun. The instrumental groups that sprang up with the surf scene kept the sound and spirit of fifties rock & roll alive and, at the same time, anticipated the shift to self-contained, guitar-based groups ushered in by the British Invasion. Important fifties precursors of the instrumental style included Bill Doggett's "Honky Tonk," Bill Justis' "Raunchy," the Champs' "Tequila," Johnny and the Hurricane's "Crossfire," Dave "Baby" Cortez' "The Happy Organ," Link Wray's "Rumble," and "Rebel-'Rouser," "Ramrod" and recordings by **Duane Eddy**, whose twangy, reverberated guitar style formed a model for surf band guitarists.

The lack of vocals inspired—necessitated—experimenting with sounds and with beat-driven arrangements so powerful that no one would miss the voices. While the guitar virtually disappeared as a lead instrument in early sixties pop, the surf bands took their cue from Chuck Berry and the rockabillies and reaffirmed its central role. After all, who wanted to dance to a string section? Even the good old saxophone couldn't come close to the power of a cranked up guitar & amp—a few turns of the knob and anyone could get a tremolo that sounded like a wave or a drenching reverb that echoed around the dancehall like the very voice of the Surf God. Aggressive drumming was, of course, another key ingredient of the surf band sound, and was taken to a maniacal extreme by the Surfaris ("Wipe Out") and other surf bands (and surf descendants like Who drummer Keith Moon).

The Ventures and Dick Dale

The Seattle-based **Ventures** solidified the two guitars, bass and drums line-up and the tight, heavily-reverbed band sound of surf rock with "Walk Don't Run" and "Perfidia," both national hits in 1960. Though not originally presented as a "surf" band, their polished dance arrangements, memorable guitar melodies and bright sound made them favorites of the surf crowd and de facto surfers. The Ventures responded with a surf-oriented remake of "Walk Don't Run" in 1964 (and returned to the charts later in the decade with the "Theme from "Hawaii Five-O.")

Southern California produced its own instrumental star in **Dick Dale**, the "King of the Surf Guitar," who began recording in 1961. Dale never scored a national hit but he was a popular local star and had a big influence on the bands that followed. "Let's Go Trippin'," "Misirlou" and other Dale outings exaggerated Duane Eddy's twang/reverb sound and added rapid-fire runs that sought to capture the daredevil thrill of surfing. With his band, the Del-Tones, Dale tied the music—embellished occasionally with surf slang lyrics—explicitly to surfing and defined "surf rock" as a musical style and lifestyle. Surf bands appeared in garages all over Southern California, inspired by Dick Dale and assured of a loyal regional audience and of access to the many small record labels located nearby.[6]

The Garage Bands

A few of the surf instrumentals managed to make the national charts, including the Chantays' "Pipeline," the Pyramids' "Penetration," the Marketts' "Out of Limits" and the Surfaris' 1963 classic "**Wipe Out.**" "Wipe Out" is a great example of the ragged "garage band" style of the neighborhood surf groups: a 12-bar blues in form, though certainly not in spirit, "Wipe Out"'s incessant guitar riff, half-crazed drums, flailing cymbals and live-in-the-school-gym sound were a sharp, gleeful contrast to the carefully crafted pop of the time. So was the *other* garage classic of the year, "**Louie Louie.**" Originally recorded by Richard Berry in 1956, the Kingsmen emerged from the Seattle club scene the Ventures had founded and spat out their hit version with an impeccably slurred "singing" style that made deciphering the song's lyrics one of the great fun pastimes of 1963. (Could they really be saying *that*?) Just in case, the Governor of Indiana banned "Louie Louie" and the U.S. Congress launched a full-scale investigation to find out what kind of smut was hidden in the grooves. As the nation waited breathlessly, the Congressmen slowed down, sped up and scientifically analyzed the record and finally declared it "incomprehensible at any speed," leaving the song's interpretation open to the active imaginations of the teenagers. Actually, the lyrics are quite tame, but the music was nasty, and the mere fact that adults *worried* about it was reason enough to love it.

The radio and record charts may have surrendered to the teen idols, but bands like the Surfaris and Kingsmen kept the original spark and spirit of rock & roll alive at a grassroots level. They inspired the same type of enthusiastic thrashing from hometown bands thousands of miles from the nearest ocean, and led the way for later garage classics like "Wooly Bully," "96 Tears," "Hang On Sloopy," "Gloria," Wild Thing," "Dirty Water," "Double Shot of My Baby's Love," "Psychotic Reaction" and other records that kept rock & roll honest and within the reach of any group of kids with guitars, drums and something burning inside.

The Beach Boys

The popularity of the instrumental bands faded as the enormous success of the Beach Boys and Jan & Dean subsumed other styles and made bright harmonies and falsetto voices as central to surf music as guitars and drums. Their songs were full of in-group surfing references that sounded positively exotic to the rest of the country, along with celebrations of hotrods, drag races, dance parties, going steady and other rites of teenage life that anyone could relate to or at least fantasize about. Their high, clear vocals complemented the brittle bite of the surf guitars, while their lyrics brought California to life as a collective dream for teenage America.

The Beach Boys made their first record, "Surfin'," in 1961, and rose to prominence in 1962 and 1963 with a string of national hits: "Surfin' Safari," "Surfin' USA," "Surfer Girl," "Shut Down," "Little Deuce Coup" and "Be True to Your School." **Brian Wilson**, the Beach Boys' songwriter and guiding spirit, combined the spirited group singing of doo-wop and the girl groups with the sophisticated jazz-pop harmonies of the Four Freshmen, then layered it all on top of a Dick Dale-meets-Chuck Berry guitar band. His songs presented an idyllic worldview, cut with a nervous self-questioning, that transplanted Berry's celebration of teenage life to the beach and to a new generation. Although the group's initial fame—and its continuing popularity as a nostalgia band—derived from their surf and hotrods hits, Wilson's vision and enormous talents carried the Beach Boys through the British Invasion and through the 1960's as America's answer to the Beatles. (In fact, the Beach Boys' influence on the Beatles' music rivaled Dylan's effect on their lyrics, as both Lennon and McCartney credited their 1966 *Pet Sounds* album with being the primary inspiration for *Sgt. Pepper*.)

Jan & Dean

As the Beach Boys abandoned the beach for more adventurous productions and personal statements, their friends Jan Berry and Dean Torrence stayed around and enjoyed the surf and sun a little longer. Unlike the Beach Boys, Jan & Dean actually *looked* like surfers, and they became the most visible representatives of the scene their songs glorified. **Surf City**," written by Jan Berry and Brian Wilson, hit #1 on the national charts in 1963 and filled the hearts of every teenage guy with the California Dream and the promise of "two girls for every boy!" Full of "woodies," wet suits, surf boards and surfer girls, "Surf City" seemed like Heaven: a magic place where "there's always something goin'—they're either out surfin' or they got a party growin'." Phil Spector influence.

Jan & Dean followed "Surf City" with "Honolulu Lulu," "Drag City," "The New Girl in School," "Little Old Lady (From Pasadena)," "Ride the Wild Surf," "Sidewalk Surfin'" and other hits that filled in the details of life in Surf City. Producer **Lou Adler** supplied a lush sound and carefully crafted arrangements that paralleled the increasingly pronounced Phil Spector influence in Brian Wilson's Beach Boys productions. **"Dead Man's Curve,"** from 1964, was a particularly effective production, with a huge, echo-laden sound and dramatic effects that evoked the thrills and danger of speeding cars and climaxed in a fiery crash.

"Dead Man's Curve" proved tragically prophetic: Jan Berry was critically injured, and three of his passengers killed, in 1966 when he lost control of his car and smashed into a parked truck just a few miles from the real Dead Man's Curve that inspired the song. Berry remained in a coma for months and suffered permanent mental and physical damage. Partially recovered, but still unable to sing, Jan reunited with Dean for a dismal 1973 comeback attempt that found the pair reduced to lip-synching their hits for hostile crowds. A 1978 television movie called *Dead Man's Curve* dramatized their lives and inspired a more authentic and warmly received comeback as the opening act for a Beach Boys tour that brought all the old surfers together again.

"THE TWIST"

Chubby Checker's "The Twist" went to #1 twice: in 1960 and again in 1962, and launched the biggest fad of the era—the dance equivalent of the skateboard and hula hoop. **"The Twist"** was written and originally recorded by R&B veteran **Hank Ballard** in 1958 and was released as merely the B-side of one of his singles. Inspired by a strange dance move that his backup band, the Midnighters, had picked up and worked into their routine, Ballard's record was a minor R&B hit and the dance became popular with black teenagers on the east coast. When one couple started twisting on *American Bandstand*, host Dick Clark frantically motioned to keep the cameras off of their grinding hips. Typically enough, though, the show's group of white "regulars" soon began mimicking the moves and Clark, sensing a fad in the making, decided to showcase "The Twist" on his show, though he wanted to push—and reap the benefits from—a new, locally produced version of the song rather than Ballard's original.

To his credit, Clark apparently resisted the temptation to hand the song over to a white teen idol (though some stories have the song offered first to Freddy Cannon and Danny & the Juniors). In any case, he eventually found a young black singer—a local chicken plucker named Ernest Evans—with a strong voice and appealing personality and had him record a note-for-note cover of "The Twist" that kept the strong dance beat and R&B feel of Ballard's original. Renamed **"Chubby Checker,"** in an obvious takeoff on "Fats Domino," Evans appeared regularly on *American Bandstand* to promote the record and give Twist instructions ("pretend you're drying your backside with a towel while putting a cigarette out with your feet"). The local dancestep quickly became a national craze and the record, released on Philadelphia's Cameo-Parkway teen label, zoomed to the top of the pop charts.

A flood of Twist records followed, highlighted by Sam Cooke's "Twistin' the Night Away," the Isley Brothers' "Twist and Shout," King Curtis' "Soul Twist," Joey Dee and the Starlighters' "Peppermint Twist," Bobby Lewis' "Tossin' and Turnin'," Chubby Checker's follow-up hit, "Let's Twist Again" ("like we did last summer"), and several great dance party records by Gary "U.S." Bonds: "New Orleans," "Quarter to Three," "School Is Out," "Dear Lady Twist," "Twist, Twist Senora."   Anything that could remotely be tied to the dance was labeled a "twist" record, since the word "twist" in a song title— "Twistin' Matilda," "Twistin' Postman," "Twistin' USA"—guaranteed sales to dance-hungry teens. In addition, many older records were remade or simply reissued as "twist" records to jump on the bandwagon. (Atlantic reissued a set of Ray Charles records on an album called *Do the Twist with Ray Charles*, and even Jerry Lee Lewis got into the act with "Whole Lot of Twistin' Goin' On.")

It was all very contrived and calculated, but "The Twist" did bring rock back to its R&B dance roots and generated a lot of excitement in the slump years of the early sixties (in the same manner that disco music took hold in the creatively fallow mid-seventies). The dance craze ushered in by "The Twist" inspired a revival of dance-based R&B styles and a slew of records that, if nothing else, at least had a good strong beat: as the teenage record-raters on *American Bandstand* put it, "It's good a good beat and you can dance to it." The Twist also, at first, gave teenagers a fad to call their own and a way to shock their parents again. The fact that couples never touched each other while twisting did little to reassure adults who viewed the movements as overtly sexual, though it did open up all kinds of possibilities for bizarre body movements that could now be called "dancing."

Dancestyle of the Rich and Famous

The Twist" kicked off a series of dance crazes: the Jerk, Locomotion, Limbo, Swim, Mashed Potatoes, Bristol Stomp, Slop, Watusi, Jerk, Frug, Fish, Fly, Pony, Monkey and a host of other dances and accompanying records from artists hoping to ignite or cash in on the latest fad. The Twist remained *the* dance, however, and shoved the others aside for an unprecedented second run at the charts and dancefloors in 1962. Along the way, a strange thing happened: the adult world quit complaining about the Twist and joined in. Having already moved from the inner city to the teen pop world, the Twist made an unlikely leap into High Society as Manhattan socialites and other jet-setters (including, rumors had it, Jackie Kennedy) decided that the dance the "kids" were doing was cute and splashed the Twist fad across the society pages and into the consciousness of mainstream America. (Chubby Checker: "God bless Zsa Zsa Gabor. She did the Twist at the Peppermint Lounge... My record came on, Zsa Zsa started dancing, Earl Wilson wrote about it, and suddenly everyone in the world was doing the Twist."[7]) New York's Peppermint Lounge became the center of the Twist world—the forerunner of Studio 54 and other trendy clubs and discos.   House band Joey Dee & the Starlighters (later to metamorphose into the Young Rascals) presided at the club and knocked Chubby Checker out of the #1 spot in 1962 with their own Twist song, "Peppermint Twist."

"The Twist" made dancing accessible to everyone: you didn't even need a partner or any discernible coordination to do the dance and, thanks to Jackie and Zsa Zsa, even respectable adults could join in and pretend to be young again. It marked the first time that adults embraced a form of rock & roll, or at least the image of youth and frivolous fun that it represented, and was the beginning of the trendy fascination with pop stars and youth culture that would mark the sixties and later years.   Silly and patronizing, to be sure, but they were— shaking their hips to a dance born in the ghettos and moving to the hard beat of an R&B band playing a 12-bar blues.

In its own peculiar way, then, the Twist was something of a victory for rock & roll, though its glib mass acceptance was more a sign of how unthreatening and easily manipulated the music scene had become, just as its periodic resurgence reflected the lifeless and fad-dominated state of the charts and airwaves.   The Twist would have been a minor diversion in better times, but it was the only "event" in the early sixties that created anything like the over-hyped excitement generated by Elvis Presley and rock & roll in the 1950's. Like the times, it quickly grew boring, but nothing replaced it until the next big "fad" hit America in 1964.   During that first triumphant trip to America, the Beatles made a well-publicized visit to the Peppermint Lounge and merrily danced on the grave they were digging for the Twist and other relics of rock's Dark Ages.

DARK BEFORE DAWN

"The darkest hour is just before dawn," as the Shirelles sang in "Dedicated to the One I Love," and it's worth remembering again that Roy Orbison, Sam Cooke, the Phil Spector productions, the great Brill Building songs and the other bright spots of the early sixties were widely scattered exceptions to the lightweight pop, dance and novelty songs that dominated the charts.   It's sad but true that "Itsy Bitsy Teenie Weenie Yellow Polkadot Bikini," "Monster Mash" and any number of "songs" by Alvin & the Chipmunks outsold Sam Cooke and Roy Orbison's greatest recordings.   So did the endless odes to self-pity that kept a constant whine on the airwaves.   Everyone, it seems, was lonely: Bobby Vinton made a career of it with "Mr. Lonely," "Long Lonely Nights" and "L-O-N-E-L-Y"; Dion was a "Lonely Teenager," Paul Anka was a "Lonely Boy" and even older and wiser Elvis was a "Lonely Man"; Gary Stites was "Lonely for You," Conway Twitty was "Lonely Boy Blue," Jack Nitzsche the "Lonely Surfer," Ricky Nelson lived in "Lonesome Town," Charlie

Rich had "Lonely Weekends," Herb Alpert & The Tijuana Brass gave us the "Lonely Bull" and Ruby & the Romantics consoled them all with "Hey There Lonely Boy." Then, of course, there was Roy Orbison, for whom mere "loneliness" would have been a major improvement.

At least Roy Orbison really *sounded* lonely. The emotional content of most early sixties pop was as calculated and contrived as the promotional campaigns for latest teen idols and dance crazes. The emotion was manipulated to absurd and morbid heights in the string of popular "death rock" songs ushered in by Ray Peterson's car crash melodrama "Tell Laura I Love Her" and Mark Dinning's "Teen Angel" (where the singer's girlfriend rushes back to their stalled car to save his high school ring and is promptly flattened by an oncoming train). The genre reached a wonderfully macabre peak in 1964 with the squealing tires and shattering glass climax of the Shangri-Las' "Leader of the Pack." It could just as easily have been the sound of an era crashing to a halt, with the leather-jacketed hero taking the early sixties with him to a well-deserved fiery death, for by then the airwaves were filled with an undeniable and wholly unexpected life that no longer had to be contrived or fabricated by the music industry. Rock & roll was suddenly, unbelievably, alive again.

The British Are Coming!

The Beatles? A *British* band?! The very idea seemed strange, even ludicrous. Only a few fluke novelty hits had ever managed to cross the Atlantic westward and dent the American charts. British youth, on the other hand, had developed a passion for all things American—styles and fashions, slang expressions, movies and movie stars, Cowboys & Indians and, above all, rock & roll. They had followed rock & roll from its inception and from a distance that in many ways afforded them a clearer view of the music and inspired an even greater fervor for it. England was not saturated with the 'round the clock, 'round the dial radio that American fans took for granted. Their link to rock came from the precious singles shipped in from America and the scant rock programming available on the government controlled BBC radio and, when the atmospheric conditions were right, distant stations like Radio Luxembourg. The limited availability of rock & roll contributed to the excitement—the type of excitement that young white Americans had discovered late at night with their radios tuned to far off R&B stations in rock's earliest days.

As rock & roll came ashore in the mid-fifties, an added craze for "**skiffle**" music gave teenagers in England a movement of their own. Skiffle was an amateurish mixture of folk, blues and other traditional styles sung and played hootenanny style on folk guitars, washboards, spoons, tin cans and anything else that was available. Popularized by Lonnie Donegan's "Rock

Island Lines" in 1956, skiffle's appeal lay largely in the fact that anyone could play it, and thousands did, laying the foundations for the grass-roots live music scene that spawned British rock. Skiffle also established a tradition of self-contained, guitar-based bands, and when the fad died many of the groups discovered that rock & roll wasn't much harder to play than the skiffle songs they were used to, and they turned to their American heroes and began playing rock & roll with the same thrilling sense of liberation that fueled the music in its homeland.

In the early sixties, while America turned toward lighter pop, teen idols and the Twist, a large segment of the British audience kept their taste for authentic rock & roll and R&B (being 4,000 miles beyond the range of *American Bandstand* had its advantages). Rock & roll may have "died" in America, but it was very much alive in England, where a generation of bands had already staked their own claim to rock's heritage and now set about reshaping the music in their own image. By 1964, the Beatles, Rolling Stones, Dave Clark Five, Animals, Kinks, Searchers, Hollies, Manfred Mann, Gerry and the Pacemakers, Billy J. Kramer & the Dakotas, Freddy & the Dreamers and many other groups had made England the rock capital of the world. After years of looking to America, England had a vital music scene all its own and it was America's turn to follow.

The British Invasion of 1964 brought America's music—reinvented and revitalized—back home, and a new generation of rock fans responded as if it was brand new (which, to them, it was). Given up for dead or at least brain-dead and docile, rock & roll sprang back to life with new heroes, new possibilities and a new sense of rebellious fun. Parents across the country let out a collective groan—"here we go again"—and the battle was resumed, launching an era that would soon take rock music and youth culture into realms unimaginable in 1964. The sixties had finally arrived.

---

[1] The Everly Brothers had just decided on their "Cathy's Clown" as their next release; Elvis had just returned from the army and was impossible to reach.

[2] The sinister undercurrent of "In Dreams"--"In dreams you're mine, ALL the time"--was wonderfully exploited in the David Lynch's film *Blue Velvet*.

[3] Liner notes for "For the Lonely: 18 Greatest Hits," Rhino compact disk, 1988.

[4] Ian Whitcomb, "Whole Lotta Shakin'" (London: Arrow Books, 1982).

[5] from "History of Rock and Roll," syndicated radio show.

[6] The lack of a music industry center prevented a similar musical movement from developing around the beach scene of the Carolina coast, where the dance grooves of R&B and soul music, including Mar-keys' "Last Night," Booker T. and the MG's "Green Onions" and other instrumental hits, were favored.

[7] Joe Smith, "Off the Record," p. 196.

Photo courtesy of Steve Aker and Vicki Timm.

B.G. "Ramblers" with "Beatles"